Pierre-François-Xavier de Charlevoix

Letters to the Dutchess of Lesdiguieres

Giving an account of a voyage to Canada, and travels through that vast country, and Louisiana, to the Gulf of Mexico, undertaken by order of the present king of France

Pierre-François-Xavier de Charlevoix

Letters to the Dutchess of Lesdiguieres
Giving an account of a voyage to Canada, and travels through that vast country, and Louisiana, to the Gulf of Mexico, undertaken by order of the present king of France

ISBN/EAN: 9783337344894

Printed in Europe, USA, Canada, Australia, Japan

Cover: Foto ©ninafisch / pixelio.de

LETTERS

TO THE

Dutchess of LESDIGUIERES;

Giving an Account of a

VOYAGE to CANADA,

AND

TRAVELS through that vast Country,

AND

LOUISIANA, to the Gulf of MEXICO.

UNDERTAKEN

By Order of the present KING of *FRANCE*,

By FATHER *CHARLEVOIX*.

Being a more full and accurate Description of *Canada*, and the neighbouring Countries than has been before published; the Character of every Nation or Tribe in that vast Tract being given; their Religion, Customs, Manners, Traditions, Government, Languages, and Towns; the Trade carried on with them, and at what Places; the Posts or Forts, and Settlements, established by the *French*; the great Lakes, Water-Falls, and Rivers, with the Manner of navigating them; the Mines, Fisheries, Plants, and Animals of these Countries.

With Reflections on the Mistakes the *French* have committed in carrying on their Trade and Settlements; and the most proper Method of proceeding pointed out.

Including also an Account of the Author's Shipwreck in the Channel of *Bahama*, and Return in a Boat to the *Mississippi*, along the Coast of the Gulf of *Mexico*, with his Voyage from thence to *St. Domingo*, and back to *France*.

Printed for R. GOADBY, and Sold by R. BALDWIN in PATER-NOSTER-ROW, LONDON. 1763.

THE

CONTENTS.

D

Dance

Foun-

Jugglers,

Q

R

River,

By the Tranſlator's being at a Diſtance from the Preſs, the following ERRATA have happened.

Page 10 line 19 read *Ray* inſtead of *Race*. Page 18 line 9 *Breton* inſtead of *Britain*. Page 20 line 4 *des* inſtead of *de*. Page 24 line 41 *Chaplain* inſtead of *Almoner*. Page 36 (the Note) *A Livre is* 10*d. Halfpenny* inſtead of *A Livre is* 1*s.* 8*d.* Page 40 line 33 *broad* inſtead of *round*. Page 60 line 19 *Chaudiere* inſtead of *Chandiere*. Page 61 the laſt line *Plane* inſtead of *Plain*. Page 64 laſt line *Shamois* inſtead of *Shamios*. Page 68 line 44 *againſt the Wind* inſtead of *with the Wind*. Page 70 line 31 after the Word *Kind* read *of*. Page 74 laſt line read *la* before *Flecke*. Page 81 line 38 *Bete* for *Beet*. Page 85 line 28 *turning* for *burning*. Page 95 line 11 *Soleil* for *Soliel*. Page 97 line 40 read *no* after the Word *Time*. Page 99 line 4 read *it* before *is*. Page 103 line 23 *fruitful* inſtead of *faithful*. Page 111 line 32 *Scandinavia* inſtead of *Scardinaria*. Page 115 line 9 *not* inſtead of *no*. Page 136 line 16 read 100 *Poles* for 70 *Yards*. Page 175 line 16 read *Grandmother* inſtead of *Great Grandmother*. Page 183 line 21 *Grandmother* inſtead of *Great Grandmother*. Page 190 line 27, 100 *Poles* inſtead of 70 *Yards*. Page 204 line 44 *Chaplains* inſtead of *Almoners*. Page 205 line 12 *Chaplain* inſtead of *Almoner*. Page 232 read Letter XXII. inſtead of XXVI. Page 238 line 45 *Maiz* inſtead of *Wheat*. Page 239 line 14 read *Maſs* inſtead of *Meſs*. Page 269 line 36 *Wood of White Fir* inſtead of *Wood of Epinette*. Page 283 line 8 *is* inſtead of *his*. Page 284 line 8 *Stragglers* inſtead of *Stagglers*. Page 325 line 5 read *Seine* for *Siene*. Page 338 read *Great Gainers by* inſtead of *Great by Gainers*. In ſeveral Places from Page 345 read *Biloxi* inſtead of *the Bilexi*. Page 373 line 18 read *in* inſtead of *the*. Page 376 line 25 *reckoned* inſtead of *reckened*. Page 379 line 3 *by East* inſtead of *by North Eaſt*.

Advertisement of the Translator.

ALthough theſe Letters were begun to be written in the Year 1720, yet the Writer has, by Notes, taken Notice of what material Alterations have been made ſince.---It is, beyond Doubt, the moſt perfect Account of *Canada* that is extant. And it is ſaid that it was from this Work in particular that our Miniſters formed their Notions of the Importance of *Canada*, and the vaſt Advantages which might be derived therefrom. And at the ſame Time it gives the moſt accurate Deſcription of the Country, it affords much Entertainment, by the particular Account it gives of the Manners, Cuſtoms, *&c.* of the various Inhabitants of theſe vaſt Countries.

AN

HISTORICAL JOURNAL

OF

TRAVELS in North America:

Undertaken

By Order of the King of FRANCE.

LETTER I.

A Voyage from ROCHELLE *to* QUEBEC. *Some Remarks upon the Voyage, the Great Bank of* NEWFOUNDLAND, *and the River* ST. LAURENCE.

MADAM, QUEBEC, *Sept.* 24.

I Arrived in this City after a tedious and troubleſome Paſſage of 83 Days: We had however but 1000 Leagues to make, ſo that you ſee we don't always go Poſt at Sea, as M. the Abbot *de Choiſy* uſed to ſay. I made no Journal of this Voyage, becauſe I ſuffered greatly by the Sea Sickneſs above a Month. I flattered myſelf that I ſhould have been free from it, becauſe I had ſuffered it twice before; but there are ſome Conſtitutions which cannot ſympathize with this Element, and ſuch is mine. And in the Condition we find ourſelves under this Sickneſs, it is not poſſible to attend to what paſſes in the Ship: On the other Hand, nothing is more barren than a Voyage like this; for the chief Obſervation to be made, is, whence the Wind blows, how much the Ship gets forward, and if it keeps in the right Courſe; for during two thirds of the Way there is nothing to be ſeen but Sky and Water. However, I ſhall proceed to inform you of what I can remember, that is moſt likely to give you ſome Minutes Amuſement; to keep, as well as I can, the Promiſe I made you.

We ſtaid in the Road of *Aix* the 1ſt of July, and the 2d we got under Sail by Favour of a ſmall Breeze from the North-Eaſt. The three firſt Days we had ſcarce any Wind, but yet it was in our Favour, and we comforted ourſelves, becauſe this made the Sea very pleaſant. It looked as if it wanted to flatter us, before it ſhewed itſelf in it's worſt Humour. The 4th or the 5th the Wind changed, and came directly againſt us, the Sea ran high, and for near ſix Weeks we were toſſed in a very extraordinary Manner; the Winds changed continually, but they were oftner againſt than for us, and we were almoſt always obliged to ſail as near the Wind as poſſible.

A Deſcription of the Great Bank.

The 9th of Auguſt our Pilots thought themſelves upon the *Great Bank of Newfoundland*, and they were not much miſtaken. But from the 9th to the 16th we made ſcarce any Way. What they call the *Great Bank of Newfoundland*, is properly a Mountain hid under Water, about 600 Leagues from *France* to the Weſt. The Sieur *Denys*, who has given us a very good Work of *North America*, and a very inſtructive Treatiſe on the Cod Fiſhery, makes this Mountain extend 150 Leagues from North to South; but according to the moſt exact Sea Charts, it begins on the South Side, in 41 Degrees North *Latitude*, and it's Northern End is in 49 Degrees 25 *Minutes*. The Truth is, it's two extremities grow ſo narrow, that it is difficult to mark it's Bounds. It's greateſt Width from Eaſt to Weſt, is about 90 *French* and *Engliſh* Sea Leagues; between 40 and 49 Degrees of Longitude. I have heard ſome Seamen ſay, that they have caſt Anchor in five Fathom Water, which is againſt the Sieur *Denys*, who ſays, that he never found leſs than 25 on the Bank; it is certain that in many Places there are above 60. About the Middle of it's Length on the Side of *Europe*, it forms a kind of Bay, which they call the *Pit*; and this is the Reaſon, that of two Ships which are upon the ſame Line, and in Sight of each other, one ſhall find Ground, and the other none.

Before we arrive at the *Great Bank* we meet with a ſmaller one, which is called the *Jacquet Bank*: Some ſay there is another before this, which is of a conical Figure; but I have ſeen ſome Pilots who of the three make but one, and they anſwer the Objections which are made to this, by ſaying that there are Hollows in the *Great Bank*, the Depth of which has deceived thoſe who make three of it, becauſe they did not let out Line ſufficient. Whatever may be the Figure and Extent of this Mountain, which it is impoſſible to know exactly, they find here a prodigious Quantity of Shells, and many kinds of Fiſh of all Sizes;

the greatest Part of which serve the Cod for Food; the Number of which seem to equal the Grains of Sand that cover the Bank. For above two Centuries they have loaded two or three hundred Ships every Year, and the Number scarce appears to be lessened. But they would do well to discontinue this Fishery now and then, especially as the Gulf of *St. Laurence*, the River itself for above 60 Leagues, the Coasts of *Acadia*, of *Isle Royal* †, and of *Newfoundland*, are almost as well stock'd with this Fish as the *Great Bank*. These are, Madam, real Mines, which are more valuable, and require much less Expence, than those of *Mexico* and *Peru*.

The Cause of the Winds and Fogs about the Bank.

We suffered greatly all the Time that the contrary Winds kept us upon the Frontiers of this Kingdom of Cod Fish, for it is the most disagreeable and inconvenient Part of the whole Ocean. The Sun scarce ever shews himself, and the greatest Part of the Time we have thick and Cold Fogs; which is such a Sign of approaching the Bank, that they cannot be mistaken. What can be the Cause of a Phænomenon so remarkable and constant? Can it be the Neighbourhood of the Land and the Woods that cover it? But, besides that *Cape Race*, which is the nearest Land to the *Great Bank*, is Thirty-five Leagues distant, the same Thing does not happen upon all the other Sides of the Island; for the Island of *Newfoundland* is not subject to Fogs but on the Side of the *Great Bank*, every where else its Coasts enjoy a pure Air, and a serene Sky. It is therefore probable, that it is the Nearness of the *Great Bank* that causes Fogs that cover *Cape Race*, and we must seek for the Cause upon the Bank itself. The following are my Conjectures upon it, which I submit to the Judgment of the Learned.

I begin by observing that we have another Sign of approaching the *Great Bank*, which is that upon all its Extremities, which they commonly call its deep Shores or Precipices; the Sea is always rough, and the Winds high. May we not look upon this as the Cause of the Fogs which reign here, and say that the Agitation of the Water, the Bottom of which is mingled with Sand and Mud, thickens the Air, and makes it greasy and that the Sun draws only the thick Vapours from it, which it can never disperse: It may be ask'd me, Whence comes this Agitation of the Sea upon the Borders of the *Great Bank*, whilst every where else, and upon the Bank itself, there reigns a profound Calm? This is the Cause if I mistake not: We find every Day in these Seas, Currents which run sometimes one Way, and sometimes another. The Sea, irregularly driven by these Currents, and striking impetuously against the Sides of the Bank, which are almost every where perpendicular, is repulsed with the same Violence; which causes the Agitation we find here.

† This is what we call *Cape Breton*.

If the fame Thing does not happen upon the Approach of all deep Coafts, it is becaufe all have not fuch a great Extent as this; that they have no Currents about them, or that they are not fo ftrong; or that they do not crofs one another; that they do not meet fuch fteep Coafts, and are not repulfed with fo much Force. Skilful Mariners agree, that the Agitation of the Sea, and the Mud which it ftirs, contribute greatly to thicken the Air; but that the Winds occafioned hereby do not reach far; and upon the *Great Bank*, at fome Diftance from its Sides, the Sea is as calm as in a Road, unlefs there is a ftrong Wind coming from fome other Part.

A Storm. It was on Friday the 17th of *Auguft*, at feven o'Clock in the Evening, we found ourfelves upon the Bank, in 75 Fathom Water. Our Ship's Crew longed for frefh Cod; but as the Sun was fet, and the Wind was fair, it was thought beft to take Advantage of it. About eleven o'Clock at Night we had a ftrong Wind at South Eaft, which with a Mizen Sail alone would have driven us 3 Leagues in an Hour. If this had been all, by furling all our other Sails, which was inftantly done, we fhould have had no Caufe of Complaint; but there followed fuch a heavy Rain, as if all the Cataracts of Heaven were opened, attended with Thunder and Lightening, which fell fo near us that the Rudder remained unmoveable, and all the Seamen who worked the Ship felt the Blow. It redoubled afterwards, and a Hundred Pieces of Cannon fired together would not have been louder: We could not hear one another; one Clap fucceeding another, before the firft was over. We could not fee each other in the midft of the Lightening, becaufe it dazzled our Eyes; in fhort, during an Hour and a half we feemed to be in the hotteft Fire of a Trench; the Hearts of the Boldeft trembled, for the Thunder always remained over our Heads; and if it had fallen a fecond Time upon us, we might have gone to feed the Cods, at whofe Expence we reckoned foon to have feafted. Had not what is called *St. Elmo's* * *Fire* given us Notice of this Hurricane, we might have been furprized and overfet under Sail.

After an Hour and a Half the Rain ceafed, the Thunder grumbled only at a Diftance, and the Lightenings were only weak Flafhes in the Horizon. The Wind was ftill fair, but not fo ftrong, and the Sea appeared as fmooth as Glafs; then every one wanted to lay down, but all their Beds were wetted; the Rain had penetrated thro' the imperceivable Cracks, which is inevitable when the Veffel is greatly loaded: We fhifted as we could, and thought ourfelves happy to come off fo well. Whatever

* Thefe Fires moft commonly appear upon the Yards, at the Approach of a Storm.

is

is violent never lasts long, especially the South East Wind; at least in these Seas. The Calm returned with the Day, we made no Way; but we made ourselves Amends by Fishing.

Of the Cod and the Fishery.

Every Thing is good in the Cod while it is fresh; it looses nothing of its Goodness, and becomes something firmer when it has been two Days in Salt; but it is the Fishers only who eat the best Parts of it; *that is to say*, the Head, the Tongue, and the Liver: To preserve all these Parts would take up too much Salt; so they throw all into the Sea which they cannot consume at the Time of Fishing. The largest Cod that I saw was not 3 Feet long; yet those on the *Great Bank* are the largest; but there is perhaps no other Creature in Proportion to its Bigness, that has so wide a Mouth, or that is more voracious. We find in the Stomach of this Fish, Pieces of broken Pots, and Bits of Iron and Glass. Some People fancy they digest all this, but this is discovered to be a Mistake, which was founded upon finding in them some Pieces of Iron half worn away. Now we are convinced, that the Cod can turn itself Inside-out like a Pocket, and that the Fish frees itself from any Thing that troubles it by this Means. The Fish of the *Great Bank* is what is salted; and this is what they call *White Cod*, or more commonly *Green Cod*. M. *Denys* says, he has seen as fine Salt made in *Canada*, as they bring from *Brouage*; but after they had made the Expriment in Marshes, which they had dug for that Purpose, they stopped them up again. Those who most exclaimed that this Country was good for nothing, have been more than once the very People that have hindered us from making any Advantage of it. The Dry Cod cannot be made but upon the Coast; and this requires great Care and Experience. M. *Denys*, who allows that all those that he has seen carry on this Trade in *Acadia*, had ruined themselves by it, proves perfectly, and makes it appear very plain, that it was wrong to conclude from hence, that there was not a Plenty of Cod. But he alledges, that to carry on the Fishery with Success, the Fishermen must be settled in the Country; and these are his Reasons. Every Season is not fit for this Fishery, it can only be carried on from the Beginning of *May* to the End of *August*. Now if you have Seamen from *France*, either you must pay them for the whole Year, and the Charges will eat up the Profit; or you will only pay them during the Time of the Fishing, and that will not do for them. To think of employing them the rest of the Time in sawing Planks, and cutting Wood, is quite a wrong Notion, for it would not answer the Expence.* But if they

* This Remark, if a just one, may put us out of Fear of the *French* rivalling us at present in the Fishery by what is allowed to them by the late Treaty.

are Inhabitants, you will be better ſerved; and it will be their own Faults if they don't thrive: They will take their Time for the Fiſhery; they will chuſe the beſt Places; they will gain much during four Months, and the reſt of the Year they will work for themſelves, in their Habitations. If this Method had been taken a hundred and fifty Years ago, *Acadia* had now been one of the moſt powerful Colonies in *America*. For whilſt they affected to publiſh in *France*, it was impoſſible to make any Thing of this Country, it enriched *New England*, by the Fiſhery alone; altho' the *Engliſh* had not all the Advantages there, which we could have had.

When we are paſſed the *Great Bank*, we meet with ſeveral ſmaller ones, almoſt equally abounding with Fiſh as the *Great Bank*. There are indeed few or none of thoſe Fiſh which require warmer Seas; but there are a great Number of Whales, Spouting Fiſh, Porpoiſes, *&c.* and many others of leſs Value. We have more than once had the Diverſion of the Fight between the Whale and the Sword Fiſh, and nothing is more entertaining: The Sword Fiſh is as thick as a Cow, ſeven or eight Feet long, gradually leſſening towards the Tail. It takes its Name from its Weapon, a Kind of Sword three Feet long, and four Inches wide; it is fixed above its Noſe, and has a Row of Teeth on each Side an Inch long, at an equal Diſtance from each other: This Fiſh is good with any Sauce, and is excellent eating; its Head is better eating than a Calf's, and is bigger and ſquarer; and the Eyes are very large.

Fight of the Whale and the Sword Fiſh.

The Whale and the Sword Fiſh never meet without fighting, and the latter, they ſay, is always the Aggreſſor. Sometimes two Sword Fiſh join againſt a Whale, and then it is not an equal Match: The Whale has neither Weapon offenſive nor defenſive but its Tail; to make Uſe of it againſt her Enemy, ſhe plunges her Head under Water, and if ſhe can ſtrike her Enemy ſhe kills him with a Blow of her Tail; but he is very dexterous to ſhun it, and inſtantly falls upon the Whale, and runs his Weapon in its Back; moſt commonly it pierces not to the Bottom of the Fat, and ſo does it no great Injury. When the Whale can ſee the Sword Fiſh dart to ſtrike him, he plunges; but the Sword Fiſh purſues him in the Water, and obliges him to appear again: Then the Fight begins again, and laſts till the Sword Fiſh looſes Sight of the Whale, which fights always retreating, and ſwims beſt on the Surface of the Water.

The *Flettan* or *Hallibut* is like a large Plaice; what they call the *Flet*, is a ſmaller Kind; it is dark coloured on the Back, and white under the Belly; it is generally four or five Feet

Feet long, and at leaſt two Feet broad, and a Foot thick; it has a large Head: Every Part of it is extremely good and tender; they get a Juice out of the Bones, which is better than the fineſt Marrow. The Eyes and the Edges of the two Sides, which they call *Relingues*, are very delicate Bits. They throw the whole Body into the Sea to fatten the Cod, whoſe moſt dangerous Enemy is the *Flettan*, who will eat three of them at a Meal. — I ſhall ſay nothing of the various Kinds of Birds which live upon theſe Seas, and ſubſiſt only by Fiſhing; for here all are Fiſhers. Many Travellers have deſcribed them, and have ſaid nothing on this Head that deſerves to be repeated.

The 18th, the Wind fair, we think the Winds have carried us a little too much to the South, and we ſteer Weſt North Weſt, to get into our Latitude. The Reaſon is, we have not ſeen the Sun theſe ten or twelve Days, and therefore could not obſerve our Latitude. This frequently happens, and is what cauſes the greateſt Danger of this Voyage. About eight in the Morning we ſaw a ſmall Veſſel, which ſeemed to make towards us; we met it, and when we were near we enquired in what Latitude we were: It was an *Engliſh* Ship, and the Captain anſwered in his own Language: We thought we underſtood him that we were in 45 Degrees; we could not greatly truſt to this Account, for he might be under the ſame Miſtake as ourſelves: However, we took Courage, and as the Wind continued fair, we flattered ourſelves, if it did not change, we ſhould have paſſed the Gulph in two Days.

Error of the Pilots, and the dangerous Conſequences of it.

About four in the Afternoon the Wind fell, which was a Concern to us; however, this ſaved us. At eleven at Night the Horizon appeared very dark before us, tho' every where elſe the Sky was very ſerene: The Sailors of the Watch * made no ſcruple to ſay it was Land; the Officer made a Jeſt of it, but when he found they perſiſted in the ſame Opinion, he began to think they might be in the right. By good Fortune there was very little Wind; ſo that we hoped Day would appear, before we ſhould come too near the Land. At Midnight the Watch changed; the Sailors who ſucceeded the firſt, were directly of their Opinion; but their Officer undertook to prove by good Reaſons, that the Land could not be there, and what they ſaw was only a Fog, which would diſperſe in the Morning; he could not make them think ſo, and they continued poſitive in their Opinion, that the Sky

* A Ship's Company is divided into four Bands, each of which are on Duty four Hours; each Band is commanded by an Officer.

was too clear to have any Fog on that Side, if there was no Land.

At Day-break they all cried out that they saw Land, the Officer would not vouchsafe so much as to look that Way, but shrugged up his Shoulders, and four o'Clock striking, he goes to Bed, affirming that when he waked, they would find this pretended Land melted away. The Officer that succeeded, who was the Count *de Vaudreuil*, being more wary, began furling some Sails, and soon saw this Precaution was necessary. As soon as it was Day-light they saw the Horizon almost all bordered with Land; and they discovered a small *English* Vessel at Anchor, about the Distance of two Cannon Shot from us. M. *de Voutron*, who was informed of it, immediately sent for the incredulous Officer, who came out of his Cabin with much Reluctance, where he still persisted that we could not be so near Land; he came, however, after two or three Summonses, and at Sight of the Danger we had been exposed to by his Obstinacy, he stood astonished. He is, notwithstanding, the most skilful Man in France to navigate these Seas; but too much Skill sometimes does Harm, when we rely too much upon it.

Neverthelefs, Madam, if the Wind had not failed the Day before, at four in the Afternoon, we had certainly been lost in the Night; for we were running full Sail upon some Breakers, from whence we could not have escaped. The Difficulty was to know whereabouts we were; it was certain we were not in 45 Degrees the Day before, but were we more to the South or North? On this we were divided in our Opinions. One of our Officers affirmed, that the Land we saw before us was *Acadia*; that he had been there before, and remembered it: Another asserted, that it was the Isles of St. *Peter*: But what Probability is there that we are so far advanced? It is but twenty-four Hours since we were upon the *Great Bank*, and it is more than 100 Leagues from the *Great Bank* to the Isles of St. *Peter*. The Pilot *Chaviteau* maintained it was *Cape Race*: What a Mistake, says he, is there in our Reckoning! there is no Doubt of it, and it is no Wonder, as it is impossible to make Allowances for Currents we do not know, and which vary continually, as we have had no Observation to correct our Errors; but there is no Probability that we should be either on the Coasts of *Acadia*, or on the Isles of St. *Peter*. His Reasons appeared * good, yet we should have been

* About 5 Years after, the same *Chaviteau* mistook in his Reckoning in a Manner much more fatal; he was still Master of the *Camel*, and having been several Days without an Observation, the Night of the 25th of *August*, this Ship was wrecked upon a Rock near *Louisbourg*, in *Isle Royal*, and no Person was saved. They found by the Journals of the Pilots, that they reckoned themselves 70 Leagues from that Place.

been very glad if he had been miſtaken; for we conceived how vexatious it would be to be Wind-bound under *Cape Race.* In this Uncertainty, we reſolved to enquire of the Captain of the *Engliſh* Ship, and *Chaviteau* had Orders to do it: At his Return he reported, that the *Engliſh* were as much ſurprized as we to find themſelves in this Bay, but with this Difference, that it was the Place they were bound to: That *Cape Race* was before us, and *Cape Brolle* ten Leagues lower; that from the midſt of thoſe Breakers, upon which we had run a Riſk of being loſt, there iſſued a River, at the Entrance of which there was an *Engliſh* Village, whither this little Veſſel was carrying Proviſions.

About 15 Years ſince, there happened to us in the ſame Place, a very ſingular Adventure, which put us in as much Danger as that which I have juſt now mentioned. It was in *Auguſt*, and we had till then felt the Weather very hot: One Morning when we roſe, we were ſo pierced with the Cold, that every Body put on their Winter Garments. We could not conceive from whence it could proceed, the Weather being fine, and no North Wind. In ſhort, the third Day at four o'Clock in the Morning, a Sailor cried as loud as he could, *Luff*; that is to ſay, turn the Helm to the Windward; he was obeyed, and the Moment after they perceived a vaſt floating Piece of Ice, which ran cloſe by the Ship's Side, and againſt which we ſhould have been wrecked, if the Sailor had not had good Eyes, and if the Steerſman had not directly turned the Helm.

I did not ſee this Ice, for I was not yet up; but all who were then upon Deck aſſured us, that it ſeemed as high as the Towers of *Notre Dame* at *Paris*, and was for certainty much higher than the Maſts of the Ship. I have often heard it affirmed that ſuch a Thing was impoſſible, becauſe it muſt have been prodigiouſly deep to riſe ſo high above the Sea; and that it was not poſſible that a Piece of Ice ſhould acquire that Height: To this I anſwer in the firſt Place, that to deny the Fact we muſt give the Lie to many People, for it is not the firſt Time that ſuch floating Rocks have been ſeen in the Sea. The Ship called the *Mother* of the *Incarnation*, making the ſame Courſe as we did, ran the ſame Danger in open Day; the Rock of Ice which nearly occaſioned its Loſs, for Want of Wind to ſhun it, was ſeen by the whole Ship's Company, and judged to be much greater ſtill, than that which we met. They add that the General Abſolution was given, as in Caſes of the greateſt Danger.

It is certain in the ſecond Place, that in *Hudſon's Bay* there are ſome of theſe Rocks of Ice formed by the Fall of Torrents, which come from the Tops of the Mountains, and which break away with a vaſt Noiſe during the Summer, and are afterwards driven about by the Currents. The Sieur *Jeremy* who lived many Years this Bay, says he had the Curiosity to sound at the Foot of one of these Rocks of Ice which was aground, and that they let out an hundred Fathoms of Line without reaching the Bottom. But I return to our Voyage.

Of Cape Race.

Cape Race Madam, is the South East Point of the Island of *New-foundland*; it is situated in 46 Degrees, and about 30 Minutes North Latitude; the Coast runs from thence 100 Leagues to the West, making a little to the North, and terminates at *Cape Race*, which is in 47 Degrees. About half Way is the great Bay of *Placentia*, which makes one of the finest Ports in *America*. West South West of this Bay, there is a high Land, which is seen at a great Distance, and serves to make it known: It is called *le Chapeau rouge* (the Red Hat) because at a Distance it appears in the Shape of a Hat, and is of a reddish Colour. The 23d at Noon we were over against it, and in the Evening we came up with the Isles of St. *Peter*, which were on our right Hand.

The Isles of St. Peter.

They are three Islands, the two first of which are very high, and from the Side on which we were, they appeared to be nothing but Mountains covered with Moss. They say that this Moss covers in several Places fine Porphyry. On the Side of *New-foundland* there are some Lands which may be cultivated; and a pretty good Port, were we formerly had some Habitations. The greatest and most Western of the three, which is most commonly called the Isle *Miquelon*, is not so high as the other two, and appears very level; it is about three quarters of a League long. The 24th at Day break, it was 5 or 6 Leagues behind us; but after Midnight we had no Wind: About four o'Clock in the Morning, there arose a small Breeze from the South East. Waiting till it was strong enough to fill our Sails, we amused ourselves with Fishing, and took a pretty large Quantity of Cod. We stopt two Hours longer than we should have done, for this Fishery, and we had soon Cause enough to repent it: It was eight o'Clock when we got under Sail, and we run all the Day in Hopes of discovering *Cape Ray*, which was on our right, or the little Isle of St. *Paul*, which we were to leave on the left, and which is almost over against *Cape Ray*; but the Night came on before we could discover either. We heartily wished then, we had made Use of the Time we had lost. What was the more vexatious we had about Midnight another Storm, much like that on the *Great Bank*, and knowing that we were near one of those two Islands which we were to pass between, we did not dare to make Use of the Wind, which would have carried us on at a great Rate. So, contrary to the Opinion of *Chaviteau*, who engaged to go forward without Danger, we lay by.

At break of Day we discovered *Cape Ray*, upon which the Currents

Currents bore us, and to encreafe our Misfortune, we had no Wind to keep us off: We were almoft upon it, when about half an Hour paft five in the Morning a fmall Breeze from the North Weft, came in very good Time to our Affiftance. We loft nothing of it, and we got out of Danger. The North Weft after having done us this good Office, would have obliged us extremely, if it had given Place to fome other Wind; but it did not, and for two Days kept us at the Entrance of the Gulf of *St. Laurence*. On the third Day we paffed between the Ifle of *St. Paul*, and Cape *St. Laurence*, which is the moft northerly Point of Ifle *Royal*; this Paffage is very narrow, and we do not hazard ourfelves in it, when the Air is foggy. The Paffage which is between the Ifle of *St. Paul* and *Cape Ray*, is much wider; but our Sails were fet to take the other, and we made Ufe of it.

Of the Gulf of St. Laurence, *and the Bird Iflands.*

The Gulf of *St. Laurence* is 80 Leagues long, which we paffed with a good Wind in twenty-four Hours, by the help of the Currents. About half Way we meet with the *Bird Iflands*, which we paffed within Cannon Shot, and which muft not be confounded with thofe which *James Cartier* difcovered near the Ifland of *Newfoundland*. Thefe I fpeak of, are two Rocks, which appeared to me to rife perpendicular, about 60 Feet above the Sea; the largeft of which is not above 2 or 300 Paces in Circumference: They are very near each other, and I believe there is not Water enough between them for a large Boat. It is difficult to fay what Colour they are, for the Dung of the Birds entirely cover their Surface and Sides: Yet we difcovered in fome Places, Veins of a reddifh Colour. They have been often vifited, and Boats have been entirely loaded here with Eggs of all Sorts: They fay that the Stench is infupportable. They add, that with the *Penguins*, which come from the neighbouring Lands, they find many other Birds which can't fly. The Wonder is, that in fuch a Multitude of Nefts, every Bird immediately finds her own. We fired a Gun, which gave the Alarm thro' all this flying Commonwealth, and there was formed above the two Iflands, a thick Cloud of thefe Birds, which was at leaft two or three Leagues round.

The next Day, about the Dawn, the Wind dropt all at once. In two Hours more we could have doubled *Cape Rofiers*, and have entered the River *St. Laurence*, which runs North Eaft and South Weft, and the North Weft Wind which rofe foon after, would have ferved us; but we loft two Hours of the twenty-four in Fifhing, and in Confequence, two Days at the Entrance of the Gulf; and we were obliged to wait here till the North Weft dropped, which was not in five Days, in which we made only five Leagues.

Cape *Rosiers* is properly the Entrance of the River *St. Laurence*, and from hence we must measure the Width of its Mouth, which is about 30 Leagues. A little on this Side, more to the South, are the Bay and Point of *Gaspe*, or *Gachepe*. Those who pretend that the River *St. Laurence* is 40 Leagues wide at its Mouth, measure it probably from the Eastern Point of *Gaspe*. Below the Bay we perceive a Kind of Island, which is only a steep Rock, about 30 Fathoms long, 10 high, and 4 in Breadth: It looks like Part of an Old Wall, and they say it joined formerly to *Mount Joli*, which is over against it on the Continent. This Rock has in the midst of it an Opening like an Arch, under which a Boat of *Biscay* may pass with its Sail up, and this has given it the Name of the *pierced* Island: Sailors know they are near it, when they perceive a flat Mountain stand above others, and which is called *Rowland's Table*. The Island of *Bonaventure* is a League distant from the pierced Island; about the same Distance is the Island *Miscou*, which is eight Leagues in Compass, and has a very good Haven. Not far from this Island, there rises out of the Sea a Spring of Fresh Water, which bubbles up, and makes a Jet like a Fountain pretty high.

All these Coasts are excellent for their Fishery, and the Anchorage is good every where. It would be easy also to establish Magazines here for the Use of *Quebec*. But we have lost a great deal of Time in pursuing the Fur Trade, which we should have employed in the Fishery for Cod and many other Sorts of Fish, with which this Sea abounds, and in fortifying ourselves in those Ports, the Importance of which we have discovered too late.

But to return to our Voyage: It was natural upon having near us such safe and convenient Retreats, that we should have made Use of them, to wait for the Return of a fair Wind; but they hoped it would return every Minute, and they wanted to take Advantage of it immediately.

At length, on Thursday the 10th of *September*, the North West Wind dropt about Noon, when finding we could not advance, or scarcely work the Ship, we amused ourselves with fishing, and this Amusement was again hurtful to us; for the Steersman minding his fishing more than his Helm, let the Wind come upon his Sails: During the Calm, we had driven much upon the Isle of *Anticoste*, and this Neglect of the Steersman brought us so near, because the Currents carried us that Way, that we saw plainly all the Breakers with which the Island is bordered. To compleat our Misfortune, the little Wind which was just risen failed us in our Necessity.

Had this Calm continued but a short Time, we had been lost. A Moment after our Sails swelled a little, and we endeavoured

to

to change our Course, but the Ship, contrary to what is usual, would not come to the Wind, and this twice together: A certain Proof, that the Current by which it was carried was very strong. We thought ourselves lost without Resource, because we were very near the Rocks: To run the Risk of turning about with the Wind in our Poop was extremely hazardous; but after all, there was nothing else to be done; so we set ourselves to work, rather to have nothing to reproach ourselves with, then in Hopes of saving ourselves; and in an Instant we found by Experience, that God comes to the Assistance of those that endeavour to help themselves. The Wind changed to the North, it freshened by Degrees, and about seven o'Clock at Night we cleared the Point of *Anticosie*, which had put us in so much Fear.

Description of the Isle of Anticoste.

This Island extends about 40 Leagues North East, and South West, about the Middle of the River *St. Laurence*, but has little Breadth. It was granted to the Sieur *Joliet*, upon his Return from the Discovery of the *Mississippi*, but they made him no great Present. It is absolutely good for nothing: It is poorly wooded, its Soil is barren, and it has not a single Harbour where a Ship may be in Safety. There was a Report some Years ago, that there was a Mine of Silver discovered in this Island; and for Want of Miners, they sent from *Quebec* (where I was at that Time) a Goldsmith to make the Proof of it; but he did not go far. He soon perceived by the Discourse of the Person who raised the Report, that the Mine existed only in his own whimsical Brain.

The Coasts of this Island are pretty well stored with Fish; nevertheless, I am persuaded, that the Heirs of the Sieur *Joliet* would willingly change their vast Lordship, for the smallest Fief of *France*.

When we have passed this Island, we have the Pleasure to see Land on both Sides, and to be assured of the Way we make; but we must sail with a great deal of Caution up the River. *Tuesday* the 3d, we left on the left Hand the Mountains of *Notre Dame*, and Mount *Louis*; it is a Chain of very high Mountains, between which there are some Vallies, which were formerly inhabited by Savages. The Country round about Mount *Louis* has some very good Land, and some *French* Habitations. They might make here a very good Settlement for the Fishery, especially for Whales; and it would be convenient for Ships which come from *France*, to find Assistance here, which they sometimes extremely want. The next Night the Wind encreased, and was very near playing us an ugly Trick. We were not far from *Trinity Point*, which we were to leave upon our right; and the Steersman thought us wide enough from it to be out of Danger; but M. *de Voutron* started up in a Fright, crying

crying out to the Steersman to keep off the Shore. If this Order had been deferred a Quarter of an Hour, the Ship had run upon the Point, which appeared some Moments after. The 4th at Night, we anchored for the first Time, a little below what they call the *Paps* of *Matane*. They are two Heads of the same Mountain, which is ab~ut two Leagues within Land. I do not think one can see a wilder Country; there is nothing to be seen but poor Woods, Rocks, Sands, and not one Inch of good Land; there are indeed some fine Springs, and Plenty of good Wild-Fowl; but it is impossible for any but Savages and *Canadians* to follow their Game in such a Place. On the other Side of the River is the Shoal of *Manicouagan*, famous for more than one Ship-wreck, which advances two Leagues into the River. It takes its Name from a River which rises in the Mountains of *Labrador*, makes a pretty large Lake, which bears the same Name, but more commonly that of *St. Barnabas*, and discharges itself into the River *St. Laurence* across the Sand: Some of our Maps call it *la Rivure Noire* (the *Black River*.)

The 8th we set Sail, but it was not worth our while for the Way we made; but Variety of Amusement and Exercise is good for Sailors. In the Night of the 10th we made 15 Leagues; and in half a League more we had cleared the most difficult Passage of the River. We also should have got into the strong Tides, for to this Place they are hardly yet perceivable but at the Shores: But the Wind changed suddenly to the South West, and obliged us to seek for Shelter, which we found under Isle *Verte* or *Green Island*, where we remained five Days. We wanted nothing here, but at the End of this Time, we resolved to try if we could not find on the North Side, as we were made to hope, some Land Winds, which would carry us into the great Tides.

We went therefore, and anchored at *MoulinBaude (Baude Mill)*

Of Saguenay, *and the Port of* Tadoussac.

the Traverse is five Leagues over. Upon arriving here, I asked to see the Mill, and they shewed me some Rocks, from whence issued a stream of clear Water. They might build a Water-Mill here, but it is not likely it will ever be done. There is not perhaps a Country in the World less habitable than this. The *Saguenay* is a little higher; it is a River which the largest Vessels may go up 25 Leagues; at the Entrance we leave the Port of *Tadoussac* to the Right. The greatest Part of our Geographers have here placed a Town, but where there never was but one *French* House, and some Huts of Savages who came there in the Time of the Trade, and who carried away their Huts or Booths, when they went away; and this was the whole Matter. It is true that this Port has been a long Time the Resort of all the Savage Nations of the North and East, and that

that the *French* resorted hither as soon as the Navigation was free, both from *France* and *Canada*; the Missionaries also made Use of the Opportunity, and came to trade here for Heaven: And when the Trade was over, the Merchants returned to their Homes, the Savages took the Way to their Villages or Forests, and the Gospel Labourers followed the last, to compleat their Instructions. Yet some Accounts, and some Travellers, have spoken much of *Tadoussac*; and the Geographers have supposed it was a Town; and some Authors have given it a Jurisdiction.

Tadoussac in other Respects, is a good Port, and they assured me that 25 Men of War might lay here sheltered from all Winds; that the Anchorage is safe, and Entrance easy. Its Shape is almost round, some steep Rocks of a prodigious Height surround it on all Sides, and a small Stream runs from them, which may supply the Ships with Water. All the Country is full of Marble; but its greatest Riches would be the Whale Fishery. In 1705, being at Anchor with the *Herce* in this Place, I saw four of these Fish, which were between Head and Tail, almost as long as our Ship. The *Biscaniers* have followed this Fishery formerly with Success, and there is still upon a little Island of their Name, and which is little lower than Isle *Verte (Green Island)* some Remains of the Furnaces, and the Ribs of the Whales. What a Difference is there betwixt a fixt Fishery, which they might follow quietly in a River, and that which they go to *Greenland* for with so much Danger and Expence. The two following Days there was no Land Wind, and we greatly regretted our first Anchorage, near which there were some *French* Habitations, whereas here we saw neither Man nor Beast: In short, the 3d Day at Noon we weighed Anchor, and we cleared the Passage of *L'Isle Rouge (Red Island)* which is difficult. You must first bear upon the Island as if you would land on it, this is to shun the *Pointe aux Allouetts (Lark Point)* which is at the Entrance of *Saguenay* upon the Left, and which advances greatly into the River; having done this, we change our Course. The Passage on the South of *L'Isle Rouge* is much safer, but to do this we must have gone back, and the Wind might have failed us. *L'Isle Rouge* is only a Rock a little above Water, which appears red, and upon which more than one Ship has been lost.

Of the Isle aux Condres, *and the Gulf.*

The next Day with little Wind and Tide, we came to an Anchor above the Island *Coudres*, which is 15 Leagues from *Quebec* and *Tadoussac*; and this Passage is dangerous, when the Wind is not to our Desire; it is rapid, straight, and a Mile long. Formerly it was much safer, but in 1663 an Earthquake rooted up a Mountain, and threw it upon the Isle of *Coudres*, which was made one half larger than before, and in the Place of the Mountain

Mountain there appeared a Gulf, which it is not safe to approach. We might have passed on the South of the Island *Coudres*, and this Passage would have been safe and easy; it bears the Name of M. *d'Iberville*, who tryed it with Success, but it is the Custom to pass by the North, and Custom is an absolute Law for the Generality of Mankind.

Of the Bay of St. Paul.

Above the Gulph I have just mentioned is the Bay of *St. Paul*, where the Habitations begin on the North Side; and there are some Woods of Pine-Trees, which are much valued: Here are also some red Pines of great Beauty. Messrs. of the Seminary of *Quebec* are Lords of this * Bay. Six Leagues higher, there is a very high Promontory, which terminates a Chain of Mountains, which extend above 400 Leagues to the West: It is called Cape *Torment*, probably because he that gave it this Name, suffered here by a Gust of Wind. The Anchorage is good, and we are surrounded by Islands of all Sizes, which afford a very good Shelter. The most considerable is the Isle of *Orleans*, the Fields of which being all cultivated, appear like an Amphitheatre, and terminate the Prospect very pleasingly. This Island is about 14 Leagues in Compass; and in 1676 it was made a Title of Honour, and first gave Title of Count to *Francis Berthelot*, Secretary General of the Ordinance, by the Stile of Count *St. Laurence*; who purchased it of *Francis de Laval*, first Bishop of *Quebec*. It contained then four Villages, but it has now six Parishes pretty well peopled. Of the two Channels made by this Island, that of the South only is navigable for Ships: Even Boats cannot pass that of the North but at high Water: So that from Cape *Torment* we must traverse the River to go to *Quebec*, and this Traverse has its Difficulties; we meet with some moving Sands, on which there is not always Water enough for large Vessels, so that this is never attempted but whilst the Tide flows. But this Difficulty might be shunned by taking the Passage of M. *d'Iberville*. Cape *Torment*, from which we pass to make the Traverse, is 110 Leagues from the Sea, and yet the Water is a little brackish: It is not fit to drink, but at the Entrance of the two Canals, which form the Isle of *Orleans*. This is a Phœnomenon pretty hard to explain, especially if we consider the great Rapidity of the River, notwithstanding its Breadth. The Tide flows here regularly 5 Hours, and ebbs seven. At *Tadoussac* it ebbs and flows six Hours; and the higher we go up the River, the more the Flood diminishes, and the Ebb increases. At twenty Leagues above *Quebec* it flows three Hours, and ebbs nine. Higher up the Tide is not perceivable. When it is

* A very good Lead Mine has been found here lately.

half

half Flood in the Port of *Tadoussac*, and at the Entrance of *Saguenay*, it is but just beginning to flow at *Checoutimi*, twenty-five Leagues higher up the River *Saguenay*; and yet it is high Water at the three Places at the same Time: This happens no Doubt because the Rapidity of the River *Saguenay*, greater than that of *St. Laurence*, running against the Tide, makes an Equilibrium for some Time between *Checoutimi*, and the Entrance of the *Saguenay* into the Great River. This Rapidity was not so great but since the Earthquake of 1663. This Earthquake overthrew a Mountain in the River, which straitened its Bed, and formed a Peninsula, which they call *Checoutimi*, above which the Stream is so strong, that Canoes can't get up it. The Depth of *Saguenay*, from its Mouth up to *Checoutimi*, is equal to its Rapidity: So that it would not be safe to anchor in it, if they could not make fast their Vessels to the Trees that cover the Banks of this River.

It is also found that in the Gulf of *St. Laurence*, at eight or ten Leagues from the Land, the Tides are different, according to the various Situations of the Land, or the Difference of the Seasons; that in some Places they follow the Winds, and in others they run against the Wind; that at the Mouth of the River, at certain Months of the Year, the Currents always run to the Sea, and in others always towards the Land; and lastly, that in the River itself, till near the seven Islands, *that is to say*, sixty Leagues, there is no Flux on the South Side, nor any Reflux on the North Side. It is not easy to give any good Reasons for all this; all that can be said, with the greatest Probability, is, that there are some Motions under Water, which produce these Irregularities, or that there are some Currents which come and go from the Surface to the Bottom, and from the Bottom to the Surface, in the Manner of Pumps. Another Observation to be made here is, that the Variation of the Compass (which in some Ports of *France*, is but two or three Degrees North West) continues always decreasing till we come to the *Azores*, where there is no longer any Variation; but from thence it increases in such a Manner, that upon the *Great Bank* of *Newfoundland* it is twenty-two Degrees and more; afterwards it begins to decrease, but slowly, since it is still sixteen Degrees at *Quebec*, and twelve in the Country of the *Hurons*, where the Sun sets thirty-three Minutes later than at *Quebec*.

Of the Isle of Orleans.

Sunday the twenty-second, we cast Anchor by the Isle of *Orleans*, where we went to take an Airing, till the Return of the Tide. I found this Country fine, the Soil good, and the Inhabitants pretty well at their Ease. They have the Character of being given to Witchcraft; and they are consulted, they say, upon future Events, and concerning what passes in distant Places.

For Inſtance: If the Ships of *France* do not arrive ſo ſoon as uſual, they are conſulted to hear News of them, and it is ſaid they have ſometimes anſwered pretty true; *that is to ſay*, having gueſſed right once or twice, and having out of Diverſion made People believe that they ſpoke from a certain Knowledge, People fancied they had conſulted the Devil.

When *James Cartier* diſcovered this Iſland, he found it full of Vines, and named it the Iſle of *Bacchus*. This Navigator was a *Britain*. After him there came ſome *Normans*; who plucked up the Vines, and ſubſtituted *Pomona* and *Ceres* in the Room of *Bacchus*. In Fact, it produces good Wheat and excellent Fruit. They alſo begin to cultivate Tobacco, and it is not bad.—At length, on *Monday* the 23d, the *Camel* anchored before *Quebec*, where I arrived two Hours before in a Canoe of Bark. I have a thouſand Leagues to travel in theſe brittle Vehicles: I muſt uſe myſelf to them by Degrees.———This is, Madam, all that I could recollect of the Particulars of my Voyage.---I ſhall have ſomething of more Conſequence to write hereafter.

I am, &c.

LETTER II.

A Deſcription of QUEBEC, *Character of the Inhabitants, and the Manner of Living in the* FRENCH COLONY.

MADAM, QUEBEC, *Oct.* 28, 1720.

I Am going to ſpeak of *Quebec*.---All the Deſcriptions I have hitherto ſeen of it are ſo different, that I thought it would be a Pleaſure to you to ſee a true Picture of this Capital of *New France*. It really deſerves to be known, were it only for the Singularity of its Situation; for it is the only City in the World that can boaſt of a Port in freſh Water a hundred and twenty Leagues from the Sea, and capable of containing one hundred Ships of the Line. It is alſo ſituated on the moſt navigable River in the World.

Whence the Name of Quebec *is derived.*

This River, up to the Iſle of ORLEANS, *that is to ſay*, one hundred and ten, or one hundred and twelve Leagues from the Sea, is never leſs than four or five Leagues wide; but above the Iſland it grows narrower all at once, ſo that before *Quebec* it is but a Mile broad, which gave it the Name of *Quebeio*, or *Quebec*; which, in the *Algonquin* Language, ſignifies *Contraction*. The *Abenaquis*, whoſe Language is a Dialect of the *Algonquin*,

Algonquin, call it *Quelibec*, which ſignifies ſomething *ſhut up*; becauſe, at the Entrance of the little River *Chaudiere*, by which the Savages came to *Quebec* from the Neighbourhood of *Acadia*, the Point of *Levi* which advances upon the Iſle of *Orleans*, entirely hides the South Channel, and the Iſle of *Orleans* hides the North; ſo that the Port of *Quebec* appears only like a great Bay.

The Fall of Montmorenci.

The firſt Thing that appears upon entering the Road, is a fine Sheet of Water, about thirty Feet wide, and forty Feet high. It is directly at the Entrance of the little Channel of the Iſle of *Orleans*, and it is ſeen from a long Point of the South Coaſt of the River; which, as I ſaid before, ſeems to bend upon the Iſle of *Orleans*. This Caſcade is called the *Fall of Montmorenci*, and the Point bears the Name of *Levi*; for *New France* had ſucceſſively for Viceroys, the Admiral *Montmorenci*, and the Duke *de Ventadour* his Nephew. Every Body would judge that ſuch a large Fall of Water, which runs continually, was the Diſcharge of ſome fine River, but it is only derived from an inconſiderable Current which in ſome Places is not Ancle deep; but it runs continually, and has its Riſe from a Lake about twelve Leagues from the Fall.

The Situation of Quebec.

The City is a League higher, and on the ſame Side, in the very Place where the River is narroweſt; but between the City and the Iſle of *Orleans*, there is a Baſon a full League in Extent every Way, into which the River *St. Charles* diſcharges itſelf, which comes from the North-Weſt. *Quebec* is between the Mouth of this River and *Diamond Cape*, which advances a little into the River *St. Laurence*. The Moorings are over-againſt the City. There is twenty-five Fathom Water, and good Anchorage; yet, when the North-Eaſt blows hard, Ships ſometimes drive upon their Anchors, but without Danger.

Deſcription of Quebec.

When *Samuel de Champlain* founded this City in 1608, the Tide roſe ſometimes to the Foot of the Rock. Since that Time the River has retired by Degrees, and left a great Space dry, where they have built the lower City, which is at preſent high enough above the Shore to ſecure the Inhabitants againſt the Inundations of the River. The firſt Thing we find at landing, is a pretty large Spot of an irregular Figure, which has in Front a Row of Houſes pretty well built, their Backſide cloſe to the Rock, ſo that they have but little Depth: They make a pretty long Street, which takes up the whole Breadth of the Place, and extends from Right to Left to two Ways, which lead to the upper City. The Place is bounded on the Left by a ſmall Church, and on the Right by two Rows of Houſes built on a Parallel. There is one Row on the other Side between the Church and the Port; and at the Turning of Cape *Diamond*, there is another pretty long Range of Houfes on the Side of a fmall Bay, which is called the *l'Anfe de Meres, (Mother's Bay.)* This Quarter may be reckoned a Kind of Suburb to the lower City.

Between this Suburb and the great Street we afcend to the upper City, by a Way fo fteep, that they have been obliged to make Steps, fo that we can only afcend on Foot: But taking the Right Hand Side, they have made a Way which is not fo fteep, and which is bordered by Houfes: 'Tis at the Spot where the two Ways meet, that the upper City begins on the Side towards the River *St. Laurence*; for there is another lower City on the Side of the River *St. Charles*. The firft remarkable Building we find to the Right of the firft Side, is the Bifhop's Palace: All the Left is bordered with Houfes. Twenty Paces further, we arrive at two pretty large Squares, or Openings: That on the Left is the Place of Arms, which is before the Fort, where the Governor-General refides. The *Recollets* are over-againft it, and fome pretty good Houfes are built on the other Side of the Square.

In that on the Right Hand, we meet firft the Cathedral, which alfo ferves as a Parifh Church to all the City. The Seminary is on one Side, upon the Angle made by the River *St. Laurence* and the River *St. Charles*. Over-againft the Cathedral, is the *Jefuits* College, and between both there are pretty good Houfes. From the Place of Arms, we enter two Streets, which are croffed by a third, which is entirely taken up by the Church and Convent of the *Recollets*. The fecond Opening has two Defcents to the River *St. Charles*; one very fteep on the Side of the Seminary, where there are few Houfes; the other, by the Side of the *Jefuits* Inclofure, which winds very much, and has the *Hotel Dieu* about the Mid-way, is bordered by fmall Houfes, and ends at the Palace of the Intendant. On the other Side of the *Jefuits* College, where the Church is, there is a pretty long Street, in which are the *Urfulines*.---To conclude, all the upper City is built on a Foundation of Marble and Slate. *(a)*

This is, Madam, the Topography of *Quebec*; which, as you fee, has a pretty large Extent. Moft of the Houfes are built of Stone; and yet it is reckoned to contain but about feven thoufand Souls.—But to give you a juft Idea of this City, I fhall defcribe its principal Buildings more particularly, and then I fhall give an Account of its Fortifications.---The Church of the lower City was built in Confequence of a Vow made during the Siege

(a) This City is confiderably increafed within the laft twenty Years.

of

of *Quebec*, in 1690. It is dedicated to *Our Lady of Victory*, and ſerves the Inhabitants of the lower City. It is a very plain Building: All its Ornament is a modeſt Neatneſs. Some Siſters of a Congregation which I ſhall mention hereafter, are lodged between this Church and the Port. There are but four or five, and keep a School.

This Epiſcopal Palace is finiſhed, excepting the Chapel, and half the Buildings of the Deſign, which was intended to be a long Square. If it is ever finiſhed, it will be a very fine Building. The Garden extends to the Brow of the Rock, and commands all the Road.—When the Capital of *New France* ſhall be as flouriſhing *(a)* as that of the *Old*, (we muſt deſpair of nothing, *Paris* was a long Time much leſs than *Quebec* is now,) as far as the Eye can reach they will ſee only Towns, Caſtles, Country Houſes; and all this is already ſketched out: And the River *St. Laurence*, that majeſtically rolls her Waters, and brings them from the Extremity of the North or the Weſt, will be covered with Veſſels. The Iſle of *Orleans*, and the two Banks of the two Rivers that form this Port, will diſcover fine Meadows, rich Hills, and fertile Fields; and nothing is wanting for this End, but to be more peopled. A Part of a charming Valley (which the River *St. Charles* winds pleaſingly through) will, no Doubt, be joined to the City, of which it will certainly make the fineſt Quarter: And when they have bordered all the Road with noble Quays, and we ſhall ſee three or four hundred Ships loaded with Riches which hitherto we have not known how to value, and bringing back in Exchange thoſe of the Old and New World, you will acknowledge, Madam, that this Terraſs will afford a Proſpect that nothing can equal.

The Cathedral and the Seminary.

The Cathedral would not be a fine Pariſh Church in one of the ſmalleſt Towns in *France*. Judge, then, if it deſerves to be the Seat of the only Biſhoprick which is in all the *French* Empire in *America*, of greater Extent, than was ever that of the *Romans*. The Architecture, the Choir, the great Altar, the Chapels of this Cathedral, appear only fit for a Country Church. The moſt tolerable Thing belonging to it, is a very high Tower or Steeple, ſolidly built, and which at a Diſtance makes ſome Appearance. The Seminary, which joins to the Church, is a large Square, the Buildings of which are not finiſhed: What is built,

(a) The Event of Things has ſhewn, that this Author had not a true Prophetic Spirit. How muſt the *French* be mortified, to find all their fond Hopes of raiſing *Quebec* to ſuch a Height of Magnificence, fruſtrated by the Valour of the *Engliſh* Arms; and to ſee that vaſt Empire, which they flattered themſelves they ſhould be able to eſtabliſh in *North America*, all transferred and annexed to the Imperial Crown of *Britain*!

is well done, and with all the Conveniencies necessary in this Country. This is the third Time of building this House. It was burnt entirely in 1703. And in *October*, 1705, when it was just rebuilt, it was almost totally destroyed by Fire. From the Garden there is a Prospect of the Road, and the River *St. Charles*, as far as the Eye can reach.

The Fort and Cape Diamond.

The Fort is a fine Building, which is to be flanked with two advanced Pavillions. There is but one built at present. They say the other is to be built very soon. *(a)* The Entrance is a large and regular Court; but it has no Garden, because the Fort is built upon the Edge of the Rock. A fine Gallery, with a Balcony that runs the whole Length of the Building, makes some Amends for this Defect. It commands the Road; to the Middle of which one may easily make oneself heard with a speaking Trumpet; and the lower City appears under your Feet. Coming out of the Fort, and passing to the Left, we enter into a pretty large Esplanade; and, by a gentle Ascent, we arrive at the Top of *Diamond Cape*, which is a very fine Platform. Besides the Pleasure of the Prospect, we breathe in this Place the purest Air, we see Numbers of Porpoises, white as Snow, play on the Surface of the Water, and sometimes pick up Stones which are more beautiful than those of *Alençon*, or *Bristol*. I have seen some as well formed as if they came out of the Hands of the best Workman. Formerly they were common, and this gave the Name to the Cape. At present they are very scarce.------The Descent to the Country here is more gentle than on the Side of the Esplanade.

The Recollets, *and the* Ursulines.

The *Recollets* have a large and fine Church, which would be an Honour to them at *Versailles*. It is neatly roofed, adorned with a large Gallery (something heavy) of Wood, well wrought, which goes all round; in which are made the Confessionals. In short, it wants nothing; but they should take away some Pictures that are very poorly painted. Father *Luke* has placed some here that do no Credit to the Place. The House is answerable to the Church: It is great, solidly built, and convenient, accompanied with a large Garden well cultivated. The *Ursuline* Nuns have suffered twice by Fire, as well as the Seminary: And withal they have such a slender Provision, and the Portions they receive with the Maids of this Country are so small, that the first Time their House was burnt, they had Thoughts of sending them back to *France*: However, they have made a Shift to re-establish themselves both Times, and their Church is quite finished.

(a) It is now finished.

They

They are neatly and conveniently lodged: It is the Fruit of the good Name they have acquired in the Colony by their Piety, Œconomy, Sobriety, and Labour: They gild and embroider. All are usefully employed; and whatever comes from their Hands, is generally of a good Taste.

The Jesuits *College.*

You have seen, without Doubt, Madam, in some of the Relations, that the College of the *Jesuits* is a very fine Building. It is certain, that when this City was a rude Heap of *French* Barracks, and Savage Cabins, this House (the only one with the Fort that was built of Stone) made some Figure. The first Travellers, who judged by Comparison, have represented it as a very fine Building. Those who followed them, and who, according to Custom, copied after them, spoke the same Language: But the Cabins have disappeared, and the Barracks are changed to Houses, most of them well built; so that the College is now a Disgrace to the City, and is in a very ruinous Condition. *(a)*

The Situation is bad: It is deprived of the greatest Advantage it could have, which is the Prospect. It had at first the View of the Road, and its Founders were good enough to fancy that they would be allowed to enjoy it, but they were deceived. The Cathedral and the Seminary make a Mask that leaves them nothing but the View of the Square, which has nothing to make Amends for what they have lost. The Court of the College is small and dirty; nothing resembles more a Farm Yard. The Garden is large and well kept, and is bounded by a little Wood, a precious Remain of the antient Forest that formerly covered this whole Mountain.

The Church has nothing fine on the Outside, but a pretty Sort of a Steeple: It is entirely covered with Slate, and is the only one of *Canada* that has this Advantage, for every Thing here is covered with Shingles. The Inside is well adorned: It has a fine Gallery, bordered with an Iron Balustrade, painted, gilt, and well contrived; a Pulpit entirely gilt, and well wrought in Wood and Iron; three handsome Altars; some good Pictures; the Roof not arched, but flat, and pretty well ornamented; no Pavement, but a good Floor, which makes this Church more supportable in Winter, whilst People are frozen with Cold in the others. I do not mention *the four great cylindric massive Columns, made of one Block of a certain Porphyry black as Jet, without Spots or Veins*, with which it pleased the Baron *de la Hontan* to enrich the grand Altar. They would certainly be much better than those they have, which are hollow, and coarsely covered with Marble. But this Author might easily obtain Pardon, if he had disguised the Truth, only to adorn the Churches.

(a) The College is since rebuilt, and is now very fine.

The Hospital has two large Halls, one for the Men and the other for the Women; the Beds are well kept, the Sick are well attended, and every Thing is convenient, and very neat. The Church is behind the Woman's Hall, and has nothing remarkable but the great Altar, the Altar-piece of which is very fine. This House is served by some Nuns of St. *Austin*, the first of which came from *Dieppe*. They have begun a good House here, but it is very likely they will not soon finish it for Want of a Fund. As their House is situated on the Midway of a Hill, on a Spot that advances a little upon the River *St. Charles*, they have a very pretty Prospect.

The Hospital.

The House of the Intendant is called the *Palace*, because the Chief Council meets there. It is a Grand Pavillion, the Ends of which project some Feet, to which we ascend by a double Flight of Steps. The Front towards the Garden is much pleasanter than that of the Entrance, having a View of the little River. The Royal Magazines are on the right Side of the Court, and the Prison is behind. The Gate at the Entrance is masked by the Mountain, on which the upper City stands, and which presents in this Place only a steep Rock, very disagreeable to the Sight. It was much worse before the Fire, which some Years ago entirely destroyed this (*a*) Palace, for it had no Court in Front, and the Buildings stood upon the Street, which is very narrow. Going down this Street, or more properly speaking, this Way, we come into the Country, and about half a Mile distant stands the General Hospital. It is the finest House in *Canada*, and would be no Disgrace to our greatest Cities of *France*. The *Recollets* formerly possessed this Place: M. *de St. Vallier*, Bishop of *Quebec*, removed them into the City, bought the Ground, and spent 100,000 Crowns in Buildings, Furniture, and a Fund for its Support. The only Defect of this Hospital is, its being built in a Marsh; however, they hope to remedy it by draining the Marsh; but the River *St. Charles* makes an Elbow in this Place, and the Waters do not easily run off, and this can never be well mended.

The General Hospital.

The Prelate, who is the Founder, has his Apartment in the House, and makes it his ordinary Residence; he lets out his own Palace, which is also his own Work, for the Benefit of the Poor. He did not disdain to serve as Almoner to the Hospital, as well as to the Nuns, and he performed the Duty of this Office with a Zeal and Assiduity, which would be admired in a common Priest, who was to live by this Employment. Artists or

(*a*) This Palace was again entirely burnt down.

others

thers, whom great Age or Infirmities have deprived of getting their living, are received into this Hospital, to a certain Number of Beds that are appropiated for this Purpose, and thirty Nuns are employed to attend them. It is a Copy of the *Hotel Dieu* of *Quebec*, but to distinguish the Nuns, the Bishop has given them some particular Regulations, and makes them wear a Silver Cross upon their Breasts. The greatest Part of them are of good Families, and as they are not of the richest of the Country, the Bishop has given Portions to many.

Of the Fortifi-actions.

Quebec is n t regularly fortified, but they have been long employed in making it a defensible Place: This City is not easy to be taken in its present Condition. The Port is flanked by two Bastions, which at the high Tides, are almost level with the Water, *that is to say*, about twenty-five Feet high, for the Equinoctial Tides rise so high. A little above the Bastion on the right, they have made a half Bastion in the Rock, and higher up, by the Side of the Gallery of the Fort, there is a Battery of twenty-five Pieces of Cannon. There is alittle square Fort called the Citadel still above this; and the Ways to go from one Fortification to another are very steep. To the left of the Port, all along the Road up to the River *St. Charles*, there are good Batteries of Cannon, and some Mortars.

From the Angle of the Citadel, which looks towards the City, they have made an *Oreille* of a Bastion, from whence they have made a Curtain at right Angles, which runs to join a very high Cavalier, upon which there is a Mill fortified. Descending from this Cavalier, we meet, at about the Distance of Musket Shot, a first Tower with Bastions, and at the same Distance from this a second. The Design was to cover all this with a Stone facing, which was to have the same Angles as the Bastions, and which was to terminate at the End of the Rock over against the Palace, where there is a little Redoubt, as well as on the *Diamond Cape*. I know not why this has not been executed. Such was, Madam, pretty near the State of the Place in 1711, when the *English* fitted out a great Fleet for the Conquest of *Canada*, which failed of Success through the Rashness of the Commander, who, contrary to the Advice of his Pilot, came too near the seven Isles, and lost all his largest Ships, and three thousand Men of his best Troops.

After having mentioned what is most material in our Capital, I must say a Word or two of its Inhabitants; this is its Beauty. And if upon considering only its Houses, Squares, Streets, and public Buildings, we may reduce it to the Rank of the smallest Cities of *France*, the Worth of those who inhabit it, secures it the Title of Capital.

Of the Inhabitants.

I have already said that they reckon scarcely at *Quebec* seven thousand Souls; but we find here a little chosen World, which wants nothing to make an agreeable Society. A Governor General (*a*) with his Attendants, Nobility, Officers of the Army, and Troops: An Intendant (*b*) with an upper Council, and the inferior Jurisdictions: A Commissary of the Marine (*c*): A Grand Provost (*d*): A Grand Surveyor of Highways, and a Grand Master of the Waters and Forests (*e*) whose Jurisdiction is certainly the most extensive in the World: Rich Merchants, or who live as if they were such: A Bishop and a numerous Seminary: *Recollets* and *Jesuits*: Three Societies of Maidens, well composed: Circles as brilliant as in any other Place, at the Governor's, and the Intendant's Ladies. Here seems to me to be every Thing for all Sorts of People to pass their Time very agreeably. And so they do in Reality, and every one endeavours to contribute what they can towards it. They play, they make Parties of Pleasure, in Summer, in Chariots, or Canoes; in Winter, in Sledges on the Snow, or skeating on the Ice. Shooting is much followed; Gentlemen find this their only Resource to live plentifully. The News current is but little, because the Country furnishes scarce any, and the News from *Europe* comes all together; but this affords Conversation for great Part of the Year: They make political Remarks on Things past, and raise Conjectures on future Events: The Sciences and the fine Arts have their Turn, and Conversation never grows dull. The CANADIANS, *that is to say*, the *Creoles* of *Canada*, breath at their Birth an Air of Liberty, which makes them very agreeable in the Commerce of Life; and our Language is no where spoken with greater Purity.

There is nobody rich here, and 'tis Pity, for they love to live generously, and no one thinks of laying up Riches. They keep good Tables, if their Fortunes will afford it, as well as to dress handsomely; if not, they retrench the Expence of their Table to bestow it on Dress; and indeed we must allow that our *Creoles* become their Dress. They are all of good Stature, and the best Complexion in the World in both Sexes. A pleasant Humour, and agreeable and polite Manners are common to all; and Clownishness, either in Language or Behaviour, is not known among them.

(*a*) The Marquis *de Vaudreuil*. (*b*) M. *Begon*. (*c*) M. *Clerambaut d'Aigremont*. (*d*) M. *Denys de St. Simon*. (*e*) M. le Baron *de Bekancourt*.

Difference between the English *and* French *Colonies.*

It is not ſo, as they ſay, with the *Engliſh* our Neighbours, and they who know the two Colonies only by the Manner of living, acting and ſpeaking of the Inhabitants, would certainly judge ours to be the moſt flouriſhing. In *New England*, and the other Provinces of the Continent of *America*, ſubject to the *Britiſh* Empire, there prevails an Opulence, of which they ſeem not to know how to take the Benefit; and in *New France*, a Poverty diſguiſed by an Air of Eaſe, which does not ſeem conſtrained. Commerce, and the Culture of Plantations, ſtrengthen the former; the Induſtry of the Inhabitants ſupports the latter, and the Taſte of the Nation diffuſes an unbounded Agreeableneſs. The *Engliſh* Coloniſt gathers Wealth, and never runs into any ſuperfluous Expence: The *French* enjoys what he has, and often makes a Shew of what he has not. One labours for his Heirs; the other leaves them in the Neceſſity in which he found himſelf, to ſhift as well as they can. The *Engliſh Americans* are entirely averſe to War, becauſe they have much to loſe; they do not regard the Savages, becauſe they think they have no Occaſion for them. The Youth of the *French*, for the contrary Reaſons, hate Peace, and live well with the Savages, whoſe Eſteem they gain during a War, and have their Friendſhip at all Times. I could carry the Parallel further, but I muſt finiſh: The King's Ship is ready to ſail, and the Merchant Ships are preparing to follow it; and perhaps in three Days there will not be a ſingle Ship in our Road.

I am, &c.

LETTER III.

Of the Huron Village: *What has hindered the Progreſs of the* French Colony *of* Canada: *Of the Money current there.*

Madam, Quebec, *Feb.* 15.

I Am returned from a little Journey of Devotion, of which I ſhall give you an Account, but I muſt firſt acquaint you, that I was miſtaken at the End of my laſt Letter, when I ſaid the Road of *Quebec* would be empty in three Days. A Ship from *Marſeilles* lies here ſtill, and has found Means to be under Shelter of the Ice, with which this River is covered. This is a Secret which may be of ſome Uſe. It is good to have ſome Reſource againſt any Accident that may happen. The Captain of this Ship weighed Anchor the 22d in the Evening, and after he had

had made about a League, he anchored again to wait for some of his Passengers, who embarked in the Middle of the Night: He then gave Orders to prepare for sailing as soon as the Tide should begin to fall, and went to Bed in pretty good Time. About Midnight they waked him, to let him know that the Vessel was filling with Water: They pumped, but to no Purpose: The Water increased continually, instead of diminishing. In short, every one began to think of saving himself, and it was Time. The last were not yet ashore when the Ship disappeared. A Bark loaded with Merchandize from *Montreal* met with the same Fate at the Lake *St. Pierre, (St. Peter,)* but they hope to get them both up again, when the fine Weather returns; and they flatter themselves that the greatest Part of the Loading of these two Vessels will not be lost,——The Affair of the Ship of *Marseilles* may have some Consequences; for the Captain suspects that some Body play'd him a Trick.

I now come to my Pilgrimage. Three Leagues from hence, to the North-East, there is a little Village of *Christian Hurons*, whose Chapel is built after the Model, and with all the Dimensions, of the *Santa Casa* of *Italy*, or the House of *Loretto*; from whence they sent to our new Converts an Image of the *Virgin*, like that which is in that celebrated Place. They could not well have chosen a wilder Place for this Mission: Nevertheless, the Concourse here is very great; and whether it be Fancy, Devotion, or Prejudice, or what you please, many Persons have assured me that they were seized upon their Arrival here with a secret and holy Horror, which they could not resist: But what makes a still greater Impression, is the solid Piety of the Inhabitants of this Desart.

A Description of Loretto.

They are Savages, but they retain nothing of their Birth and Original but what is valuable; *that is to say*, the Simplicity and Freedom of the first Age of the World, with the Addition of Grace; the Faith of the Patriarchs, a sincere Piety, that Rectitude and Docility of Heart, which is the Character of Saints, an incredible Innocence of Manners, a pure Christianity, on which the World has never breathed the contagious Air that corrupts it, and often Actions of the most heroic Virtue. Nothing is more affecting than to hear them sing in two Choirs, the Men on one Side, and the Women on the other, the Prayers of the Church, and Hymns in their own Language. Nothing is comparable to the Fervour and Modesty which they make appear in all their Exercises of Religion. I never saw any Person who was not touched with it to the Bottom of his Soul.

The Zeal of the Savages.

This Village was formerly more populous; but Diseases, and something, I know not what, that reduces insensibly to nothing all

all the Nations of this Continent, have greatly diminiſhed the Number of Inhabitants. The Age and Infirmities of ſome of their antient Paſtors had alſo made ſome Breaches in their firſt Fervour; but it was not difficult to recover them; and he that governs them at preſent, has nothing to do but to keep Things upon the Footing he found them. It is true, that they take all Manner of Precautions to hinder their falling off again. Strong Liquors, the moſt common, and almoſt the only Stumbling-Block, which makes the Savages fall, are forbid by a ſolemn Vow, the Tranſgreſſion of which is puniſhed with publick Penance, as well as every other Fault which cauſes Scandal; and the ſecond Offence generally ſuffices to baniſh the Guilty, without Hope of Return, from a Place which ought to be the impenetrable Aſylum of Piety and Innocence. Peace and Subordination reign here intirely; and the whole Village ſeems to make but one Family, regulated upon the pureſt Maxims of the Goſpel. This always ſurprizes every one who knows how far theſe People (and the *Hurons* eſpecially) do naturally carry Pride and the Spirit of Independence.

The greateſt, and perhaps the only Trouble of a Miſſionary here, is to find Proviſion for his Flock. The Diſtrict they poſſeſs, cannot ſufficiently ſupply them; and there are good Reaſons why they do not permit them to abandon it.—Monſieur and Madam *Begon* were of our Pilgrimage, and were received by theſe good People with a Reſpect due to Perſons of their Rank, and who never let them want Neceſſaries. After a Reception entirely military on the Part of the Warriors, and the Shouts of the Multitude, they began the Exerciſes of Piety, which was mutually edifying: They were followed by a general Feaſt, at the Expence of Madam *Begon*, who received all the Honours of it. The Men, according to Cuſtom, eat in one Houſe, and the Women and Children in another: I ſay Houſe, and not Cabin; for theſe Savages are lately lodged after the *French* Manner. The Women on theſe Occaſions uſed only to ſhew their Gratitude by their Silence and Modeſty; but becauſe it was a Lady of the firſt Rank that was then in the Colony, who treated the whole Village, they granted the *Huron* Women an Orator, by whom they diſplayed to their illuſtrious Benefactreſs all the Sentiments of their Hearts. As for the Men, after the Chief had made a Speech to the Intendant, they danced and ſung as long as we pleaſed. Nothing, Madam, is leſs diverting, than theſe Songs and Dances: Firſt, all are ſeated upon the Earth like Apes, without any Order. From Time to Time a Man riſes up and comes forward ſlowly into the Midſt of the Place, always keeping Time, as they ſay, he turns his Head from Side to Side,

ſigns

sings an Air, which is far from being melodious to any one but a Savage born, and pronounces some Words which have no great Meaning. Sometimes it is a Song of War, sometimes a Song of Death, sometimes an Attack or a Surprize; for as these People drink nothing but Water, they have no drinking Songs, and they have not yet thought of singing their Amours. Whilst they sing, all the Company never cease to beat Time by drawing from the Bottom of their Breast an *He*, which never varies. The Connoisseurs say they always keep Time exactly. I refer it to them. When one has ended, another takes his Place: And this continues till the Assembly returns them Thanks; which would soon happen, without a little Complaisance, which it is good to have for this People. It is in Fact a very tiresome and disagreeable Musick, at least to judge by what I have heard. Throats of Iron, always in one Tone; Airs which have always something fierce, or mournful. But their Voice is quite different when they sing at Church. As for the Women, their Voices have a surprizing Sweetness; they have also a good deal of Taste and Inclination for Musick.

Upon these Occasions, the Speech is the best Thing. They explain in few Words, and generally very ingeniously, the Occasion of the Feast; to which they never fail to give some high Motives. The Praises of the Founder are never forgotten; and they take the Opportunity of the Presence of some Persons (especially when they speak before the Governor-General or the Intendant) to ask some Favour, or to make some Representation.

The Orator of the *Hurons*, on that Day, said such witty Things, that we suspected that the Interpreter (who was the Missionary himself) had lent him his Wit and Politeness with his Voice; but he protested that he had added nothing of his own; and we believed him, because he is known to be one of the most open and sincere Men in the World. *(a)*

Before I had taken this little Journey, I had made several Excursions about this City; but as the Earth was every where covered with Snow, five or six Feet deep, I could thereby learn nothing of the Nature of the Soil; but I have been over it formerly in all Seasons, and I can assure you that it is very rare to see Lands more fruitful, or of a better Quality. I applied myself very diligently this Winter, to inform myself of the Advantages which might be made of this Colony, and I will communicate to you the Fruit of my Labours.——*Canada* does not enrich *France*; this is a Complaint as old as the Country, and it is not without Foundation. It has no rich Inhabitants: This is also true. Is this the Fault of the Country, or is it not owing also to the first Settlers? I shall endeavour to make you able to decide this Point.

(a) Father *Peter-Dan. Ricker*.

The

The first Source of the ill Fortune of this Country, which is honoured with the Name of *New France*, was the Report which was at first spread through the Kingdom, that it had no Mines; and they did not enough consider that the greatest Advantage that can be drawn from a Colony, is the Increase of Trade: And to accomplish this, it requires People; and these Peoplings must be made by Degrees, so that it will not appear in such a Kingdom as *France*: And that the two only Objects which presented themselves first in *Canada* and *Acadia*, (I mean the Furs and the Fishery,) required that these Countries should be peopled: If they had been so, they had perhaps given greater Returns to *France*, than *Spain* has drawn from the richest Provinces of the New World; especially if they had added Ship-building: But the Lustre of the Gold and Silver which came from *Mexico* and *Peru* so dazled the Eyes of all *Europe*, that a Country which did not produce these precious Metals, was looked upon as a bad Country. Let us hear upon this Subject a sensible Author, who had been in these Places.

The false Notions People had of Canada.

" The common Questions they make (says *Mark Lescarbot*) " are these: Is there any Gold or Silver? And no Body asks, " Are these People inclined to hear the *Christian* Doctrine? " And as to the Mines, there are some indeed, but they must be " wrought with Industry, Labour, and Patience. The finest " Mine that I know of, is that of Corn and Wine, and the " breeding of Cattle. They who have this, have Money; and " we do not live upon Mines. The Sailors who go from all " Parts of *Europe* to get Fish at *Newfoundland* and beyond, eight " or nine hundred Leagues distant from their Country, find there " good Mines, without breaking the Rocks, digging into the " Bowels of the Earth, and living in the Darkness of Hell. " They find, I say, good Mines at the Bottom of the Waters, " and in the Trade of Fur and Skins, of which they make good " Money."

They not only gave *New France* a very bad Name without knowing it; but those who thought to get some Profit by it, took no Measures for this Purpose. First, they were a long Time before they settled upon a Place: They cleared the Land without having first well examined it: They sowed it, and raised Buildings upon it; and then, without knowing why, they often abandoned it, and went to some other Place. This Inconstancy was the great Cause of our losing *Acadia*, and hindering us from making any Thing of it, whilst we were in Possession of that fine Country.—The Author I have already cited, and who was a Witness of our Want of Resolution, was not afraid

Mistakes that were made at the first Settlement.

afraid to blame thoſe who were moſt guilty in this Affair. " It " is thus (ſays he) that at all Times we make much ado about " nothing, that we purſue new Enterprizes with great Heat, and " that we project fine Beginnings, and then quit every Thing. " In Reality, for ſuch Undertakings there muſt be a Subſiſtence " and Support; but we muſt alſo have Men of Reſolution, who " will not ſoon be diſheartened, and have this Point of Honour " in View, *Victory or Death*, that Death being great and glorious " which happens in executing a great Deſign; ſuch as laying " the Foundation of a New Kingdom, and eſtabliſhing the " *Chriſtian* Faith among People where GOD is not known."

I come now to Trade.——The Trade of *Canada* has been a long Time ſolely in the Fiſhery and Skins. The Cod Fiſhery was carried on upon the *Great Bank*, and upon the Coaſts of *Newfoundland*, a long Time before they diſcovered the River of *St. Laurence:* They bethought themſelves too late, of making a Settlement upon the Iſland; and we had ſuffered the *Engliſh* to be before-hand with us. At length we took Poſſeſſion of the Port and Bay of *Placentia*. The Militia of *Canada* have performed here many warlike Exploits, equal to thoſe of the boldeſt *Buccaneers* of *St. Domingo*. They have often deſtroyed the Inhabitants, and ruined the Trade of the *Engliſh* in this Iſland: But they who ſuffered their ſtrongeſt Places to be eaſily taken from them, knew their Enemy too well to be diſheartened. Accuſtomed to ſee the *Canadian* Fire break out amidſt the Northern Ice, and die away of itſelf in the Midſt of what ought to have given it more Power, they behaved themſelves at the Approach of our Heroes like a ſkilful Pilot upon the Approach of a Storm. They prudently yielded to the Tempeſt, and afterwards repaired without any Hindrance the Damage which had been done to their Poſts; and by this Conduct tho' they were always beat in *Newfoundland*, either when they attacked or defended themſelves, they have always carried on a much greater Trade than their Conquerors, and have at laſt remained the ſole Maſters and quiet Poſſeſſors of this Iſland. We have behaved ſtill worſe in *Acadia*. This great and rich Province has been a long Time divided amongſt divers private Perſons, none of which are grown rich, whilſt the *Engliſh* have made an immenſe Profit of the Fiſhery upon the Coaſts.

The Settlements which theſe Proprietors made here, not being upon a ſolid Foundation, and wanting themſelves Judgment, and ruining one another, they left the Country in much the ſame Condition they found it; and with ſuch an ill Name, that it never recovered till the Moment we loſt it. But our Enemies have made us know the Value of it.

The

Ill Conduct in Respect to the Skin Trade.

The Trade to which they confined themſelves ſolely for a long Time in *Canada*, was that of Skins or Furs. It is impoſſible to relate the Faults which have been here committed. The Genius of our Nation never, perhaps, was ſhewn more than on this Occaſion. When we diſcovered this vaſt Continent, it was full of Deer and other Beaſts of the Chace: But a Handful of *Frenchmen* have within a ſingle Age found Means to make them almoſt entirely diſappear, and there are ſome Species of them entirely deſtroyed. They killed the *Orignals*, or Elks, for the ſole Pleaſure of killing them, and to ſhew they were good Markſmen. No Body thought of interpoſing the King's Authority to put a Stop to ſuch an extravagant Diſorder: But the greateſt Evil proceeded from the inſatiable Covetouſneſs of private Perſons, who applied themſelves ſolely to this Trade. They came for the moſt Part from *France*, like Simonides; *that is to ſay*, poſſeſſing only what they had upon their Backs; and they were impatient to appear in a better Condition. At firſt, this was eaſy: The Savages did not know the Treaſure their Woods contained, but by the Eagerneſs the *French* ſhewed to get the Skins out of their Hands, they got from them a prodigious Quantity, by giving them Things which ſome People would not pick up: And even ſince they have been better informed of the Value of this Merchandize, and expected to be ſomething better paid for it, it was very eaſy for a long Time to ſatisfy them at a ſmall Expence: With a little Conduct, this Trade might have been continued on upon a tolerably good Foundation. It would be difficult, however, to name a ſingle Family, at this Time, that has been enriched by this Trade. We have ſeen ſome Fortunes, as immenſe as ſudden, raiſed and diſappear almoſt at the ſame Time; like thoſe moving Mountains of Sand which ſome Travellers ſpeak of, and which a Whirlwind raiſes and levels again in the Plains of *Africa*. Nothing is more common in this Country, than to ſee People ſuffer a languiſhing old Age under Miſery and Contempt, after having had it in their Power to have made a handſome Settlement for themſelves.

After all, Madam, theſe private Perſons who have miſſed making Fortunes which they did not deſerve, would have been unworthy of the Public Concern, if the Effects of it did not fall upon the Colony; which ſoon found itſelf reduced to ſuch a State, as to ſee entirely dried up, or running in another Channel, a Spring from whence ſo many Riches might flow into its Boſom.

Its Ruin begun by its Plenty. By Means of heaping up Beaver Skins, which were always the principal Object of this Trade, there was found ſuch a vaſt Quantity in the Magazines,

F that

that they could not be disposed of: Whence it happened, that the Dealers not being willing to take them, our Adventurers, whom they call here *Coureurs de Bois, (Forest Rangers)* carried them to the *English*, and many of them settled in *New York*. Several Attempts were made to hinder these People from deserting the Colony, but with little Success; on the contrary, those who went over to our Neighbours for the Sake of Interest, were detained there by the Fear of Punishment; and some Vagabonds, who had taken a Liking to Independency, and a wandering Life, remained among the Savages; from whom they could not be distinguished, but by their Vices. Recourse was had several Times to the publishing of Pardon to all that would return; which at first had little Effect; but at length this Method, managed with Prudence, answered the expected End.

Of Licences, and their Abuses.

They made Use of another Method, which was still more effectual. This was, to allow a Number of Persons, whom they thought they could confide in, to go and trade in the Countries of the Savages, and prohibit all other Persons to go out of the Colony. The Number of these Licences were limited, and they were distributed to poor Widows and Orphans, who could sell them to the Traders for more or less, according to the Value of the Trade; *that is*, according to the Places where the Licences permitted them to go; for they had taken the Precaution to mark out the Places, to hinder them from going all one Way.

Besides these Licences, (the Number of which was settled by the Court, and the Distribution of which belongs to the Governor General) there are some for the Commanders of Posts, and for extraordinary Occasions; and the Governor gives some also by Name of *simple Permissions*: So that a Part of the young Men are continually roving the Woods; and though they do not commit any longer, or at least so openly, the Disorders which have so much disgraced this Profession, yet they still contract a loose vagrant Habit, of which they are never entirely cured: They lose at least an Inclination for Labour; they waste their Strength, and become incapable of the least Restraint; and when they are no longer able to bear the Fatigues of these Journies, (which soon happens, because these Fatigues are very great) they remain without any Resource, and are no longer fit for any Thing. From hence it proceeds, that Arts have been a long Time neglected, that much good Land lies still uncultivated, and that the Country is not peopled. It has been often proposed to abolish these pernicious Licences, and to make some *French* Settlements in some chosen Places, and where it would be easy to assemble the Savages, at least at certain Seasons of the Year. By this Means the Trade would be rendered more flourishing. These vast Countries would be insensibly peopled; and this would perhaps be the only Means to execute what the Court has had so long at Heart, to *frenchify* these Savages. I believe I may at least assert, that if this Project had been followed, *Canada* would have been at this Time much more populous than it is; that the Savages, attracted and retained by the Help and kind Treatment they would have found in our Habitations, would have been less roving, less miserable, and in Consequence would have encreased in Number, (instead of which their Numbers are surprisingly diminished) and they would have been attached to us in such a Manner, that we might have made the like Use of them by this Time, as of the Subjects of the Crown; and the more so, as the Missionaries would have found much less Difficulty in their Conversion.——What we now see at *Loretto*, and in some Measure amongst the *Iroquois*, the *Algonquins*, and the *Abenaquis*, who live in the Colony, leaves no Room to doubt of the Truth of what I advance; and there is no Person amongst those who have been most conversant with the Savages, who does not agree that we can never depend on these People till they are *Christians*. I will cite no other Example than the *Abenaquis*; who, though few in Number, were during the two last Wars the principal Bulwark of *New France* against *New England*.

This Project, which I have laid before you, Madam, is as old as the Colony, it was that of M. *de Champlain* its Founder, and it was the Desire of almost all the Missionaries whom I have known, and whose painful Labours in the Situation in which, Things have been a long while, do not produce any great Fruit in the Missions which are at any Distance. It would be in Fact very late to take up this Design now with Respect to the Savages, who disappear in such a Manner, as is scarce conceivable. But what should hinder us from following it, with Respect to the *French*, and to continue the Colony from one Neighbourhood to another, till it can reach out a Hand to that of *Louisiana*, to strengthen each other. By this Means the *English* in less than an Age and a half have peopled above five hundred Leagues of Country, and have formed a Power on this Continent, which we cannot help beholding without Fear when we take a near View of it.————*Canada* may and does sometimes carry on a pretty considerable Trade with the Isles of *America*, in Flour, Planks, and other Wood fit for Buildings; as there is not perhaps a Country in the World that has more Variety of Wood, nor a better Sort: Judge what Riches this may one Day produce. It appears that few People understand this Article; I do not understand it enough myself to enter into a more particular Account: I have something more Knowledge in the Article of Oils, of which I shall soon take Notice. Being in Haste to finish my Letter, I have only Time to compleat what concerns the Trade in general.

Nothing has more contributed to distress the Trade than the frequent Changes which have been made in the Money; this is the History of it in few Words. In 1670, the West-India Company, to whom the King had given the Domain of the Islands of the Continent of *French America*, had leave to send to these Islands a hundred thousand Livres *(a)* in small Money, marked with a particular Legend, that was proper to it. The King's Edict is dated in *February*, by which this Species was to be current only in the Islands. But upon some Difficulties which arose, the Council made an Order *November* 18, 1672, that the said Money, and all other Species that was current in *France*, should pass also, not only in the *French* Islands, but also on the Continent of *America* subject to the Crown, with an Augmentation of one fourth Part; *that is to say*, the Pieces of fifteen Sous for twenty, and the rest in Proportion. The same Order decreed that all Contracts, Notes, Accounts, Sales, and Payments, should be made according to the Rate of the Money, without making Use of Exchanges, or accounting in Sugar or other Merchandize, on the Penalty of making all such Acts void. And for all past it was ordered, that all Contracts, Notes, Debts, Dues, Rents in Sugar, or other Merchandize, should be paid in Money, according to the Currency of the said Species. In the Execution of this Order, Money encreased one fourth in *New France*, which soon occasioned many Difficulties. In Fact, M. *de Champigny Noroy*, who was made Indendant of *Quebec* in 1684, and who is now Intendant at *Havre-de-Grace*, found himself soon embarrassed, both in the Payment of the Troops, and other Expences of the King in this Colony.

Various Changes in the Money.

Besides this, the Funds which were sent from *France*, almost always came too late; and by the first of *January* the Officers and Soldiers were to be paid, and other Payments to be made, which were equally indispensable. To satisfy the most pressing Demands, M. *de Champigny* made Notes to supply the Place of Money, observing always the Augmentation. And by Order of the Governor and the Intendant, they set on every Piece of this Money (which was a Card) the Treasurer's Sign Manual, the Arms of *France*, and the Seals of the Governor and Intendant in Wax; they afterwards got them printed in *France*, on Pasteboard, with the same Marks as the current Money of the Kingdom; and it was ordered that they should be presented every Year before the Arrival of the Ships from *France*, to add a Mark, to prevent Counterfeits.

(a) A Livre is about 1s. 8d. of our Money.

This

This Pasteboard Money did not last long, and they made Use again of Cards, on which they graved new Devices. The Intendant signed all that were of four Livres Value and above, and only made a Flourish upon the others. In latter Times the Governor General signed all that were of six Livres or more. In the Beginning of the Autumn, all the Cards were carried to the Treasurer, who gave for their Value Bills of Exchange upon the Treasurer General of the Marines, or his Clerk at *Rochfort*, on the Account of the Expences for the next Year. Those which were damaged or defaced were burnt, after they had taken a proper Account of them. So long as these Bills of Exchange were faithfully paid, these Cards were preferred to Money; but when the Bills were not paid, the Cards were no longer carried to the Treasurer; so that in 1702, M. *de Champigny* gave himself a great deal of Pains to no Purpose, to call in those he had made. His Successors were obliged to make new ones every Year to pay Officers, which multiplied them to such a Degree, that they fell to no Price, and nobody would receive them any longer. Trade was hereby entirely ruined, and the Disorder went so far, that in 1713 the Inhabitants proposed to lose half, on Condition that the King would take them again and pay the other half: This Proposal was accepted the Year following, but the Orders given in Consequence, were not entirely executed till 1717. An Order was then made to abolish the Money of Cards, and they begun to pay in Silver the Officers of the Colony. The Augmentation of one fourth was also abolished at the same Time: Experience having made it appear that the Augmentation of the Species in a Colony, is not the Way to keep it in it, which was the Thing proposed; and that Money can never circulate greatly in a Colony, but when they pay in Merchandize for all they have from the Mother Country. In Fact, in this Case, the Colony keeps the Species, instead of which, if it has not Merchandize sufficient to answer the whole Demands upon it, it is obliged to pay the Surplus in Money, and how will it come back again?

In short, Madam, you will be surprized to hear, that in 1706, the Trade of the oldest of our Colonies was carried on with a Fund of only six hundred and fifty thousand Livres, and Things are not much changed since that Time. Now this Sum dispersed amongst thirty thousand Inhabitants, cannot set them at their Ease, nor afford them Means to purchase the Merchandize of *France*. So the greatest Part of them go naked, especially those who are in the distant Settlements. They do not even sell the Surplus of their Merchandize to the Inhabitants of the Towns, because the latter are obliged for a Subsistence to have Lands in the Country, and to improve them themselves.

When

When the King took *Canada* out of the Hands of the Companies, his Majesty spent much more for some Years than he has done since; and the Colony, during this Time, sent to *France* near the Value of a Million of Livres in Beaver Skins every Year, tho' it was less peopled than it is now: But it has always had more from *France* than it could pay, and has acted like a private Person, who has thirty thousand Livres a Year Estate, and who spends forty thousand or more. By this Means its Credit is fallen, and in falling, has brought on the Ruin of its Trade; which, since the Year 1706, has consisted in nothing more than small Peltry. All the Dealers sought for them, and this was their Ruin, because they often bought them dearer of the Savages, than they sold them in *France*.

I am, &c.

LETTER IV.

Of the BEAVERS *of* CANADA, *how they differ from the* BEAVERS *of* EUROPE: *Of their Manner of Building: The Manner of hunting the* BEAVERS: *Of the Advantage to be made of them. Of the* MUSK RAT.

MADAM, QUEBEC, *March* 1. 1721

I Was to go from hence a Day or two after I had closed my last Letter, but I must still stop for Want of Carriage. The best I can do in the mean Time, is to entertain you with the Curiosities of this Country; and I begin with what is most singular, that is, the Beaver. The Spoils of this Animal has hitherto furnished *New France* with the principal Object of its Trade. It is of itself one of the Wonders of Nature, and it may be to Man a great Example of Foresight, of Industry, Skill, and Constancy in Labour.

The Difference of the Beaver of Canada, *from that of* Europe.

The Beaver was not unknown in *France* before the Discovery of *America*, and we find in some ancient Writings of the Hatters of *Paris*, some Regulations for making Beaver Hats: The Beaver or Castor is entirely the same Creature; but either that the *European* Beaver is become extreamly scarce, or its Fur was not so good as that of the *American* Castor, we hear little Mention now but of the last, unless it be with Respect to *Castoreum*, of which I shall say a few Words at the End of this Letter. I do not know that any Author has spoken of this Animal as being any Thing curious; perhaps it was for Want of observing it attentively; perhaps also that the

Castors

tors or Beavers of *Europe* are like the Land Castors, the Difference of which from the others I shall presently make you understand.

However that may be, Madam, the Beaver of *Canada* is an amphibious Quadrupede, which cannot however remain a long Time in the Water, and can do without being in it, provided it has the Opportunity of washing itself sometimes: The largest Beavers are something under four Feet long, about fifteen Inches from one Hip to the other, and weigh about sixty Pounds. The Colour of this Animal is different, according to the different Climates where it is found. In the most distant Parts of the North they are generally quite black, though sometimes they are found there white. In the more temperate Countries they are brown, and by Degrees, as they advance towards the South, their Colour grows more and more light. Amongst the *Ilinois*, they are almost of a fallow Colour, and some have been found of a straw Colour. It it further observed, that the less black they are, the less they are furnished with Fur, and of Consequence their Skins are less valuable. This is an Effect of Providence, which defends them from the Cold, as they are the more exposed to it. Their Fur is of two Sorts all over the Body, except the Feet, where there is but one Sort very short. The longest Sort is about eight or ten Lines, or Parts of an Inch long, suppose an Inch to be divided into twelve Parts. It is even two Inches long on the Back, but diminishes by Degrees towards the Head and Tail. This Fur is stiff and glossy, and is what gives the Colour to the Creature. Upon viewing it with a Microscope, the middle Part of it is found to be the clearest, which proves that it is hollow; this Fur is of no Use. The other Fur is a very fine Down, very thick, and at most not above an Inch long, and this is what is made Use of. It was formerly called in EUROPE, *Muscovy* Wool. This is properly the Cloathing of the Beaver, the first serves him only for Ornament, and perhaps helps him in swimming.

Of the Fur of the Beaver.

They say that the Beaver lives from fifteen to twenty Years; that the Female goes four Months with Young; and has commonly four Young ones; some Travellers make the Number amount to eight, but I believe this seldom happens: She has four Dugs, two on the great Pectoral Muscle, between the second and third Ribs, and two about four Inches higher. The Muscles of this Animal are very strong, and bigger than seems necessary to its Size. Its Intestines on the contrary are very tender; its Bones are very hard, its two Jaws, which are almost even, have a very great Strength; each Jaw is furnished with ten Teeth, two cutting ones and eight Grinders. The upper cutting

An Anatomical Description of this Animal.

ting Teeth are two Inches and a half long, the lower are above three Inches, and follow the Bend of the Jaw, which gives them a Strength which is admirable in ſuch little Animals. It is obſerved alſo, that the two Jaws do not meet exactly, but that the upper reach over the lower, ſo that they croſs like the Edges of a Pair of Sciſſars; and laſtly, that the Length of all their Teeth is exactly the third Part of the Roots of them. The Head of a Beaver is nearly like the Head of a Field Rat, the Snout is ſomewhat long, the Eyes little, the Ears ſhort and round, covered with Down on the Outſide, and naked within; its Legs are ſhort, particularly thoſe before, they are ſeldom above four or five Inches long, and like thoſe of a Badger; its Nails are as it were cut ſloping, and are hollow like a Quill. The hind Legs are quite different, they are flat, and furniſhed with a Membrane; ſo that the Beaver goes but ſlowly on Land, but ſwims as eaſily as any other Water Animal: And on the other Hand, by its Tail, it is entirely a Fiſh; and ſo it has been declared by the College of Phyſicians at *Paris*, and in Conſequence of this Declaration, the Doctors of Divinity have agreed, that the Fleſh might be eaten on Faſt Days. M. *Lemery* was miſtaken, when he ſaid that this Deciſion was only confined to the Tail of the Beaver. It is true that we can make but little Advantage of this Condeſcenſion: The Beavers are ſo far from our Habitations at preſent, it is rare to have any that are eatable. The Savages who dwell amongſt us, keep them after they have been dryed in the Smoak, and I aſſure you, Madam, that I know of nothing more ordinary. We muſt alſo, when the Beaver is freſh, put it in ſome Broth to make it loſe a wild and nauſeous Taſte; but with this Precaution there is no Meat lighter, more dainty, or wholſome: They ſay that it is as nouriſhing as Veal: Boiled it wants ſomething to give it a Reliſh, but roaſted it it wants nothing.

What is ſtill moſt remarkable in the Shape of this Animal, is the Tail. It is near four Inches round at its Root, five in the midſt, and three at the End, (I ſpeak always of the large Beavers) it is an Inch thick, and a Foot long. Its Subſtance is is a hard Fat, or a tender Sinew, which pretty much reſembles the Fleſh of a Porpoiſe, but which grows harder upon being kept a long Time. It is covered with a ſcaly Skin, the Scales of which are hexagonal, half a Line thick, and three or four Lines long, which lay one upon another like thoſe of a Fiſh; they lay upon a very tender Skin, and are fixt in ſuch a Manner, that they may be eaſily ſeparated after the Death of the Animal. This is, Madam, in few Words, the Deſcription of this curious amphibious Creature.

The

The true Testicles of this Animal were not known to the Ancients, probably, because they are very small, and hid under the Groin. They had given this Name to the Purses or Bags of the *Castoreum*, which are very different, and four in Number, in the lower Belly of the Beaver. The two first, which they call the upper, because they are higher than the others, have the Shape of a Pear, and communicate with each other like the two Pockets of a Wallet. The two others, which are called the lower, are rounded at the Bottom. These contain a resinous, soft, glewy Matter, mixt with small Fibres, of a greyish Colour without, and a yellowish within; of a strong Smell, disagreeable and penetrating, and which is easily inflammable. This is the true *Castoreum*: It grows hard in the Air in a Month's Time, and becomes brown, brittle, and friable. If we are in a hurry to harden it, it need only be hung in the Chimney.

Of the Castoreum.

They say that the *Castoreum* which comes from *Dantzic*, is better than that of *Canada*, I refer to the Druggists; it is certain that the Bags of the latter are smaller, and that here also the largest are esteemed. Besides their Bigness, they should be heavy, of a brown Colour, of a penetrating and strong Smell, full of a hard brittle and friable Matter, of the same Colour, or yellow, interweaved with a thin Membrane, and of a sharp Taste. The Properties of *Castoreum*, are to attenuate viscous Matter, to strengthen the Brain, to remove Vapours, to provoke the Menses, to hinder Corruption, and to evaporate bad Humours by Transpiration; it is used also with Success against the Epilepsy, the Palsy, the Apoplexy, and Deafness.

The lower Bags contain an unctuous fat Liquor like Honey. Its Colour is a pale Yellow, its Odour fetid, little differing from that of *Castoreum*, but something weaker and fainter. It thickens with keeping, and takes the Consistence of Tallow. This Liquor is resolving, and strengthens the Nerves; for this Purpose, it need only be applied to the Part affected. It is a Mistake to say, as some Authors do still, upon the Credit of the ancient Naturalists, that when the Beaver is pursued, it bites off these pretended Testicles, and leaves them to the Hunters to save his Life. It is of his Fur which he ought rather to deprive himself, for in Comparison of his Fleece, the rest is hardly of any Value. But however, it is this Fable, which has given it the Name of Castor. The Skin of this Animal, deprived of its Fur, is not to be neglected; they make Gloves and Stockings of it; but as it is difficult to get off all the Fur without cutting the Skin, they seldom use any but those of the Land Beaver. You have heard, perhaps, Madam, of the fat and dry Beaver Skins; the Difference is this, the dry Skin is the Skin of a Beaver that has never been used;

the fat Skin is what has been worn by the Savages, which, after they have been well ſcraped within, and rubbed with the Marrow of certain Animals which I do not know, to make it more pliable, they ſew ſeveral together, and make a Kind of Mantle, which they call a Robe, with which they wrap themſelves up with the Fur inwards. They wear it continually in Winter, Day and Night; the long Hair ſoon falls off, and the Down remains, and grows greaſy: In this Condition it is much fitter for the Uſe of the Hatters; they cannot not even uſe the dry Sort, without mixing ſome of the other with it. They ſay that it muſt be worn fifteen or ſixteen Months to be in Perfection. I leave you to judge, if at firſt they were weak enough to let the Savages know, that their old Clothes were ſuch a precious Merchandize. But a Secret of this Nature, could not be long hid from them; it was truſted to Covetouſneſs, which is never long without betraying itſelf.

Another Uſe of the Beaver.

About three Years ago one *Guigues*, who had the Farm of the Beaver Skins, finding himſelf burdened with a prodigious Quantity of theſe Skins, thought to encreaſe the Conſumption, by having the Fur ſpun and carded with Wool; and with this Compoſition he made Cloths and Flannels, and wove Stockings, and ſuch-like Works, but with little Succeſs.

It is evident by this Tryal, that the Beaver Fur is good for nothing but to make Hats. It is too ſhort to be ſpun alone, it muſt be mixt with above half Wool; ſo that there is but little Profit to be made of theſe Works. There is, however, ſtill one of theſe Manufactures in *Holland*, where they make Cloths and Druggets; but theſe Stuffs are dear, and do not wear well. The Beaver Fur ſeparates ſoon, and forms a Kind of Down upon the Surface, which takes off all their Beauty. The Stockings which were made of it in *France*, had the ſame Fault.

The Induſtry and Labours of the Beavers.

This is, Madam, all the Advantage this Colony can receive from the Beavers, with Reſpect to its Trade. The Induſtry of the Beavers, their Foreſight, the Unity and Subordination ſo much admired in them, their Attention to procure themſelves Conveniencies, the Comforts of which, we thought formerly Brutes were not ſenſible of, furniſh to Man more Inſtruction than the Ant, to which the Holy Scriptures ſend the Idle. They are at leaſt amongſt Quadrupedes, what the Bees are amongſt flying Inſects. I never heard that they had a King or a Queen, and it is not true that when they are at work together in Companies, that they have a Chief who commands and puniſhes the idle: But by Virtue of that Inſtinct given to Animals, by him whoſe Providence governs them, every one knows what he has

to

to do, and every Thing is done without Confusion, and with so much Order as can never be sufficiently admired. Perhaps, after all, we are so much astonished but for Want of looking up to that Supreme Intelligence, who makes Use of these Beings, who want Reason, the better to display his Wisdom and Power, and to makes us know that our Reason itself is frequently, by our Presumption, the Cause of our going astray.

The first Thing that is done by these Creatures, when they want to make a Habitation, is, to assemble themselves: Shall I say in Tribes or Societies? It shall be what you please: But there are sometimes three or four hundred together, making a Town, which might be called a little *Venice.* (a) At first they chuse a Place were they may find Plenty of Provisions, and Materials for their building: Above all, they must have Water. If there is no Lake or Pond near, they supply the Defect, by stopping the Course of some Brook or Rivulet, by the Means of a Dyke; or, as they call it here, a Causey. For this End they go and cut down some Trees above the Place where they intend to build: Three or four Beavers set themselves about a great Tree, and cut it down with their Teeth. This is not all: They take their Measures so well, that it always falls on the Side towards the Water, that they may have the less Way to carry it when they have cut it to Pieces; as they are sensible their Materials are not so easily transported by Land as by Water. They have nothing to do after, but to roll these Pieces into the Water, and guide them to the Place where they are to be fixed. These Pieces are thicker or thinner, longer or shorter, as the Nature and Situation of the Place require; for one would say that these Architects conceive at once every Thing that relates to their Design. Sometimes they employ large Trunks of Trees, which they lay flat: Sometimes the Causey is made only of Stakes; some as thick as a Man's Thigh, or less; which they drive into the Earth very near each other, and interweave with small Branches; and every where the hollow Spaces are filled up with Clay so well applied, that not a Drop of Water can pass through. It is with their Paws that the Beavers prepare the Clay; and their Tail does not only serve them for a Trowel to build with, but for a Hod to carry this Mortar. To place and spread this Clay, they first make Use of their Paws, then their Tail. The Foundation of the Dams are generally ten or twelve Feet thick; but they decrease in Thickness upwards: So that a Dam which is twelve Feet thick at the Bottom, is not above two at the Top. All this is done in exact Proportion, and, as one may say, according to the Rules of Art; for it is observed, that the Side towards the Cur-

(a) The City of VENICE is built in the midst of Waters.

rent of the Water is always sloping, in order to break the Pressure of the Water, and the other Side perfectly perpendicular. In a Word, it would be difficult for our best Workmen to make any Thing more solid and regular. The Construction of their Cabins is not less wonderful. They are generally made upon Piles in the midst of these little Lakes, which the Dykes have made: Sometimes by the Side of a River, or at the Extremity of a Point that advances into the Water. Their Shape is round or oval; and the Roof is arched. The Walls are two Feet thick, built with the same Materials as the Causey, but less, and every where so well plaistered with Clay on the Inside, that the least Breath of Air cannot enter. Two thirds of the Building is out of the Water, and in this Part every Beaver has a separate Place, which he takes Care to strew with Leaves, or small Branches of Firs. It is always free from Ordure; and for this End, besides the common Door of the Cabin, and another Outlet by which these Creatures pass to bathe themselves, there are several Openings by which they can dung into the Water. The common Cabins lodge eight or ten Beavers, some have been found which held thirty, but this is uncommon. They are all near enough each other, to have an easy Communication.

Their Foresight.

The Beavers are never surprized by the Winter; all the Works I mention, are finished by the End of *September*, and then every one provides his Store for the Winter. Whilst they go backwards and forwards in the Woods or Fields, they live upon Fruits, the Bark and Leaves of Trees; they also catch Cray-Fish and other Fish: Then they have Variety of Food. But when they are to provide themselves for the whole Season, that the Earth being covered with Snow supplies them with nothing, they content themselves with soft Woods, such as the Poplar and the Aspen, and such-like. They pile it up in such a Manner, that they can always take those Pieces which are soaked in the Water. It is always observed, that these Piles are larger or smaller, as the Winter will prove longer or shorter; and this is an Almanack for the Savages, which never deceives them in Regard to the Cold. The Beavers before they eat the Wood, cut it in very small Pieces, and carry it into their separate Lodges; for every Cabin has but one Magazine for all the Family. When the melting of the Snow is at its Height, as it never fails to cause great Floods, the Beavers leave their Cabins, which are no longer habitable, and every one takes which Way he likes best. The Females return as soon as the Waters are run off, and then bring forth their Young: The Males keep the Country till towards the Month of *July*, when they re-assemble to repair the Breaches which the Floods have made in their Cabins or Dykes. If they

have

have been destroyed by the Hunters, or if they are not worth the Trouble of repairing, they make others: But many Reasons oblige them to change their Abode frequently, the most common is the Want of Provision; they are also obliged to do it by the Hunters, or Beasts of Prey, against which they have no other Defence than Flight. We might think it strange, that the Author of Nature has given less Power of Defence to the greatest Part of useful Animals, than to those which are not useful; if this Circumstance did not the more display his Wisdom and Power, in that the former, notwithstanding their Weakness, multiply much more than the latter.

There are some Places which the Beavers seem to have taken such an Affection to, that they cannot leave them, though they are continually disquieted. In the Way from *Montreal* to Lake *Huron*, by the great River, they never fail to find every Year in the same Place, a Lodgment which these Animals build or repair every Summer. For the first Thing Passengers do who pass this Way, is to break down the Cabin, and the Causey which furnishes it with Water. If this Causey had not kept up the Water, they would not have enough to continue their Way, and they would be obliged to make a Portage; so that it looks as if these officious Beavers posted themselves here solely for the Convenience of Passengers. The same Thing, as they say, is to be seen near *Quebec*, where the Beavers labouring for themselves, supply Water to a Mill for sawing Planks.

Of the Land Beavers.

The Savages were formerly persuaded, if we believe some Relations, that the Beavers were a reasonable Kind of Creatures, which had their Laws, their Government, and their particular Language: That this amphibious People chose Commanders, who in their common Labours appointed to every one his Task, placed Centinels to give Notice of the Approach of an Enemy, and punished or banished the idle. These pretended Exiles are probably those which they call the *Land Beavers*, which in Fact live apart from the others, do not labour, and live under Ground, where their whole Care is to make themselves a covered Way to go to the Water. They are known by the little Fur they have upon their Backs, which proceeds no doubt from their rubbing it constantly against the Earth; and withal they are lean, the Effect of their Sloth: More of these are found in the South than in the North. I have already observed, that our Beavers of *Europe* are more like these, than the others. In Fact, M. *Lemery* says, they live in Holes and Cavities on the Banks of Rivers, especially in *Poland*. There are some also in *Germany* upon the *Elbe*, and in *France* upon the *Rhone*, the *Isere*, and the *Oise*. It is certain, that we do not find in the *European* Beavers

Beavers those extraordinary Qualities which so much distinguish those of *Canada*. 'Tis a great Pity, Madam, that none of these wonderful Creatures were found in the *Tyber*, or in the Territories of *Parnassus*, what fine Things would the *Greek* and *Roman* Poets have said on this Subject.

It appears that the Savages of *Canada* did not disturb them greatly till our Arrival in their Country. The Skins of the Beavers were not the most used by these People for Garments, and the Flesh of Bears, Elks, and other wild Creatures was more approved by them. They hunted them, nevertheless, and this Chace had its Season, and its peculiar Ceremonies; but when they hunted only for what was merely necessary for a present Supply, they made no great Ravages; and indeed when we came to *Canada*, we found a prodigious Number of these amphibious Creatures in the Country.

Of hunting the Beaver.

There is no Difficulty in hunting the Beaver, for this Animal has not in any Degree the Strength to defend himself, nor the Skill to shun the Attacks of his Enemy, which it discovers in providing for itself Lodging and Provisions. It is during Winter they make War against him in Form; *that is to say*, from the Beginning of *November* till *April*. Then it has, like all other Animals, more Fur, and the Skin is thinner; this hunting is performed four different Ways, with Nets, with the Gun, the Trench, and the Trap; the first is generally joined to the third, and they seldom make Use of the second, because the Eyes of this little Animal are so piercing, and his Ears are so quick, that it is difficult to approach near enough to shoot him, before he gets into the Water, which he never goes far from during this Season, and into which he immediately plunges. They would lose him also if he were wounded before he gets into the Water, because he never comes up again if he dies of his Wound; it is therefore the Trench or the Trap that are generally used.

Though the Beavers have made their Provision for the Winter, they still continue to make some Excursions into the Woods to find some fresher and tenderer Food, and this Daintiness costs many their Lives. The Savages set up Traps in their Way, made almost like a Figure of 4, and for a Bait they put little Pieces of soft Food newly cut; as soon as the Beaver touches it, a great Log falls upon him and breaks his Back, and the Hunter coming up makes an End of him without any Trouble. The Trench requires more Caution, and they proceed in this Manner: When the Ice is but half a Foot thick, they cut an Opening with an Ax, the Beavers come here to breathe more freely; the Hunters wait for them, and perceive them coming at at a good Diſtance, becauſe in blowing they give a conſiderable Motion to the Water; ſo that it is eaſy to take their Meaſures to kill them as ſoon as they appear above Water: But for the greater Certainty, and not to be ſeen by the Beavers, they throw upon the Hole which they make in the Ice ſome broken Reeds or Stalks of *Indian* Wheat, and when they find that the Animal is within Reach, they ſeize him by one of his Paws, and throw him upon the Ice, where they knock him on the Head before he has recovered of his Surprize.

If the Cabin is near ſome Rivulet, they are taken with leſs Trouble, they make a Cut acroſs the Ice to let down their Nets, then they go and break down the Cabin. The Beavers that are in it never fail to run into the Rivulet, and are caught in the Net, but they muſt not be left there long, for they would ſoon make their Way out by gnawing it. Thoſe which have their Cabins in the Lakes have, at three or four hundred Paces from the Shore, a Kind of Country-houſe, where they may breathe a better Air: Then the Hunters divide themſelves in two Parties, one goes to break down the Country Cabin, and the other Party falls upon that of the Lake; the Beavers which are in the latter (and the Hunters take the Time when they are all there) fly for Refuge to the other; but they find nothing there but Duſt, which has been thown in on Purpoſe, and which blinds them ſo that they are eaſily taken. Laſtly, in ſome Places, they make a Breach in the Cauſey; by this Means the Beavers ſoon find themſelves aground, and without Defence, or elſe they immediately run to remedy the Evil of which they do not know the Authors, and as they are well prepared to receive them, the Beavers ſeldom eſcape, or at leaſt ſome of them are taken.

Some Particularities of this Creature.

There are ſome other Particularities of the Beavers which I find in ſome Memoirs, the Truth of which I cannot warrant. They pretend, that when theſe Animals have diſcovered any Hunters, or any of thoſe Beaſts that prey upon them, they dive, ſtriking the Water with their Tail, with ſuch a great Noiſe, that they may be heard half a League off: This is probably to give Notice to the reſt to be upon their Guard. They ſay alſo that they have the Senſe of ſmelling ſo exquiſite, that being in the Water they ſmell a Canoe at a great Diſtance. But they add, that they only ſee Side-ways like a Hare, and that through this Defect they often fall into the Hands of the Hunter whom they ſeek to ſhun. And laſtly they affirm, that when a Beaver has loſt his Mate, they never couple again with another, as is reported of the Turtle Dove. The Savages take great Care to hinder their Dogs from touching the Bones of the Beaver, becauſe they are ſo hard they would ſpoil their Teeth; they ſay the ſame

Thing

Thing of the Bones of the Porcupine. The Generality of the Savages give another Reason for this; it is, they say, not to enrage the Spirits of these Animals, which would hinder at another Time the Chace from being successful. For the rest, Madam, I wonder they have not tried to transport some of these wonderful Creatures into *France*; we have Places enough where they might find Food enough, and Materials for building, and I believe they would multiply there presently.

Of the Musk Rat.

We have here also a little Animal much of the same Nature as the Beaver, which in many Respects seems to be a smaller Species, and is called the *Musk Rat*. It has, in Fact, almost all the Properties of the Beaver, the Shape of the Body, and especially of the Head of both, is so alike, that one would take the Musk Rat for a little Beaver, if his Tail was cut off, which is almost like that of our Rats; and if its Testicles were taken away, which contain a most exquisite Musk. This Animal, which weighs about four Pounds, is much like that which Mr. *Ray* describes under the Name of *Mus Alpinus*. It takes the Field in the Month of *March*, and its Food is then some Bits of Wood, which it peals before eating them. After the Snows are melted, it lives upon the Roots of Nettles, then on the Stalks and Leaves of this Plant. In Summer it feeds mostly on Rasberries and Strawberries, and afterwards on other autumnal Fruits. During this Season, the Male is seldom seen without the Female: When Winter begins they separate, and each goes to find a Lodging in some Hole, or the Hollow of a Tree, without any Provisions; and the Savages affirm that as long as the Cold lasts they eat nothing.

They build also Cabins, something like those of the Beavers, but very far from being so well built. As to their Situation, it is always by the Water Side, so they have no Occasion to make any Dams. They say that the Fur of the Musk Rat may be mixt with that of the Beaver in making Hats, without any Prejudice to the Work. Its Flesh is not bad but in rutting Time; then it is not possible to deprive it of a Muskiness, which is not so pleasant to the Taste as to the Smell. —— I was very much inclined, Madam, to give you an Account of the other Chaces of the Savages, and of the Animals that are peculiar to this Country, but I must defer it to another Opportunity. I am just now informed that my Carriage is ready, and I am going to set out.

I am, &c.

LET-

LETTER V.

A Journey from QUEBEC *to* TROIS RIVIERES *(the Three Rivers:) How they go Post upon the Snow. Of the Lordships or Manors of* NEW FRANCE. *A Description of* BECKANCOURT. *The Tradition in regard to the Name of the River* PUANTE *(the Stinking River.), A Description of* TROIS RIVIERES. *A Continuation of the several Huntings of the Savages.*

MADAM, TROIS RIVIERES, *March* 6.

I Arrived Yesterday in this Town, after two Days Journey, and though it is twenty-five Leagues distant from *Quebec*, I could have performed the Journey in twelve Hours, because I came in a Sledge, which the Snow and Ice makes a very easy Way of travelling in this Country during the Winter, and which does not cost more than the common Carriages. The Sledge runs so smoothly, that a single Horse suffices to draw it, and always goes a Gallop. One finds at different Places fresh Horses at a cheap Rate. In Case of Need one might travel this Way threescore Leagues in twenty-four Hours, much more conveniently than in the best Post-Chaises.

Of the Lordships of Canada.

I lay the the first Night at *Pointe aux Trembles*, *(Aspen Tree Point)* seven Leagues from the Capital, which I left but one Hour before Night. This is one of the good Parishes of this Country. The Church is large and well built, and the Inhabitants in good Circumstances. In general, the old Inhabitants are richer here than the Lords of the Manors, and this is the Reason: *Canada* was but a great Forest when the *French* first settled it. Those who obtained Lordships, were not People to improve the Land themselves; they were Officers, Gentlemen, and Companies, who had not Funds sufficient to establish a proper Number of Labourers for this Purpose. They were therefore obliged to settle Inhabitants, who, before they could get a Subsistence, were obliged to labour much, and to advance all the Charges; so that they paid their Lords but a very slender Rent; and all the usual Fines of a Manor amount here but to a small Sum. A Lordship of two Leagues in Front, and of an unlimited Depth, brings in but a small Income in a Country so thinly peopled, and where there is so little Trade in the inward Parts.

This was without Doubt, one of the Reasons that engaged *Lewis* the XIVth to allow *all Nobles and Gentlemen settled in* Canada, *to trade both by Sea and Land, without being liable to be troubled on this Account, or reputed to have derogated from their Birth and Family.* These are the Terms of the Order, which was made by the Council, the 10th of *March* 1685. And further, there are no Lordships in this Country, even of those which give Titles of Honour, to which the Right of Patronage belongs; for upon the Claim of some Lords, founded upon their having built a Parish Church, his Majesty being present in Council, declared the same Year, 1685, that this Right belonged only to the Bishop, as well because he is more capable than any other of judging who are the fittest Persons, as because, that the proper Allowance of the Curates, is paid out of the Tythes that belong to the Bishop. The King in the same Order declares, that the Right of Patronage is not to give any Rank of Honour.

Of the Right of Patronage. Gentlemen are allowed to Trade.

I departed from *Pointe aux Trembles* before Day, with a one eyed Horse, I changed him afterwards for a lame one, and then him for a broken winded one. With these three Relays, I went seventeen Leagues in seven or eight Hours, and I arrived early at the Baron *de Beckancourt*'s, chief Surveyor of the Highways of *New France*, who would by no Means suffer me to go forward. This Gentleman has a Village of *Abenaquis*, under the Direction of a *Jesuit* in Matters of Religion, to whom I was very glad to pay my Respects by the Way. The Baron lives at the Entrance of a little River that comes from the South, which runs entirely through his Lordship, and bears his Name. The Life which M. *de Beckancourt* leads in this Desert (for here are no other *French* Inhabitants as yet but the Lord) naturally brings to Mind the antient Patriarchs, who did not disdain to divide with their Servants the Labours of their Country, and lived almost in as plain a Manner as they. The Advantage which he makes by the Trade with the Savages his Neighbours, by buying Skins of them at the first Hand, is more than the Profits he could make of Inhabitants, to whom he should divide his Land. In Time, it will be his own Fault if he has no Vassals, and he will make more advantageous Conditions when he has cleared all his Land. The River *Beckancourt* was formerly called *Riviere Puante*, or the *Stinking River*. I enquired the Cause of this Name, for the Water appeared to me very fine, and they assured me that it is very good, and that there is no bad Smell in all this Quarter. Yet some told me it was so called on Account of the bad Qualities of the

Of the Situation of Beckancourt.

Waters:

Waters: Others attributed it to the great Number of Musk Rats that are found in it, the Scent of which the Savages cannot bear; but here is a third Reason, which they who have made the greatest Researches into the antient History of the Country say, is the true one.

Some *Algonquins* were at War with the *Onnontcharonnons*, better known by the Name of the *Iroquet* Nation, which antiently dwelt in the Island of *Montreal*. The Name it bears proves, that it was of the *Huron* Language; but they say it was these *Hurons* who drove them from their antient Habitation, and who have in Part destroyed them: However that may be, this Nation was at the Time I speak of, at War with the *Algonquins*, who, to make an End at once of the War, which they began to be weary of, contrived a Stratagem, which succeeded. They set themselves in Ambush on the two Sides of a little River, which is now called *Beckancourt*. Then they detached some Canoes, which made a Shew of Fishing in the Great River. They knew that their Enemies were not far off, and they made no Doubt that they would soon fall upon these pretended Fishermen: And in Fact, they soon saw a Fleet of Canoes coming in Haste to attack them; they seemed to be afrighted, fled, and got up the River. They were followed very close by the Enemy, who thought to make a very easy Conquest of this Handful of Men; and to draw them on, they affected to be greatly terrified. This Feint succeeded, the Pursuers still kept advancing, and making most hideous Cries, according to the Custom of these Barbarians, they thought they were instantly going to seize their Prey.

Then a Shower of Arrows from behind the Bushes which bordered the River threw them into Confusion, which they gave them no Time to recover. A second Discharge which followed close upon the first, entirely routed them. They strove to fly in their Turn,. but they could no longer use their Canoes, which were every where pierced with Arrows: They leaped into the Water, hoping to save themselves by swimming, but besides that the greatest Part were wounded, they met at landing the Death they fled from, and not one escaped the *Algonquins*, who gave no Quarter, and did not even amuse themselves with making of Prisoners: The *Iroquet* Nation never recovered this fatal Blow, and though some of these Savages have been seen since the Arrival of the *French* in *Canada*, at present there are none remaining. In the mean Time the Number of dead Bodies which remained in the Water and upon the Sides of the River infected it in such a Manner, that it still retains the Name of *Riviere Puante, (the Stinking River.)*

Of the Abenaqui *Village of* Beckancourt.

The *Abenaqui* Village of *Beckancourt* is not so populous as it was some Years ago, yet they would be of great Assistance to us in Case of a War. These Savages are always ready to make Inroads into *New England*, where their Name alone has often carried Terror even into *Boston*. They would also serve us as effectually against the *Iroquois*, to whom they are no ways inferior in Valour, and are better disciplined. They are all *Christians*, and they have a pretty Chapel, where they practise with much Edification all the Exercises of the *Christian* Religion. We must, nevertheless, acknowledge, that they are greatly fallen from the Fervour which appeared in them the first Years of their Establishment amongst us. They carried them Brandy, which they took a great Liking to, and the Savages never drink but to get drunk. We have learnt by fatal Experience, that in Proportion as these People depart from God, in the same Measure they pay less Respect to their Pastors, and grow more in the Interest of the *English*. It is greatly to be feared that the Lord will permit them to become our Enemies, to punish us for having contributed, for a sordid Interest, to render them vicious, as it has already happened to some other Nations.

Situation of the Town of Trois Rivieres.

After having embraced the Missionary of *Beckancourt*, *(a)* visited his Village, and made with him some sorrowful Reflections which naturally arise from the Disorders I have mentioned, and for which he is often reduced to groan in the Sight of God, I crossed the River *St. Laurence* to come to this Town. Nothing is more charming than its Situation. It is built upon a gentle Hill of Sand, which is only barren for the Space it may occupy, if it ever becomes a considerable Town; for at present it is but of little Consequence. It is surrounded by whatever can render a Town agreeable and wealthy. The River, which is near half a League wide, runs at the Bottom. Beyond, we see a cultivated fruitful Country, that is crowned with the finest Forests in the World. A little below, and on the same Side as the Town, the Great River receives another tolerably fine River, which before it mixes its Water with the first, receives at the same Time two others, one to the right and the other to the left, which has given the Name of *Trois Rivieres (Three Rivers)* to the Town.

Of the Lake of St. Pierre (St. Peter.)

Above, and at about the same Distance, begins the Lake of *St. Pierre*, which is about three Leagues wide, and seven long: So that nothing bounds the Sight on that Side, and the Sun appears to set in the Waves. This Lake, which is only an Enlargement of the River *St. Laurence*, receives

(a) Father *Eustache Le Sueur.*

many

Rivers. It appears probable, that it is these Rivers that in a Course of Years have eaten away the low and light Soil, through which they run. This is most apparent in the River *St. François*, the Mouth of which hath may little Islands interspersed in it, which probably were formerly joined to the Continent. And moreover, in all the Lake, unless in the midst of the Channel where the Strength of the Current of the Great River has preserved its Depth, there is no passing but in Canoes. There are also some Places where great Canoes, if they are but lightly loaded, cannot easily pass. But it is every where full of Fish, and the Fish are excellent.

A Description of the Town.

They reckon but about seven or eight hundred People in the Town of *Trois Rivieres*, but it has in its Neighbourhood wherewithal to enrich a great City; *that is to say*, very good Iron Mines, which may be wrought with Profit at at any Time *(a)*. Upon the whole, though this Town is but thinly peopled, its Situation renders it of great Consequence, and it is one of the oldest Settlements in the Colony. From the first, this Post has had a Governor, he has a thousand Crowns Salary, and an *Etat Major* (a certain Number of General Officers of the Army under him.) Here is also a Convent of *Recollets*, a pretty good Parish Church served by this Society, and a very fine Hospital, joined to a Nunnery of *Ursulines*, to the Number of forty, who are employed as Nurses to the Hospital. This is also a Foundation of M. *de St. Vallier*. From the Year 1650, the *Senechal* (whose Office and Power was afterwards abolished and invested in the Superior Council of *Quebec*, and the Intendant) had a Lieutenant at *Trois Rivieres*: At present, this Town has a common Court of Justice, the Chief of which is a Lieutenant General.

The first Cause of its Establishment.

It owes its Origin to the great Resort of Savages of different Nations to this Place. At the Beginning of the Colony there came down many, especially from the farthest Parts of the North, by the three Rivers, which have given the Name to this Town, and by which they go up a great Way. The Situation of the Place, joined to the great Trade that was carried on here, engaged some *French* to settle here; and the Neighbourhood of the River *de Sorel*, then called the *Iroquois River*, (which I shall mention soon) induced the Governor General to build a Fort here, where was maintained a good Garrison, and which had from the first a Governor of its own. This Post was then looked

(a) They are actually wrought at this Time, and produce the best Iron in the World.

upon

upon, as one of the most important in *New France*. After some Years, the Savages being tired of being continually harrassed by the *Iroquois*, from whom the *French* themselves had Trouble enough to defend themselves, and having no longer the Liberty of the Passes, where these proud Enemies laid wait for them continually, and not being safe even in Sight of, and under the Cannon of our Fort, they forebore to bring hither their Peltry or Skins. The *Jesuits* with all their new Converts retired three Leagues lower, upon some Lands that were given them by the Abbot *de la Madeleine*, one of the Members of the Society of the hundred Associates, formed by the Cardinal *de Richlieu*, from whence this Place took the Name of *Cape de la Madeleine*, which it bears to this Day *(a)*.

Of Cape Madeleine.

The Mission which was transported hither, did not subsist a long Time. This was partly the Effect of the Fickleness of the Savages, but principally the Consequence of the Wars and Diseases which have almost entirely destroyed this rising Church. There are still in the Neighbourhood a Company of *Algonquins*, the greatest Part of whom were baptized in their Infancy, but have now no regular Exercise of Religion. The Gentlemen of the *West-India* Company, who have now the Beaver Trade, have in vain endeavoured to draw them to *Checoutime*, where they have already re-united several Families of the same Nation, and of the Nation of the Mountains, under the Direction of a *Jesuit* Missionary. Others wanted to unite them with the *Abenaquis* of *St. François*. All their Answer to these Invitations was, that they could not resolve to quit a Place where the Bones of their Fathers rest. But some People believe, and not without Foundation, that this Refusal proceeds less from themselves, than from some People to whom their Neighbourhood is advantageous; and who, without Doubt, do not sufficiently consider that they sacrifice the Salvation of these Savages to a little Interest.

I have just been informed, Madam, that in a few Days I shall have an Opportunity of sending this Letter to *Quebec*, from whence it may go early to *France* by the Isle *Royal*. I shall fill it up with what concerns the Huntings of the Savages.——The hunting of the Beaver, as I have before observed, was not their principal Concern, till they saw the Value which the *French* set upon the Skin of this Animal. Before this, the hunting of the Bear held the first Place, and was performed with the greatest Superstition. This is what is observed at this Day in this Chace, amongst those who are not *Christians*.

(a) Besides the Iron Mines, which are very plentiful at *Cape Madeleine*, there have been discovered some Years ago, several Springs of Mineral Waters.

It

Of hunting the Bear.

It is always a War-Chief who fixes the Time, and has the Care of inviting the Hunters. This Invitation, which is made with great Ceremony, is followed with a Faſt of eight Days; during which they muſt not drink even a Drop of Water. And I will tell you by the Way, Madam, that what the Savages call faſting, is to take abſolutely nothing at all. Still more, in Spite of the extreme Weakneſs which ſuch an Abſtinence one may ſuppoſe cannot fail to cauſe, they never ceaſe ſinging all the Time it laſts. They obſerve this Faſt, in order to induce the Genii, or Spirits, to diſcover the Places where they may find many Bears. Many even do much more to deſerve this Favour. Several have been ſeen to cut their Fleſh in ſeveral Places of their Body, to render their Genii, or Spirits, more propitious. But it is proper to obſerve, that they do not aſk their Aſſiſtance to conquer theſe furious Animals: It ſuffices them to be informed where they are. As *Ajax* did not aſk of *Jupiter* to give him the Victory over his Enemies, but only Day enough to make an End of his Conqueſt.

The Savages ſupplicate alſo on the ſame Account the Manes of the Beaſts which they have killed in former Huntings; and as their Thoughts run wholly on the Matter whilſt they are awake, it is natural that during their Sleep (which can't be very ſound upon ſuch empty Stomachs) they ſhould often dream of Bears. But this is not enough to determine them: It is neceſſary that all, at leaſt the greateſt Number, ſhould in their Sleep have ſeen Bears in the ſame Place: And how (you will ſay) ſhould all their Dreams agree in this? The Caſe ſeems to be thus: Provided a ſkilful Hunter has thought he has dreamt two or three Times together of ſeeing Bears in a certain Place, either through Complaiſance, or through continual talking of it, their chimerical Brain at laſt takes the Impreſſion, and every Body preſently dreams the ſame, or feign that they have dreamt ſo, and a Reſolution is taken to go to that Place.——The Faſt being over, and the Place of the Hunt ſettled, the Chief who is choſen for the Chace gives to all thoſe who are to be of the Party a great Feaſt; but no Perſon dares be preſent, without having firſt bathed; *that is to ſay*, without having plunged into the River, let the Weather be ever ſo ſevere, provided the River is not frozen. This Feaſt is not like many others, in which they are obliged to eat up all: Though they have faſted ſo long before it, (and perhaps it is for this Reaſon) they eat moderately. He who gives the Feaſt, eats nothing; and all his Employment, whilſt the others are at Table, is to relate his former Atchievements in hunting: Freſh Invocations of the Manes of dead Bears, finiſhes the Feaſt. Then they begin their March, equipp'd as for War, and their Faces besmeared with Black, amidst the Acclamations of the whole Village; for the Chace, amongst these People, is as noble as War. The Alliance of a good Hunter is more sought after than that of a famous Warrior, because the Chace provides the whole Family with Provision and Cloathing, and the Savages desire nothing more: But a Man is not esteemed a great Hunter, till he has killed twelve great Beasts in one Day.

These People have two great Advantages over us in this Exercise; for, in the first Place, nothing stops them, neither Bushes, Ditches, Torrents, Ponds, nor Rivers. They always go forward upon a strait Line. In the second Place, there are few, or rather no Creatures, which they cannot overtake in running: They have been seen, as it is said, entering a Village, leading Bears in a Wythe, (which they had tired by running down) as if they had been leading a Flock of Sheep; and the nimblest Deer is not swifter than they are. Lastly, the chief Hunter must make little Advantage himself of his Game: He is oblig'd to be very liberal of it: If they even prevent his Gift, and take it away from him, he must suffer the Loss without saying any Thing, and be contented with the Glory of having labour'd for the Public. Nevertheless, it is not complained of, if in the Distribution which he makes of the Game, he gives the first Part to his own Family. But we must confess, that those Savages with whom we have most Commerce, have lost something of that antient Generosity, and that wonderful Disinterestedness which they were remarkable for.---Nothing is more contagious than the Spirit of Interest, and nothing more capable of altering the Manners of a People.

The Bear is six Months without eating.

Winter is the Season for hunting the Bear: Then these Animals are hid in hollow Trees; or if they find any blown down, they shelter themselves under the Roots of them, and stop up the Entrance with Branches of Pine, so that they are perfectly screened from the Rigour of the Season; otherwise, they make a Hole in the Earth, and take great Care, when they are in, to stop up the Opening. Some have been found at the Bottom of a Cavern, hid in such a Manner as not to be perceived, though looked very narrowly for. But in what Manner soever the Bear is lodged, he never leaves his Retreat for the whole Winter: This is no longer doubted of. It is as certain that he never makes any Provision for the Winter, and of Consequence, that during all that Time he never eats or drinks: As to his living all this Time by sucking his Paws, as some Authors have affirmed, every one is allowed to believe what he pleases: But this is certain, that they have been kept chained up during the he Winter, without having any Thing given them to eat or to drink, and at the End of ſix Months they were as fat as before. It is without Doubt ſurprizing that a Creature cloathed with ſuch a good Fur, and who has not the Appearance of being very tender, ſhould take ſuch Precautions againſt the Cold, which no one elſe would think there was any Need of. This ſhews we muſt not judge by Appearances: Every one beſt knows his own Wants.

The Manner of hunting the Bear.

There is no Need of running much to catch the Bear: It is only neceſſary to know the Places where the greateſt Number is hid. As ſoon as the Hunters think they have found ſuch a Place, they form a Circle of a Quarter of a League in Circumference, or more or leſs, according to the Number of Hunters: Then they advance, coming ſtill cloſer and cloſer together; and every one looks before him, to find out the Retreat of ſome Bear; ſo that if there is any, it is difficult for one to eſcape, for our Savages are excellent Ferrets. The next Day the ſame Manœuvre begins again at ſome Diſtance from thence, and all the Time of the Chace is employed in this Manner.

A ridiculous Ceremony when a Bear is killed.

When a Bear is killed, the Hunter puts the End of his lighted Pipe between his Teeth, blows into the Bowl; and thus filling the Mouth and Throat of the Beaſt with Smoak, he conjures its Spirit to bear no Malice for what he has juſt done to the Body, and not to oppoſe him in his future Huntings: But as the Spirit does not anſwer, the Hunter (to know if his Prayer is granted) cuts the String under the Bear's Tongue, and keeps it till he returns to the Village: Then they all throw, with great Ceremony, and after many Invocations, theſe Strings into the Fire: If they crackle, and ſhrink up, as ſeldom fails to happen, this is taken for a certain Sign that the Spirit of the Bear is appeaſed; if not, they believe they are enraged, and that the Chace of next Year will not be ſucceſsful, unleſs they can find a Way to reconcile them; for, in ſhort, there is a Remedy for every Thing.

How the Hunters are received at their Return.

The Hunters make good Cheer, as long as the Chace laſts; and even if they have but little Succeſs, they carry off with them enough to treat their Friends, and feed their Families a long Time. This Fleſh is in Reality no great Ragout, but every Thing is good to the Savages. To ſee how they are received, the Praiſes they give them, the pleaſed and ſelf-ſufficient Airs they take upon themſelves, one would ſay they were returning from ſome grand Expedition, loaded with the Spoils of a whole Nation deſtroyed. The People of the Village ſay, *It must be a Man* (and the Hunters say so themselves) *to fight with and conquer Bears in this Manner.*—Another Thing for which they receive no less Praise, and upon which they as much pride themselves, is to leave nothing of the great Feast which is given them at their Return from the Chace by the chief Hunter. The first Service that is presented, is the largest Bear they have taken; and they serve it up whole, with all its Entrails: It is not even skinned; they only singe the Skin as one does that of a Hog for Bacon. This Feast is performed to a certain Spirit, whose Anger they think they should incur if they did not eat all: They must not even leave any of the Broth in which the Meat was boiled, which is scarce any Thing but Fat melted and reduced to Oil: Nothing can be worse; and it generally kills some of them, and makes many of them very sick.

Some Particularities of the Bear.

The Bears are not mischievous in this Country, but when they are hungry, or when they are wounded; however, People are on their Guard when they approach them. They seldom attack; they even generally run away as soon as they see any Person, and there needs only a Dog to make them scour quite away. The Bear ruts in *July*: He then grows so lean, & his Flesh is so insipid and ill tasted, that even the Savages who often eat those Things, the Sight of which would turn our Stomachs, can hardly touch it. Who would believe that this Passion should waste an Animal of this Kind and Shape more in one Month, than a total Abstinence from Food for six Months? It is less surprizing that he should then be so fierce and ill-natured, that it is not safe to meet him in his Way. This is the Effect of his Jealousy.

This Season being over, the Bear grows fat again, and nothing contributes more to it than the Fruits which he finds in the Woods, of which he is very fond. Above all, he is fond of Grapes; and as all the Forests are full of Vines, which grow to the Tops of the highest Trees, he makes no Difficulty to climb up them: But if a Hunter finds him there, his Daintiness costs him his Life. When he has thus well fed upon Fruits, his Flesh has a very good Taste, and keeps it till Spring: It has, nevertheless, always a great Fault; it is too oily; and if it is not used with Moderation, it causes the Bloody Flux. On the other Hand, a Bear's Whelp is as good as a Lamb.

Of the Dogs the Savages use for hunting.

I forgot, Madam, to tell you that the Savages always carry a great Number of Dogs with them when they hunt; they are the only Domestic Creatures which they bring up, and they bring them up only for Hunting: They all seem to be of the same Species: Their Ears stand upright; their Nose is long, like that of a Wolf; but they are very faithful and attached

tached to their Masters; who, nevertheless, feed them but poorly, and never fondle them: They break them betimes to that Kind of Chace they are intended for, and they are excellent Hunters. I have not Time to add any Thing more, for they call me to depart.

I am, &c.

LETTER VI.

A Description of the Country, and the Islands of Richlieu *and* St. François. *Of the* Abenaqui *Village. Of the antient Fort of* Richlieu, *and of those that have been built in each Parish. A brave Action of two* Canadian *Ladies.*

MADAM, St. FRANÇOIS, *March* 11.

I Departed on the 9th from *Trois Rivieres*, and crossed the Lake of *St. Peter*, inclining a little to the South. I performed this Journey in a Sledge, because the Ice was still strong enough to bear all Sorts of Carriages; and I arrived at Noon at *St. François*. I employed the Afternoon, and all Yesterday, to visit this Quarter; and I shall now give you an Account of what I observed here.

At the West End of Lake *St. Pierre*, there is a vast Number of Islands of all Sizes, which they call the *Islands of Richlieu*; and turning to the Left, when we come from *Quebec*, we find six others, which border a pretty deep Bay, into which a River discharges itself, the Spring Head of which is in the Neighbourhood of *New York*. The Islands, the River, and all the Country it waters, bear the Name of *St. François*. Each of these Islands are about a Mile long; their Breadth is unequal: The greatest Part of those of *Richlieu* are smaller: They were all formerly full of Stags, Deer, Goats, and Elks: Here was also a surprizing Plenty of wild Fowl, which is not now very scarce; but the great Beasts have disappeared.

Of the Islands of Richlieu, *and of* St. François.

We get also excellent Fish in the River of *St. François*, and at its Mouth. In Winter they make Holes in the Ice, and let down their Nets of five or six Fathom long, and they seldom take them up empty. The Fish which they commonly take, are the gilt Fish, *Achigans*, and particularly the *Masquinongez*, which are a Kind of Pike: It hath a Head larger than ours, and the Mouth under a hooked Snout, which gives them an odd Look. The Lands of *St. François*, if we may judge by the Trees that grow here, and by that which is already cultivated, are very good. The Inhabitants are, notwithstanding, poor enough; and many would be reduced to the greatest Indigence, if the Trade with the Savages, their Neighbours, did not help them a little. But is it not this Trade that hinders them from mending their Circumstances, by making them lazy?

Of the Abenaquis *Village.*

The Savages I speak of, are the *Abenaquis*, amongst which there are some *Algonquins*, and also *Sckokis* and *Mahingans*, better known by the Name of the *Wolves*. This Nation was formerly settled upon the River of *Manhatte*, in *New York*, and it appears that they were antient Inhabitants of that Country. The *Abenaquis* came to *St. François* from the Southern Parts of *New France*, which are nearest *New England*. Their first Station, upon leaving their Country to come to live amongst us, was a little River that discharges itself into the River *St. Laurence*, almost over-against SYLLERY; *that is to say*, about a League and a half above *Quebec*, on the South Side. They seated themselves in the Neighbourhood of a Fall, which was called the Fall *de la Chandiere*, (the *Kettle.*) They are now situated on the Bank of the River *St. François*, two Leagues from its Mouth, in the Lake *St. Pierre*. The Place is very pleasant; but the Misfortune is, that these People do not enjoy the Pleasures of a fine Situation, and the Cabins of the Savages, especially of the *Abenaquis*, do not adorn a Country. The Village is well peopled, and is inhabited only by *Christians*. This Nation is docible, and were at all Times well affected to the *French (a)*; but the Missionary has no less Trouble on their Account, than his Brother of *Beckancourt*, and for the same Reasons.

Of the Maple Juice.

I was treated here with Maple Juice: This is the Season in which it is drawn. It is delicious, of wonderful Coolness, and very wholesome. The manner of drawing it is very easy. When the Sap begins to rise, they make a Jag or Notch in the Trunk of the Maple, and by the Means of a bit of Wood which they fix in it, the Water runs as by a Spout: This Water is received into a Vessel, which they set under it. To make it run plentifully, there must be much Snow upon the Ground, the Night must be frosty, the Sky clear, and the Wind not too cold. Our Maples would have perhaps the same Virtue, if we had in *France* as much Snow as in *Canada*, and if it lasted as long. By Degrees, as the Sap thickens, it runs less, and after some Time it stops entirely. It is easy to judge, that after such a Bleeding, the Tree is not the more healthy: They affirm, however, that it can bear this many Years together. They would do better perhaps, to let

(a) Father *Joseph Aubery*.

let it rest a Year or two, that it might recover its Strength. But at last, when it is worn out, it serves to cut down, and its Wood, Roots, and Knots, are fit for many Things. This Tree must be very plenty here, for they burn much of it.

The Water of the Maple is pretty clear, though a little whitish; it is very cooling, and leaves in the Mouth a Taste like that of Sugar, very agreeable. It is a very good Pectoral; and in what Quantity soever it is drank, though you are never so much heated, it never does Harm; for it has not that Rawness which causes the Pleurisy; but on the contrary, a balsamick Virtue, which sweetens the Blood, and a certain Salt, which keeps up the Heat of it. They add that it never congeals; but if they keep it a certain Time, it becomes an excellent Vinegar. I do not warrant this for Fact, and I know that a Traveller ought not to take every Thing for Truth which he hears. It is very probable that the Savages, who are well acquainted with the Virtues of all their Plants, have at all Times made the same Use of this Water, which they do at this Day; but it is certain they did not know how to make a Sugar of it, which we have since taught them. They were contented to let it boil a little, to thicken it something, and make a Sort of Syrup, which is pretty enough. What is further required to make Sugar of it, is to let it boil till it takes a proper Consistence, and it purifies itself without any foreign Mixture. There needs only Care not to boil it too much, and to scum it well. The greatest Fault in making it, is to let it harden too much in its Syrup, which makes it oily, and to keep a Taste of Honey, which renders it less palatable, unless it is refined.

This Sugar made with Care, and it requires much less than ours, is natural, pectoral, and does not burn the Stomach. Besides, the making of it is very cheap. It is commonly thought that it is impossible to refine it, like that which is made from Canes; but I do not see the Reason of this; and it is certain, that as it comes out of the Hands of the Savages, it is purer and much better than the Sugar of the Islands, which has undergone no more Management. I gave some to a Sugar Baker of *Orleans*, who found no other Defect in it, than that which I have already mentioned, and which he attributed solely to its not being sufficiently purified. He thought it also of a better Kind than the other, and made some Lozenges of it, which I had the Honour to present to you, Madam, and which you found so excellent. It will be objected, that if it was of such a good Quality, it would have become an Object of Trade, but there is not enough made for this Purpose; but perhaps they are in the wrong in not trying what may be done. There are many other Things besides this, that are neglected in this Country.---The Plain-Tree, the

the small Cherry, the Ash, and the Walnut-Trees of different Sorts, give also a Water that makes Sugar, but in less Quantity, and the Sugar is not so good. Yet some People give the Preference to that which is drawn from the Ash, but there is very little made. Could you have believed, Madam, that we should find in *Canada*, what *Virgil* says in foretelling the Renewal of the golden Age, that Honey should flow from the Trees *(a)*.

Of Fort Richlieu.

All this Country has been a long Time the Theatre of many bloody Scenes, because during the War with the *Iroquois*, it was the most exposed to the Excursions of those Barbarians. They came down upon the Colony, by a River that discharges itself into the River *St. Laurence*, a little above Lake *St. Pierre*, on the same Side as that of *St. François*; and to which, for this Reason, they at first gave their Name. It has been since for some Time called *Richlieu*, and is now called the River *de Sorel*. The Islands of *Richlieu*, which they came to first, served them equally for their Ambushes, and for a Retreat; but when we had shut up this Passage by a Fort, built at the Entrance of the River, they took their Way by the Lands above and below, and threw themselves especially on the Side of *St. François*, where they found the same Advantages to exercise their Robberies, and where they have committed Cruelties which are horrible to relate.

Other Forts in all the Parishes.

They spread themselves afterwards through the whole Colony, and they were obliged in order to defend themselves from their Fury, to build in every Parish a Kind of Fort, where the Inhabitants may take Refuge on the first Alarm. They kept in each Fort one or two Centinels, who did Duty Night and Day, and they had all some Field-Pieces, or at least some Pattereroes, as well to disperse the Enemy, as to give Notice to the Inhabitants to be upon their Guard, and to inform when they wanted Succours. These Forts are only Inclosures, defended with Pallisadoes, with some Redoubts: The Church and the Manor-House are always in this Inclosure; and there is still Room enough left, in case of need, to give Refuge to the Women and Children, and the Cattle. This has been found sufficient to preserve them from any Insult; for I never heard the *Iroquois* took any of these Forts.

They very seldom block them up, and scarce ever attack them to take them by Assault. One is too dangerous for Savages, who have no defensive Arms, and do not love a Victory stained with their Blood: The other Way does not agree with their Manner of making War. Two attacks of the Fort *de Vercheres*, are never-

(a) *Et duræ Quercus sudabunt roscida mella.*

theless

theless famous in the Annals of *Canada*; and it looks as if the *Iroquois* had attempted it twice, contrary to their Custom, only to display the Valour and Intrepidity of two Amazons.

Gallant Actions of two Canadian *Ladies.*

In 1690, these Savages being informed that Madam *de Vercheres* was almost alone in her Fort, approached it without being seen, and attempted to scale the Pallisadoes: Some Musket Shot that were fired to good Purpose, upon the first Noise they made, dispersed them; but they soon returned, and they were again repulsed; and what suprised them the more was, that they saw only a Woman, and her they saw every where. This was Madam *de Vercheres*, who kept up as good a Countenance as if she had had a numerous Garrison. The Hope which the Besiegers had conceived at first, to take a Place easily, which they knew was without Men, made them return several Times to the Charge; but the Lady with the Help of the Women with her, always beat them off. She fought in this Manner two Days, with such Bravery and Presence of Mind, as would have done Honour to an old Warrior; and at last she obliged the Enemy to retire, for Fear of having their Retreat cut off, greatly ashamed of being forced to fly before a Woman.

Two Years after another Party of the same Nation, much more numerous than the other, appeared in Sight of the same Fort, whilst all the Inhabitants were abroad, and the greatest Part employed in the Fields. The *Iroquois* finding them thus dispersed, without any Suspicion of an Enemy, seized them all one after another, then marched towards the Fort. The Daughther of the Lord, who was at most but fourteen Years old, was about two hundred Paces off the Fort. At the first Cry she heard, she ran to get in: The Savages pursued her, and one of them came up with her just as she got to the Door; but having seized her by a Handkerchief that was about her Neck, she let it slip from her, and so got in, and shut to the Gate.

There was nobody in the Fort but a young Soldier and a Company of Women; who, at the Sight of their Husbands whom the Savages were binding and carrying away Prisoners, sent forth most lamentable Cries. The young Lady lost neither her Judgment nor Courage. She began by pulling off her Cap, she tied up her Hair, put on a Hat and a Jacket, and locked up all the Women, whose Cries and Tears could but encourage the Enemy. Then she fired a Cannon and some Musket Shot, and shewing herself with her Soldier sometimes in one Redoubt, and sometimes in another, changing frequently their Dress, and firing to good Purpose whenever she saw the *Iroquois* approach the Pallisade, the Savages fancied there were many People in the Fort, and when the Chevalier *de Crisay*, upon hearing the firing,

came

came to succour the Place, the Enemy was already marched off.

Of the Elk, or Orignal.

Let us now return to the Chase.——That of the Orignal would not have been less profitable to us at present, than that of the Beaver, if our Predecessors in this Country had given more Attention to the Profits which might have been made of it, and had not almost entirely destroyed the Species, at least in those Places which are within our Reach.

A Description of the Orignal.

What they call here the Orignal, is what in *Germany*, *Poland*, and *Muscovy*, they call the Elk or Great Beast. This Animal here, is as big as a Horse, or a Mule of *Auvergne*. The hind Quarters are large, the Tail but only an Inch long, the Hams very high, the Legs and Feet like those of a Hart: a long Hair covers the Withers, the Neck, and the upper Part of the Hams: The Head is above two Feet long, and he carries it out, which gives him an ill Look: Its Muzzle is large, and lessens in the upper Part like that of a Camel, and its Nostrils are so large one may easily thrust in half ones Arm. Its Horns are not less long than those of a Hart, and much wider: They are flat and forked like those of a Deer, and are renewed every Year; but I know not if upon the new Growth, they make an Increase which denotes the Age of the Animal.

They say that the Orignal is subject to the Epilepsy, and when the Fits seize him, he gets over them by scratching his Ear with his left hind Foot till he draws Blood, which has made the Hoof of this Foot be esteemed a Specific against the falling Sickness. It is applied to the Heart of the Patient, and they do the same to cure the Palpitation of the Heart: They put it also into the left Hand of the Person who is disordered, and rub his Ear with it: But why should they not draw Blood from him also, as the Orignal does? This Hoof is also reckoned very good against the Pleurisy Cholick Pains, the Flux, the Vertigo, and the Purples, by reducing it to Powder, and giving it in Water. I have been told that the *Algonquins*, who formerly made the Flesh of this Animal their common Food, were very much subject to the Epilepsy, and never used this Remedy: Perhaps they had better. The Hair of the Orignal is a Mixture of light grey and dark red. It grows hollow as the Beast grows old, and never loses its elastic Power: Beat it ever so long it springs up again. Mattresses are made of it, and Saddles. Its Flesh is well tasted, light, and nourishing; it would be a Pity that it should cause the Epilepsy; but our Hunters, who have lived upon it whole Winters, never found that it had any bad Quality. Its Skin is strong, soft and substantial; it is made into Shamios, and excellent

excellent Beef, which is very light. The Savages look upon the Original as a Creature of good Omen, and believe that those who dream frequently of it, may flatter themselves with long Life: But they think quite the contrary with Regard to dreaming of the Bear, except in the Time when they are disposed to hunt those Creatures. There is also current among these Barbarians, a comical Tradition of a great Original, near which all the rest appear but as Ants: They say his Legs are so long, that eight Feet Depth of Snow is no Hindrance to him; that his Skin is Proof against all Sorts of Arms, and that he has a Kind of Arm which grows out of his Shoulder, which he makes Use of as we do of our's; that he never fails to have after him a great Number of Originals, who form his Court, and who render him all the Services he requires of them. Thus the Antients had their Phœnix, and their Pegasus: And the *Chinese* and the *Japanese* have their Kirin, their Foe, their Water Dragon, and their Bird of Paradise.—*Every Country has its ridiculous Notions.*

The proper Time to hunt the Original.

The Original loves cold Countries; he feeds on Grass in Summer, and in Winter he gnaws the Trees. When the Snows are high, these Animals troop together into some Pine-Grove, to shelter themselves under the Verdure from the bad Weather, and they continue there as long as they find Food. Then it is easy to hunt them; but easier still, when the Sun begins to have Strength enough to melt the Snow; for the frosty Nights making a sort of Crust upon the Snow melted in the Day, the Original (which is an heavy Creature) breaks it with his cloven Foot, fleas his Legs, and has some Trouble to get out of the Holes he makes. Without this, and especially when there is but little Snow, they cannot approach him without Trouble, nor without Danger; because, when he is wounded, he grows furious, turns suddenly upon the Hunter, and tramples him under his Feet. The Way to escape this, is for the Hunter to throw him his Coat, upon which he discharges all his Fury; whilst the Hunter, hid behind a Tree, can take his Measures to kill him. The Original always goes a great Trot, which is near equal to the Speed of the Buffaloe, and he holds it a long Time: But yet the Savages can out-run him. They say that he kneels down to drink, to eat, and to rest himself, and that there is in his Heart a little Bone, which being reduced to Powder, and taken in Broth, appeases the Pains of Child-birth, and facilitates Delivery.

Various Ways of his Chace.

The most Northern Nations of *Canada* have a Way of performing this Hunt which is very easy, and without Danger. The Hunters divide themselves into two Companies: One embarks in

K Canoes;

Canoes; and theſe Canoes keeping at ſome Diſtance from each other, form a large Semicircle, the two Ends of which touch the Shore: The other Company that remains on the Land, performs much the ſame Operation, and encloſe a large Space. Then theſe Hunters let go their Dogs, and rouze all the Orignals that are in that Space; and driving them forward, oblige them to run into the River, or the Lake. They are no ſooner in the Water, than they fire upon them from all the Canoes: Every Shot takes Place, and very ſeldom even a ſingle Orignal eſcapes.

Champlain ſpeaks of another Manner of hunting not only the Orignals, but alſo Harts and Caribous, which is ſomething like this Way. They incloſe (ſays he) a Part of a Foreſt with Stakes, interwoven with Branches of Trees, and leave but one narrow Opening, where they lay Snares made of raw Skins. This Space is triangular, and from the Angle of the Entrance they draw another Triangle, much larger: So theſe two Incloſures communicate together by the two Angles: The two Sides of the ſecond Triangle are alſo ſhut up with Stakes, and the Hunters ranged upon a Line form the Baſe. Then they advance, without breaking the Line; and drawing nearer and nearer to each other, they make a great Shouting, and ſtrike upon ſomething that makes a great Noiſe. The Beaſts being driven forward, and not able to eſcape either to Right or Left, and being affrighted with the Noiſe, know not where to fly, but into the other Incloſure; and many, as they enter it, are caught by the Horns or the Neck. They ſtruggle greatly to get looſe, and ſometimes they carry with them or break the Snares: Sometimes alſo they ſtrangle themſelves, or at leaſt give the Hunters Time to ſhoot them at their Eaſe. Thoſe which eſcape this, fare no better: They are incloſed in too ſmall a Space to ſhun the Arrows which the Hunters let fly at them from all Sides.

How the Carcajou, or wild Cat, hunts the Orignal.

The Orignal has other Enemies than the Savages, and which make a no leſs rough War againſt him. The moſt terrible of all is the Carcajou, or Quincajou, a Sort of wild Cat; whoſe Tail is ſo long, that it can twiſt it ſeveral Times round its Body: Its Hair is a reddiſh brown. As ſoon as this Hunter can come up with an Orignal, he leaps upon him; and fixing upon his Neck, twiſts its long Tail round it; after which, it tears the Jugular Vein. The Orignal has but one Way to eſcape this Misfortune; *that is*, to get into the Water as ſoon as he is ſeized by this dangerous Enemy. The Carcajou, who cannot bear the Water, lets go his Hold immediately. But if the Water is too far off, it has Time to kill the Orignal before he can get into it. Commonly this Hunter, whoſe Smell is not the beſt, brings three Foxes to the Chace, and ſends them out upon the

the Discovery. As soon as they have smelt out an Orignal, two place themselves at his Sides, and the third behind him, and they all three make such a fine Manœuvre, harrassing the Beast, that they oblige him to go where they have left the Carcajou, with which they agree afterwards about dividing the Game.---Another Stratagem of the Carcajou, is to climb up a Tree: There lying along upon an extended Branch, he waits for the passing by of an Orignal, and leaps upon him as soon as he is within his Reach.

Many People have imagined, Madam, that the Relations of *Canada* give the Savages more Wit and Sense than they have. They are, nevertheless, Men: And under what Climate shall we find Brutes that have an Instinct more ingenious than the Beaver, the Carcajou, and the Fox?

Of the Hart and the Caribou.

The Hart of *Canada* is absolutely the same as in *France*, perhaps commonly a litttle larger. It does not appear that the Savages disturb him much; at least, I do not find that they make War against him in Form, and with any Preparations. It is not the same with Regard to the Caribou *(a)*. This is an Animal not so high as the Orignal, which has more of the Ass than the Mule in its Shape, and which equals the Hart in Swiftness. Some Years ago, one appeared upon Cape *Diamond*, above *Quebec*: It was, no Doubt, flying from the Hunters, but he perceived soon he was not in a Place of Safety, and he made almost but one Leap from thence into the River. A wild Goat of the *Alps* could not have done more: Then he swam very swiftly across the River; but it was all to no Purpose: Some *Canadians*, who were going to make War, and who were encamped near the Point of *Levi*, having discovered him, waited for his landing, and killed him. They greatly esteem the Tongue of this Animal, which herds most about *Hudson's Bay*. The Sieur *Jeremy*, who has passed many Years in these Northern Parts, says, that between the *Danes* River and Port *Nelson*, during the whole Summer, they see prodigious Numbers of them; which being driven from the Woods by the Flies and Gnats, come to refresh themselves by the Sea Side; and that for the Space of forty or fifty Leagues they meet almost continully with Herds of ten thousand at least.

It appears that the Caribou has never been in any great Numbers in the most frequented Places of *Canada*; but the Orignals abounded every where when we first discovered the Country; and it might have made an Article of Trade, and a great Convenience of Life, if they had been careful to preserve the Breed: But this they have not done; and, either because they have

(a) It differs not from the Rain-Deer, but in its Colour; which is brown, or a little reddish.

thinned the Species, by killing great Numbers, or that by frightening them they have been driven to some other Country, nothing is more scarce at present.

Of hunting the Buffaloe.

In the Southern and Western Parts of *New France*, on both Sides the *Mississippi*, the most famous Hunt is that of the Buffaloe, which is performed in this Manner: The Hunters range themselves on four Lines, which form a great Square, and begin by setting Fire to the Grass and Herbs, which are dry and very high: Then as the Fire gets forwards they advance, closing their Lines: The Buffaloes, which are extremely afraid of Fire, keep flying from it, and at last find themselves so crouded together, that they are generally every one killed. They say that a Party seldom returns from hunting without killing Fifteen Hundred or Two Thousand. But lest the different Companies should hinder each other, they all agree before they set out about the Place where they intend to hunt. There are also some Penalties appointed against those who transgress this Rule, as well as against those who, quitting their Post, give way to the Beasts to escape. These Penalties consist in giving a Right to every Person to strip those who are guilty, and to take away even their Arms, which is the greatest Affront that can be given to a Savage; and to pull down their Cabins. The Chiefs are subject to this Penalty, as well as the others, and if any were to endeavour to exempt them from this Law, it would raise a Civil War amongst them, which would not end soon.

Description of the wild Bull, or Buffaloe.

The Bull, or Buffaloe, of *Canada* is bigger than ours; his Horns are low, black, and short; he has a great Beard of Hair under his Muzzle, and a great Tuft of Hair upon his Head, which falls down upon his Eyes, and gives him a hideous Look. He has a great Bump upon his Back, which begins at his Hips, and goes increasing up to his Shoulders; and this Bump is covered with Hair, something reddish, and very long; the rest of the Body is covered with black Wool, which is much valued. They say that the Skin of a Buffaloe has eight Pounds of Wool on it. This Animal has a large Chest, the hind Parts small, the Tail very short, and one can scarce see any Neck it has, but its Head is bigger than that of the *European* Bulls. He runs away generally at the Sight of any Person, and one Dog is enough to make a whole Herd take to a full Gallop. The Buffaloe has a good Smell, and to approach him without being perceived near enough to shoot him, you must go with the Wind. When he is wounded he is furious, and turns upon the Hunters. He is as furious when the Cows have newly calved. His Flesh is good, but they seldom eat any but that of

 the

the Cows, becauſe the Buffaloes are too tough. As for his Skin, there are none better; it is eaſily dreſſed, and tho' very ſtrong, it becomes ſupple, like the beſt Shamois. The Savages make Shields of it, which are very light, and which a Muſket Ball will not eaſily pierce.

Of the Muſk Bull.

They find about *Hudſon's Bay* another Bull, whoſe Skin and Wool are the ſame with thoſe I have already deſcribed. This is what M. *Jeremy* ſays of it: "Fifteen Leagues from the *Danes* River, "is the River of *Seals*, ſo called becauſe there are many in this "Place. Between theſe two Rivers there is a Kind of Bulls which "we call the *Muſk Bulls*; becauſe they have ſo ſtrong a Smell of "Muſk, that at ſome certain Times there is no ſuch Thing as "eating their Fleſh. Theſe Animals have a very fine Wool, and "it is longer than that of the *Barbary* Sheep. I brought ſome to "*France* in 1708, of which I had ſome Stockings made, which "were finer than thoſe made of Silk. Theſe Bulls, though "they are ſmaller than our's, have Horns much thicker and "longer: Their Roots join on the Crown of the Head, and "deſcend by the Side of the Eyes almoſt as low as the Throat; "afterwards the End riſes up, and forms a Kind of Creſcent. "There are ſome ſo large, that I have ſeen of them, which be"ing ſeparated from the Skull, weighed both together ſixty "Pounds: Their Legs are very ſhort, ſo that their Wool "drags upon the Ground when they walk; which makes them "ſo deformed, that it is difficult at a little Diſtance to know "which Way the Head ſtands. There are not many of theſe "Animals; ſo that the Savages would ſoon deſtroy them, if "they were to hunt them. Moreover, as their Legs are very "ſhort, when there is much Snow they kill them with Lances, "as they are not able then to make any Speed."

Of the Roe-Buck.

The moſt common Quadrupede at this Time in *Canada*, is the Roe-Buck, which differs in nothing from our's. It is ſaid that it ſheds Tears when it is run down by the Hunters. Whilſt it is young its Hair is ſtriped with many Colours lengthwiſe: Afterwards this Hair falls off, and another grows up of the Colour of the common Roe-Buck. This Creature is not fierce, and is eaſily tamed, and ſeems naturally to have an Affection for Man. The Female that is uſed to the Houſe, retires into the Woods in rutting Time, and as ſoon as it has coupled with the Male, returns again to the Houſe of her Maſter. When her Time is come to bring forth, ſhe returns into the Woods, and remains there ſome Days with her Young; then ſhe returns again to her Maſter; but continues to viſit her Young very aſſiduouſly: When they think proper, they follow her and take her Young, and ſhe brings

brings them up in the House. It is something strange that all our Habitations have not whole Herds of them. The Savages hunt them but seldom.

Of the Wolves and Foxes.

There are also in the Woods of *Canada* many Wolves, or rather wild Cats, for they only resemble the Wolves in a Kind of Howling: In every Thing else, says Mr. *Sarrasin*, they are *ex genere felino* (of the Cat Kind.) They are true Hunters, which live only on the Animals they catch, and which they pursue to the Tops of the highest Trees. Their Flesh is white and good to eat. Their Skins are well known in *France*; it is one of the finest Furs of this Country, and one of the greatest Articles of its Trade.

There are a Sort of black Foxes in the northern Mountains, whose Skins are much valued, but they are very scarce. There are some that are more common, the Hair of which is black or grey, and others of a tawny red. They find some going up the *Mississippi* that are very beautiful, the Fur of which is of a Silver Colour. We also meet with here Tygers, and Wolves of a smaller Kind than our's. The Foxes here catch Water-Fowl in a very ingenious Manner. They go a little Way into the Water, and come out again, and make a thousand Capers upon the Bank of the River. The Ducks, the Bustards, and the like Birds who are pleased with this Sport, approach the Fox: When he sees them within his Reach, he keeps himself very quiet at first, not to scare them; he only wags his Tail to draw them nearer, and the silly Birds give into the Snare so far as to pick his Tail. Then the Fox leaps upon them, and seldom misses his Aim. Some Dogs have been broke to this Way with Success, and these Dogs make a sharp War with the Foxes.

Of the small Peltry.

Here is a Kind Pole-Cat, which they call *Enfant de Diable* or *Bete Puante* (the Child of the Devil, or stinking Beast) because when it is pursued, it makes a Urine which stinks the Air for half a Mile round. It is in other Respects, a very pretty Animal. It is about as high as a small Cat, but bigger round, has bright Hair inclining to grey, with two white Lines, which form on the Back an oval Figure from its Head to the Tail. Its Tail is bushy like a Fox's, and it carries it like a Squirrel. Its Fur is like that of the Pekans, another Kind of wild Cat, about the same Bigness of our's. Otters Skins, common Pole-Cat's, the *Pitois* or Stote, the Field Rat's, the Ermine's, and the Marten's, are what we call the small Peltry. The Ermine is about the Size of our Squirrel, but something longer; its Hair is a fine white, and it has a very long Tail, the End of which is as black as Jet. The Martens in *Canada* are not so red as those of

France

France, and have a finer Fur. They keep generally in the midst of the Woods, out of which they never come but once in two or three Years; but they always come out in great Troops. The Savages believe that the Year when they see them come out, will be good for Hunting; *that is to say*, that there will be a deep Snow. The Martens Skins are actually sold here at a Crown a-piece, I mean the common ones, for those that are brown fetch up to twenty-four Livres, and more. The *Pitci* or Stote differs nothing from the Pole-Cat, but in that the Fur is blacker, longer, and thicker. These two Animals make War with the Birds, even with the largest, and make great Ravages in Hen-Roosts and Dove-Houses. The Field Rat is twice as big as ours, and has an hairy Tail, and its Fur is of a very fine Silver grey. There are some which are entirely white, and a very beautiful White. The Female has a Purse under the Belly, which opens and shuts when she will. She puts her young ones in it when she is pursued, and saves them with herself. As to the Squirrels, they give them very little Disturbance here, so that there are a prodigious Number in this Country. They distinguish them into three Sorts; the red, which does not differ from ours, the *Swiss*, which are a little smaller, and are so called because their Fur is striped lengthwise with red, black, and white, much like the *Swiss* of the Pope's Guard; and the flying Squirrels, of much the same Size as the *Swiss*, whose Fur is a dark grey. They call them flying, not because they really fly, but because they leap from one Tree to another, the Distance of forty Paces at least. When they leap from a high Place to a lower, they leap twice as far. What enables them to make such Leaps, are two Skins which they have on their Sides, between the fore and hind Feet, and which stretch to the Breadth of two Inches. They are very thin, and only covered with Down. This little Animal soon grows familiar; it is very lively when it does not sleep; but it often sleeps in any Place it can creep into, as a Pocket, Sleeve, or Muff. It soon grows fond of its Master, and will find him out amongst twenty Persons. The Porcupine of *Canada* is as thick as a middling Dog, but shorter, and not so high; its Quills are about four Inches long, about the Thickness of a small Straw, white, hollow, and very strong, particularly on the Back. These are its Arms, both offensive and defensive. It darts them directly at those who attempt its Life, and if it enters ever so little in the Flesh, it must be drawn out instantly, or else it sinks in entirely. Its for this Reason, that they are very careful to hinder their Dogs from approaching these Animals. Their Flesh is good eating. A roasted Porcupine, is as good as a sucking Pig. The Hares and Rabbits here are like those of *Europe*, excepting that their hind Legs are longer. Their Skins

are

are of no great Use, because they shed their Fur continually; which is a Pity, for their Fur is very fine, and would do no Damage in the Hat Manufacture. In Winter these Animals turn grey, and seldom come out of their Holes, where they live upon the smallest Branches of the Birch Tree. In Summer, their Fur is of a yellowish red. The Foxes make a sharp War with them in all Seasons, and the Savages take them in Winter in Gins, when they go out to seek for Food.

I am, &c.

LETTER VII.

A Description of the Country between Lake ST. PIERRE, *and* MONTREAL: *In what it differs from* QUEBEC. *A Description of the Island and Town of* MONTREAL, *and its Environs. Of the Fishery for Seals, the Sea Cow, Porpoise, and Whale.*

MADAM, MONTREAL, *March* 20.

Of the Islands of Richlieu.

I Departed the 13th from *St. François*, and the next Day I arrived in this Town. I had not in passing here, which is about twenty Leagues, the Pleasure I had formerly in coming this same Route in a Canoe, in the finest Weather in the World, to see open before me by Degrees as I advanced, Canals that reached out of Sight, between a prodigious Number of Islands, which at a Distance seemed to make one Land with the Continent, and stop the River in its Course, those pleasing Views, which changed every Moment like the Decorations of a Theatre, and which one would think were contrived on Purpose to recreate a Traveller: But I had some Recompence in the Singularity of the Sight of an *Archipelago*, that was become in some Manner a Continent; and by the Convenience of travelling in a Sledge, or Kind of Calash, upon Canals between Islands, which appeared as if they had been plac'd by a Line like Orange Trees.

Difference between the Country of Quebec, *and that of* Montreal.

As for the Prospect, it is not fine in this Season. Nothing is more melancholy than that White which covers every Thing, and which takes the Place of that beautiful Variety of Colours which is the greatest Ornament of the Country; than Trees, which appear planted in the Snow, and which present to our Sight only hoary Heads, and Branches loaded with Isicles.——In other Respects, Madam, the Lake of *St. Pierre* is here what the River *Loire* is in *France*. On the Side

Side of *Quebec* the Lands are good; but in general you ſee nothing that can recreate the Sight. Moreover, the Climate is very ſevere; for the more we go down the River, and the more we advance towards the North, of Conſequence the Cold is more piercing. *Quebec* is in 47. 56. Latitude. *Trois Rivieres* is in 46. and ſome Minutes: And *Montreal* between 44. and 45. The River *St. Laurence*, above the Lake of *St. Pierre*, making an Elbow to the South. It ſeems therefore, when we are paſt the *Iſlands of Richlieu*, as if we were tranſported all at once into another Climate. The Air is ſofter, the Land more level, the River finer; and its Banks have a *Je ne ſcai quoi*, more pleaſing. We meet from Time to Time with Iſlands, ſome of which are inhabited; the others, in their natural State, offer to the Sight the fineſt Landſcapes in the World. In a Word, it is *Touraine* and *la Limagne* of *Auvergne*, compared with *Maine* and *Normandy*.

Deſcription of the Iſle of Montreal.

The Iſle of *Montreal*, which is as it were the Centre of this fine Country, is ten Leagues long from Eaſt to Weſt, and near four Leagues over in its greateſt Breadth. The Mountain from which it takes its Name, and which has two Heads of unequal Height, is almoſt in the Midſt of the Length of the Iſland, but it is but half a League from the South Coaſt, upon which the Town is built. This Town was called *Ville-Marie*, by its Founders; but this Name hath never been brought into common Uſe: It is only mentioned in public Writings, and amongſt the Lords, who are very tenacious of it. Theſe Lords, who have the Domain not only of the Town, but alſo of the whole Iſland, are Miſſionaries of the Seminary of St. *Sulpice*: And as all the Lands here are very good, and well cultivated; and as the Town is as well peopled as *Quebec*, we may affirm that this Lordſhip is worth half a Dozen of the beſt in *Canada*. This is the Fruit of the Labour and good Conduct of the Lords of this Iſland; and certainly twenty private Perſons, amongſt whom this might have been divided, would not have put it in the State we now ſee it, nor have made the People ſo happy. The Town of *Montreal* has a very chearful Aſpect: It is well ſituated, open, and well built. The Agreeableneſs of its Environs, and its Proſpects, inſpires a certain Gaity, of which every one feels the Effect. It is not fortified: A ſingle Palliſade, which is but poorly kept up, is all its Defence; with a bad Redoubt upon a little Eminence, which ſerves for a Bulwark, and which terminates with a gentle Slope at a little Square. This is what we meet with at firſt, in coming from *Quebec*. It is not forty Years ago, ſince the Town was quite open, and expoſed to be burnt by the Savages or the *Engliſh*. It was the Chevalier *de Callieres*, Brother of the Plenipotentiary of *Riſwick*, who enclosed

closed it whilst he was Governor. They have talked some Years of surrounding it with Walls *(a)*; but it will not be easy to engage the Inhabitants to contribute towards it: They are brave, and not rich; and are hard to be persuaded of the Necessity of this Expence, being fully convinced that their Valour is more than sufficient to defend the Town against any Enemy that should dare to attack it. Our *Canadians*, on this Article, have all a pretty good Opinion of themselves, and we must allow it is not ill founded; but in Consequence of the Confidence which this gives them, it is not so difficult to surprize them, as to conquer them.

Montreal is a long Square, situated on the Bank of the River; which rising insensibly, divides the Town in its Length into High and Low; but the Ascent from one to the other is scarcely perceiveable. The *Hotel Dieu*, and the King's Magazines, are in the Lower Town, and almost all the Traders live there. The Seminary and the Parish Church, the *Recollets*, the *Jesuits*, the Maids of the Congregation, the Governor, and greatest Part of the Officers, are in the Higher Town. Beyond a little Rivulet, which comes from the North West, and bounds the Town on that Side, there are some Houses and the Hospital General; and going to the Right, beyond the *Recollets*, whose Convent is at the End of the Town, on the same Side, there begins to be formed a Kind of Suburb, which in Time will make a very fine Quarter.

The *Jesuits* here have but a very little House; but their Church, which is just finished, is large and well built. The Convent of the *Recollets* is much larger, and the Society more numerous. The Seminary is in the Centre of the Town: It appears that they studied more to make it solid and convenient, than fine; but yet it has the Air of belonging to the Lords of the Place: It communicates with the Parish Church, which has much more the Appearance of a Cathedral than that of *Quebec*. The Service is performed here with a Modesty and Dignity which inspires Respect for the Majesty of the God who is here adored.

The House of the Maids of the Congregation, though one of the largest in the Town, is yet still too little to lodge so numerous a Society: It is the Chief of an Order, and the Noviciate of an Institution, which ought to be so much dearer to *New France*, and to this Town in particular, because it took its Rise here, and because all the Colony feels the Advantages of this fine Foundation. The *Hotel Dieu* is served by Nuns, the first of which were taken from *Fleche* in *Anjou*.

(a) This is now done.

They are poor, yet their Poverty does not appear in their Hall; which is large, and well furniſhed with Beds and other Furniture; nor in their Church, which is fine and well adorn'd; nor in their Houſe, which is well built, neat and convenient: But they have but a poor Maintenance, though they are all indefatigably employed in the Inſtruction of Youth, and in the Care of the Sick.

The Hoſpital General owes its Foundation to a private Perſon, named *Charron*, who aſſociated himſelf with many pious Perſons, not only for this good Work, but alſo to furniſh the Country Pariſhes with School-Maſters, who ſhould inſtruct the Boys, as the Siſters of the Congregation do the Girls: But the Society was ſoon diſſolved: Some left it for other Affairs, and ſome through Fickleneſs; ſo that the Sieur *Charron* was left alone. However, he was not diſcouraged; he emptied his own Purſe, and found Means to open thoſe of ſome powerful Perſons: He built a Houſe, and procured a Number of School-Maſters, and Perſons to attend the Hoſpital. The Public took a Pleaſure to aſſiſt and give Authority to a Man who ſpared neither his own Subſtance, nor his Pains, and whom nothing could diſcourage. In ſhort, before his Death, which happened in 1719, he had the Comfort to ſee his Project out of all Danger of failing, at leaſt with Reſpect to the Hoſpital General. The Houſe is fine, and the Church very pretty. The School-Maſters are not yet well eſtabliſhed in the Pariſhes; and the Order they have received from Court, forbidding them to wear an uniform Habit, or to engage themſelves by Vows, may hinder their Eſtabliſhment.

Of the Iſland of Jeſus, *and the River* des Prairies, (of the Meadows)

Between the Iſland of *Montreal* and the Continent on the North Side, there is another Iſland about eight Leagues long, and two Leagues over: It was firſt named the Iſland of *Montmagny*, from the Name of a Governor General of *Canada*: It was afterwards granted to the *Jeſuits*, who called it the Iſland of *Jeſus*; and it has preſerved this laſt Name, though it has paſſed from the Hands of the *Jeſuits* to Meſſieurs of the Seminary of *Quebec*, who have begun to place ſome Inhabitants here; and as the Lands are good, there is Room to hope that the whole Iſland will ſoon be cleared.

The Fall of the Recollets.

The Channel which ſeparates the two Iſlands, is called the River *des Prairies*, (*Meadows*) becauſe it runs in the Midſt of fine Meadows. Its Courſe is impeded towards the Middle by a Torrent which they call *the Recollet's Fall*, in Memory of one of that Order, who was drowned here. The Eccleſiaſtics of the Seminary of *Montreal*, for a long Time, had a Miſſion of Savages near this Place, which they have ſince removed to another Part.

Of the Environs of Montreal.

The third Arm of the River is ſtrewed as it were with ſuch a prodigious Number of Iſlands, that there is almoſt as much Land as Water. This Channel is called *Milles-iſles*, or River of *St. Jean*, (*thouſand Iſlands*, or *St. John's* River.) At the Head of the Iſland *Jeſus*, is the little Iſland *Bizard*, ſo called from the Name of a *Swiſs* Officer, to whom it belonged, and who died a Major at *Montreal*. A little higher towards the South, is the Iſland *Perrot*; thus called by Mr. *Perrot*, who was the firſt Governor of *Montreal*, and the Father of Madam the Counteſs *de la Roche-Allard*, and of Madam the Preſidenteſs of *Lubert*. This Iſland is near two Leagues every Way, and the Lands are good, and they begin to clear them. The Iſle *Bizard* terminates the Lake *des deux Montagnes* (of the two Mountains) and the Iſland *Perrot* ſeparates the ſame Lake from that of *St. Louis*.

The Lake of the two Mountains is properly the Mouth of the *Great River*, otherwiſe called the River of the *Outaouais*, into the River *St. Laurence*. It is two Leagues long, and near as wide. The Lake of *St. Louis* is ſomething larger, but it is in Fact nothing more than an Enlargement of the River *St. Laurence*. Till lately, the *French* Colony extended no farther to the Weſt; but they begin to make ſome new Habitations a little higher, and the Lands are every where excellent.

Of the Fall of St. Louis.

That which has been the Security of *Montreal* and its Environs during the laſt Wars, are two Villages of *Iroquois Chriſtians*, and the Fort *de Chambly*. The firſt of the two Villages is that of the Fall of *St. Louis*, ſituated on the Continent on the South Side, three Leagues above the Town of *Montreal*. It is very populous, and has always been eſteemed one of our ſtrongeſt Barriers againſt the *Heathen Iroquois*, and the *Engliſh* of *New York*. It has already been twice removed within the Space of two Leagues. Its ſecond Situation, where I ſaw it in 1708, was over-againſt the Fall of *St. Louis*; and it keeps this Name, though it is now a good Diſtance from it. It looks as if they had fixed it now; for the Church, which is juſt finiſhed, and the Houſe of the Miſſionaries are, each in its Kind, two of the fineſt Buildings in the Country. The Situation is charming: The River *St. Laurence*, which is very wide here, is alſo hereabouts full of Iſlands, which have a very fine Effect. The Iſland of *Montreal*, entirely peopled, is a Perſpective on one Side; and the View has ſcarce any Bounds on the other Side, on Account of the Lake *St. Louis*, which begins a little higher.

The

The second Village is called *de la Montagne*, (of the Mountain) because it was a long Time on the Mountain which gave the Name to the Island. It has since been removed to the *Recollet's* Fall, as I said before. It is now on the Continent, over-against the West End of the Island. It is governed by the Ecclesiastics of the Seminary of *Montreal*. These two Villages have produced many brave Men, and their Fervour in Religion was admirable before the Avarice of our Traders had introduced Drunkenness, which has made still greater Ruin here than in the Missions of *St. François* and *Beckancourt*.

Of the Iroquois *of the Mountain.*

The Missionaries have in vain employed all their Industry and Vigilance to put a Stop to this Disorder. It was to no Purpose that they called in the Aid of the Magistrates, threatened the Wrath of Heaven, and offered the most persuasive Reasons: All signified nothing. Even the most fatal Accidents, in which the Hand of GOD evidently appeared heavy on the Authors of this Evil, have not been sufficient to open the Eyes of some *Christians*, whom a Thirst after sordid Gain hath blinded. One sees even in the Squares and Streets of *Montreal*, the most frightful Spectacles, the certain Consequences of the Drunkenness of these Barbarians: Husbands and Wives, Fathers, Mothers and their Children; Brothers and Sisters, taking each other by the Throat, tearing off each other's Ears, and biting one another like furious Wolves. The Air resounds in the Night with Howlings, more horrible than those which the wild Beasts make in the Woods.

Disorders occasioned by the Brandy Trade in these two Villages.

Those who have most to reproach themselves with for these horrible Disorders, are the first to ask, If these People are *Christians?* We may answer them, Yes, they are *Christians*, and new Converts, who know not what they do: But those who cooly, and knowing the certain Effect, bring them by their Avarice to this Condition, have they any Religion? They know that the Savages would give all they have for a Glass of Brandy: This is a Temptation to the Traders; against which, neither the Cries of the Pastors, nor the Zeal and Authority of the Magistrates, nor Respect of the Laws, nor the Severity of the Sovereign Jurisdiction nor the Fear of GOD's Judgments, nor the Thoughts of Hell, (a Representation of which is seen in the Drunkenness of these Savages) have been able to restrain them.——But let us turn away our Eyes from these disagreeable Objects.

The great Trade for Skins, after the Town of *Trois Rivieres* was no longer frequented by the Nations of the North and West, was carried on several Years at *Montreal*, whither the Savages resorted at certain Seasons from all Parts of *Canada*. This was a

Kind

Kind of Fair, which brought many *French* to this Town. The Governor General, and the Intendant, came hither alſo, and they took Advantage of this Occaſion to accommodate the Difference that might have happened between our Allies. But if you meet, Madam, by Chance, with the Book of *La Hontan*, where Mention is made of this Fair, I would have you take Care how you give Credit to what he ſays of it: He does not even preſerve Probability. The Women of *Montreal* never gave any Foundation for what this Author reports of them, and there is no Fear that their Honour ſhould ever ſuffer any Blemiſh from the Savages. There is no Example that any have ever taken the leaſt Liberty with the *French* Women, even when they were their Priſoners: They not even ſeem to have an Inclination to it; and it were to be wiſhed that the *Frenchmen* had the ſame Diſlike to the Savage Women. *La Hontan* could not be ignorant of what is ſo publickly known in this Country; but he wanted to give a Gaiety to his Memoirs, and for this Purpoſe he ſaid any Thing. We are always ſure to pleaſe certain Perſons, when we give no Bounds to a Liberty of inventing Stories, and of ſlandering.

One ſees now and then little Fleets of Savages arrive at *Montreal*; but nothing in Compariſon of former Times. It is the *Iroquois* War that has interrupted this great Concourſe of Nations in the Colony. To make Amends for this Failure of the Savages coming to *Montreal*, they have eſtabliſhed amongſt the greateſt Part of them Magazines and Forts, where there are always an Officer and Soldiers enough to ſecure the Merchandize. The Savages will always have a Gunſmith in theſe Places; and in many there are Miſſionaries; who would do more Good if there were no other *French* there. There is Reaſon to believe it would be better to ſet Things upon the antient Footing, ſince Peace has been eſtabliſhed both within and without the Colony: This would be the Means to reſtrain the Wood-Rangers, whoſe Covetouſneſs (not to mention the Diſorders cauſed by their Licentiouſneſs) makes them every Day guilty of mean Actions, which render us deſpicable in the Sight of the Savages, have lower'd our Merchandizes, and raiſed the Price of Skins. Beſides, the Savages, naturally proud, are grown inſolent, ſince they find that we ſeek after them.

Of the Seal Fiſhery.

The Fiſhery might much more enrich *Canada* than the Chace; and this does not depend on the Savages: Two weighty Reaſons for following it, which yet have not been ſufficient to engage our Coloniſts to make it the principal Object of their Trade.——I have nothing to add to what I have already ſaid on the Cod Fiſhery, which alone would be worth more to us than *Peru*, if the Founders

ders of *New France* had taken proper Meaſures to ſecure the Poſſeſſion of it to ourſelves.---I begin with the Fiſhery for Seals, Sea Cows, and Porpoiſes, which may be carried on every where in the Gulph of *St. Laurence*, and a great Way up the River.

The Sea Wolf, or the Seal, takes its Name from its Cry, which is a Sort of howling; for in its Shape it reſembles not the Wolf, nor any Land Animal that we know. *Leſcarbot* aſſerts, that he has heard ſome cry like Screech-Owls; but theſe might be only young ones, whoſe Cry was not quite formed. They make no Heſitation here, Madam, to place it in the Rank of Fiſhes; though it is not mute, though it is brought forth on the Land, and lives as much on it as in the Water, and is covered with Hair: In a Word, though it wants nothing to make it to be conſidered as an amphibious Creature. But we are in a new World, and it muſt not be required of us always to ſpeak the Language of the Old; and Cuſtom, againſt which there is no reaſoning, is here in Poſſeſſion of all its Rights. So that the War they make with the Seals, though it is often on Land, and with the Gun, is called a Fiſhery; and that which they make with the Beavers in the Water, and with Nets, is called a Chace.

Deſcription of the Seal.

The Head of a Seal is ſomething like a Bull-Dog's: He has four Legs, very ſhort, eſpecially thoſe behind: In every other Reſpect it is a Fiſh. It drags itſelf rather than walks upon its Feet. Its Legs before have Nails, thoſe behind are like Fins: His Skin is hard, and covered with ſhort Hair of divers Colours. There are ſome Seals all white, and they are all ſo at firſt; but ſome, as they grow up, become black, others tawny: Many are of all theſe Colours mixed together.

Of the ſeveral Species of Seals.

The Fiſhermen diſtinguiſh ſeveral Species of Seals: The largeſt weigh up to two thouſand Pounds, and they ſay their Noſe is more pointed than the others. There are ſome that only friſk about in the Water: Our Sailors call them *Braſſeurs, (Brewers.)* They have given the Name of *Nau* to another Sort; for which I can give no Reaſon, nor know the Meaning of the Word. Another Sort they call *Groſſes Tetes, (Great Heads.)* There are ſome ſmall ones that are very lively and ſkilful in cutting the Nets they are taken in: They are of a Tyger Colour; they are full of Play and Spirit, and as pretty as Creatures of this Shape can be. The Savages learn theſe to follow them like little Dogs, and eat them notwithſtanding.

M. *Denys* ſpeaks of two Sorts of Seals that are found upon the Coaſts of *Acadia*. One Sort (ſays he) are ſo big, that their Young are larger than our largeſt Porkers. He adds, that ſoon after

after they are brought forth, the old ones carry them to the Water, and from Time to Time bring them ashore again to suck: That the Time of sucking them is the Month of *February*; when the young ones, which they aim chiefly to catch, go scarce any more into the Water: That at the first Noise the old ones fly, making a great Noise to give Notice to the young ones to follow them; which they never fail to do, if the Fishermen do not make Haste to give them a Blow on the Nose with a Stick, which is enough to kill them.---The Number of these Animals must be very great upon these Coasts, if it true, as the same Author affirms, that in one Day they take sometimes eight hundred of the young ones.

The second Species of these Seals, which M. *Denys* speaks of, is very small, and has little more Oil but what it has in its Bladder. These last never go far from the Shore, and there is always one that stands Centinel: At the first Signal he gives, they all throw themselves into the Sea: After some Time they approach the Land, and raise themselves upon their hind Feet to see if there is nothing to fear: But in Spite of all their Precautions, they surprize a great Number of them on Shore, and it is almost impossible to take them any other Way.

Use of the Flesh and Skin of the Seal.

It is agreed, that the Flesh of the Seal is not bad to eat, but it is more profitable to make Oil of it: This is not difficult. They melt the Fat on the Fire, and it dissolves into an Oil. Sometimes they only put the Fat of a great many Seals on Square Planks; and leave it to dissolve of itself, a Hole being made at the Bottom, for the Oil to run through. This Oil whilst it is new is very good for Kitchen Uses; but that of the young Seals soon grows rank, and the other dries too much, upon keeping any time: They then use it to burn, or to dress Skins with. It keeps clear a long Time, has no Smell, and leaves no Lee, nor any Kind of Foulness at the Bottom of the Vessel.

At the first settling the Colony, they used a great Quantity of Seal Skins to make Muffs; but that is now out of Fashion; and their chief Use now is to cover Trunks, *&c.* When they are tanned they have almost the same Grain as *Morocco* Leather: They are not so fine, but they are stronger, and wear better. They make of them very good Shoes, and Boots; which will not take Water. They are also used to cover Seats of Chairs, the Frames of which are sooner worn out than the Covers. They tan these Skins here with the Bark of the Spruce Fir, and in the Tincture, they use to dye them black, they mix a Powder, drawn from certain Stones they find upon the Banks of the Rivers; which are called *Thunder Stones*, or Marcasites.

The

The Seals couple upon the Rocks, and ſometimes upon the Ice, where alſo the Females bring forth their Young. They have commonly two, and they ſuckle them pretty often in the Water, but oftener upon the Land. When they would accuſtom them to ſwim, they carry them, as they ſay, on their Backs in the Water, and let them off from Time to Time into the Water, then take them again, and continue this Practice till the young ones can ſwim alone. If this Fact is true, this is a ſtrange Fiſh, which Nature has not taught what the greateſt part of Land Animals are capable of almoſt as ſoon as they come into the World. The Seal has its Senſes very quick, and this is its ſole Defence; but this does not hinder them from being often ſurprized, as I have before remarked; but the moſt common Method of fiſhing for them is this: The Cuſtom of this Animal, when it is in the Water, is to come with the Tide into the Creeks. When they have diſcovered the Creeks, where a great Number come, they ſhut them up with Stakes and Nets; they only leave a ſmall Space open by which the Seals enter. When the Tide is up, they ſtop this Opening, ſo that after the Tide is out, theſe Fiſh remain on the Shore, and they have only the Trouble to knock them on the Head. They follow them alſo in a Canoe, in Places where there is Plenty of them, and when they put their Heads out of the Water to breathe, they ſhoot them. If they are only wounded, they eaſily take them; but if they are ſhot dead, they ſink directly to the Bottom, like as the Beavers do. But they have great Dogs, which are train'd to fetch them up at the Depth of ſeven or eight Fathom.

Some Particularities of theſe Animals.

Our Fiſhermen take but few Sea-Cows on the Coaſts of the Gulph of *St. Laurence*; I know not whether they have taken any in other Places. The *Engliſh* formerly eſtabliſhed a Fiſhery for them at the Iſle of *Sable*; but they made no great Advantage of it. The Shape of this Animal is not very different from the Seals. What is peculiar to it, are two Teeth, of the Bigneſs and Length of a Man's Arm, a little bent back at Top, and which appear at a Diſtance like Horns; this is probably the Reaſon they are called Sea-Cows. Our Sailors call them more plainly *la beet a la grande dent*, (the great toothed Beaſt) theſe Teeth are of very fine Ivory, as well as all thoſe which are in the Jaw of this Fiſh, and which are four Inches long.

There are in the River *St. Laurence* Porpoiſes of two Colours: In the Salt Water; *that is to ſay*, till a little below the Iſle of *Orleans*, they do not differ from thoſe found in the Sea: In the freſh Water they are all white, and as big as a Cow. The firſt go generally in Companies, I have have not obſerved the ſame of the others,

Porpoiſes of two Colours.

others, though I have seen many of them playing in the Port of *Quebec*. They seldom go higher than this City, but there are many on the Coasts of *Acadia*, as well as of the first Kind; so that the Difference of their Colour does not proceed from the Difference of the salt and fresh Water. The white Porpoises yield a Hogshead of Oil, and this Oil is little different from that of the Seals: I never saw any Person who had eaten the Flesh of this Animal; but as to the Black Porpoise, they say, that they are not bad eating: They make Puddings and Chitterlings of their Entrails, the Harslet is excellent in Fricassee, and the Head better than that of a Sheep, but not so good as a Calf's.

Use of their Skins.

The Skins of both Sorts are tan'd like *Merocco* Leather. At first it is soft like Fat, and is an Inch thick, they scrape it a long Time, and it becomes like a transparent Leather; and how thin soever it is, even so as to be fit for Waistcoats and Breeches, it is always very strong and Proof against a Musket Ball. There are some eighteen Feet long, and nine wide; they say that there is nothing better to cover the Tops of Coaches. They have lately established two Fisheries below *Quebec* for Porpoises, one in the Bay of *St. Paul*, and the other seven or eight Leagues lower, over-against a Habitation called *Camourasca*, from the Name of certain Rocks that rise considerably above the Water. The Expences are not great; and the Profits would be considerable, if the Porpoises were Animals settled in a Place: But either through Instinct, or Caprice, they often break the Measures of the Fishermen, and take another Route than that where they wait for them. Moreover, these Fisheries, which would only enrich some few Persons, have occasioned an Inconvenience which made the common People complain; which is, that they have greatly diminished the Eel Fishery, which is a great Help to the poor Inhabitants. For the Porpoises, finding themselves disturbed below *Quebec*, are retired to some other Place; and the Eels, finding no longer these great Fish in their Way, which obliged them to return back, go down the River without any Hindrance; whence it happens, that between *Quebec* and *Trois Rivieres*, where they took a prodigious Number every Year, they now scarce take any.

The Way of fishing for Porpoises is much the same as that I have been mentioning for Seals. When the Tide is out, they set Stakes in the Mud, or Sand, pretty near one another, and they fasten Nets to them in the Shape of Funnels, the Opening of which is pretty large, and made in such a Manner, that when once the Fish has entered, he can't find his Way out again. They take Care to put upon the Tops of the Stakes Branches of Greens. When the Tide rises, these Fish giving Chace to

Her-

Herrings, which always run to the Sides, and being allured by the Greens which they greatly love, are engaged in the Nets, and find themſelves ſhut up: As the Tide ſinks, it is pleaſant to ſee their Trouble, and their fruitleſs Attempts to eſcape: At laſt they remain on dry Land, and often one upon another in ſuch great Numbers, that one Blow with a Stick kills two or three of them. They ſay that there have been found ſome among the white Sort, which weighed three thouſand Pounds.

Of the Whale.

Every one knows the Nature of the Whale Fiſhery, therefore I ſhall ſay nothing of it. It is ſaid here, that the *Biſcayners*, who carried it on formerly in the River *St. Laurence*, diſcontinued it only to apply themſelves entirely to the Fur-Trade, which required not ſo much Expence or Labour, and the Profits of which were then more conſiderable, and of a quicker Return. On the other Hand, they had not all the Conveniencies for this Fiſhery, which may be had at preſent, now there are Habitations very near the Gulf. Some Years ago they tried to re-eſtabliſh it, but without Succeſs: The Undertakers either had not a ſufficient Fund to make the neceſſary Advances, or expected their Charges to be reimburſed ſooner than the Thing would allow, or elſe they wanted Perſeverance. It appears nevertheleſs certain that this Fiſhery might be a great Article in the Trade of this Colony *(a)*, and might be carried on with leſs Expence and Danger than on the Coaſts of *Greenland*; and what ſhould hinder to fix it here, as M. *Denys* propoſed to do that of the Cod-Fiſhery in *Acadia*. —— This is, Madam, all that concerns the Fiſheries, that may enrich *Canada*.

I am, &c.

LETTER VIII.

Of the Fort of CHAMBLY: *Of the Fiſh; of the Birds: And of ſome Animals, peculiar to* CANADA. *Of the Trees which are the ſame with thoſe of* FRANCE; *and of thoſe which are peculiar to this Country.*

MADAM, CHAMBLY, *March* 1.

ONE of the chief Defences of *Montreal* againſt the *Iroquois* and *New York*, is Fort *Chambly*: It is from this Fort I have the Honour to write to you. I came hither to pay a Viſit

(a) It is to be hoped that we ſhall now eſtabliſh a Whale Fiſhery in theſe Parts; as there ſeems great Probability that a vaſt Advantage may be reaped from it.

to the Commandant, who is M. *de Sabrevois*, of one of the best Families of *Beauce*, my Friend, my Companion in the Voyage, and a good Officer. I shall describe this important Fort, and the Situation of it, in a few Words.

In the first Years of our Settlement in this Country, the *Iroquois*, to make their Incursions into the very Centre of our Habitations, came down a River which discharges itself into the River *St. Laurence*, a little above Lake *St. Pierre*, and which for this Reason, was called first the *Iroquois* River. It has been since called the River of *Richelieu*, from a Fort which bore this Name, and which was built at its Mouth. This Fort being in a ruinous Condition, M. *de Sorel*, Captain in *Carignan-Salicres* Regiment, built another, which he called by his own Name. This Name communicated itself to the River, and it is still called so, tho' the Fort has not been standing for a long Time. When we have gone up the River about seventeen Leagues, going always towards the South, but a little to the South West, we find a Torrent or Water-fall, and over against it a Kind of little Lake, formed by the River itself. It is by the Side of the Water-fall, and over against the Lake, that the Fort is situated. It was first built of Wood, by M. *de Chambly*, at the same Time that M. *de Sorel* built his Fort, but it has been since built of Stone, and flanked with four Bastions, and there is always a pretty good Garrison kept in it. The Lands round it are very good, and they begin to establish some Habitations here, and many People think that in Time, they will build a Town in this Place. From *Chambly* to Lake *Champlain*, it is but eight Leagues. The River *Sorel* crosses the Lake; and there is perhaps no Part of *New France* which is more fit to be peopled. The Climate is milder than any other Part of the Colony, and the Inhabitants will have the *Iroquois* for Neighbours, who at the Bottom are a good Sort of People, who will not seek to quarrel with us, when they see us in a Condition not to be afraid of them, and who will find their Account I believe still better from this Neighbourhood, than from that of *New York*. Many other Reasons ought to engage us in this Settlement, but if I should write all, I should have nothing to say when I have the Honour to see you again. I shall take Advantage of the Leisure Hours I have here, to continue to entertain you with the Particularities of this Country. I have already given an Account of what the Gulf and the River of *St. Laurence* may supply for the Trade of *New France*; it remains for me to speak of the Resources which the Inhabitants may find here for the Support of Life.

Wherever

Fish which are taken in the Gulf and River of St. Laurence.

Wherever the Water of the River is salt, *that is to say*, from Cape *Torment* to the Gulf, one may take almost all Fish that live in the Sea, as Salmon, Tunny, Shad, Trout, Lamprey, Smelts, Conger Eels, Mackerel, Soals, Herrings, Anchovies, Pilchards, Turbots, and many others that are not known in *Europe*. They are all taken with a Sein, or other Nets. In the Gulf they take Hallibuts, three Sorts of Thornbacks, the common, the curled Sort, which they say is better than in *France*, and another Sort that is not esteemed; *Lencornets*, a Kind of Cuttle Fish, St. *Peter*'s Fish, *Requiems*, Sea Dogs, a Kind of *Requiems* much less mischievous whilst alive, and beyond Comparison better when dead, than the common Sort. Oysters are very plenty in Winter on the Coasts of *Aacida*, and the Manner of fishing for them is something singular. They make a Hole in the Ice, and they thrust in two Poles together in such a Manner, that they have the Effect of a Pair of Pinchers, and they seldom draw them up without an Oyster. The *Lencornet* is, as I have said, a Kind of Cuttle Fish, but however, it is very different from the common Cuttle Fish. It is quite round, or rather oval; at the End of its Tail is a Sort of Ledge, which makes him a Kind of Shield, and his Head is surrounded with Barbs half a Foot long, which he makes Use of to catch other Fish. There are two Kinds, which differ only in Bigness; the smaller Sort is about a Foot long. They take few but of the last Sort, and those by the Light of a Flambeau: They love the Light much, they shew it them on the Shore when the Tide is at Height, but just upon burning, they approach it, and so are left aground. The *Lencornet* roasted, boiled, or fricasseed, is very good eating, but makes the Sauce quite black.

Of St. Peter's *Fish. Of the Salmon Trout, and the Turtle, &c.*

The St. *Peter*'s Fish is like a small Cod, has the same Taste, and is dried also like that. It has two black Spots on the Sides of its Head, and the Sailors say, this is the Fish in which St. *Peter* found the Piece of Money to pay the Tribute to the *Roman* Emperor, for our Lord and himself; and that its two Spots are the two Places by which he took hold of it: For this Reason they call it St. *Peter*'s Fish. The Sea Plaice is firmer and better than the River Plaice. They catch them as well as Lobsters with long Sticks armed with a sharp Iron, which is notched to prevent the Escape of the Fish. In short, in many Places, especially towards *Acadia*, the Ponds are full of Salmon Trouts, and Turtles two Feet in Diameter, the Flesh of which is excellent, and the Top Shell streaked with white, red, and blue.

Among

Among the Fish with which the Lake *Champlain*, and the Rivers which flow into it, abound, M. *Champlain* observed one pretty singular, which he calls *Chaousarou*, probably from the Name given it by the Savages. It is a particular Species of the Armed Fish, which is found in many Places. This has a Body nearly of the same Shape as a Pike, but it is covered with Scales that are Proof against the Stab of a Dagger: Its Colour is a silver grey, and there grows under his Mouth a long bony Substance, jagged at the Edges, hollow, and with a Hole at the End of it; which gives Reason to judge, that it breaths by it: The Skin that covers it is tender: The Length of it is proportioned to that of the Fish, of which it makes a third Part. It is two Fingers in Breadth in the smallest. The Savages assured M. *Champlain* that some of these Fish were eight or ten Feet long, but the largest he saw were but five Feet, and about as thick as a Man's Thigh.

Of the Armed Fish.

One may easily conceive that such an Animal is a Ravager among the Inhabitants of the Water, but one would not imagine that it should make War with the Inhabitants of the Air; which he does, however, with much Art, in this Manner: He hides himself in the Reeds in such a Manner, that only this Instrument of his is to be seen, which he thrusts out of the Water in an upright Position; the Birds that want to rest themselves take this for a dry Reed, or Piece of Wood, and perch upon it. They are no sooner on it, than the Fish opens his Mouth, and makes such a sudden Motion to seize his Prey, that it seldom escapes him. The Teeth which edge the Instrument that he uses to such good Purpose, are pretty long and very sharp. The Savages say, that they are a sovereign Remedy against the Head-Ach, and that pricking with one of these Teeth where the Pain is sharpest, takes it away instantly.

How this Fish catches Birds.

These People have a wonderful Skill in striking Fish in the Water, especially in the Torrents. They fish also with the Sein, and they have an odd Ceremony before they use this Net. They marry it to two young Maids, and during the Wedding Feast they place it between the two Brides. They exhort it very seriously to take a great many Fish, and they think to engage it to do so by making great Presents to its pretended Fathers-in-Law.

The Marriage of the Sein.

The Sturgeon here is a Sea and a fresh Water Fish; for they take it upon the Coasts of *Canada*, and in the great Lakes which cross the River *St. Laurence*. Many People think it is the real Dolphin of the Antients; if this is true, it was fitting that this

Of fishing for Sturgeon.

King

King of Fish should reign equally in the Ocean and the Rivers. Be that as it may, we see here Sturgeons of eight, ten, and twelve Feet long, and big in Proportion. This Animal has on the Head a Sort of Crown raised about an Inch, and it is covered with Scales of half a Foot Diameter, almost oval, and sprinkled with small Figures which something resemble the Flower de Luce of the Arms of *France*. The Savages take them in the Lakes in this Manner: Two Men are at the two Ends of a Canoe; he behind steers, and the other stands up, holding a Dart in one Hand, to which a long Cord is fastened, the other End is tied to one of the Bars of the Canoe. As soon as he sees the Sturgeon in his Reach, he throws his Dart, and endeavours to strike where there are no Scales; if the Fish is wounded it flies, and draws the Canoe also pretty swiftly, but after having swam about 150 Paces it dies, then they draw up the Cord and take it. There is a small Kind of Sturgeon, the Flesh of which is very tender and delicate.

Fish peculiar to Canada.

The River *St. Laurence* produces many Fish which are not known in *France*: The most esteemed are the *Achigan*, and the *Poisson-doré* (the *Gilt Fish*); the other Rivers of *Canada*, and especially those of *Acadia*, are as well stocked as this River, which has perhaps the most Fish of any in the World, and of the most various Kinds, and the best of the Sorts. There are some Seasons when the Fish alone might feed the whole Colony; but I know not what Credit may be given to what I have seen in the Manuscript of an antient Missionary, who affirms that he saw a Mer-man in the River *de Sorel*, three Leagues below *Chambly*. The Relation is written with much Judgment, but the better to state the Fact, and to shew that the first Appearance did not deceive him, the Author should have added to his Account a Description of this Monster. We are sometimes seized at the first Glance with a Resemblance, which upon viewing more attentively immediately vanishes. Furthermore, if this Fish in human Shape came from the Sea, it came a long Way to get so near *Chambly*, and it is something strange that it was not seen but in this Place.

Two Sorts of Eagles.

Our Forests are not so well stocked with Birds as our Lakes and Rivers are with Fish; however, here are some which have their Merit, and are peculiar to *America*. We see here two Sorts of Eagles, the largest has the Neck and Head almost white; they prey upon the Hares and Rabbits, which they take in their Talons, and carry to their Magazines and their Nests. The others are all grey, and are contented to make War with the Birds: And they are all pretty good Fishers. The Falcon, the

Gofs Hawk, and the Taffel, are entirely the fame as in *France*; but we have a fecond Sort of Falcons which live only on Fifh.

Three Sorts of Partridges.

Our Partridges are of three Kinds, grey, red, and black; the laft are the leaft efteemed, they have too much Tafte of the Grape, Juniper, and Fir: Their Head and Eyes are like the Pheafant's, and their Flefh is brown. They all have a long Tail, and fpread it as a Fan, like the Turkey Cock: Thefe Tails are very fine, fome are mixed with red, brown, and grey; and others of a light and dark grey. I faid that the black Partridges were not moft efteemed, but fome People prefer them to the red. They are all bigger than in *France*, but fo filly, that they fuffer themfelves to be fhot, and even approached, without fcarce ftirring.

Other Birds.

Befides the Snipes, which are excellent in this Country, and the fmall Game of the Rivers, which is every where plenty, they find fome Woodcocks about the Springs, but in a fmall Number. Amongft the *Ilinois*, and in all the fouthern Parts of *New France*, they are more common; M. *Denys* afferts, that the Crows of *Canada* are as good to eat as a Fowl. This may be true on the Side of *Acadia*, but I do not find in thefe Parts that they are much of this Opinion. They are bigger than in *France*, and fomething blacker, and have a different Cry. The Ofprey on the contrary is fmaller, and its Cry is not fo difagreeable. The Screech-Owl of *Canada* differs from that of *France* only by a little white Ruff about the Neck, and a particular Cry: Its Flefh is good to eat, and many People prefer it to a Fowl. Its Provifion for the Winter is Field Mice; whofe Feet it breaks, and then nourifhes and fattens them with Care till it has Occafion to feed upon them. The Bat is bigger here than in *France*. The Blackbirds and Swallows are here Birds of Paffage, as in *Europe*. The firft are not black, but inclining to red. We have three Sorts of Larks, the fmalleft of which are as big as a Sparrow. The Sparrow is but little different from our's, and has the fame Inclinations, but an ugly Sort of a Look. We fee in this Country a prodigious Quantity of Ducks, they reckon twenty-two different Species. The moft beautiful, and thofe whofe Flefh is moft delicate, are the *Branch Ducks*: They call them fo becaufe they perch on the Branches of Trees; their Plumage is very much varied, and very brilliant. Swans, Turkies, Water-hens, Cranes, Teal, Geefe, Buftards, and other great River Birds fwarm every where except in the Neighbourhood of the Habitations, which they never approach. We have Cranes of two Colours, fome white, and others gridelin. All of them make excellent

excellent Soup. Our Wood-Peckers are very beautiful; there are ſome which are of all Colours, others are black or a dark brown all over except the Head and the Neck, which are of a very fine red.

The Nightingale of *Canada*, is much the ſame as that of *France* for Shape, but it has but half its Song: The Wren has robbed it of the other Half. The Goldfinch has not ſo fine a Head as in *Europe*, and all its Plumage is mixt with Yellow and Black. As I never ſaw any of them in a Cage, I can ſay nothing of their Song. All our Woods are full of a Sort of Birds, which are Yellow all over, about the Bigneſs of a Linnet, which has a pretty Note, but its Song is very ſhort, and not varied. It has no other Name but that of its Colour, being called the Yellow Bird. A kind of Ortolan, whoſe Plumage is of an Aſh Colour on the Back, and White under the Belly, and which they call the White Bird, is the beſt Songſter of all the Inhabitants of our Woods: It is little inferior to the Nightingale of *France*, but it is the Male only that ſings, the Female which is of a deeper Colour is ſilent even in a Cage. This little Bird has a very pretty Plumage, and is well called an Ortolan for its Taſte. I know not where it retires during the Winter, but it is always the firſt to proclaim to us the Return of Spring. As ſoon as the Snow is melted in ſome Places, they come in great Flocks, and we take as many of them as we pleaſe.

Of the Cardinal Bird.

It is ſeldom, but at a hundred Leagues from hence towards the South, that we begin to ſee the *Cardinal Bird*. There are ſome at *Paris*, that were tranſported from *Louiſiana*, and I believe they will make their Fortune in *France*, if they can breed them there like the Canary-Birds. The Sweetneſs of its Song, the Brilliancy of its Plumage, which is of a fine Scarlet, a little Tuft of Feathers they have upon the Head, and which pretty well reſembles the Crowns which Painters give to *Indian* Kings and *Americans*, ſeems to confirm to them, the Empire of the Air. They have nevertheleſs a Rival here who would have all the Votes for it, if it pleaſed the Ear as much as it charms the Sight. This is what they call in this Country *l'Oiſeau Mouche*, (the Fly-Bird.) It is thus called

Of the Fly-Bird, with its Feathers.

for two Reaſons: The firſt, on Account its Smallneſs, for it is but little bigger than the common May-Bug, or Chaffer. The ſecond, is on Account of a pretty loud Humming, which it makes with its Wings; which is much like that of a great Fly. Its Legs, which are about an Inch long, are like two Needles, its Bill is the ſame, and it puts out of it a little Trunk, which it thruſts into the Flowers, to draw out their Juice, upon which it feeds. The Female has nothing brilliant, a pretty fine White under the Belly, and an Aſh Colour on the reſt of her Body, is all its Ornament; but the Male is a perfect Beauty. It has on the Top of the Head, a little Tuft of a beautiful Black, the Throat red, the Belly white, the Back, the Wings, and the Tail of a green like that of Roſe Leaves; a Lay of Gold ſpread over all this Plumage gives it a great Brilliancy, and a little imperceptible Down, gives it the fineſt Shades that can be ſeen.

How it differs from the Humming-Bird.

Some Travellers have confounded it with the Humming-Bird, of the Iſlands; and in Fact it appears to be a Species of it; but that is a little bigger, its Plumage is not ſo brilliant, and its Bill bent a little downward. I may however be deceiv'd in regard to the Brilliancy of the Humming-Bird's Plumage, becauſe I have never ſeen any alive. Some have ſaid it has a very melodious Song, if this is true, it has a great Advantage over our Fly-Bird, which Nobody has heard ſing. But I have heard myſelf a Female, which whiſtled in a harſh and diſagreeable Note. This Bird has a very ſtrong Wing, and flies with ſurprizing Swiftneſs; you ſee it upon a Flower, and in a Moment it riſes up to a great Height in the Air, almoſt perpendicular. It is an Enemy to the Crow, and a dangerous one too. I heard one ſay, who was worthy of Credit, that he has ſeen one ſuddenly quit a Flower it was ſucking, riſe up as ſwift as Lightning, and go and thruſt itſelf under the Wing of a Crow, that was floating very high in the Air, with its Wings ſpread out, and peircing it with its Trunk, made it fall down dead; either kill'd by the Fall, or the Wound.

The Fly-Bird ſeeks Flowers, which have the ſtrongeſt Smell; and it ſucks them, keeping always upon the Fluttering: But it reſts itſelf from Time to Time; and then one may view it perfectly: They have been kept ſome Time upon ſugared Water, and Flowers; I kept one formerly for 24 Hours: It ſuffered itſelf to be taken, and handled, and feigned itſelf dead; as ſoon as I let it go, it took its Flight, and kept fluttering about my Window: I made a Preſent of it to one of my Friends, who the next Morning found it dead; and that Night there had been a little Froſt. Theſe little Animals take Care to ſhun the firſt cold Weather, It is very probable, that they return towards *Carolina*; and it is aſſured that they are not there but in the Winter. They make their Neſts in *Canada*, where they hang them to a Branch of a Tree, and turn them in ſuch Manner, that they are ſheltered from all the Injuries of the Weather. Nothing is ſo neat as theſe Neſts. The Bottom is made of very little Bits of Wood, platted like a Baſket; and the Inſide is lined with I know not what Sort of Down, which appears like Silk. The Eggs are about the Big-

neſs

neſs of a Pea, and have yellow Spots upon a white Ground. They ſay they have commonly three, and ſometimes five Eggs.

Of the Rattle-Snake.

Amongſt the Reptiles of this Country, I know of none but the Rattle-Snake that deſerves any Attention. There are ſome of theſe as big as a Man's Leg, and ſometimes bigger, and they are long in Proportion: But there are ſome, and I believe the greateſt Number, that are not bigger nor longer than our largeſt Adders in *France*: Their Shape is pretty ſingular. Upon a flat and very thick Neck they have but a ſmall Head: Their Colours are lively, without being brilliant; a pale Yellow predominates, with ſome Clouds that are pretty enough.

But what is moſt remarkable in this Animal, is its Tail, which is ſcaly like a Coat of Mail, a little flat; and they ſay that it grows every Year one Ring or Row of Scales, ſo that they know its Age by its Tail, as we do that of a Horſe by his Teeth. In moving, it makes the ſame Noiſe as a Cricket in flying: For you know, without Doubt, Madam, that the pretended Singing of a Cricket is only the Noiſe of its Wings. And the Reſemblance I ſpeak of is ſo alike, that I have often been deceived by it myſelf: It is this Noiſe that has given this Serpent the Name it bears.

The Bite of this Serpent is mortal, if a Remedy is not applied immediately; but Providence has provided a Remedy. In all the Places where this dangerous Reptile is found, there grows a Plant which is called *Rattle-Snake Herb*; the Root of which is a certain Antidote againſt the Venom of this Serpent: It need only be pounded or chewed, and applied like a Poultice upon the Wound: It is a beautiful Plant, and eaſily known: Its round Stalk, a little bigger than a Gooſe's Quill, riſes to the Height of three or four Feet, and ends in a yellow Flower of the Shape and Bigneſs of a common Daiſey: This Flower has a very ſweet Smell. The Leaves of the Plant are oval, and are ſupported five together, like the Claw of a Turkey, by a Stalk of an Inch long.

The Rattle-Snake ſeldom attacks the Paſſenger that does not meddle with it. I have had one at my Feet, which was certainly more afraid than myſelf; for I did not perceive it till it was running away: But if you tread upon it, you are immediately ſtung; and if you purſue it, if it has but a little Time to recover itſelf, it folds itſelf round with the Head in the Middle, and then darts itſelf with great Violence and Fury againſt its Purſuer: Nevertheleſs, the Savages chace it, and find its Fleſh very good. I have even heard ſome *Frenchmen*, who had taſted it, ſay, that it was not bad eating; but they were Travellers, and ſuch People think every Thing good, becauſe they are often hungry.

hungry. But this is at least certain, that it does no Harm to those that eat it.

Of the Woods of Canada.

I know not, Madam, whether I should undertake to speak to you of the Woods of *Canada*. We are in the Midst of the greatest Forests in the World. In all Appearance they are as old as the World itself, and were not planted by the Hands of Men. Nothing is more magnificent to the Sight; the Trees lose themselves in the Clouds; and there is such a prodigious Variety of Species, that even among those Persons who have taken most Pains to know them, there is not one perhaps that knows half the Number. As to their Quality, and the Uses to which they may be employed, the Sentiments are so different in this Country, and in *France*, that I even despair of ever being able to give you that Satisfaction which I could wish upon this Article: At least, for the present, I must confine myself to some Observations which I have made myself, and have had from other People, who have more Skill and Experience in this Matter than myself.

Of the two Species of Pines.

What struck my Sight most the first Time I came into this Country, were the Pines, the Firs, and the Cedars, which are of surprizing Height and Bigness. There are here two Sorts of Pines. They all produce a Rosin which is very fit to make Pitch and Tar: The white Pines, at least some of them, have at the very Tops of them a Kind of Mushroom, which the Inhabitants call *Guarigue*, and which the Savages make Use of with Success against Disorders of the Breast and Bloody-Fluxes. The red Pines are fullest of Gum, and the heaviest Wood, but they do not grow so large. The Lands which produce both Sorts, are not the best to produce Grain; they generally consist of Gravel, Sand, and Clay.

Four Species of Firs.

There are four Species of Fir in *Canada*; the first resembles our's: The other three Sorts are the White, the Red, and the Spruce: The second and the fourth Sort grow very high, and are fit for Masts, especially the White, which is also fit for Carpenters Work: It grows generally in wet and black Lands; but which being drained, may bear all Sorts of Grain: Its Bark is smooth and shining; and there grows upon it some little Bladders, the Bigness of a Kidney-Bean, which contain a Kind of Turpentine, most excellent for Wounds, which it cures in a short Time; and even for Fractures. They affirm, that it allays Fevers, and cures the Disorders of the Stomach and Lungs. The Way to use it, is to put two Drops of it into Broth: It has also a purging Quality. This is what they call at *Paris*, the *White Balsam*.

The

The red Fir has ſcarce any Reſemblance with the white: Its Wood is heavy, and may be employed for Building. The Lands where it grows are only Gravel and Clay. The Spruce Fir is gummy, but does not throw out enough Gum to be made Uſe of: Its Wood laſts a long Time in the Earth without rotting, which renders it very fit to make Incloſures: Its Bark is very fit for the Tanners; and the Savages make of it a Dye, which is pretty near a deep Blue. The greateſt Part of the Land where this Tree grows, is Clay. I have nevertheleſs ſeen ſome very large in a ſandy Soil, but perhaps under the Sand there might be Clay.

Two Species of Cedars.

The Cedars are of two Species, White and Red: The firſt are the largeſt: They make Pales of it; and this Wood is what they generally make Shingles with, becauſe of its Lightneſs. There diſtills from it a Kind of Incenſe, or Perfume; but it bears no Fruit like that of Mount *Lebanon*. The red Cedar is ſmaller: The moſt ſenſible Difference between one and the other is, that the Smell of the firſt is in its Leaves, and of the other in the Wood; but the laſt is by much the moſt agreeable. The Cedar, at leaſt the White, grows only in a very good Soil.

Of the Oaks, Maples, wild Cherry, Beach, Walnut, &c.

There are every where in *Canada* two Species of Oaks, diſtinguiſhed by the Names of White and Red. The firſt are often found in a low, wet, and fertile Soil, which is fit to produce Grain and Pulſe. The Red, whoſe Wood is leſs eſteemed, grows in a dry and ſandy Soil: Both Kinds bear Acorns.---The Maple is very common in *Canada*, and ſome are very large, of which they make handſome Furniture: They grow on high Grounds, which are fitteſt for Fruit-Trees. They call the Female Maple here *Rheue*, the Wood of which is wav'd, but paler than that of the Male: In other Reſpects it has the ſame Shape and Qualities; but it requires a wet and fruitful Soil.——The wild Cherry-Tree, which grows promiſcuouſly with the Maple and the White Wood, makes very fine Furniture: It yields more Water or Juice than the Maple; but it is bitter, and the Sugar made of it never loſes its Bitterneſs. The Savages make Uſe of its Bark in certain Diſorders that happen to Women.

There are in *Canada* three Sorts of Aſh; the True, the Mongrel, and the Baſtard: The firſt Sort, which grows amongſt the Maples, is fit for the Carpenters Uſe, and to make Caſks for dry Goods: The ſecond has the ſame Properties, and grows as the Baſtard Kind does, only in a low and good Soil.

They reckon alſo in this Country three Kinds of Walnuts; the hard, the ſoft, and a third Kind which has a very thin Bark: The

The hard Kind bears very ſmall Nuts, good to eat, but hard to ſhell: Its Wood is good for nothing but to burn. The ſoft Kind bears long Nuts, as big as thoſe of *France*, but the Shells are very hard: The Kernels are excellent. The Wood is not ſo fine as our's; but to make Amends, it ſcarce ever decays, either in Earth or in Water, and is with Difficulty conſumed in the Fire. The third Sort bears Nuts of the Bigneſs of the firſt, but in a greater Quantity; which are bitter, and incloſed in very ſoft Shells. They make very good Oil of theſe Nuts. This Tree yields ſweeter Water than the Maple, but in a ſmaller Quantity: It grows only, like the ſoft Walnut, in the beſt Soils.

Beach Trees are very plentiful here. I have ſeen ſome on ſandy Hills, and in very fruitful low Lands: They bear much Maſt, from which it would be eaſy to extract an Oil. The Bears make it their principal Food, as do alſo the Partridges. The Wood is very ſoft, and fit to make Oars for Boats; but the Rudders of Canoes are made of Maple. The White Wood, which grows amongſt the Maple and the wild Cherry, is very plenty. Theſe Trees grow large and ſtrait: They make Boards and Planks of them, and alſo Caſks for dry Goods: It is ſoft, and eaſy to work. The Savages peel off the Bark to cover their Cabins.

Two Species of Elms.

Elms are very common through the whole Country. There are white and red. The Wood of the firſt is hardeſt to work, but laſts longeſt. The *Iroquois* make their Canoes of the Bark of the red Elm: There are ſome of a ſingle Piece, which will hold twenty Men. There are alſo ſome hollow Elms, where the Bears and wild Cats retire from *November* to *April*. The Aſpen-Tree commonly grows here by the Sides of Rivers and Marſhes.

Trees peculiar to this Country.

They find in the thickeſt Woods a great Number of Plumb-Trees, loaded with Fruit, but very ſour. The *Vinegar-Tree* is a Shrub very pithy, which yields Bunches of a ſharp Fruit, of an Ox-Blood Colour. By infuſing them in Water they make a Kind of Vinegar. The *Pemine* is another Kind of Shrub which grows by the Side of Brooks, and Meadows. It bears a Bunch of Fruit of a lively red, which is aſtringent. There are three Sorts of Gooſberries that grow naturally in this Country. They are the ſame as in *France*. The Sloe grows here as in *France*: This Fruit is wonderful for curing the Bloody-Flux in a very ſhort Time. The Savages dry them as we do Cherries in *France*.

The *Atoca* is a Fruit with Kernels as big as a Cherry: This Plant, which runs upon the Ground in the Marſhes, produces its

its Fruit in the Water. The Fruit is ſharp, and they make Sweet-Meats of it. The White-Thorn is found by the Sides of Rivers, and produces much Fruit with three Kernels. This is the Food of many wild Beaſts. They call here the Cotton-Tree a Plant which ſhoots up like Aſparagus, to the Height of about three Feet, at the Top of which grow many Tufts of Flowers. In the Morning, before the Dew is off, they ſhake theſe Flowers, and there falls off with the Water a Kind of Honey, which is made into Sugar by boiling. The Seed grows in a Bladder, which contains a very fine Sort of Cotton. The *Soliel* (the Sun) is another Plant very common in the Fields of the Savages, and which grows ſeven or eight Feet high. Its Flower, which is very large, is in the Shape of a Marigold, and the Seed grows in the ſame Manner. The Savages by boiling it draw out an Oil, with which they greaſe their Hair. The Plants which theſe People principally cultivate are Maiz, or *Turkey* Wheat, Kidney-Beans, Gourds, and Melons.——They have a Kind of Gourd leſs than our's, which has a ſweet Taſte. They boil them whole, or roaſt them under the Aſhes, and eat them thus without any thing with them. The Savages before our Arrival here had the common Melons, and the Water Melons. The firſt are as good as our's in *France*, eſpecially in this Iſland, where they are very plenty. Hops and Maiden-Hair are the natural Growth of this Country; but the Maiden-Hair grows higher here, and is infinitely better than in *France*. ————Here is a Letter, Madam, in which you will eaſily diſtinguiſh a Traveller who ranges thro' the Woods and Plains of *Canada*, and who is entertained with every thing that preſents itſelf to his View.

I am, &c.

LETTER IX.

Of the Causes of the Cold of CANADA. *Of the Resources they have for Subsistence. Of the Character of the* FRENCH CANADIANS.

MADAM, MONTREAL, *April* 22.

IT is surprising that in *France*, where they so often see Persons who have passed a good Part of their Lives in *Canada*, they should have such a wrong Idea of this Country. This proceeds without Doubt from the Information of those People who know it by its worst Side. The Winter generally begins before the Vessels sail for *France*, and it begins in a Manner that astonishes those who are not used to it. The first Frost fills the Rivers with Ice in a few Days, and the Earth is soon covered with Snow, which lasts six Months, and always rises six Feet high where the Wind has not Power.

Canada *is not known in* France, *but by its worst Side.*

There is indeed no Want of Wood to provide against the Cold, which soon becomes excessive, and lasts till the Spring is pretty forward: But it is very melancholy not to be able to stir out without being frozen, or without being wrapt up in Furs like a Bear. Besides, What a Sight is the Snow, which dazzles one's Eyes, and hides all the Beauties of Nature! There is no longer any Difference between the Rivers and the Fields, no more Variety, even the Trees are covered with a Rime, and all their Branches are hung with Isicles, under which it is not safe to stand. What can one think when we see the Horses have Beards of Ice a Foot long? And how can one travel in a Country, where the Bears for six Months dare not venture out of their Holes? And indeed, I never passed a Winter in this Country, but I saw some People who were carried to the Hospital, to have their Legs and Arms cut off that were frozen. In Fact, if the Sky is clear, there blows from the western Parts a Wind that cuts the Face. If the Wind turns to the South or the East, the Weather grows a little milder, but there falls such a thick Snow, that you cannot see ten Paces at Noon Day. If there comes a thawing Air, adieu to all the Capons, Quarters of Beef and Mutton, the Fowls and the Fish, which had been laid up in the Store-Rooms: So that in Spight of the Rigour of the excessive Cold, they are still obliged to wish for its Continuance. It is to no Purpose to say the

Excessive Cold.

the Winters are not so cold as they were eighty Years ago, that in all Appearance they will grow milder hereafter. The Misfortune of those who came before us, and the good Fortune of those who shall come after us, is no Cure for the present Evil which we suffer. A *Creole* of *Martinico*, who should have landed the first Time in *France* during the great Frost in 1709, would he have been much relieved by hearing me say, who came at that Time from *Quebec*, that the Cold was not so sharp as in *Canada*? For though I spoke the Truth, and had good Evidences of it, yet he might have answered me, that he did not find the Cold of *France* less piercing by hearing that it was sharper still in *Canada*. Nevertheless, as soon as the Month of *May* is come, the Scene is soon changed, the Sweetness of this End of the Spring is so much the more pleasing, as it succeeds a more rigorous Season. The Heat of the Summer, which in less than four Months Time shews us both Seed-Time and Harvest *(a)*, the Serenity of the Autumn, in which we enjoy a Course of fine Days, which are seldom seen in most of the Provinces of *France*: All this, added to the Liberty which they enjoy in this Country, is a Compensation which makes many People think an Abode here, at least as agreeable as in the Kingdom where they were born; and it is certain, that our *Canadians* do not scruple to give it the Preference.

The Inconveniencies of the great Cold.

After all, there are in this excessive and long Cold, some Inconveniencies which can never be well remedied: I shall Place in the first Rank, the Difficulty of feeding Cattle, which during the whole Winter can find absolutely nothing in the Fields, and of Consequence cost much to feed, and the Flesh of which, after six Months dry Food, has scarce any Taste. The Fowls require also a great deal of Care, and much Corn, to preserve them during so long and severe a Winter. If we save the Expence by killing at the End of *October*, all the Animals we are to eat till *May*, one may easily judge that such Meat is very insipid, and in the Manner that I have said they take Fish under the Ice, they cannot be very plenty; besides that, they are immediately frozen. So that it is almost impossible to have them fresh in the Season when it is most difficult to do without. We should also be very much embarrassed during Lent, without Cod and Eels. There is at that Time fresh Butter and Eggs; and there is but little Nourishment to be expected in eating the

(a) They plow the Fields in Summer, they sow from the midst of *April* to the 10th of *May*, they cut the Corn from the 15th of *August* to the 20th of *September*. The Lands that are not plowed till the Spring bear less, because they are not so well impregnated with the nitrous Parts of the Snow.

Pulſe, and Roots, which they preſerve in Store-Rooms as well as they can, but which has ſcarce any Virtue when they have been kept there ſome Months.

Add to this, that excepting Apples, which are excellent here, and the ſmall Summer Fruits which do not keep, the Fruits of *France* have not ſucceeded in *Canada*. Theſe, Madam, are the Diſadvantages which are cauſed by the great Cold. We are, notwithſtanding, as near the Sun as they are in the moſt ſouthern Provinces of *France*, and as we advance in the Colony, we come nearer ſtill. From whence can this different Temperature of the Air proceed under the ſame Parallels? This is what, in my Opinion, no Perſon has yet well explained.

Reflexion on the Cauſes of the great Cold.

The greateſt Part of the Authors, who have treated on this Matter, have ſatisfied themſelves with ſaying, that this long and ſevere Cold proceeds from the Snow's laying ſo long on the Ground, that it is impoſſible that the Ground ſhould be well warmed again. But this Anſwer makes the Difficulty ſtill greater, for one may aſk what is it that produces this great Quantity of Snow, in Climates as hot as *Languedoc*, and *Provence*, and in Parts that are much more diſtant from any Mountains. The Sieur *Denys*, whom I have cited ſeveral Times before, aſſerts, that the Trees grow green before the Sun is high enough above the Horizon to melt the Snow, and to warm the Earth; that may be true in *Acadia*, and on all the Sea Coaſts, but every where elſe it is certain that all the Snow is melted in the thickeſt Foreſt before there is a Leaf upon the Trees. This Author ſeems not to have any better Authority for ſaying, that the Snow melts rather by the Heat of the Earth, than that of the Air, and that it is always at the Bottom that it begins to melt: For who can be perſuaded that the Earth, covered with a frozen Water, ſhould have more Heat than the Air, which receives immediately the Heat of the Rays of the Sun. Beſides, it does not Anſwer the Queſtion, what is the Cauſe of this Deluge of Snow, which overflows vaſt Countries in the midſt of the temperate Zone?

There is no Doubt but that, generally ſpeaking, the Mountains, Woods, and Lakes, contribute much to it; but it appears to me, that we muſt ſtill ſeek for other Cauſes. Father *Joſeph Breſſani*, an *Italian Jeſuit*, who paſt the beſt Years of his Life in *Canada*, has left us in his native Tongue, a Relation of *New France*, in which he endeavours to clear up this Point of Philoſophy: He cannot allow that we ſhould attribute the Cold, of which we ſeek the Cauſe, to any of the Cauſes I have juſt mentioned, *viz.* the Mountains, Woods, and Lakes, with which

this

this Country abounds; but he seems to go too far; for there is nothing to answer against Experience, which makes us sensible of the Abatement of the Cold, in Proportion as the Country is cleared of the Woods, altho' is not in so great a Proportion as it ought to be, if the Thickness of the Woods was the principal Cause of it. What he allows himself, that it is common to see a Frost in Summer after a very hot Day, appears to me a Demonstration against him; for how can we explain this Phœnomenon otherwise, than by saying that the Sun having opened in the Day Time the Pores of the Earth, the Moisture that was inclosed in it, and the nitrous Particles which the Snow left in it in great Quantities, and the Heat which is continued after the setting of the Sun, in an Air so subtil as that we breathe in this Country, form these little Frosts in the same Manner as we make Ice on the Fire: Now the Moisture of the Air is evidently a great Part of the Cause of the Cold; and from whence should this Moisture come in a Country where the Soil is generally mixt with much Sand, if it was not from the Lakes and the Rivers, from the Thickness of the Forests, and from Mountains covered with Snow, which in melting water the Plains, and from Winds which carry the Exhalations every where.

But if Father *Bressani* was mistaken, as I think, from excluding all these Things from the Causes of the excessive Cold of *Canada*, what he substitutes in Lieu thereof, seems to me to contribute greatly towards it. There are, says he, in the hottest Climates, some moist Lands, and there are some very dry in the coldest Countries: But a certain Mixture of dry and moist makes Ice and Snow, the Quantity of which makes the Excess and Duration of the Cold. Now if one was to travel but very little in *Canada*, we should perceive this Mixture in a very remarkable Manner. It is without Contradiction a Country where there is the most Water of any Country in the World, and there are few, where the Soil is more mixt with Stones and Sand. Add to this, it seldom rains here, and the Air is extremely pure and healthy; a certain Proof of the natural Dryness of the Earth. In Fact, Father *Bressani* affirms, that during sixteen Years that the Mission subsisted in the Country of the *Hurons*, there lived there at the same Time sixty *Frenchmen*, many of whom were of a tender Constitution; that they all fared very hardly in Point of Diet, and suffered in other Respects beyond all Imagination, and that not one died.

In Fact, this prodigious Multitude of Rivers and Lakes, which occupy as much Space in *New France* as half the Lands n *Europe*, one would imagine should furnish the Air with new Vapours; but, besides that the greatest Part of these Waters

O 2 are

are very clear, and on a ſandy Bottom, their great and continual Agitation blunt the Rays of the Sun, hinder it from raiſing many Vapours, or cauſes them to fall again in the Fogs; for the Winds excite upon theſe freſh Water Seas as frequent and as violent Storms as upon the Ocean: And this alſo is the true Reaſon why it ſeldom rains at Sea.

The ſecond Cauſe of the exceſſive Cold of *Canada*, according to Father *Breſſani*, is the Neighbourhood of the Northern Sea, covered with monſtrous Heaps of Ice above eight Months in the Year. You may here recollect, Madam, what I ſaid in my firſt Letter of the Cold we felt in the Dog Days, from the Neighbourhood of a floating Iſland of Ice, or rather from the Wind which blew upon us from the Side where it was, and which ceaſed the Moment it was under the Wind. It is moreover certain, that is does not ſnow here, but with a North Eaſt Wind, which comes from the Quarter where the Ice of the North lies; and though we do not feel ſo great Cold while the Snow falls, there is no Doubt but it contributes greatly to render ſo piercing the Weſt and North Weſt Winds, which come to us acroſs vaſt Countries, and a great Chain of Mountains which are covered with Snow.

Laſtly, if we take the Opinion of this *Italian* Miſſionary, the Height of the Land is not the leaſt Cauſe of the Subtilty of the Air which we breathe in this Country, and conſequently of the Severity of the Cold. Father *Breſſani* takes great Pains to prove this Elevation by the Depth of the Sea, which increaſes, ſays he, in Proportion as we approach *Canada*, and by the Number and Height of the Falls of the Rivers. But it ſeems to me that the Depth of the Sea proves nothing at all, and that the Falls of the River *St. Laurence*, and of ſome Rivers in *New France*, prove no more than the Cataracts of the *Nile*. On the other Hand, we do not obſerve that from *Montreal*, where the Falls begin, down to the Sea, that the River *St. Laurence* is much more rapid than ſome of our Rivers in *Europe*. I think therefore, we muſt keep to the Neighbourhood of the Ice of the North, as the Cauſe of the Cold, and that even in Spite of this Neighbourhood, if *Canada* was as free from Woods, and as well peopled as *France*, the Winters here would not be ſo long and ſo ſevere. But they would be always more ſo than in *France*, becauſe of the Serenity and Purity of the Air: For it is certain that in Winter, all other Things being equal, the Froſt is keener when the Sky is clear, and the Sun has rarified the Air.

Of the Eel Fiſhery.

When the Winter is paſt, Fiſhing, Shooting, and Hunting, abundantly ſupplies thoſe with Proviſions who take the Pains for it: Beſides the Fiſh and Wild Fowl, which I have already mentioned, the River *St. Laurence* and the Foreſt, furniſh the Inhabitants

bitants with two Sorts of Manna, as we may call it, which are a great Support to them. From *Quebec* to *Trois Rivieres*, they take in the River a prodigious Quantity of great Eels, which come down, as they say, from Lake *Ontario*, where they are bred in some Marshes, on the Side of the Lake; but as they meet, as I before remarked, with white Porpoises, which chase them, the greatest Part strive to return again, and this is the Reason they take such a great Number. They fish for them in this Manner: Upon a Part of the Shore which is covered at high Water, and which is left dry when the Tide falls, they place Boxes at certain Distances, and fix them against a Fence of Ozier Hurdles, which leaves no Passage open for the Eels. Large Nets, or Baskets of the same Matter, are fixed by the narrowest End into these Boxes, and the other End, which is very wide, lies against the Hurdles, upon which they place at Intervals some Bunches of Greens. When all is covered with the Tide, the Eels, which always run to the Side, and which are enticed by the Greens, come in great Numbers along this Fence, and enter into the Baskets, which conduct them to the Prisons prepared for them. And often in one Tide the Boxes are filled.

These Eels are bigger than our's, and yield a great deal of Oil. I have already observed, that with whatsoever Sauce they are eaten, they always retain a rank Taste, to which we cannot reconcile ourselves but with Difficulty: Perhaps this is the Fault of our Cooks. Their Bones all terminate in a Point a little bent, which I do not remember to have seen in those of *France*. The best Method of dressing this Fish is to hang it up in the Chimney, and there let it roast slowly in its Skin: This Skin comes off of itself, and all the Oil runs out. As they provide great Store of them during the three Months that the Fishery lasts, they salt them, and put them in Barrels like Herrings. The other Manna I spoke of, is a Kind of Wood-Pigeons, which come here in the Months of *May* and *June*. It is said that formerly they darkened the Air by their Multitudes, but it is not the same now. Nevertheless, there still comes into the Neighbourhood of the Towns a pretty large Number to rest upon the Trees. They commonly call them *Tourtes*, and they differ in Fact from Wood-Pigeons, Turtles, and the common Pigeons of *Europe*, enough to make a fourth Species. They are smaller than our largest Pigeons of *Europe*; but have their Eyes, and the like Clouds of their Neck. Their Plumage is of a dark brown, except their Wings, where they have some Feathers of a very fine blue.

One would think that these Birds sought to be killed, for if there is any dry Branch on a Tree, they chuse that to perch upon;

upon; and they range themselves in such a Manner, that the worst Marksman may knock down six at least with one Shot. They have also found a Way to take many alive, and they feed them till the first Frost; then they kill them, and lay them up in their Store-Rooms, where they keep all the Winter.

The happy Condition of the Inhabitants of Canada.

It follows from hence, Madam, that every one here has the Necessaries of Life: They pay little to the King; the Inhabitant knows neither Land-Tax nor Poll-Money; he has Bread cheap; Meat and Fish are not dear; but Wine and Stuffs, and every Thing they have from *France*, is very dear. The most to be pitied are the Gentlemen and Officers here, who have only their Salaries, and are burthened with Families: The Women seldom bring any other Portions to their Husbands than much Wit, Love, Agreeableness, and Fruitfulness. But as God gives to the Marriages of this Country the Blessing which he gave to the Patriarchs, they ought also, in order to subsist such numerous Families, to live like the Patriarchs; but those Times are past. In *New France* there are more Gentlemen than in all the rest of our Colonies together. The King maintains here twenty-eight Companies of Marines, and three *Etats Majors*. Many Families have been enobled here, and there have remained here several Officers of the Regiment of *Carignan-Salieres*, which have peopled the Country with Gentlemen, the greatest Part of which find it hard to live. It would be harder with them still, if they were not allowed to trade, and if every one here had not a common Right to fish, shoot, and hunt.

Many know not how to make Advantage of this.

After all, if they suffer Want, they are a little to blame themselves. The Land is good almost every where, and Agriculture does not degrade a Gentleman. How many Gentlemen in all the Provinces of *France* would envy the common Inhabitants of *Canada* if they knew it; and those who languish here in a shameful Indigence, can they be excused for not embracing a Profession, which the sole Corruption of Manners and weak Maxims have degraded from its antient Honour? We do not know in the World a Country more healthy than this: There prevails here no particular Disease; the Fields and Woods are full of Herbs of wonderful Virtue, and the Trees distill most excellent Balsams. These Advantages ought at least to keep those in this Country who are born here; but Fickleness, and Aversion to diligent and regular Labour, and a Spirit of Independency, have driven out a great Number of young People, and have hindered the Colony from being peopled.

These,

These, Madam, are the Failings of which they accuse, with the most Foundation, the *French* of *Canada*. The Savages have also the same; one would think that the Air which they breathe in this vast Continent contributes to it; but the Example and Company of the natural Inhabitants, who place all their Happiness in Liberty and Independence, are more than sufficient to form this Character. They accuse also our *Creoles* of being very greedy, and of heaping up Riches, and truly for this Purpose, they perform Things one would not believe without seeing: The Journies they undertake, the Fatigues they endure, the Dangers they expose themselves to, the Efforts they make, exceed all Imagination. There are, notwithstanding, few Men less covetous, who dissipate more easily what has cost them so much Pains to acquire, and who shew less Concern for having lost it. And there is no Room to doubt, but that they generally undertake these painful and dangerous Journies through Inclination. They love to breathe an open Air, they are accustomed betimes to live a roving Life; it has Charms for them that makes them forget the past Dangers and Fatigues; and they pride themselves in braving them anew. They have much Wit, (especially the Women, whose Wit is brilliant and easy). They are faithful in Expedients, bold, and capable of conducting Affairs of the greatest Moment. You have known, Madam, more than one of this Character, and you have often expressed to me your Surprize at it. I do assure you, that the greatest Part here are such; and they are the same in all Ranks.

Good and bad Qualities of the Creoles *of* Canada.

I know not whether I should place among the Failings of the *Canadians*, the good Opinion they have of themselves. It is certain at least that it inspires them with a Confidence that makes them undertake and execute what would seem impossible to many others. We must allow, on the other Hand, that they have excellent Qualities. They are of a good Stature, and well shaped in Body. Their Strength of Constitution is not always answerable thereto; and if the *Canadians* live long, they are old and worn out betimes. This is not entirely their own Fault, it is partly that of their Parents, who for the most Part do not watch enough over their Children to hinder them from ruining their Health in an Age, in which, when it is ruined, there is no Resource. Their Agility and Dexterity are without equal; the most skilful Savages do not guide their Canoes better in the most dangerous Torrents, and are not better Marksmen.

Many People are persuaded that they are not fit for the Sciences, which require much Application, and a Course of Study. I cannot say whether this Prejudice is well or ill founded,

founded, for we have had no *Canadian* yet who has undertaken to confute it. Perhaps they are ſo only from the looſe diſſipated Way they are brought up in. But every one muſt acknowledge, that they have a wonderful Genius for Mechanics: They have ſcarce any Need of Maſters to excel in them, and we ſee every Day ſome who ſucceed in all Trades without having ſerved an Apprenticeſhip. Some charge them with Ingratitude, yet they have appeared to me to have Hearts good enough, but their natural Levity often hinders them from conſidering the Duties that Gratitude requires. It is ſaid they make bad Valets; this is becauſe they are too high ſpirited, and love their Liberty too much to ſubmit to Servitude. On the other Hand, they are very good Maſters. This is quite contrary to what is ſaid of thoſe from whom the greateſt Part take their Origin. They would be perfect Men, if with their own good Qualities, they had preſerved thoſe of their Anceſtors. Some have complained that they are inconſtant Friends: This is far from being generally true, and in thoſe who have given Room for this Complaint, this proceeds from their not being uſed to any Reſtraint, even in their own Affairs. If they are not eaſy to be diſciplined, this comes from the ſame Principle; or becauſe they have a Diſcipline of their own, which they think the propereſt to make War with the Savages, in which they are not altogether in the wrong. On the other Hand, they ſeem not to be Maſters of a certain Impetuoſity, which makes them fitter for a *Coup de Main*, or a ſudden Expedition, than for the regular and ſettled Operations of a Campaign. It has alſo been remarked, that amongſt a great Number of brave Men, who have diſtinguiſhed themſelves in the late Wars, there have been few found who had Talents to command. This was perhaps, becauſe they had not ſufficiently learnt how to obey. It is true that when they are well headed, there is nothing they cannot accompliſh, either by Land or Sea; but for this End, they muſt have a great Opinion of their Commander. The late M. *d'Iberville*, who had all the good Qualities of his Country, without any of its Defects, would have led them to the End of the World.

There is one Thing upon which it is not eaſy to excuſe them, which is, the little Regard they have for their Parents; who on their Side, have a Tenderneſs for them that is not juſtifiable. The Savages fall into the ſame Error, and it produces amongſt them the ſame Effects. But what above all Things ſhould make us value our *Creoles* is, that they have a great deal of Piety and Religion, and that nothing is wanting in their Education on this Point. It is alſo true, that out of their own Country they retain ſcarce any of their Faults. As with this, they are extremely

tremely brave and dexterous, they might be rendered very serviceable for War, for the Sea, and for the Arts; and I believe it would be for the Good of the State to promote their Increase more than has hitherto been done.——Men are the principal Riches of a Sovereign; and *Canada*, though it could be of no other Use to *France*, but for this Purpose, would still be, if it was well peopled, one of the most important of our Colonies.

I am, &c.

LETTER X.

Of the IROQUOIS *Village. Of the* FALL *of* ST. LOUIS; *and of the different People who inhabit* CANADA.

MADAM, FALL OF ST. LOUIS, *May* 21.

THIS Village was at first placed by St. *Magdalen*'s Meadow, about a League lower than the *Fall of St. Louis*, towards the South. The Lands not being found fit for producing Maiz, it was removed over-against the Fall itself, from whence it took the Name it still bears, though it has been removed again a few Years ago a League still higher. I have already said that its Situation is charming, that the Church and the House of the Missionaries are two of the finest Buildings in the Country; from which we may conclude, that effectual Measures have been taken not to be obliged to make more Removals. I reckoned, when I came here, to go away immediately after the *Easter* Holidays; but nothing is more subject to Disappointments of all Kinds, than these Sort of Journies. I am yet uncertain of the Day of my Departure; and as we must make Advantage of every Thing, when we make such Excursions as mine, I have endeavoured to make Use of this Delay: I have passed the Time in conversing with some antient Missionaries, who have lived a long Time with the Savages, and have had from them many Particulars concerning various People who inhabit this vast Continent; which, Madam, I shall now communicate to you.

Of the Inhabitants of Newfoundland.

The first Land of *America* that we meet with coming from *France* to *Canada*, is the Island of *Newfoundland*, one of the largest that we know. It could never be known for Certainty, whether it had any Native Inhabitants: Its Barrenness, supposing it every where as real as it is thought to be, is not a sufficient Proof that it has had no Native Inhabitants;

P for

for Fishing and Hunting is sufficient to maintain Savages. This is certain, that here was never seen any but *Eskimaux*, who are not Natives of this Country. Their real Country is *Labrador*, or *New Britain*: It is there at least that they pass the greatest Part of the Year; for it would be prophaning the Name of *Native Country*, to apply it to wandering Barbarians, who having no Affection for any Country, travel over a vast Extent of Land. In Fact, besides the Coasts of *Newfoundland*, which the *Eskimaux* range over in the Summer, in all the vast Continent which is between the River *St. Laurence* and *Canada*, and the North Sea, there has never been seen any other People than the *Eskimaux*: They have been met with also a good Way up the River *Bourbon*, which runs into *Hudson's Bay*, coming from the West.

The original Name of these People is not certain; however, it is very probable that it comes from the *Abenaqui* Word *Esquimantsic*, which signifies *an Eater of raw Flesh*.—The *Eskimaux* are in Fact the only Savages known that eat raw Flesh, though they have also the Custom of dressing it, or drying it in the Sun: It is also certain, that of all the People known in *America*, there are none who come nearer than these to compleat the first Idea which *Europeans* had of Savages. They are almost the only People where the Men have any Beard; and they have it so thick up to their Eyes, that it is difficult to distinguish any Features of the Face: They have besides something hideous in their Look: Little Eyes, looking wild; large Teeth, and very foul: Their Hair is commonly black, but sometimes light, much in Disorder, and their whole outward Appearance very rough. Their Manners and their Character do not disagree with their ill Look: They are fierce, surly, mistrustful, and uneasy, always inclined to do an Injury to Strangers, who ought therefore to be upon their Guard against them. As to their Wit and Understanding, we have had so little Commerce with this People, that we can say nothing concerning them; but they are however cunning enough to do Mischief. They have often been seen to go in the Night to cut the Cables of Ships that were at Anchor, that they might be wrecked upon the Coast; and they make no Scruple of attacking them openly in the Day, when they know they are weakly mann'd. It was never possible to render them more tractable; and we cannot yet treat with them, but at the End of a long Pole. They not only refuse to approach the *Europeans*, but they will eat nothing that comes from them; and in all Things, they take on their Part such Precaution, as shews a great Diffidence, which gives Room to mistrust reciprocally every Thing that comes from them. They are tall, and pretty well shaped: Their Skin is as white as Snow, which

which proceeds without Doubt from their never going naked in the hotteſt Weather. Their Hair, their Beards, the Whiteneſs of their Skin, the little Reſemblance and Commerce they have with their neareſt Neighbours, leaves no Room to doubt that they have a different Origin from other *Americans*: But the Opinion which makes them deſcended from the *Biſcayners*, ſeems to me to have little Foundation, eſpecially if it is true, as I have been aſſured, that their Language is entirely different. For the reſt, their Alliance would do no great Honour to any Nation; for if there was no Country on the Face of the Earth leſs fit to be inhabited by Men than *Newfoundland* and *Labrador*, there is perhaps no People which deſerve more to be confined here than the *Eſkimaux*. For my Part, I am perſuaded they came originally from *Greenland*.

Theſe Savages are covered in ſuch a Manner, that you can hardly ſee any Part of their Face, or the Ends of their Fingers. Upon a Kind of Shirt made of Bladders, or the Guts of Fiſh cut in Slips, and pretty well ſewed together, they have a Coat made of Bear or Deer Skins, and ſometimes of Birds Skins. A Capuchin of the ſame Stuff, and which is faſtened to it, covers their Head; on the Top of which there comes out a Tuft of Hair, which hangs over their Forehead: The Shirt comes no lower than their Waiſt; their Coat hangs behind down to their Thighs, and terminates before in a Point ſomething below the Waiſt; but the Women wear them both before and behind, to the Middle of the Leg, and bound with a Girdle, from which hang little Bones. The Men have Breeches of Skins, with the Hair inwards, and which are covered on the Outſide with the Skins of Ermine, or ſuch-like: They wear alſo Socks, with the Hair inwards, and over this a Boot, furred in like Manner on the Inſide; then a ſecond Sock and ſecond Boots: And they ſay that theſe Coverings for the Feet are ſometimes three or four-fold; which does not, however, hinder theſe Savages from being very nimble. Their Arrows, which are the only Arms they uſe, are armed with Points made of the Teeth of the Sea-Cow, and they ſometimes make them of Iron, when they can get it. It appears that in Summer they keep in the open Air Night and Day, but in the Winter they lodge under Ground in a Sort of Cave, where they all lie one upon another.

Of the People of Port Nelſon.

We are little acquainted with the other People which are in the Environs, and above *Hudſon's Bay*. In the Southern Part of this Bay, they trade with the *Miſtaſſins*, the *Monſonis*, the *Criſtinaux*, and the *Aſſiniboils*. Theſe laſt came here from a great Diſtance, ſince they inhabit the Borders of a Lake which is to the North or the North Weſt of the *Sioux*, and their Language is a Dialect of the *Sioux*. The other three uſe the *Algonquin* Language. The *Criſtinaux*, or *Killiſtinons*, come from the North of the upper Lake. The Savages of the River *Bourbon (a)*, and the River *Sainte Thereſe*, have a Language entirely different from either: It is probable they are more acquainted with the *Eſkimaux* Language. It is obſerved, that they are extremely ſuperſtitious, and offer ſome Sort of Sacrifices. Thoſe who are the moſt acquainted with them affirm, that they have, like thoſe of *Canada*, a Notion of a good and evil Spirit; that the Sun is their great Deity; and that when they deliberate on an important Affair, they make him as it were ſmoke; which they perform in this Manner: They aſſemble at Day-break in a Cabin of one of their Chiefs; who, after having lighted his Pipe, preſents it three Times to the riſing Sun; then he guides it with both Hands from the Eaſt to the Weſt, praying the Sun to favour the Nation. This being done, all the Aſſembly ſmoke in the ſame Pipe. All theſe Savages, though they are of five or ſix different Nations, are known in the *French* Relations by the Name of the *Savenois*, becauſe the Country where they inhabit is low, marſhy, poorly wooded, and becauſe in *Canada* they call *Savanes (b)* thoſe wet Lands which are good for nothing.

Going to the North of the Bay, we find two Rivers; the firſt of which is called the *Danes River*, and the ſecond the *River of Seals*. There are ſome Savages on the Sides of theſe Rivers, to whom they have given (I know not why) the Name, or rather the Nick-Name, of the *flat Sides of Dogs*. They are often at War againſt the *Savanois*, but neither one nor the other treat their Priſoners with that Barbarity which is uſual amongſt the *Canadians*; they only keep them in Slavery. The *Savanois* are often reduced by Want to ſtrange Extremities: Either through Idleneſs on their Part, or that their Land produces nothing at all, they find themſelves, when the Chace and the Fiſhery fail, without any Proviſions; and then it is ſaid, they make no Difficulty to eat one another: The Weakeſt, no Doubt, go firſt. It is alſo ſaid, that it is a Cuſtom amongſt them, that when a Man is arrived to an Age in which he can be of no longer Service to his Family, but on the contrary a Burden to it, he puts a Cord himſelf about his Neck, and preſents the two Ends of it to him of his Sons whom he is moſt fond of, who ſtrangles him as ſoon as he can: He even thinks that in this he does a good Action,

(a) They ſay that when they have gone one hundred Leagues up this River, it is no longer navigable for fifty Leagues, and that afterwards it runs in the midſt of a very fine Country, and this laſts to the Lake of the *Aſſiniboils*, where it riſes.

(b) The *Engliſh* call them *Swamps*.

not only because he puts an End to the Sufferings of his Father, but also because he is persuaded he hastens his Happiness; for these Savages imagine that a Man who dies in old Age, is born again in the other World at the Age of a sucking Child; and that on the contrary, those who die young, are old when they come into the Country of Souls. The Daughters of these People never marry, but with the Consent of their Parents, and the Son-in-Law is obliged to live with his Father-in-Law, and be subject to him in every Thing, till he has Children. The Sons leave their Father's House early. These Savages burn their Dead, and wrap up their Ashes in the Bark of a Tree, which they bury in the Earth: Then they raise over the Grave a Kind of Monument with Poles, to which they fasten Tobacco, that the Deceased may have wherewith to smoke in the other World. If he was a Hunter, they hang up also his Bow and Arrows. Tho' the Mothers weep for their Children twenty Days, the Fathers receive Presents, and in Return make a Feast. War is much less honourable amongst them than the Chace; but to be esteemed a good Hunter, they must fast three Days together without taking the least Nourishment, having their Faces smeared with Black all this Time. When the Fast is over, the Candidate sacrifices to the *Great Spirit* a Piece of each of the Beasts he hath been wont to hunt; this is commonly the Tongue and the Muzzle, which at other Times is the Hunter's Share: His Family or Relations don't touch it; and they would even sooner die with Hunger than eat any of it, it being appropriated to the Hunter to feast his Friends and Strangers with. As to the rest, they say that these Savages are perfectly disinterested, and are of most inviolable Fidelity; that they cannot bear a Lye, and look upon all Deceit with Horror.

This is, Madam, all that I could learn of these Northern People, with whom we never had a settled Intercourse, and whom we never saw but *en passant*.———Let us come to those we are better acquainted with.—One may divide them into three Classes, distinguished by their Language, and their particular Genius.

The Extent of New France.

In that Extent of Country which is commonly called *New France*, which has no Bounds to the North, but on the Side of *Hudson's Bay*, which was dismembered from it by the Treaty of *Utrecht*, which has no other on the East but the Sea, the *English* Colonies on the South, *Louisiana* to the South-East, and the *Spanish* Territories to the West: In this Extent of Country, there are but three Mother Tongues, from which all the others are derived: These are the *Sioux*, the *Algonquin*, and the *Huron*. We know but little of the People that speak the first of these Languages, and no Body knows how far it extends. We have hitherto had

no

no Commerce but with the *Sioux* and the *Assiniboils*, and this has not been greatly followed.

Of the Sioux.

Our Missionaries have endeavoured to make a Settlement among the *Sioux*; and I knew one who greatly regretted that he had not succeeded, or rather, that had not remained longer among these People, who appeared to him docible. There are none perhaps from whom we may gain more Information concerning all that is to the North West of the *Mississippi*, as they have an Intercourse with all the Nations of these vast Countries. They dwell commonly in Meadows, under Tents made of Skins, and well wrought: They live on wild Oats, which grow in Abundance in their Marshes and Rivers, and by hunting, especially of the Buffaloes that are covered with Wool, and which are in Herds of Thousands in their Meadows: They have no fixed Abode, but travel in great Companies like the *Tartars*, and never stay in one Place any longer than the Chace detains them.

Our Geographers distinguish this Nation into *wandering Sioux*, and *Sioux of the Meadows*, into *Sioux of the East*, and *Sioux of the West*. These Divisions don't appear to me to be well grounded: All the *Sioux* live after the same Manner; whence it happens that a Village which was last Year on the East Side of the *Mississippi*, shall next Year be on the West Side; and that those who were at one Time by the River *St. Pierre*, are perhaps now far enough from it in some Meadow. The Name of *Sioux*, which we have given to these Savages, is entirely our own making, or rather is the two last Syllables of *Nadouessioux*, as they are called by many Nations: Others call them *Nadouessis*. They are the most numerous People we know in *Canada*: They were peaceable enough, and little used to War, before the *Hurons* and *Outaouais* took Refuge in their Country, flying from the Fury of the *Iroquois*. They derided their Simplicity, and made them Warriors to their own Cost.

The *Sioux* have several Wives, and they severely punish those that fail of Conjugal Fidelity. They cut off the End of their Noses, and cut a Circle in a Part of the Skin on the Top of their Head, and pull it off. I have seen some People who are persuaded that these Savages had a *Chinese* Accent: It would not be dificult to know the Truth of this, nor to know if their Language has any Affinity with the *Chinese*.

Of the Assiniboils.

Those who have been amongst the *Assiniboils* say, that they are tall, well made, strong, nimble, inured to the Cold and all Manner of Fatigues; that they prick themselves all over the Body, and mark out Figures of Serpents, or other Animals, and that they undertake very long Journies. There is nothing in this that distinguishes

guishes them much from the other Savages of this Continent, whom we know; but what is particular in their Character is, that they have a great deal of Gravity; at least they appear so, in Comparison of the *Cristinaux*, with whom they have some Intercourse. The *Cristinaux* are in Fact of an extraordinary Vivacity; they are always singing and dancing; and they speak with such a Volubility and Precipitation, that has never been observed of any other Savages.

Of the Lake of the Assiniboils.

The Native Country of the *Assiniboils* is about a Lake which bears their Name, and which is little known. A *Frenchman* whom I have seen at *Montreal*, assured me he had been there, but that he had seen it as they see the Sea in a Port and *en passant*. The common Opinion is, that this Lake is six hundred Leagues in Compass, that we cannot go to it but by Ways which are almost impassable, that all the Borders of it are charming, that the Air here is very temperate, though they place it to the North West of the upper Lake, where the Cold is extreme, and that it contains such a Number of Islands, that they call it in these Parts the *Lake of Islands*. Some Savages call it *Michinipi*, which signifies the *Great Water*; and it seems in Fact to be the Source of the greatest Rivers and all the great Lakes of *North America*: For by several Evidences, they make the River *Bourbon* to rise out of it, which runs into *Hudson's Bay*; the River *St. Laurence*, which carries its Waters to the Ocean; the *Mississippi*, which discharges itself into the Gulph of *Mexico*; the *Missouri*, which mingles with the last; and which, to the Place where they join, is in no Respect inferior to it; and a fifth which runs, as they say, to the West, and which of Course must go into the South Sea. It is a great Loss that this Lake was not known to the Learned, who have sought every where for the terrestial Paradise. It would have been at least as well placed here as in *Scandinaria*. But I do not warrant, Madam, all these Facts for Truth, which are only founded upon the Reports of Travellers; much less what some Savages have reported, *viz.* that about the Lake of the *Assiniboils* there are Men like the *Europeans*, and who are settled in a Country where Gold and Silver is so plenty, that it serves for the most common Uses.

Father *Marquette*, who discovered the *Mississippi* in 1673, says in his Relation, that some Savages not only spoke to him of the River, which taking its Rise from this Lake, runs to the West, but that they also added, that they had seen great Ships in its Mouth. It appears in the old Maps under the Name of *Poualaks*, and of whom some Relations say that their Country is the Boundary to that of the *Cristinaux*, or *Killistinons*.

The

Of the People of the Algonquin *Language.*

The *Algonquin* and *Huron* Languages have between them almost all the Savage Nations of *Canada* that we are acquainted with. Whoever should well understand both, might travel without an Interpreter above one thousand five hundred Leagues of Country, and make himself understood by one hundred different Nations, who have each their peculiar Tongue. The *Algonquin* especially has a vast Extent: It begins at *Acadia* and the Gulf of *St. Laurence*, and takes a Compass of twelve hundred Leagues, twining from the South East by the North to the South West. They say also, that the *Wolf* Nation, or the *Mahingans*, and the greatest Part of the *Indians* of *New England* and *Virginia*, speak *Algonquin* Dialects.

Of the Abenaquis *Nations, and the lower* Algonquins.

The *Algonquins*, or *Canibas*, who are Neighbours to *New England*, have for their nearest Neighbours the *Etechemins*, or *Malecites*, about the River *Pentagoët*; and more to the East are the *Micmaks*, or *Souriquois*, whose proper or Native Country is *Acadia*, the Continuance of the Coast of the Gulf of *St. Laurence*, up to *Gaspé*, (from whence one Writer calls them *Gaspesians*) and the neighbouring Islands. In going up the River *St. Laurence*, we meet with at present no Savage Nation, till we come to *Saguenay*. Nevertheless, when *Canada* was first discovered, and many Years afterwards, they reckoned in this Space many Nations, which spread themselves in the Island *Anticoste*, towards the Hills of *Notre-dame*, and along the North Side of the River. Those which the antient Relations speak most of, are the *Bersiamites*, the *Papinachois*, and the *Montagnez*. They call them also (especially the last) the *lower Algonquins*, because they inhabited the lower Part of the River with Respect to *Quebec*. But the greatest Part of the others are reduced to some Families, which we meet with sometimes in one Place, and sometimes in another.

Of the Savages of the North.

There were some Savages who came down into the Colony from the North, sometimes by *Saguenay*, and oftener by *Trois Rivieres*, of whom we have heard nothing for a long Time. There were amongst others the *Altikameques*: These Savages came from far, and their Country was surrounded by many other Nations, who extended themselves about the Lake *St. John*, and to the Lakes of the *Mistassins* and *Nemiseau*. They have been almost all destroyed by the Sword of the *Iroquois*, or by Distempers that were the Consequence of the Sufferings to which the Fear of these Barbarians reduced them. This is a great Loss: They had no Vices; they were of a very mild Disposition, easily converted, and very affectionate to the *French*.

Between

Between *Quebec* and *Montreal*, towards *Trois Rivieres*, we meet still with some *Algonquins*, but who do not make a Village, and who trade with the *French*. At our first Arrival here, this Nation occupied all the Northern Side of the River from *Quebec* (where M. *de Champlain* found them settled, and made an Alliance with them) up to the Lake *St. Pierre*.

Of the Algonquins, *the* Outaouais, *and other higher* Algonquins.

From the Isle of *Montreal*, going towards the North, we meet with some Villages of *Nipissings*, of *Temiscamings*, of *Tetes de Boules*, *(Round Heads)* of *Amikoues*, and of *Outaouais (a)*. The first are the true *Algonquins*, and who have alone preserved the *Algonquin* Language, without any Alteration: They have given their Name to a little Lake situated between Lake *Huron* and the River of the *Outaouais*. The *Temiscamings* occupy the Borders of another little Lake, which bears their Name, and which appears to be the real Source of the River *Outaouais*. The *Round Heads* are not far off: Their Name comes from the Shape of their Heads: They think a round Head to be a great Beauty; and it is very probable that the Mothers give this Shape to the Heads of their Children in their Infancy. The *Amikoues*, which they call also the Nation of the *Beavers*, are reduced almost to nothing: The Remains of them are found in the Island *Manitoualin*, which is in the Lake *Huron*, towards the North. The *Outaouais*, formerly very numerous, were settled on the Borders of the great River which bears their Name, and of which they pretended to be Lords. I know but of three Villages of this Nation, and those but thinly peopled, which I shall speak of hereafter.

Between Lake *Huron* and the upper Lake in the Streight itself, by which the second flows into the first, is a Torrent, or Fall, which is called *Saulte Sainte Marie, (the Fall St. Mary.)* Its Environs were formerly inhabited by Savages who came from the South Side of the upper Lake, whom they call *Saulteurs*; THAT IS TO SAY, *the Inhabitants of the Fall*. They have probably given them this Name, to save the Trouble of pronouncing their true Name; which it is not possible to do, without taking Breath two or three Times *(b)*. There is no Nation settled (at least that I know of) on the Borders of the upper Lake; but in the Posts which we possess there, we trade with the *Cristinaux*, who come here from the North East, and who belong to the *Algonquin* Tongue, and with the *Assiniboils*, who are to the North West.

(a) Many write and pronounce *Outaouaks*.

(b) *Pauoirigoucieuhak*.

Of the Pouteouatamis, *and other Savages of the Bay.*

The Lake *Michigan*, which is almost parallel with Lake *Huron*, into which it discharges itself, and which is separated from it but by a Peninsula one hundred Leagues long, which grows narrower continually towards the North, has few Inhabitants on its Banks. I do not know even that any Nation was ever settled here, and it is without any Foundation called in many Maps the Lake of the *Ilinois*. In going up the River *St. Joseph*, which runs into it, we find two Villages of different Nations, which came from other Parts not long since. This Lake has on the West Side a great Bay, which extends twenty-eight Leagues to the South, and which is called the *Bay des Puans*, or simply, *the Bay*. Its Entrance is very wide, and full of Islands, some of which are fifteen or twenty Leagues in Compass. They were formerly inhabited by the *Pouteouatamis*, whose Name they bear, excepting some which we leave to the Right, where there are still some Savages called *Noquets*. The *Pouteouatamis* possess at present one of the smallest of these Islands; and they have besides two other Villages, one in the River *St. Joseph*, and another in the Streight. In the Bottom of the Bay there are some *Sakis* and *Otchagras*. These last are called *Puans*, (*stinking*), but for what Reason I know not. Before we come to them, we leave upon the Right another little Nation, called *Malhomines*, or *Folles Avoines*, (*wild Oats.*)

Of the Outagamis, *the* Mascoutins, *and the* Kicapous.

A little River, much ruffled with Torrents, discharges itself into the Bottom of the Bay: It is known by the Name of the River *des Renards*, (*of the Foxes*). All this Country is very beautiful; and that is still more so, which extends from the South to the River of the *Ilinois*. It is notwithstanding only inhabited by two little Nations, which are the *Kicapous* and the *Mascoutins*. Some of our Geographers have been pleased to call the last the *Nation of Fire*, and their Country the *Land of Fire*. An equivocal Word gave Rise to this Name.

Of the Miamis *and the* Ilinois.

Fifty Years ago, the *Miamis* were settled at the South End of the Lake *Michigan*, in a Place called *Chicagou*, which is also the Name of a little River which runs into the Lake, the Spring of which is not far from that of the *Ilinois*. They are at present divided into three Villages, one of which is on the River *St. Joseph*, the second on another River which bears their Name, and runs into Lake *Erie*, and the third upon the River *Ouabache*, which runs into the *Mississippi*. These last are more known by the Name of *Ouyatanons*. There is scarce any Doubt but that this Nation and the *Ilinois* were, not long since, one People, consider-

ing

ing the Affinity of their Languages. I ſhall be able to ſpeak with more Certainty, when I have been among them. For the reſt, the greateſt Part of the *Algonquin* Nations, excepting thoſe which are more advanced towards the South, employ themſelves but little in cultivating the Lands, and live almoſt wholly upon Hunting and Fiſhing; ſo that they are not fixed to any Place. Some of them allow Plurality of Wives; yet, far from multiplying, they decreaſe every Day. There is not any one of theſe Nations that conſiſts of ſix thouſand Souls, and ſome no of two thouſand.

Of the People of the Huron *Language.*

The *Huron* Language is not by far ſo extenſive as the *Algonquin*: The Reaſon of which is, without Doubt, that the People who ſpeak it have been leſs roving than the *Algonquins*: I ſay the *Huron* Language, in Conformity to the common Opinion; for ſome maintain that the *Iroquois* is the Mother Tongue. Let that be as it will, all the Savages which are to the South of the River *St. Laurence*, from the River *Sorel* to the End of the Lake *Erie*, and even pretty near *Virginia*, belong to this Language: And whoever underſtands the *Huron*, underſtands them all. The Dialects are indeed extremely multiplied, and there are almoſt as many as there are Villages. The five Cantons which compoſe the *Iroquois* Commonwealth, have each their own Language; and all that was formerly called without any Diſtinction the *Huron*, was not the ſame Language. I cannot find out to what Language the *Cherokees* belong, a pretty numerous People, which inhabit the vaſt Meadows which are between the Lake *Erie* and the *Miſſiſſippi*.

But it is worth while to obſerve, that as the greateſt Part of the Savages of *Canada* have at all Times been converſant with each other, ſometimes as Allies, and ſometimes as Enemies, although the three Mother Tongues which I have ſpoken of, have no Manner of Affinity or Agreement with each other, theſe People have nevertheleſs found Means to treat together without the Help of an Interpreter: Either that long Cuſtom makes it eaſy to underſtand each other by Signs, or that they have formed a Kind of common Jargon, which they learn by Uſe.— I have juſt received Notice that I muſt embark: I ſhall finiſh this Article at my firſt Leiſure.

I am, &c.

LETTER XI.

Voyage to CATAROCOUI. *A Description of the Country, and of the Falls of the River* ST. LAURENCE. *Description and Situation of the Fort* CATAROCOUI. *Of the Languages of* CANADA, *and of the People that speak them. The Occasion of the War between the* IROQUOIS *and the* ALGONQUINS.

MADAM, CATAROCOUI, *May* 14.

I Departed from the *Fall St. Louis* the Day after I had closed my last Letter, and went to lie at the Western Point of the Isle of *Montreal*, where I did not arrive till Midnight. The next Day I employed all the Morning in visiting the Country, which is very fine. In the Afternoon I crossed the Lake *St. Louis* to go to the *Cascades*, where I found those of my People who went hither in a direct Way: I found them busy in mending their Canoe, which they had let fall in carrying it on their Shoulders, and which was split from one End to the other.——This is, Madam, the Convenience and Inconvenience of these little Carriages: The least Thing breaks them, but the Remedy is ready and easy. It suffices to furnish one's self with Bark, Gums, and Roots; and there are very few Places where one does not find Gums and Roots fit to sew the Bark.

Description of the Falls of the River St. Laurence.

What they call *the Cascades*, is a Water-fall situated exactly above the Island *Perrot*, which makes the Separation of the Lake *St. Louis*, and the Lake *des deux Montagnes, (of the two Mountains)*. To avoid it, we go a little Way to the Right, and make the Canoes pass empty in a Place they call *le Trou, (the Hole)*: Then they draw them to Land, and make a Portage of half a Quarter of a League; *that is to say*, they carry the Canoe with all the Baggage on their Shoulders. This is to avoid a second Fall called *le Buisson, (the Bush)*. This is a fine Sheet of Water, which falls from a flat Rock about half a Foot high. They might ease themselves of this Trouble, by deepening a little the Bed of a small River which runs into another above the *Cascades*: The Expence would not be great.

Above the *Buisson*, the River is a Mile wide, and the Lands on both Sides are very good, and well wooded. They begin to clear those which are on the North Side, and it would be very easy to make a Road from the Point, which is over against the Island *Montreal*, to a Bay which they call *la Galette*. They will shun by this forty Leagues of Navigation, which the Falls render almost impracticable, and very tedious. A Fort would be much better situated and more necessary at *la Galette* than at *Catarocoui*, because a single Canoe cannot pass here without being seen, whereas at *Catarocoui*, they may slip behind the Islands without being observed: Moreover, the Lands about *Galette* are very good, and they might in Consequence have always Provisions in plenty, which would save many Charges. Besides this, a Bark might go in two Days with a good Wind to *Niagara*. One of the Objects which they had in View in building the Fort *Catarocoui*, was the Trade with the *Iroquois*; but these Savages would come as willingly to *la Galette*, as to *Catarocoui*. They would have indeed something further to go, but they would avoid a Passage of eight or nine Leagues, which they must make over the Lake *Ontario*: In short, a Fort at *la Galette* would cover the whole Country, which is between the great River of the *Outaouais*, and the River *St. Laurence*; for they cannot come into this Country, on the Side of the River *St. Laurence*, because of the Falls; and nothing is more easy than to guard the Banks of the River of the *Outaouais*. I have these Remarks from a Commissary of the Marine *(a)*, who was sent by the King to visit all the distant Posts of *Canada*.

Reflexion on the Fort of Catarocoui, *and on the Way they take to go thither.*

The same Day, *May* the third, I went three Leagues, and arrived at the *Cedars*; this is the third Fall; which has taken its Name from the Quantity of Cedars that grew in this Place; but they are now almost all cut down. On the fourth, I could go no farther than the fourth Fall, which is called the *Coteau du Lac*, *(the Hill of the Lake)* tho' it is but two Leagues and half from the other; because one of the Canoes burst. You will not be surprised, Madam, at these frequent Wrecks, when you know how these Gondola's are made. I believe that I have already told you that there are two Sorts of them, the one of Elm Bark, which are wider and more clumsily built, but commonly bigger. I know none but the *Iroquois* who have any of this Sort. The others are of the Bark of Birch Trees, of a Width less in Proportion than their Length, and much better made: It is these that I am going to describe, because all the *French*, and almost all the Savages, use them.

(a) M. *de Clerambaut, d' Aigremont.*

They

They lay the Bark, which is very thick, on flat and very thin Ribs made of Cedar: These Ribs are confined their whole Length by small Cross-Bars, which separate the Seats of the Canoe; two main Pieces of the same Wood, to which these little Bars are sew'd, strengthen the whole Machine. Between the Ribs and the Bark they thrust little Pieces of Cedar, which are thinner still than the Ribs, and which help to strengthen the Canoe, the two Ends of which rise by Degrees, and insensibly end in sharp Points that turn inwards. These two Ends are exactly alike; so that to change their Course, and turn back, the Canoe-Men need only change Hands. He who is behind steers with his Oar, working continually; and the greatest Occupation of him who is forward, is to take Care that the Canoe touches nothing to burst it. They sit or kneel on the Bottom, and their Oars are Paddles of five or six Feet long, commonly of Maple; but when they go against a Current that is pretty strong, they must use a Pole, and stand upright. One must have a good deal of Practice to preserve a Ballance in this Exercise, for nothing is lighter, and of Consequence easier to overset, than these Canoes; the greatest of which, with their Loading, does not draw more than half a Foot Water.

Description of the Canoes of Bark.

The Bark of which these Canoes are made, as well as the Ribs and the Bars, are sew'd with the Roots of Fir, which are more pliable, and dry much less than the Ozier. All the Seams are gum'd within and without, but they must be viewed every Day, to see that the Gum is not peeled off. The largest Canoes carry twelve Men, two upon a Seat; and 4000 *l.* Weight. Of all the Savages, the most skilful Builders of Canoes are the *Outaouais*; and in general the *Algonquin Nations* succeed herein better than the *Hurons*. Few *French* as yet can make them even tolerably; but to guide them, they are at least as safe as the Savages of the Country; and they practise this Exercise from their Childhood. All the Canoes even the smallest carry a Sail, and with a good Wind can make twenty Leagues in a Day. Without Sails they must be good Canoe-Men to make twelve Leagues in a dead Water.

From the *Hill of the Lake* to Lake *St. François*, is but a good half League. This Lake which I passed the fifth is seven Leagues long, and three Leagues wide at the most in its greatest Breadth. The Lands on both Sides are low, but they seem to be pretty good. The Course from *Montreal* to this Place is a little to the South West; and the Lake of *St. François* runs West South West, and East North East. I encamped just above it, and in the Night I was wakened by some piercing Cries, as of People complaining. I was frightened at first, but soon recovered myself, when they

Of the Lake St. François.

they told me they were *Huars*, a kind of *Cormorants*; they added that these Cries were a certain Sign of Wind the next Day, which proved true.

The sixth I passed the *Chesnaux du Lac*, they call thus some *Canals*, which form a great Number of Islands, that almost cover the River in this Place. I never saw a Country more charming, and the Lands appear good. The rest of the Day we employed in passing the Falls, the most considerable of which they call the *Moulinet*; it is frightful to look at, and we had a great deal of Trouble to get thro' it. I went however that Day near seven Leagues, and I encamped at the Bottom of the *Long Fall*; this is a Torrent half a League long, which the Canoes cannot go up but with half their Loading; we passed it at seven in the Morning, then we sailed till three o'Clock in the Afternoon; but then the Rain obliged us to encamp, and detained us all the next Day: There fell the eighth a little Snow, and at Night it froze as it does in *France* the Month of *Jan.* we were nevertheless under the same Parallels as *Languedoc.* The ninth we passed the Flat Fall, about seven Leagues distant from the Long Fall, and five from the *Galots*, which is the last of the Falls. *La Galette* is a League and a half further, and we arrived there the tenth. I could not sufficiently admire the Country which is between this Bay and *les Galots*, it is impossible to see finer Forests, and I observed especially some Oaks of an extraordinary Height.

Other Falls.

Five or six Leagues from *la Galette*, there is an Island called *Tonihata*, the Soil of which appears pretty fertile, and which is about half a League long. An *Iroquois*, whom they call the *Quaker*, I know not why, a very sensible Man, and well affected to the *French*, obtained the Domain of it from the late *Count de Frontenac*, and he shews the Writing of this Grant to any one that will see it; he has nevertheless sold the Lordship, for four Pots of Brandy; but has reserved to himself all other Profits of the Land, and has assembled here eighteen or twenty Families of his Nation. I arrived the twelvth in his Island, and I paid him a Visit; I found him working in his Garden, which is not the Custom of the Savages; but he affects all the Manners of the *French*: He received me very well, and would treat me, but the Fineness of the Weather obliged me to go forward; I took my Leave of him, and went to pass the Night two Leagues further, in a very fine Place. I had still thirteen Leagues to *Cataracoui*; the Weather was fine, the Night very clear, and this engag'd us to embark at three in the Morning. We passed thro' the midst of a Kind of *Archipelago*, which they call *Mille Isles*, *(the Thousand Isles,)* and I believe there are above five hundred: When we are

Of the Island Tonihata.

passed

paſſed theſe we have a League and half to arrive at *Catarocoui*; the River is more open, and is at leaſt half a League wide; then we leave upon the Right three great Bays pretty deep, and the Fort is built in the third.

A Deſcription of Fort Catarocoui.

This Fort is a Square with four Baſtions built with Stone, and the Ground it occupies is a Quarter of League in Compaſs, its Situation has really ſomething very pleaſant; the Sides of the River preſent every Way a Landſcape well varied, and it is the ſame at the Entrance of Lake *Ontario*, which is but a ſmall League diſtant; it is full of Iſlands of different Sizes, all well wooded, and nothing bounds the Horizon on that Side: This Lake was ſome Time called *St. Louis*, afterwards *Frontenac*, as well as the Fort of *Catarocoui*, of which the Count *de Frontenac* was the Founder; but inſenſibly the Lake has gained its antient Name, which is *Huron* or *Iroquois*, and the Fort that of the Place where it is built. The Soil from this Place to *la Galette* appears ſomething barren, but this is only on the Edges, it being very good farther on. There is over-againſt the Fort a very pretty Iſland in the midſt of the River; they put ſome Swine into it, which have multiplied, and given it the Name of *Iſle des Porcs*: There are two other Iſlands ſomewhat ſmaller, which are lower, and half a League diſtant from each other; one is called the *Iſle of Cedars*, the other *Iſle aux Cerfs*, (*Harts Iſland*). The Bay of *Catarocoui* is double, *that is to ſay*, that almoſt in the midſt of it there is a Point that runs out a great Way, under which there is good Anchorage for large Barks. M. *de la Sale*, ſo famous for his Diſcoveries and his Misfortunes, who was Lord of *Cataracoui*, and Governor of the Fort, had two or three here, which were ſunk in this Place, and remain there ſtill: Behind the Fort is a Marſh where there is a great Plenty of Wild Fowl: This is a Benefit to, and Employment for, the Garriſon. There was formerly a great Trade here, eſpecially with the *Iroquois*; and it was to entice them to us, as well as to hinder their carrying their Skins to the *Engliſh*, and to keep theſe Savages in Awe, that the Fort was built: But this Trade did not laſt long, and the Fort has not hindered the Barbarians from doing us a great deal of Miſchief. They have ſtill ſome Families here on the Outſides of the Place, and there are alſo ſome *Miſſiſaguez*, an *Algonquin* Nation, which ſtill have a Village on the Weſt Side of Lake *Ontario*, another at *Niagara*, and a third in the Streight.

I find here, Madam, an Opportunity of ſending my Letters to *Quebec*: I ſhall take Advantage of ſome leiſure Hours to fill up this with what I have further to ſay to you on the Difference of the Languages of *Canada*. Thoſe who have ſtudied them perfectly

perfectly, say that those three of which I have spoken have all the Characters of primitive Languages; and it is certain that they have not the same Origin; which the Pronunciation alone is sufficient to prove. The *Siou* whistles in speaking; the *Huron* has no labial Letter, which he cannot pronounce, he speaks in the Throat, and asperates almost every Syllable; the *Algonquin* pronounces with more Sweetness, and speaks more naturally. I can learn nothing particular of the first of these three Languages, but our antient Missionaries have much studied the two last, and their principal Dialects: This is what I have heard from the most skilful.

The *Huron* Language has a Copiousness, an Energy, and a Sublimity perhaps not to be found united in any of the finest that we know; and those whose native Tongue it is, tho' they are now but a Handful of Men, have such an Elevation of Soul that agrees much better with the Majesty of their Language, than with the sad State to which they are reduced. Some have fancied they found in it some Similitude with the *Hebrew*; others, and the greatest Number, have maintained it had the same Origin as the *Greek*; but nothing is more trifling than the Proofs they bring for it. We must not depend especially upon the Vocabulary of Brother *Gabriel Saghard*, a *Recollet* who hath been cited to support this Opinion; much less on those of *James Cartier* and the Baron *de la Hontan*. These three Authors took at Random some Terms, some of which were *Huron*, others *Algonquin*, which they ill retained, and which often signified quite different from what they thought. And how many Errors have been occasioned by such Mistakes of many Travellers.

Character of the Algonquin *Language.*

The *Algonquin* Language has not so much Force as the *Huron*, but has more Sweetness and Elegance: Both have a Richness of Expressions, a Variety of Turns, a Propriety of Terms, a Regularity which astonish: But what is more surprising is, that among these Barbarians who never study to speak well, and who never had the Use of Writing, there is not introduced a bad Word, an improper Term, or a vicious Construction; and even Children preserve all the Purity of the Language in their common Discourse. On the other Hand, the Manner in which they animate all they say, leaves no Room to doubt of their comprehending all the Worth of their Expressions, and all the Beauty of their Language. The Dialects which are derived from both, have not preserved all their Beauties, nor the same Force. The *Tsonnonthouans*, for Instance (this is one of the five *Iroquois* Cantons) pass among the Savages to have a vulgar or rude Language.

In the *Huron* all is conjugated; a certain Device which I cannot well explain to you, distinguishes the Verbs, the Nouns, the Pronouns, the Adverbs, &c. The simple Verbs have a double Conjugation, one absolute, and the other reciprocal; the third Persons have the two Genders, for there are but two in these Languages; *that is to say*, the noble and the ignoble Gender. As to the Numbers and Tenses, they have the same Differences as in the *Greek*: For Instance, to relate Travels, they express themselves differently according as it was by Land, or by Water. The Verbs active multiply as often as there are Things which fall under Action; as the Verb which signifies *to eat* varies as many Times as there are Things to eat. The Action is expressed differently in Respect to any thing that has Life, and an inanimate Thing; thus to see a Man, and to see a Stone, are two Verbs; to make Use of a Thing that belongs to him that uses it, or to him to whom we speak, are two different Verbs.

Particularities of the Huron *Language.*

There is something of all this in the *Algonquin* Language, tho' not the same, of which I am not able to give any Account. Notwithstanding, Madam, if from the little I have said it follows, that the Richness and Variety of these Languages renders them extremely difficult to learn; their Poverty and Barrenness produces no less Difficulty: For as these People, when we first conversed with them, were ignorant of almost every Thing they did not use, or which did not fall under their Senses, they wanted Terms to express them, or they had let them fall into Oblivion: Thus, having no regular Worship, and forming of the Deity, and of every Thing which relates to Religion, but confused Ideas, not making scarce any Reflexions but on the Objects of their Senses, and on nothing which did not concern their own Affairs, which were confined within a small Compass, and not being accustomed to discourse on the Virtues, the Passions, and many other Subjects of our common Conversation; not cultivating any Arts, but those which were necessary for them, and which were reduced to a very small Number; nor any Science, only observing what was within their Ability; and for Life, having nothing superfluous, nor any Refinement: When we wanted to speak to them of these Things, we found a great Vacuity in their Languages, and we were obliged, in order to make ourselves understood, to fill them up with Circumlocutions that were troublesome to them as well as to us: So that after having learnt of them their Language, we were obliged to teach them another, composed partly of their own Terms, and partly of our's translated into *Huron* and *Algonquin*, to make the Pronunciation easy to them. As to Characters they had none, and they supplied

Particularities of the Algonquin *Language.*

plied

plied the Defect by a Sort of Hieroglyphicks. Nothing surprised them more than to see us express ourselves as easily by writing as by speaking.

If it is asked how we know that the *Siou*, the *Huron*, and the *Algonquin*, are rather Mother Tongues than some of those which we look upon as their Dialects, I answer, that it is not easy to mistake in this, and I think there needs no other Proof than the Words of the Abbe *Duboss*, which I have already cited; but in short, as we can judge here only by Comparison, if from these Reflexions we may conclude that the Languages of all the Savages of *Canada* are derived from those three which I have noted, I allow it does not prove absolutely that these are primitive, and of the first Institu- tion of Languages. I add, that these People have in their Discourse something of the *Asiatic* Genius, which gives Things a Turn, and figurative Expressions; and this is, perhaps, what has persuaded some Persons that they derive their Origin from *Asia*, which seems probable enough.

The People of the *Huron* Language have always applied themselves more than the others to cultivating the Land; they have also extended themselves much less, which has produced two Effects: For in the first Place, they are better settled, better lodged, and better fortified; and there has always been amongst them more Policy, and a more distinguished Form of Goverment. The Quality of Chief, at least among the true *Hurons*, which are the *Tionnontates*, is Hereditary. In the second Place, till the *Iroquois* Wars, of which we have been Witnesses, their Country was more peopled, though they never allowed Polygamy. They are also reputed more industrious, more dexterous in their Affairs, and more prudent in their Resolutions; which cannot be attributed but to a Spirit of Society, which they have preserved better than the others. This is remarked particularly of the *Hurons*, that tho' scarcely any longer a Nation, and reduced to two Villages not very large, and at a great Distance one from the other; yet they are the Soul of all the Councils, when they consult on any general Affairs. It is true, that in Spite of that Difference which is not seen at the first Glance, there is much Resemblance in the Sense, the Manners, and all the Customs of the Savages of *Canada*; but this is the Consequence of the Intercourse which has been always between them for many Ages.

This would be the Place to speak to you concerning the Government of these People, of their Customs, and of their Religion; but I see nothing in this yet but a Chaos, which it is impossible for me to clear up.

There are some Travellers who make no Scruple to fill their Journals with whatever they hear said, without troubling themselves about the Truth of any Thing. You would not, doubtless, have me follow their Example, and impose upon you for Truth all the extravagant Things that have been placed to the Account of our Savages, or that have been taken as they could from their Traditions. These Traditions, on the other Hand, are so little to be relied on, and almost always contradict each other so grossly, that it is almost impossible to discover any Thing from them that may be depended on. In Fact, how could such People, as we found these, transmit faithfully down to Posterity what has passed between them for so many Ages, having nothing to help their Memory? And can we conceive that Men, who think so little of Futurity, should ever busy themselves about what is past, to make any faithful Records of it? So that after all the Enquiries that could be made, we are still at a Loss to know what was the Situation of *Canada* when we made the first Discovery thereof, about the Middle of the sixth Century.

Origin of the War which the Algonquins *and the* Hurons *have maintained against the* Iroquois.

The only Point of their History, which is derived to us with any Sort of Probability, is the Origin of the War, which M. *de Champlain* found very much kindled between the *Iroquois* on the one Side, and the *Hurons* and *Algonquins* on the other; and in which he engaged himself much more than was agreeable to our true Interest. I cannot discover the first Beginning of this War, but I do not think it was very antient. What I shall say about it, I give you Notice before Hand, I do not warrant the Truth of, though I have it from pretty good Authority.

The *Algonquins*, as I have already observed, possessed all that Extent of Country which is from *Quebec*, and perhaps also from *Tadousac* quite to the Lake of *Nipissing*, following the North Shore of the River *St. Laurence*, and going up the great River, which runs into it above the Isle of *Montreal*. By this we my judge that this Nation was then very numerous; and it is certain, that for a long Time it made a very great Figure in this Part of *America*, where the *Hurons* were alone in a Condition to dispute with them the Pre-eminence over all the rest. For the Chace they had no Equals, and for War they acknowledged no Superiors. The few who remain to this Day, have not degenerated from the antient Merit of this Nation, and their Misfortunes have not yet lessened their Reputation. The *Iroquois* had made with them a Kind of Confederacy, very useful to both Sides; but which in the Opinion of the Savages, amongst whom a great Hunter and a great Warrior are equally esteemed, gave the *Algonquins* a real Superiority over the *Iroquois*. The latter, almost wholly employed in the Culture of the Lands, had engaged to give Part of their Harvest to the *Algonquins*; who, on their Side, were

were to divide with them the Fruit of the Chace, and to defend them againſt whoever ſhould undertake to diſturb them. The two Nations lived thus a long Time in a good Underſlanding; but an ill timed Haughtineſs on one Side, and a Reſentment, which was not expected, on the other Side, broke this Union, and made a Quarrel between theſe two People that hath been never reconciled.

As Winter is the great Seaſon for the Chace, and that the Earth, then covered with Snow, gives no Employment to them who cultivate it, the two Confederate Nations joined together to winter in the Woods; but the *Iroquois* commonly left the Chace to the *Algonquins*, and contented themſelves with fleaing the Beaſts, drying the Fleſh, and taking Care of the Skins. This is at preſent every where the Work of the Women, perhaps then it was not the Cuſtom: However, the *Iroquois* made no Difficulty of it. From Time to Time, however, ſome of them took a Fancy to try themſelves in the Chace, and the *Algonquins* did not oppoſe it, in which they were bad Politicians.

It happened one Winter, that a Troop of both Nations ſtopped in a Place where they expected Plenty of Game, and ſix young *Algonquins*, accompanied with as many *Iroquois* of the ſame Age, were detached to begin the Chace. They preſently diſcovered ſome Elks, and they all prepared themſelves directly to purſue them; but the *Algonquins* would not ſuffer the *Iroquois* to follow them, and gave them to underſtand that they would have enough to do to flea the Beaſts they ſhould kill. Unfortunatély for theſe Boaſters, three Days paſſed without their being able to bring down a ſingle Orignal, though a great Number came in Sight. This bad Succeſs mortified them, and probably was no Diſpleaſure to the *Iroquois*, who earneſtly deſired to obtain Leave to go another Way, where they hoped to be more ſucceſsful. Their Propoſal was received by the *Algonquins*, as was formerly that by the Brothers of *David*, which the young Shepherd made to go and fight with the Giant *Goliah*: They told them that they were very vain to pretend to have more Skill than the *Algonquins*; it was their Buſineſs to dig the Earth, and that they ſhould leave the Chace to thoſe that were fit for it. The *Iroquois*, enraged at this Anſwer, made no Reply; but the next Night they departed privately for the Chace. The *Algonquins* were ſurpriſed in the Morning at not ſeeing them, but their Surpriſe was ſoon changed into extreme Vexation; for in the Evening of the ſame Day, they ſaw the *Iroquois* returning loaded with the Fleſh of Orignals. There are no Men in the World who are more ſuſceptible of Spite, and who carry the Effects of it further: The Reſult of that of the *Algonquins* was ſudden: The *Iroquois* were no ſooner aſleep than they were all knocked on the Head.

Such

Such an Aſſaſſination could not be long a Secret; and though the Bodies were buried privately, the Nation was ſoon informed of it. At firſt, they complained with Moderation, but inſiſted on having the Murderers puniſhed. They were too much deſpiſed to obtain this Juſtice: The *Algonquins* would not ſubmit to make even the leaſt Satisfaction.

The Sequel of this War.

The *Iroquois* in Deſpair made a firm Reſolution to be revenged for this ſcornful Treatment, which irritated them more than the Aſſaſſination of which they complained. They ſwore they would all die to the laſt Man, or have Satisfaction; but as they perceived themſelves not in a Condition to cope with the *Algonquins*, whoſe Name alone kept almoſt all the other Nations in Awe, they departed from them a great Diſtance, to make a Proof of their Arms againſt leſs formidable Enemies, which they did by Way of Diverſion; and when they thought themſelves ſufficiently inured to War, they fell ſuddenly on the *Algonquins*, and began a War of which we only ſaw the End, and which ſet all *Canada* in a Flame. It was continued on the Side of the *Iroquois* with a Fierceneſs ſo much the more terrible, as it was the more deliberate, and had nothing of that precipitate Fury which hinders Meaſures from being well taken. Moreover, the Savages do not think themſelves thoroughly revenged, but by the utter Deſtruction of their Enemies, and this is ſtill truer of the *Iroquois* than of the reſt. They ſay commonly of them, that they come like Foxes, they attack like Lions, and fly away like Birds. Thus they ſeldom fail in their Attempts; and this Conduct has made them ſo ſucceſsful, that had it not been for the *French*, there would perhaps be no Mention made at this Day of any of the Nations who have dared to oppoſe this Torrent. Thoſe who ſuffered the moſt were the *Hurons*, who were engaged as Allies or Neighbours of the *Algonquins*, or becauſe their Country lay in the Way between both. We have ſeen with Aſtoniſhment, one of the moſt numerous Nations, and the moſt warlike of this Continent, and the moſt eſteemed of all for their Wiſdom and Underſtanding, diſappear almoſt entirely in a few Years. We may alſo ſay, that there is not a Nation in this Part of *America*, which has not ſuffered greatly by the *Iroquois* being obliged to take up Arms; and I know of none but the *Abenaquis* in all *Canada*, whom they have not dared to diſturb in their own Country: For ſince they have taken a Taſte for War, they cannot remain long quiet, like Lions, who by the Sight and Taſte of Blood, increaſe their inſatiable Thirſt for it. One would hardly believe how far they have travelled to ſeek Men to fight with. Nevertheleſs, by being thus continually at War, as they have from Time to Time met with very great Checks, they find themſelves greatly diminiſhed,

minished; and were it not for the Prisoners which they have brought from all Parts, and the greatest Number of which they have adopted, their Situation would not be much more happy than that of the Nations they have subdued.

What has happened in this Respect to the *Iroquois*, maybe said with more Reason of all the other Savages of this Country, and it is not strange if, as I have already observed, these Nations decrease every Day in a very sensible Manner. For though their Wars do not appear at first so destructive as our's, they are much more so in Proportion. The most numerous of these Nations has never had perhaps more than sixty thousand Souls, and from Time to Time there is much Blood spilt. A Surprize, or a *Coup de Main*, sometimes destroys a whole Town; and often the Fear of an Irruption drives a whole Canton to forsake their Country, and then these Fugitives, to avoid dying by the Sword of their Enemies, or by Torture, expose themselves to perish by Hunger and Cold in the Woods or on the Mountains, because they seldom have Leisure or Precaution to carry Provisions with them. This has happened in the last Age to a great Number of *Algonquins* and *Hurons*, of whom we could never hear any Account.

I am, &c.

LETTER XII.

A Description of the Country up to the River of the ONNONTAGUES: *Of the Flux and Reflux in the great Lakes of* CANADA. *The Manner how the Savages sing their War-Song. Of the God of War amongst these People. Of the Declaration of War. Of the Necklaces of Shells: And of the Calumet: And of their Customs of Peace and War.*

MADAM, FAMINE BAY, *May* 16.

I Have the Misfortune to be detained here by a contrary Wind, which in all Appearance will last a long Time, and keep me in one of the worst Places in the World.

I shall amuse myself with writing to you. Whole Armies of those Pigeons they call *Tourtes* pass by here continually; if one of them would carry my Letter, you would perhaps have News of me before I leave this Place: But the Savages never thought of bringing up Pigeons for this Purpose, as they say the *Arabs* and many other Nations formerly did.

I em-

I embarked the 14th, exactly at the same Hour I arrived at *Catarocoui* the Evening before. I had but six Leagues to go to the Isle of *Chevreuils*, (*Roe-Bucks*) where there is a pretty Port that can receive large Barks; but my *Canadians* had not examined their Canoe, and the Sun had melted the Gum of it in many Places; it took Water every where, and I was forced to lose two whole Hours to repair it in one of the Islands at the Entrance of the Lake *Ontario*. After that we sailed till Ten o'Clock at Night, without being able to reach the Isle of *Chevreuils*, and we were obliged to pass the rest of the Night in the Corner of a Forest.

Departure from Catarocoui: *The Rout form thence to* Famine Bay: *A Description of the Country.*

This was the first Time I perceived some Vines in the Wood. There were almost as many as Trees; to the Top of which they rise. I had not yet made this Remark, because I had always till then stopped in open Places; but they assure me it is the same every where, quite to *Mexico*. The Stocks of these Vines are very large, and they bear many Bunches of Grapes; but the Grapes are scarcely so big as a Pea; and this must be so, as the Vines are not cut nor cultivated. When they are ripe, it is a good Manna for the Bears, who seek for them at the Tops of the highest Trees. They have, nevertheless, but the Leavings of the Birds, who have soon gathered the Vintage of whole Forests.

Of the Vines of Canada.

I set out early next Morning, and at Eleven o'Clock I stopped at the Isle *aux Gallots*, three Leagues beyond the Isle *aux Chevres*, (*of Goats*), in 43°. 33′. I re-embarked about Noon, and made a Traverse of a League and a half, to gain *the Point of the Traverse*. If to come hither from the Place where I passed the Night, I had been obliged to coast the Continent, I should have had above forty Leagues to make; and we must do this, when the Lake is not very calm; for if it is the least agitated, the Waves are as high as in the open Sea: It is not even possible to sail under the Coast, when the Wind blows hard from the Lake. From the Point of the Isle *aux Gallots*, we see to the West the River *Chouguen*, otherwise called the River *d'Onnontagué*, which is fourteen Leagues off. As the Lake was calm, and there was no Appearance of bad Weather, and we had a little Wind at East, which was but just enough to carry a Sail, I resolved to make directly for this River, that I might save fifteen or twenty Leagues in going round. My Conductors, who had more Experience than myself, judged it a dangerous Attempt; but, out of Complaisance, they yielded to my Opinion.—The Beauty of the Country which I quitted on the Left Hand, did not tempt me any more than the Salmon, and Numbers of other excellent

excellent Fish, which they take in six fine Rivers which are at two or three Leagues Distance one from the other *(a)* : We took then to the open Lake, and till Four o'Clock we had no Cause to repent of it; but then the Wind rose suddenly, and we would willingly have been nearer the Shore. We made towards the nearest, from which we were then three Leagues off, and we had much Trouble to make it. At length, at Seven at Night we landed at *Famine* Bay; thus named, since M. *de la Barre*, Governor General of *New France*, had like to have lost all his Army here by Hunger and Distempers, going to make War with the *Iroquois*.

Description of Famine *Bay.*

It was Time for us to get to Land; for the Wind blew strong, and the Waves ran so high, that one would not have ventured to pass the *Seine* at *Paris*, over-against the *Louvre*, in such Weather. As to the rest, this Place is very fit to destroy an Army, which depends on the Chace or the Fishery for their Subsistence, besides that the Air appears to be very unhealthy here. But nothing is finer than the Woods that cover the Borders of the Lake: The white and red Oaks rise up here even to the Clouds. There is also here a Tree of the largest Kind; the Wood of which is hard, but brittle, and much resembles that of the Plane-Tree: The Leaf has five Points, is of a middle Size, a very fine Green on the Inside, and whitish without. It is called here the *Cotton-Tree*, because in a Shell nearly of the Bigness of a Horse Chesnut, it bears a Kind of Cotton; which appears, nevertheless, of no Use.———As I walked upon the Side of the Lake, I observed that it loses Ground on this Side sensibly: This is evident, because for the Space of half a League in Depth the Land is much lower and more sandy than it is beyond. I have observed also in this Lake (and they assure me the same happens in all the others) a Kind of Flux and Reflux almost momentaneous; some Rocks which are pretty near the Shore being covered and uncovered several Times within the Space of a Quarter of an Hour, although the Surface of the Lake was very calm, and there was scarce any Wind. After having considered this some Time, I imagined it might proceed from Springs which are at the Bottom of the Lake, and from the Shocks of those Currents with those of the Rivers, which flow in from all Parts, and which produce these intermitting Motions.

(a) The River of the *Assumption*, a League from *the Point of the Traverse*; that of *Sables*, three Leagues further; that of *la Planche*, *(the Plank)* two Leagues further; that of *la grande Famine*, *(the great Famine)* two Leagues more; that of *la petite Famine*, *(the little Famine)* one League; that of *la grosse Ecorce*, *(the thick Bark)* one League.

But

But would you believe, Madam, that in this Seafon, and in 43 Degrees Latitude, there is not yet a Leaf upon the Trees, though we have fometimes as great Heat as you have in the Month of *July*. The Reafon of this is, without Doubt, becaufe the Earth, which has been covered with Snow feveral Months, is not yet heated enough to open the Pores of the Roots, and to make the Sap rife. For the reft, the *great* and the *little Famine* do not deferve the Name of Rivers; they are but Brooks, efpecially the laft, but are pretty well ftocked with Fifh. There are here fome Eagles of a prodigious Bignefs. My People have juft now taken down a Neft, which confifted of a Cart Load of Wood, and two Eagles which were not yet fledged, and which were bigger than the largeft Hen Turkeys: They eat them, and found them very good.

Why the Trees have no Leaves in the Month of May.

I returned to *Catarocoui*; where, the Night that I ftaid there, I was Witnefs to a Scene that was fomething curious. About Ten or Eleven o'Clock at Night, juft as I was going to Bed, I heard a Cry, which they told me was a War-Cry; and a little after, I faw a Company of *Miffifaguez* enter the Fort finging. Some Years fince, thefe Savages engaged themfelves in the War which the *Iroquois* make with the *Cherokees*, a pretty numerous People, who inhabit a fine Country to the South of Lake *Erié*, and fince that Time the young People are eager for War. Three or four of thefe Heroes, equipped as for a Mafquerade, their Faces painted in a horrible Manner, and followed by almoft all the Savages who live about the Fort, after having run thro' all their Cabins finging their War-Song to the Sound of the *Chichikoué (a)*, came to do the fame in all the Apartments of the Fort, in Honour to the Commandant and the Officers. I confefs to you, Madam, that there is fomething in this Ceremony which fills one with Horror the firft Time one fees it; and I found by it what I had not fo fenfibly perceived before, as I did then, *viz.* that I was amongft Barbarians: Their Singing has always fomething mournful and difmal; but here I found in it fomething terrifying, caufed perhaps folely by the Darknefs of the Night, and the Preparation of the Feaft, for it is one for the Savages. This Invitation was addreffed to the *Iroquois*; but they, who begin to be Lofers by the War with the *Cherokees*, or who were not in a Humour for it, demanded Time to deliberate, and every one returned to his own Home.

(a) The *Chichikoué* is a Kind of Calibafh, full of Pebbles.

It

It appears, Madam, that in these Songs they invoke the God of War, whom the *Hurons* call *Areskoui*; and the *Iroquois* call him *Agreskoué*. I know not what Name they give him in the *Algonquin* Language. But is it not something strange that in the *Greek* Word ARES, who is the *Mars*, or the God of War, in all the Countries where they have followed the Theology of *Homer*, we find the Root from which several Terms of the *Huron* and *Iroquois* Language seem to have been derived, which relate to War? *Aregouen* signifies to make War, and is thus declined; *Garego*, I make War; *Sarego*, thou makest War; *Arego*, he makes War. For the rest, *Areskoui* is not only the *Mars* of these People; he is also their chief God; or, as they express it, the *Great Spirit*, the Creator and Master of the World, the Genius who governs every Thing: But it is chiefly for Military Expeditions that they invoke him; as if the Attribute which does him the most Honour, was that of *the God of Hosts*: His Name is the War-Cry before the Battle, and in the Height of the Engagement: Upon the March also they often repeat it, by Way of Encouragement to each other, and to implore his Assistance.

Of the God of War.

To take up the Hatchet, is to declare War: Every private Person has a Right to do it, without any one having a Power to hinder him; unless it be among the *Hurons* and the *Iroquois*, with whom the Mothers of Families can declare or forbid War when they please. We shall see, in its proper Place, how far their Authority extends in these Nations. But if a Matron would engage one who has no Dependence on her, to make a Party of War, either to appease the Manes of her Husband, of her Son, or of a near Relation, or to get Prisoners to supply the Places of those in her Cabin whom Death or Captivity have deprived her of, she is obliged to make him a Present of a Collar or Necklace of Shells, and it is very seldom that such an Invitation is without Effect.

Of the Declaration of War.

When the Business is to make a War in all the Forms between two or more Nations, the Manner of expressing it is, *to hang the Kettle upon the Fire*; and it has its Origin, without Doubt, from the barbarous Custom of eating the Prisoners, and those that were killed, after they had boiled them. They say also in direct Words, that they are going to *eat a Nation*; to signify, that they will make a cruel War against it; and it seldom happens otherwise. When they would engage an Ally in a Quarrel, they send him a Porcelain; *that is to say*, a great Shell, to invite him to drink the Blood, or (according to the Meaning of the Terms they use) the Broth of the Flesh of their Enemies. After all, this Custom may be very antient; but it does not follow from hence, that these People were always Man-Eaters: It was perhaps, in the primitive Times, only an allegorical Way of speaking, such as we often find even in the Scripture. The Enemies of *David* did not, as appears, make it a Custom to eat the Flesh of their Enemies, when he said, *Ps.* xxvii. *v.* 2. *When the Wicked, even mine Enemies, came upon me to eat up my Flesh.* In after Times, certain Nations that were become savage and barbarous, substituted the Fact in the Room of the Figure.

A Digression on the Porcelain, or Venus Shell, of Canada.

I have said that the Porcelain of these Countries are Shells: They are found on the Coasts of *New England* and *Virginia*: They are channel'd, pretty long, a little pointed, without Auricles, and pretty thick. The Fish that is inclosed in these Shells, is not good to eat; but the Inside of the Shell is of such a fine Varnish, and such lively Colours, that Art cannot come near it. When the Savages went quite naked, they applied them to the same Use as our first Parents did the Fig Leaves, when they saw their Nakedness, and were ashamed of it. They hung them also about their Necks, as the most precious Thing they had; and it is at this Day one of their greatest Treasures, and finest Ornaments. In a Word, they have the same Idea of them, as we have of Gold, Silver, and precious Stones; being so much the more reasonable in this, as they need only in a Manner stoop to obtain Treasures as real as our's, since all depends upon Opinion.

James Cartier speaks in his Memoirs of a Kind of Shell something like these, which he found in the Isle of *Montreal*: He calls it *Esurgni*; and asserts, that it had the Virtue to stop bleeding at the Nose. Perhaps it is the same with that we are speaking of; but they find none about the Isle of *Montreal*, and I never heard that these Shells had the Properties which *Cartier* mentions.

Of the Strings and Necklaces of Porcelain.

They are of two Sorts, or of two Colours; one White, the other Violet: The first is the most common, and perhaps for this Reason is less esteemed. The second appears to be something of a finer Grain when it is wrought. The deeper the Colour is, the more valuable it is. They make of both Sorts little cylindrical Beads: They pierce them, and string them; and it is of this that they make *Strings and Necklaces of Porcelain.* The Strings are nothing else but four or five Threads, or little Slips of Skin about a Foot long, on which the Beads are strung. The Necklaces are a Sort of Fillet, or Diadems formed of these Strings; which are confined by Threads, which make a Texture of four, five, six, or seven Rows of Beads, and of a proportionable Length: This depends on the Importance of the Affair they treat of, and on the Dignity of the Persons to whom the Necklace is presented.

By

By the Mixture of Beads of different Colours they form what Figures and Characters they please, which often serve to express the Affairs in Question. Sometimes also they paint the Beads; at least it is certain they often send red Necklaces, when it concerns War. These Necklaces are preserved with Care, and they not only make a Part of the public Treasure, but they are also as it were Records and Annals which are laid up in the Cabin of the Chief: When there are in one Village two Chiefs of equal Authority, they keep the Treasure and Records by Turns for a Night; but this Night at present is a whole Year.

Of their Use.

It is only Affairs of Consequence that are treated of by Necklaces; for those of less Importance they use Strings of Porcelain, Skins, Coverlets, Maiz, either in whole Grains or in Flour, and other such-like Things; for the public Treasure is a Receptacle for all these. When they invite a Village or a Nation to enter into a League, sometimes instead of a Necklace they send a Flag dipt in Blood; but this Custom is modern, and it is very probable that the Savages took the Notion from the Sight of the white Flags of the *French*, and the red Flags of the *English*. It is said also that we made Use of these first with them, and that they took a Fancy to dye their Flags in Blood when they intended to declare War.

Of the Calumet, and its Use.

The Calumet is not less sacred among these People than the Necklaces of Porcelain; if you believe them, it is derived from Heaven, for they say it is a Present which was made them by the Sun. It is more in Use with the Nations of the South and West, than those of the North and East, and it is oftener used for Peace than for War. *Calumet* is a *Norman* Word, which signifies *Reed*, and the Calumet of the Savages is properly the Tube of a Pipe; but they comprehend under this Name the Pipe also, as well as its Tube. In the Calumet made for Ceremony, the Tube is very long, the Bowl of the Pipe is commonly made of a Kind of reddish Marble, very easy to work, and which is found in the Country of the *Ajouez* beyond the *Mississippi*: The Tube is of a light Wood painted of different Colours, and adorned with the Heads, Tails, and Feathers of the finest Birds, which is in all Appearance merely for Ornament. The Custom is to smoke in the Calumet when you accept it, and perhaps there is no Instance where the Agreement has been violated which was made by this Acceptation. The Savages are at least persuaded, that the Great Spirit would not leave such a Breach of Faith unpunished: If in the midst of a Battle the Enemy presents a Calumet it is allowable to refuse it, but if they receive it they must

instantly

instantly lay down their Arms: There are Calumets for every Kind of Treaty. In Trade, when they have agreed upon the Exchange, they present a Calumet to confirm it, which renders it in some Manner sacred. When it concerns War, not only the Tube, but the Feathers also that adorn it, are red: Sometimes they are only set on one Side; and they say that according to the Manner in which the Feathers are disposed, they immediately know what Nation it is that presents it, and whom they intend to attack.

There is scarce any Room to doubt but that the Savages, in making those smoke in the Calumet, with whom they would trade or treat, intend to take the Sun for Witness, and in some Measure for a Guarantee of their Treaties; for they never fail to blow the Smoke towards this Planet: But that from this Practice, and the common Use of the Calumets, one should infer as some have done, that this Pipe might well be in its Origin, the *Caduceus* of *Mercury*, does not appear to me to be probable, because this *Caduceus* had no Relation to the Sun; and because in the Traditions of the Savages, we have found nothing that gives any Room to judge, that they ever had any Knowledge of the *Greek* Mythology. It would be in my Opinion, much more natural to think that these People, having found by Experience that the Smoke of their Tobacco draws Vapours from the Brain, makes the Head clearer, rouses the Spirits, and makes us fitter to treat of Affairs, have for these Reasons introduced the Use of it in their Councils, where in Fact they have always the Pipe in their Mouths; and that after having gravely deliberated and taken their Resolution, they thought they could never find a Symbol fitter to put a Seal to their Determinations, nor any Pledge more capable of confirming the Execution of them, than the Instrument which had so much Share in their Deliberations. Perhaps it will appear to you more simple, Madam, to say that these People could not find any Signs more natural to mark a strict Union, than to smoke in the same Pipe; especially if the Smoke they draw from it, is offered to a Deity who puts the Seal of Religion to it. To smoke in the same Pipe therefore in Token of Alliance, is the same Thing as to drink in the same Cup, as has been practised at all Times by many Nations. These are Customs which are too natural, to seek any Mystery in them.

The Largeness, and the Ornaments of the Calumets, which are presented to Persons of Distinction, and on important Occasions, have nothing neither that should make us search far for the Motive of it. When Men become ever so little acquainted, and have a mutual Respect, they accustom themselves to a certain Regard for one another, chiefly on Occasions of a publick Concern;

cern; or when they strive to gain the Good-will of those with whom they treat; and from thence comes the Care they take to give more Ornament to the Presents they make. For the rest, they say that the Calumet was given by the Sun to the *Panis*, a Nation settled upon the Borders of the *Missouri*, and which extends much towards *New Mexico*. But these Savages have probably done like many other People, they have pretended something marvellous, to make a Custom esteemed, of which they were the Authors; and all that we can conclude from this Tradition is that the *Panis* were the most antient Worshippers of the Sun, or were more distinguished in their Way of Worship of it, than the other Nations of this part of the Continent of *America*, and that they were the first who thought of making the Calumet a Symbol of Alliance. In short if the Calumet was in in its Institution, the *Caduceus* of *Mercury*, it would be employed only for Peace, or for Trade; but it is certain that it is used in Treaties which concern War. These Reflexions, Madam, appeared necessary to me, to give you a perfect Knowledge of what concerns the War of the Savages, which I shall entertain you with in my Letters, till I have entirely exhausted this Subject; if they are Digressions they are not quite foreign to my Subject. Besides, a Traveller endeavours to place in the best Order he can, whatever he learns on his Route.

I am, &c.

LETTER XIII.

A Description of the Country from FAMINE BAY, *to the River of* SABLES. *Motives of the Wars of the Savages. Departure of the Warriors, and what preceeds their Departure. Their Farewell. Their Arms Offensive and Defensive. The Care they take to carry with them their* TUTELAR DEITIES. *Particulars of the Country up to* NIAGARA.

MADAM, River of SABLES, *May* 19.

I AM again detained here by a contrary Wind, which arose the Moment that we were in the fairest Way to proceed. It also surprised us so suddenly, that we should have been in a bad Condition if we had not very luckily met with this little River to shelter us. You must allow, Madam, that there are many Difficulties and Inconveniencies to get over in a Journey like this. It is very melancholy to travel sometimes two hundred Leagues without finding a House, or meeting a Man; not to be

able

able to venture a Traverſe of about two or three Leagues to ſave going twenty, without endangering one's Life by the Caprice of the Winds; to be detained, as it ſometimes happens, whole Weeks on a Point or on a barren Shore, where if it rains you muſt remain under a Canoe or under a Tent: If the Wind is high, you muſt ſeek Shelter in a Wood, where you are not without Danger of being killed by the Fall of a Tree. One might ſhun ſome of theſe Inconveniencies by building Barks, to ſail up the Lakes, but to do this the Trade ought to be of more Worth.

Deſcription of the Coaſt.

We are here upon the Edge of the *Iroquois* Cantons: We embarked Yeſterday early in the Morning, in the fineſt Weather in the World; there was not a Breath of Air, and the Lake was as ſmooth as Glaſs. About nine or ten o'Clock we paſſed the Mouth of the River *Onnontague*, which appears to me about ſeventy Yards wide. The Lands are ſomewhat low, but very well wooded. Almoſt all the Rivers which water the *Iroquois* Cantons flow into this, the Source of which is a Lake called *Gannentaha*, on the Border of which there are ſome Salt Springs. About half an Hour after eleven o'Clock, a little Wind from the North Eaſt made us ſet up our Sail, and in a few Hours carried us to the Bay of *Goyogouins*, which is ten Leagues from *Onnontague*. All the Coaſt in this Space is varied with Marſhes and high Lands, ſomething ſandy, and covered with very fine Trees, eſpecially Oak, which ſeem as if they had been planted by the Hand.

A violent Wind from the Land, which came upon us near the Bay of *Goyogouins*, obliged us to take Shelter in it. It is one of the fineſt Places I ever ſaw. A Peninſula well wooded advances in the Middle, and forms a Kind of Theatre. On the left of the Entrance, we perceived a little Iſland, which hides the Entrance of a River by which the *Goyogouins* deſcend into the Lake. The Wind did not laſt, we purſued our Courſe, and we made three or four Leagues more. This Morning we embarked before the Riſing of the Sun, and we made five or ſix Leagues. I know not how long the North Weſt Wind will keep us here; in the mean time I ſhall reſume my Account of the Wars of the Savages where I broke off.

Motives which engage the Savages to make War.

It ſeldom happens, Madam, that theſe Barbarians refuſe to engage in a War, when they are invited to it by their Allies. They have no Need in general of Invitation to take up Arms; the leaſt Motive or Trifle, even nothing, often induces them to it. Revenge eſpecially: They have always ſome old or new Injury to revenge, for Time never in them heals theſe Sorts of Wounds, how light ſoever they may be.

So

So that there is no depending upon Peace being solidly established between two Nations which have been Enemies a long Time. On the other Hand, the Desire of supplying the Place of the Dead by Prisoners, or of appeasing their Spirits, the Whim of a private Person, a Dream that he explains his own Way, and other Reasons or Pretences as frivolous, are the Causes that we often see a Troop of Adventurers set out for War, who thought of nothing less the Day before.

It is true that these little Expeditions, without the Consent of the Council, are commonly of no great Consequence, and as they require no great Preparations, little Notice is taken of them; and generally speaking, they are not much displeased to see the young People thus exercise themselves, and they must have very good Reasons who would oppose it. Authority is seldom employed for this Purpose, because every one is Master of his own Conduct. But they endeavour to intimidate some by false Reports, which they give out; they solicit others under-hand, they engage the Chiefs by Presents to break the Party, which is very easy; for to this Purpose there needs only a true Dream or a feigned one. In some Nations the last Resource is to apply to the Matrons, and this is almost always effectual; but they never have Recourse to this but when the Affair is of great Consequence.

The Manner how a War is resolved on.

A War which concerns all the Nation is not concluded on so easily: They weigh with a great deal of Thought the Inconveniencies and the Advantages of it; and whilst they deliberate, they are extremely careful to avoid every Thing that would give the Enemy the least Cause to suspect that they intend to break with them. War being resolved on, they directly consider of the Provisions and the Equipage of the Warriors, and this does not require much Time. The Dances, Songs, Feasts, and some superstitious Ceremonies, which vary much, according to the different Nations, require much more.

The Preparations of the Chief.

He who is to command does not think of raising Soldiers till he has fasted several Days, during which he is smeared with black, has scarce any Conversation with any one, invokes Day and Night his tutelar Spirit, and above all, is very careful to observe his Dreams. Being fully persuaded, according to the presumptuous Nature of these Savages, that he is going to obtain a Victory, he seldom fails of having Dreams according to his Wishes. The Fast being over, he assembles his Friends, and with a Collar of Beads in his Hand, he speaks to them in these Terms, "My "Brethren, the Great Spirit authorises my Sentiments, and in-"spires me with what I ought to do: The Blood of such a

" one is not wiped away, his Body is not covered, and I will " acquit myself of this Duty towards him." He declares also the other Motives which make him take Arms. Then he adds, " I am therefore resoved to go to such a Place, to pull off " Scalps, or to make Prisoners; or else I will eat such or such a " Nation. If I perish in this glorious Enterprize, or if any of " those who will accompany me should lose their Lives, this " Collar shall serve to receive us, that we may not continue to " lie in the Dust, or in the Dirt." By which is meant, probably, that it shall belong to him who shall take Care to bury the dead. In pronouncing these last Words, he lays the Collar on the Ground, and he who takes it up, declares himself by doing it his Lieutenant: Then he thanks him for the Zeal he shews to revenge his Brother, or to support the Honour of his Nation. Afterwards they heat Water, they wash the Face of the Chief, they set his Hair in Order, grease it, and paint it. They also paint his Face with various Colours, and put on his finest Robe. Thus adorned, he sings in a low Tone the Song of Death; his Soldiers, *that is to say*, all who have offered to accompany him, (for no Person is constrained to go) then sing out with a loud Voice, one after another, their War-Song; for every Man has his own, which no other is allowed to sing. There are some also peculiar to each Family.

The Deliberation of the Council.

After this Preliminary, which passes in a remote Place, and often in a Stove, the Chief goes to communicate his Project to the Council, which consults upon it without ever admitting to this Consultation, the Author of the Enterprize. As soon as his Project is accepted, he makes a Feast, of which the chief, and sometimes the only Dish, must be a Dog. Some pretend that this Animal is offered to the God of War before it is put into the Kettle, and perhaps this is the Custom among some Nations. For I must inform you here, Madam, that what I shall say to you on this Article, I do not warrant to be the general Custom among all the Nations. But it appears certain, that on the Occasion now mentioned, they make a great many Invocations to all the Spirits good and evil, and above all to the God of War.

The Measures they take to get Prisoners.

All this lasts many Days, or rather is repeated many Days together: And though all the People seem entirely employed in these Feasts, each Family takes their Measures to have its Share of the Prisoners that shall be made, in order to repair their Losses, or to revenge their Slain. With this View they make Presents to the Chief, who, on his Side, gives his Word and Pledges. In Case of Want of Prisoners they ask Scalps, and

and this is easier to obtain. In some Places, as among the *Iroquois*, as soon as a military Expedition is resolved upon, they set on the Fire the Kettle of War, and they give Notice to their Allies to bring something for it; in doing which they declare that they approve the Undertaking, and will go Part in it.

All those who engage themselves, give to the Chief, as a Sign of their Engagement, a Bit of Wood, with their Mark. Whoever, after this, should go back from his Word, would run a Risque of his Life, at least he would be disgraced for ever. The Party being formed, the War Chief prepares a new Feast, to which all the Village must be invited; and before any Thing is touched, he says, or an Orator for him, and in his Name, "Brethren, I know that I am not yet a Man, but you know, nevertheless, that I have seen the Enemy near enough. We have been slain, the Bones of such and such a one remain yet uncovered, they cry out against us, we must satisfy them: They were Men; how could we forget them so soon, and remain so long quiet upon our Mats? In short, the Spirit that is interested in my Glory has inspired me to revenge them. Young Men take Courage, dress your Hair, paint your Faces, fill your Quivers, and make our Forests echo with your Songs of War; let us relieve the Cares of our dead, and inform them that they are going to be revenged."

Songs and Dances, and the Feasts of the Warriors.

After this Discourse, and the Applauses that never fail to follow it, the Chief advances into the midst of the Assembly with his Fighting-Club or Head-breaker in his Hand, and sings; all his Soldiers answer him singing, and swear to support him well, or to die in the Attempt. All this is accompanied with very expressive Gestures, to make one understand that they will not fly from the Enemy. But it is to be remarked, that no Soldier drops any Expression that denotes the least Dependence. They only promise to act with a great deal of Union and Harmony. On the other Hand, the Engagement they take, requires great Returns from the Chiefs. For Instance, every Time that in the public Dances, a Savage, striking his Hatchet upon a Post set up on Purpose, puts the Assembly in Mind of his brave Actions, as it always happens, the Chief under whose Conduct he performed them, is obliged to make him a Present; at least this is the Custom among some Nations.

The Notion these People have of Courage.

The Songs are followed by Dances: Sometimes it is only walking with a proud Step, but keeping Time; at other Times they have pretty lively Motions, representing the Operations of a Campaign, and always keeping Time. At length the Feast puts an End to the Ceremony. The War-Chief is only a Spectator of it, with a Pipe in his Mouth: It is the same Thing commonly in all their Feasts of Preparation, that he who gives them, touches nothing. The following Days, and till the Departure of the Warriors, there passes many Things which are not worth Notice, and which are not constantly practised. But I must not forget a Custom which is singular enough, and which the *Iroquois* never dispense with: It appears to have been invented to discover those who have Sense, and know how to be Masters of themselves; for these People whom we treat as Barbarians, cannot conceive that any Man can have true Courage if he is not Master of his Passions, and if he cannot bear the highest Provocations: This is their Way of proceeding.

The Trial which they make of their Warriors.

The oldest of the Military Troop affront the young People in the most injurious Manner they can think of, especially those who have never yet seen their Enemy: They throw hot Coals upon their Heads, they make them the sharpest Reproaches, they load them with the most injurious Expressions, and carry this Game to the greatest Extremities. This must be endured with a perfect Insensibility: To shew on these Occasions the least Sign of Impatience, would be enough to be judged unworthy of bearing Arms for ever. But when it is practised by People of the same Age, as it often happens, the Aggressor must be well assured that he has nothing to account for himself, otherwise when the Game is done, he would be obliged to make Amends for the Insult by a Present: I say, when the Game is done; for all the Time it lasts, they must suffer every Thing without being angry, though the Joke is often carried so far as to throw Firebrands at their Heads, and to give them great Blows with a Cudgel.

The Precautions for the wounded.

As the Hope of being cured of their Wounds, if they have the Misfortune to receive any, does not contribute a little to engage the bravest to expose themselves to the greatest Dangers, after what I have related, they prepare Drugs, about which their Jugglers are employed. I shall tell you another Time what Sort of People these Jugglers are. All the Village being assembled, one of these Quacks declares that he is going to communicate to the Roots and Plants, of which he has made a good Provision, the Virtue of healing all Sorts of Wounds, and even of restoring Life to the dead. Immediately he begins to sing, other Jugglers answer him; and they suppose that during the Concert, which you may imagine is not very harmonious, and which is accompanied with many Grimaces of the Actors, the healing Virtue is communicated to the Drugs. The principal Juggler

Juggler proves them afterwards: He begins by making his Lips bleed, he applies his Remedy; the Blood, which the Impoſtor takes Care to ſuck in dexterouſly, ceaſes to run, and they cry out a *Miracle!* After this he takes a dead Animal, he gives the Company Time enough to be well aſſured that he is dead, then by the Means of a Pipe which he has thruſt under the Tail, he cauſes it to move, in blowing ſome Herbs into its Mouth, and their Cries of Admiration are redoubled. Laſtly, all the Troop of Jugglers go round the Cabins ſinging the Virtue of their Medicines. Theſe Artifices at the Bottom do not impoſe on any one; but they amuſe the Multitude, and Cuſtom muſt be followed.

Some particular Cuſtoms of the Miamis *to prepare themſelves for War.*

There is another Cuſtom peculiar to the *Miamis*, and perhaps to ſome Nations in the Neighbourhood of *Louiſiana*. I had theſe Particulars from a *Frenchman*, who was a Witneſs of them. After a ſolemn Feaſt, they placed, ſaid he, on a Kind of Altar, ſome Pagods made with Bear Skins, the Heads of which were painted green. All the Savages paſſed this Altar bowing their Knees, and the Jugglers lead the Van, holding in their Hands a Sack which contained all the Things which they uſe in their Conjurations. They all ſtrove to exceed each other in their Contorſions, and as any one diſtinguiſhed himſelf in this Way, they applauded him with great Shouts. When they had thus paid their firſt Homage to the Idol, all the People danced in much Confuſion, to the Sound of a Drum and a *Chichicoué*; and during this Time the Jugglers made a Shew of bewitching ſome of the Savages, who ſeemed ready to expire: Then putting a certain Powder upon their Lips, they made them recover. When this Farce had laſted ſome Time, he who preſided at the Feaſt, having at his Sides two Men and two Women, run through all the Cabins to give the Savages Notice that the Sacrifices were going to begin. When he met any one in his Way, he put both his Hands on his Head, and the Perſon met embraced his Knees. The Victims were to be Dogs, and one heard on every Side the Cries of theſe Animals, whoſe Throats they cut; and the Savages, who howled with all their Strength, ſeemed to imitate their Cries. As ſoon as the Fleſh was dreſſed, they offered it to the Idols; then they eat it, and burnt the Bones. All this while the Jugglers never ceaſed raiſing the pretended dead, and the whole ended by the Diſtribution that was made to theſe Quacks, of whatever was found moſt to their Liking in all the Village.

From

From the Time that the Resolution is taken to make War, till the Departure of the Warriors, they sing their War-Songs every Night: The Days are passed in making Preparations. They depute some Warriors to go to sing the War-Song amongst their Neighbours and Allies, whom they engage beforehand by secret Negociations. If they are to go by Water, they build, or repair their Canoes: If it is Winter they furnish themselves with Snow Shoes and Sledges.

A Description of the Racquets for walking upon the Snow; and of the Sledges for carrying the Baggage.

The Raquets which they must have to walk on the Snow are about three Feet long, and about fifteen or sixteen Inches in their greatest Breadth. Their Shape is oval, excepting the End behind, which terminates in a Point; little Sticks placed across at five or six Inches from each End, serve to strengthen them, and the Piece which is before is in the Shape of a Bow, where the Foot is fixed, and tied with Leather Thongs. The Binding of the Raquet is made of Slips of Leather about a sixth Part of an Inch wide, and the Circumference is of light Wood hardened by Fire. To walk well with these Raquets, they must turn their Knees a little inwards, and keep their Legs wide asunder. It is some Trouble to accustom ones self to it, but when one is used to it, one walks with as much Ease and as little Fatigue as if one had nothing on ones Feet. It is not possible to use the Raquets with our common Shoes, we must take those of the Savages, which are a Kind of Socks, made of Skins dried in the Smoke, folded over at the End of the Foot, and tied with Strings. The Sledges which serve to carry the Baggage, and in Case of Need the sick and wounded, are two little Boards, very thin, about half a Foot broad each Board, and six or seven Feet long. The fore Part is a little bent upwards, and the Sides are bordered by little Bands, to which they fasten Straps to bind what is upon the Sledge. However loaded these Carriages may be, a Savage can draw them with Ease by the Help of a long Band of Leather, which he puts over his Breast, and which they call Collars. They draw Burdens this Way, and the Mothers use them to carry Children with their Cradles, but then it is over their Foreheads that the Band is fixed.

The Farewell of of the Warriors.

All Things being ready, and the Day of Departure being come, they take their Leave with great Demonstration of real Tenderness. Every Body desires something that has been used by the Warriors, and in Return give them some Pledges of their Friendship, and Assurances of a perpetual Remembrance. They scarce enter any Cabin, but they take away their Robe to give them a better, at least one as good. Lastly, they all meet at the Cabin of the Chief: They find him armed as he was the first Day he

spoke

ſpoke to them; and as he always appeared in publick from that Day. They then paint their Faces, every one according to his own Fancy, and all of them in a very frightful Manner. The Chief makes them a ſhort Speech; then he comes out of his Cabin, ſinging his Song of Death: They all follow him in a Line, keeping a profound Silence, and they do the ſame every Morning when they renew their March. Here the Women go before with the Proviſions; and when the Warriors come up with them, they give them their Clothes, and remain almoſt naked, at leaſt as much as the Seaſon will permit.

Of their Arms, offenſive and defenſive.

Formerly the Arms of theſe People were Bows and Arrows, and a Kind of Javelin; which, as well as their Arrows, was armed with a Point of Bone wrought in different Shapes. Beſides this, they had what they call the Head-breaker: This is a little Club of very hard Wood, the Head of which is round, and has one Side with an Edge to cut. The greateſt Part have no defenſive Arms; but when they attack an Intrenchment, they cover their whole Body with little light Boards: Some have a Sort of Cuiraſs made of Ruſhes, or ſmall pliable Sticks, pretty well wrought: They had alſo Defences for their Arms and Thighs of the ſame Matter. But as this Armour was not found to be Proof againſt Fire Arms, they have left it off, and uſe nothing in its Stead. The Weſtern Savages always make Uſe of Bucklers of Bulls Hides, which are very light, and which a Muſket-Ball will not pierce. It is ſomething ſurpriſing that the other Nations do not uſe them.

When they make Uſe of our Swords, which is very ſeldom, they uſe them like Spontoons; but when they can get Guns, and Powder, and Ball, they lay aſide their Bows and Arrows, and ſhoot very well. We have often had Reaſon to repent of letting them have any Fire Arms; but it was not we who firſt did it: The *Iroquois* having got ſome of the *Dutch*, then in Poſſeſſion of *New York*, we were under a Neceſſity of giving the ſame to our Allies. Theſe Savages have a Kind of Enſigns to know one another, and to rally by: Theſe are little Pieces of Bark cut round, which they put on the Top of a Pole, and on which they have traced the Mark of their Nation, and of their Village. If the Party is numerous, each Family or Tribe has its Enſign with its diſtinguiſhing Mark: Their Arms are alſo diſtinguiſhed with different Figures, and ſometimes with a particular Mark of the Chief.

Of the Care they take to carry their Deities.

But what the Savages would ſtill leſs forget than their Arms, and which they have the greateſt Care about they are capable of, are their *Manitous*. I ſhall ſpeak of them more largely in another Place: It ſuffices to ſay here, that they are the

the Symbols under which every one represents his familiar Spirit. They put them into a Sack, painted of various Colours; and often, to do Honour to the Chief, they place this Sack in the fore Part of his Canoe. If there are too many *Manitous* to be contained in one Sack, they distribute them into several, which are entrusted to the Keeping of the Lieutenant and the Elders of each Family: They put with these the Presents which have been made to have Prisoners, with the Tongues of all the Animals they have killed during the Campaign, and of which they must make a Sacrifice to the Spirits at their Return.

In their Marches by Land, the Chief carries his Sack himself, which he calls his *Mat*; but he may ease himself of this Burthen, by giving it to any one he chuses; and he need not fear that any Person should refuse to relieve him, because this carries with it a Mark of Distinction. This is, as it were, a Right of Reversion to the Command, in Case the Chief and his Lieutenant should die during the Campaign.

But whilst I am writing to you, Madam, I am arrived in the River of *Niagara*, where I am going to find good Company, and where I shall stay some Days. I departed from the River of *Sables* the 21st, before Sun-rise; but the Wind continuing against us, we were obliged at Ten o'Clock to enter the Bay of the *Tsonnonthouans*. Half Way from the River of *Sables* to this Bay, there is a little River, which I would not have failed to have visited, if I had been sooner informed of its Singularity, and of what I have just now learnt on my arriving here.

Of the River of Casconchiagon.

They call this River *Casconchiagon*: It is very narrow, and of little Depth at its Entrance into the Lake. A little higher, it is one hundred and forty Yards wide, and they say it is deep enough for the largest Vessels. Two Leagues from its Mouth, we are stopped by a Fall which appears to be sixty Feet high, and one hundred and forty Yards wide. A Musket Shot higher, we find a second of the same Width, but not so high by two thirds. Half a League further, a third, one hundred Feet high, good Measure, and two hundred Yards wide. After this, we meet with several Torrents; and after having failed fifty Leagues further, we perceive a fourth Fall, every Way equal to the third. The Course of this River is one hundred Leagues; and when we have gone up it about sixty Leagues, we have but ten to go by Land, taking to the Right, to arrive at the *Ohio*, called *La belle Riviere*: The Place where we meet with it, is called *Ganos*; where an Officer worthy of Credit *(a)*, and

(a) M. *de Joncaire*, at present a Captain in the Troops of *New France*.

the ſame from whom I learnt what I have juſt now mentioned, aſſured me that he had ſeen a Fountain, the Water of which is like Oil, and has the Taſte of Iron. He ſaid alſo, that a little further there is another Fountain exactly like it, and that the Savages make Uſe of its Water to appeaſe all Manner of Pains.

A Deſcription of the Bay of the Tſonnonthouans.

The Bay of the *Tſonnonthouans* is a charming Place: A pretty River winds here between two fine Meadows, bordered with little Hills, between which we diſcover Vallies which extend a great Way, and the whole forms the fineſt Proſpect in the World, bounded by a great Foreſt of high Trees; but the Soil appears to me to be ſomething light and ſandy.

We continued our Courſe at half an Hour paſt One, and we ſailed till Ten o'Clock at Night. We intended to go into a little River which they called *La Rivière aux Bœufs, (Ox River)*; but we found the Entrance ſhut up by Sands, which often happens to the little Rivers which run into the Lakes, becauſe they bring down with them much Sand; and when the Wind comes from the Lakes, theſe Sands are ſtopped by the Waves, and form by Degrees a Bank ſo high and ſo ſtrong, that theſe Rivers cannot break through it, unleſs it be when their Waters are ſwelled by the melting of the Snow.

Of the River Niagara.

I was therefore obliged to paſs the reſt of the Night in my Canoe, where I was forced to endure a pretty ſharp Froſt. Indeed one could ſcarcely here perceive the Shrubs begin to bud: All the Trees were as bare as in the Midſt of Winter. We departed from thence at half an Hour paſt Three in the Morning, the 22d, being *Aſcenſion-Day*, and I went to ſay Maſs at Nine o'Clock in what they call *le Grand Marais, (the great Marſh)*. This is a Bay much like that of the *Tſonnonthouans*, but the Land here appeared to me not to be ſo good. About Two in the Afternoon we entered into the River *Niagara*, formed by the great Fall which I ſhall mention preſently; or rather, it is the River *St. Laurence*, which comes out of the Lake *Erié*, and paſſes through the Lake *Ontario*, after a Streight of fourteen Leagues. They call it the River of *Niagara* from the Fall, and this Space is about ſix Leagues. We go South at the Entrance. When we have made three Leagues, we find upon the Left Hand ſome Cabins of *Iroquois Tſonnonthouans*, and ſome *Miſſiſaguez*, as at *Catarocoui*. The Sieur *Joncaire*, a Lieutenant in our Troops, has alſo a Cabin here, to which they give before-hand the Name of *Fort (a)*; for they ſay that in Time it will be changed into a real Fortreſs.

(a) The Fort has been built ſince at the Entrance of the River *Niagara*, on the ſame Side, and exactly in the Place where M. *de Denonville* had built one, which did not ſubſiſt a long Time. There is alſo here the Beginnings of a *French* Village.

I found here ſeveral Officers, who muſt return in a few Days to *Quebec*, which obliges me to cloſe this Letter, that I may ſend it by this Opportunity. As for myſelf, I foreſee I ſhall have Time enough after their Departure to write you another; and the Place itſelf will furniſh me with enough to fill it, with that which I ſhall learn farther from the Officers I have mentioned.

I am, &c.

LETTER XIV.

What paſſed between the Tſonnonthouans *and the* Engliſh, *on the Occaſion of our Settlement at* Niagara. *The* Fire-Dance: *A Story on this Occaſion. A Deſcription of the Fall of* Niagara.

MADAM, FALL OF NIAGARA, *May* 26.

I Have already had the Honour to inform you that we have here a Project of a Settlement. To underſtand well the Occaſion of it, you muſt know, that by Virtue of the Treaty of *Utrecht*, the *Engliſh* pretend to have a Right to the Sovereignty of all the Country of the *Iroquois*, and of Conſequence to have no Bounds on that Side but the Lake *Ontario*. Nevertheleſs, it was conceived that if their Pretenſions took Place, it would ſoon be in their Power to ſettle themſelves ſtrongly in the Centre of the *French* Colony, or at leaſt to ruin their Trade entirely. It was therefore thought proper to guard againſt this Inconvenience; nevertheleſs, without any Infringement of the Treaty: And there was no Method found better than to ſeat ourſelves in a Place which ſhould ſecure to us the free Communication of the Lakes, and where the *Engliſh* had no Power to oppoſe our Settlement. The Commiſſion for this Purpoſe was given to M. *de Joncaire*; who having been a Priſoner in his Youth amongſt the *Tſonnonthouans*, gained ſo much the Favour of theſe Savages, that they adopted him: And even in the greateſt Heat of the Wars which we have had againſt them, in which he ſerved very honourably, he has always enjoyed the Privileges of his Adoption.

As ſoon as M. *de Joncaire* received his Orders for the Execution of the Project I have mentioned, he went to the *Tſonnonthouans*, and aſſembled the Chiefs; and after having aſſured them that he had no greater Pleaſure in the World than to live among his Brethren, he added alſo, that he would viſit them much oftener, if he had a Cabin among them, where he might retire when he wanted to enjoy his Liberty. They replied, that they had never

never ceaſed to look upon him as one of their Children; that he might live in any Place, and that he might chuſe the Place that he judged moſt convenient. He required no more: He came directly here, fixed upon a Spot by the Side of the River that terminates the Canton of the *Tſonnonthouans*, and built a Cabin upon it. The News was ſoon carried to *New York*, and cauſed there ſo much the more Jealouſy, as the *Engliſh* had never been able to obtain in any of the *Iroquois* Cantons what was now granted to the Sieur *Joncaire*.

The English *oppoſe this Settlement without Effect.*

They complained in a haughty Manner, and their Complaints were ſupported by Preſents, which brought the other four Cantons into their Intereſt: But this ſignified nothing, becauſe the *Iroquois* Cantons are independent of each other, and very jealous of this Independence: It was therefore neceſſary to gain the *Tſonnonthouans*, and the *Engliſh* left no Means untried for this Purpoſe; but they ſoon perceived that they ſhould never ſucceed in diſlodging M. *de Joncaire* from *Niagara*. Then they reduced their Terms to this Requeſt, that at leaſt they might be permitted to have a Cabin in the ſame Place. "Our "Land is in Peace, (ſaid the *Tſonnonthouans* to them) the *French* "and you cannot live together without diſturbing it: Fur- "thermore, (added they) it is of no Conſequence that M. *de Joncaire* dwells here; he is a Child of the Nation; he enjoys "his Right, and we have no Right to deprive him of it."

Deſcription of the Country of Niagara.

We muſt allow, Madam, that there is ſcarce any Thing but a Zeal for the public Good that can engage an Officer to live in a Country like this. It is impoſſible to ſee one more ſavage and frightful. On one Side we ſee under our Feet, and as it were in the Bottom of an Abyſs, a great River indeed; but which, in this Place, reſembles more a Torrent by its Rapidity, and by the Whirlpools which a thouſand Rocks make in it, through which it has much Difficulty to find a Paſſage, and by the Foam with which it is always covered. On the other Side, the View is covered by three Mountains ſet one upon another, the laſt of which loſes itſelf in the Clouds; and the Poets might well have ſaid, that it was in this Place the *Titans* would have ſcaled Heaven. In ſhort, which Way ſoever you turn your Eyes, you do not diſcover any Thing but what inſpires a ſecret Horror.

It is true that we need not go far to ſee a great Change. Behind theſe wild and uninhabitable Mountains we ſee a rich Soil, magnificent Foreſts, pleaſant and fruitful Hills: We breathe a pure Air, and enjoy a temperate Climate, between two

Lakes, the least *(a)* of which is two hundred and fifty Leagues in Compass.

It appears to me, that if we had had the Precaution to have secured ourselves early by a good Fortress, and by a moderate peopling of a Post of this Importance, all the Forces of the *Iroquois* and the *English* joined together, would not be capable at this Time of driving us out of it, and that we should be ourselves in a Condition to give Laws to the first, and to hinder the greatest Part of the Savages from carrying their Peltry to the second, as they do with Impunity every Day.

The Company which I found here with M. *de Joncaire*, was composed of the Baron *de Longueil*, the King's Lieutenant at *Montreal*, and the Marquis *de Cavagnal*, Son of the Marquis *de Vaudreuil*, the present Governor General of *New France*, and of M. *de Senneville*, Captain, and the Sieur *de la Chauvignerie*, Ensign, and the King's Interpreter for the *Iroquois* Language. These Gentlemen are going to negociate an Accommodation with the Canton of *Onnontagué*, and had Orders to visit the Settlement of M. *de Joncaire*, with which they were very well satisfied. The *Tsonnonthouans* renewed to them the Promise they had made to support him. This was done in a Council; where M. *de Joncaire*, as I have been told, spoke with all the Sense of the most sensible *Frenchman*, and with the most sublime *Iroquois* Eloquence.

A Description of the Fire-Dance.

The Night before their Departure, *that is to say*, the 24th, a *Missisagué* gave us an Entertainment which is something singular. He was quite naked when it began; and when we entered the Cabin of this Savage, we found a Fire lighted, near which a Man beat (singing at the same Time) upon a Kind of Drum: Another shook, without ceasing his *Chichikoué*, and sung also. This lasted two Hours, till we were quite tired of it; for they said always the same Thing, or rather they formed Sounds that were but half articulate, without any Variation. We begged of the Master of the Cabin to put an End to this Prelude, and it was with much Reluctance he gave us this Mark of his Complaisance. Then we saw appear five or six Women; who placing themselves Side by Side on the same Line, as close as they could to each other, with their Arms hanging down, sung and danced, *that is to say*, without breaking the Line, they made some Steps in Cadence, sometimes forward and sometimes backward. When they had continued this about a Quarter of an Hour, they put out the Fire, which alone gave Light to the Cabin; and then we saw nothing but a Savage, who had in his Mouth a lighted Coal, and who danced. The Symphony of the Drum and the *Chichi-*

koué

(a) The Lake *Ontario*. The Lake *Erié* is three hundred Leagues in Compass.

koué ſtill continued. The Women renewed from Time to Time their Dances and their Song. The Savage danced all the Time; but as he was only to be diſtinguiſhed by the faint Gloom of the lighted Coal which he had in his Mouth, he appeared like a Spectre, and made a horrible Sight. This Mixture of Dances, Songs, Inſtruments, and the Fire of the Coal which ſtill kept lighted, had ſomething odd and ſavage, which amuſed us for half an Hour; after which we went out of the Cabin, but the Sport continued till Day-light. And this is all, Madam, that I have ſeen of the *Fire-Dance*. I could never learn what paſſed the reſt of the Night. The Muſick, which I heard ſtill ſome Time, was more tolerable at a Diſtance than near. The Contraſt of the Voices of the Men and Women, at a certain Diſtance, had an Effect that was pretty enough; and one may ſay, that if the Women Savages had a good Manner of ſinging, it would be a Pleaſure to hear them ſing.

A Story on this Subject.

I had a great Deſire to know how a Man could hold a lighted Coal ſo long in his Mouth, without burning it, and without its being extinguiſhed; but all that I could learn of it was, that the Savages know a Plant which ſecures the Part that is rubbed with it from being burnt, and that they would never communicate the Knowledge of it to the *Europeans*. We know that Garlick and Onions will produce the ſame Effect, but then it is only for a ſhort Time *(a)*. On the other Hand, how could this Coal continue ſo long on Fire? However this may be, I remember to have read in the Letters of one of our antient Miſſionaries of *Canada* ſomething like this, and which he had from another Miſſionary who was a Witneſs thereof. This laſt ſhewed him one Day a Stone, which a Juggler had thrown into the Fire in his Preſence, and left it there till it was thoroughly heated; after which, growing, as it were furious, he took it between his Teeth, and carrying it all the Way thus, he went to ſee a ſick Perſon, whither the Miſſionary followed him. Upon entering the Cabin, he threw the Stone upon the Ground; and the Miſſionary having taken it up, he found printed in it the Marks of the Teeth of the Savage, in whoſe Mouth he perceived no Marks of Burning. The Miſſionary does not ſay what the Juggler did afterwards for the Relief of the ſick Perſon.——The following is a Fact of the ſame Kind, which comes from the ſame Source, and of which you may make what Judgment you pleaſe.

(a) They ſay that the Leaf of the Plant of the Anemony of *Canada*, though of a cauſtick Nature in itſelf, has this Virtue.

A *Huron* Woman, after a Dream, real or imaginary, was taken with a ſwimming of the Head, and almoſt a general Contraction of the Sinews. As from the Beginning of this Diſtemper ſhe never ſlept without a great Number of Dreams, which troubled her much, ſhe gueſſed there was ſome Myſtery in it, and took it into her Head that ſhe ſhould be cured by Means of a Feaſt; of which ſhe regulated herſelf the Ceremonies, according to what ſhe remembered, as ſhe ſaid, of what ſhe had ſeen practiſed before. She deſired that they would carry her directly to the Village where ſhe was born; and the Elders whom ſhe acquainted with her Deſign, exhorted all the People to accompany her. In a Moment her Cabin was filled with People, who came to offer their Services: She accepted them, and inſtructed them what they were to do; and immediately the ſtrongeſt put her into a Baſket, and carried her by Turns, ſinging with all their Strength.

Another remarkable Story of a Cure.

When it was known ſhe was near the Village, they aſſembled a great Council, and out of Reſpect they invited the Miſſionaries to it, who in vain did every Thing in their Power to diſſuade them from a Thing in which they had Reaſon to ſuſpect there was as much Superſtition as Folly. They liſtened quietly to all they could ſay on this Subject; but when they had done ſpeaking, one of the Chiefs of the Council undertook to refute their Diſcourſe: He could not effect this; but ſetting aſide the Miſſionaries, he exhorted all the People to acquit themſelves exactly of all that ſhould be ordered, and to maintain the antient Cuſtoms. Whilſt he was ſpeaking, two Meſſengers from the ſick Perſon entered the Aſſembly, and brought News that ſhe would ſoon arrive; and deſired, at her Requeſt, that they would ſend to meet her two Boys and two Girls, dreſſed in Robes and Necklaces, with ſuch Preſents as ſhe named; adding, that ſhe would declare her Intentions to theſe four Perſons. All this was performed immediately; and a little Time after, the four young Perſons return'd with their Hands empty, and almoſt naked, the ſick Woman having obliged them to give her every Thing, even to their Robes. In this Condition they entered into the Council, which was ſtill aſſembled, and there explained the Demands of this Woman: They contained twenty-two Articles; amongſt which was a blue Coverlet, which was to be ſupplied by the Miſſionaries; and all theſe Things were to be delivered immediately: They tried all Means to obtain the Coverlet, but were conſtantly refuſed, and they were obliged to go without it. As ſoon as the ſick Woman had received the other Preſents, ſhe entered the Village, carried in the Manner as before. In the Evening a public Cryer gave Notice, by her Order, to keep Fires lighted in all the

Cabins,

Cabins, becauſe ſhe was to viſit them all; which ſhe did as ſoon as the Sun was ſet, ſupported by two Men, and followed by all the Village. She paſſed through the Midſt of all the Fires, her Feet and her Legs being naked, and felt no Pain; whilſt her two Supporters, though they kept as far from the Fires as they poſſibly could, ſuffered much by them; for they were to lead her thus through more than three hundred Fires. As for the ſick Woman, they never heard her complain but of Cold; and at the End of this Courſe, ſhe declared that ſhe found herſelf eaſed.

The next Day, at Sun-riſe, they began, by her Order ſtill, a Sort of Bacchanal, which laſted three Days: The firſt Day the People ran through all the Cabins, breaking and overſetting every Thing; and by Degrees, as the Noiſe and Hurly-burly encreaſed, the ſick Woman aſſured them that her Pains diminiſhed. The two next Days were employed in going over all the Hearths ſhe had paſſed before; and in propoſing her Deſires in enigmatical Terms; they were to find them out by Gueſs, and accompliſh them directly. There were ſome of them horribly obſcene. The fourth Day the ſick Woman made a ſecond Viſit to all the Cabins, but in a different Manner from the firſt: She was in the Midſt of two Bands of Savages, who marched in a Row with a ſad and languiſhing Air, and kept a profound Silence: They ſuffered no Perſon to come in her Way; and thoſe who were at the Head of her Eſcort, took Care to drive all thoſe away that they met. As ſoon as the ſick Woman was entered into a Cabin, they made her ſit down, and they placed themſelves round her: She ſighed, and gave an Account of her Sufferings in a very affecting Tone, and made them to underſtand that her perfect Cure depended on the Accompliſhment of her Deſire, which ſhe did not explain, but they muſt gueſs: Every one did the beſt they could; but this Deſire was very complicated: It contained many Things: As they named any one, they were obliged to give it her, and in general ſhe never went out of a Cabin till ſhe had got every Thing in it. When ſhe ſaw that they could not gueſs right, ſhe expreſſed herſelf more plainly; and when they had gueſſed all, ſhe cauſed every Thing to be reſtored which ſhe had received. Then they no longer doubted but that ſhe was cured. They made a Feaſt, which conſiſted in Cries, or rather frightful Howlings, and in all Sorts of extravagant Actions. Laſtly, ſhe returned Thanks; and the better to ſhew her Acknowledgment, ſhe viſited a third Time all the Cabins, but without any Ceremony.

The Miſſionary who was preſent at this ridiculous Scene ſays, that ſhe was not entirely cured, but was much better than before: Nevertheleſs, a ſtrong and healthy Perſon would have been killed by this Ceremony. This Father took Care to obſerve

serve to them, that her pretended Genius had promised her a perfect Cure, and had not kept his Word. They replied, that in such a great Number of Things commanded, it was very difficult not to have omitted one. He expected that they would have insisted principally on the Refusal of the Coverlet; and in Fact they did just mention it; but they added, that after this Refusal the Genius appeared to the sick Woman, and assured her that this Incident should not do her any Prejudice, because as the *French* were not the natural Inhabitants of the Country, the Genii had no Power over them.———But to return to my Journey.

Description of the Fall of Niagara.

When our Officers went away, I ascended those frightful Mountains I spoke of, to go to the famous Fall of *Niagara*, above which I was to embark. This Journey is three Leagues: It was formerly five, because they passed to the other Side of the River; *that is to say*, to the West, and they did not re-embark but at two Leagues above the Fall: But they have found on the Left, about half a Mile from this Cataract, a Bay where the Current is not perceiveable, and of Consequence where one may embark without Danger. My first Care, at my Arrival, was to visit the finest Cascade perhaps in the World; but I directly found the Baron *de la Hontan* was mistaken, both as to its Height and its Form, in such a Manner as to make me think he had never seen it. It is certain that if we measure its Height by the three Mountains which we must first pass over, there is not much to bate of the six hundred Feet which the Map of M. *Delisle* gives it; who, without Doubt, did not advance this Paradox, but on the Credit of Baron *de la Hontan* and Father *Hennepin*. But after I arrived at the Top of the third Mountain, I observed that in the Space of the three Leagues, which I travelled afterwards to this Fall of Water, tho' we must sometimes ascend, we descended still more; and this is what these Travellers do not seem to have well considered. As we cannot approach the Cascade but by the Side, nor see it but in Profile, it is not easy to measure it with Instruments: We tried to do it with a long Cord fastened to a Pole; and after we had often tried this Way, we found the Depth but one hundred and fifteen, or one hundred and twenty Feet: But we could not be sure that the Pole was not stopped by some Rock which juts out; for although it was always drawn up wet, as also the End of the Cord to which it was fastened, this proves nothing, because the Water which falls from the Mountain rebounds very high in a Foam. As for myself, after I had viewed it from all the Places where one may examine it most easily, I judged one could not give it less than one hundred and forty, or one hundred and fifty Feet.

As

As to its Shape, it is in the Form of a Horſe-ſhoe, and about four hundred Paces in Circumference; but exactly in the Middle it is divided into two by a very narrow Iſland about half a Mile long, which comes to a Point here. But theſe two Parts do ſoon unite again: That which was on my Side, and which is only ſeen in Profile, has ſeveral Points which jut out; but that which I ſaw in Front, appeared to me very ſmooth. The Baron *de la Hontan* adds to this a Torrent which comes from the Weſt; but if this was not invented by the Author, we muſt ſay that in the Time of the Snow's melting, the Waters come to diſcharge themſelves here by ſome Gutter.

You may very well ſuppoſe, Madam, that below this Fall the River is for a long Way affected by this rude Shock, and indeed it is not navigable but at three Leagues Diſtance, and exactly at the Place where M. *de Joncaire* is ſituated. One would imagine it ſhould not be leſs navigable higher up, ſince the River falls here perpendicularly in its whole Breadth. But beſides this Iſle, which divides it in two, ſeveral Shelves ſcattered here and there at the Sides of, and above this Iſland, much abate the Rapidity of the Current. It is nevertheleſs ſo ſtrong, notwithſtanding all this, that ten or twelve *Outaouais* endeavouring one Day to croſs the Iſland, to ſhun ſome *Iroquois* who purſued them, were carried away with the Current down the Precipice, in Spite of whatever Struggles they could make to avoid it.

Obſervations on this Caſcade.

I have been told that the Fiſh that are brought into this Current, are killed thereby, and that the Savages ſettled in theſe Parts make an Advantage of it; but I ſaw no ſuch Thing. I have alſo been aſſured, that the Birds that attempted to fly over it, were ſometimes drawn into the Vortex which was formed in the Air by the Violence of this Torrent; but I obſerved quite the contrary. I ſaw ſome little Birds flying about, directly over the Fall, which came away without any Difficulty. This Sheet of Water is received upon a Rock; and two Reaſons perſuade me that it has found here, or perhaps has made here by Length of Time, a Cavern which has ſome Depth. The firſt is, that the Noiſe it makes is very dead, and like Thunder at a Diſtance. It is ſcarcely to be heard at M. *de Joncaire*'s Cabin, and perhaps alſo what one hears there, is only the daſhing of the Water againſt the Rocks, which fill the Bed of the River up to this Place: And the rather, becauſe above the Cataract the Noiſe is not heard near ſo far. The ſecond Reaſon is, that nothing has ever re-appeared (as they ſay) of all that has fallen into it, not even the Wreck of the Canoe of the *Outaouais* I mentioned juſt now. However this may be, *Ovid* gives us a Deſcription of ſuch a Cataract, which he ſays is in the delightful Valley of *Tempe*. The Country about *Niagara* is far from being ſo fine, but I think its Cataract is much finer *(a)*.

For the reſt, I perceived no Miſt over it, but from behind. At a Diſtance one would take it for Smoke; and it would deceive any Perſon that ſhould come in Sight of the Iſland, without knowing before-hand that there is ſuch a ſurpriſing Cataract in this Place. The Soil of the three Leagues which I travelled on Foot to come here, and which they call the Portage of *Niagara*, does not appear good: It is alſo badly wooded; and one cannot go ten Steps without walking upon an Ant-Hill, or without meeting with Rattle-Snakes.——I believe, Madam, that I told you that the Savages eat as a Dainty the Fleſh of theſe Reptiles; and, in general, Serpents do not cauſe any Horror to theſe People: There is no Animal, the Form of which is oftener marked upon their Faces, and on other Parts of their Bodies, and they never hunt them but to eat. The Bones and the Skins of Serpents are alſo much uſed by the Jugglers and Sorcerers, to perform their Deluſions, and they make themſelves Fillets and Girdles of their Skins. It is alſo true, that they have the Secret of enchanting them, or, to ſpeak more properly, of benumbing them; ſo that they take them alive, handle them, and put them in their Boſoms, without receiving any Hurt; and this helps to confirm the high Opinion theſe People have of them.

Some Circumſtances of the March of the Warriors.

I was going to cloſe this Letter, when I was informed that we ſhould not depart To-morrow, as I expected. I muſt bear it with Patience, and make good Uſe of the Time. I ſhall therefore proceed on the Article of the Wars of the Savages, which will not be ſoon finiſhed.—As ſoon as all the Warriors are embarked, the Canoes at firſt go a little Way, and range themſelves cloſe together upon a Line: Then the Chief riſes up, and holding a *Chichicoué* in his Hand, he thunders out his Song of War, and his Soldiers anſwer him by a treble *Hé*, drawn with all their Strength from the Bottom of their Breaſts. The Elders and the Chiefs of the Council who remain upon the Shore, exhort the Warriors to behave well, and eſpecially not to ſuffer themſelves to be ſurpriſed. Of all the Advice that can be given to a Savage, this is the moſt neceſſary, and that of which in general he makes the leaſt Benefit.

(a) Eſt nemus Hæmoniæ prærupta quod undiq; claudit
Sylva, vocant Tempe, per quæ Peneus ab imo
Effuſus Pindo ſpumoſis volvitur Undis.
Dejectiſque gravi tenues agitantia Fumos
Nubila conducit, ſummiſque aſpergine ſylvas
Impluit, & ſonitu pluſquam vicina fatigat.

This Exhortation does not interrupt the Chief, who continues ſinging. Laſtly, the Warriors conjure their Relations and Friends not to forget them: Then ſending forth all together hideous Howlings, they ſet off directly and row with ſuch Speed that they are ſoon out of Sight.

The *Hurons* and the *Iroquois* do not uſe the *Chichicoué*, but they give them to their Priſoners: So that theſe Inſtruments, which amongſt others is an Inſtrument of War, ſeem amongſt them to be a Mark of Slavery. The Warriors ſeldom make any ſhort Marches, eſpecially when the Troop is numerous. But on the other Hand, they take Preſages from every Thing; and the Jugglers, whoſe Buſineſs it is to explain them, haſten or retard the Marches at their Pleaſure. Whilſt they are not in a ſuſpected Country, they take no Precaution, and frequently one ſhall ſcarce find two or three Warriors together, each taking his own Way to hunt; but how far ſoever they ſtray from the Route, they all return punctually to the Place, and at the Hour, appointed for their Rendezvous.

Of their encamping.

They encamp a long Time before Sun-ſet, and commonly they leave before the Camp a large Space ſurrounded with Paliſades, or rather a Sort of Lattice, on which they place their *Manitous*, turned towards the Place they are going to. They invoke them for an Hour, and they do the ſame every Morning before they decamp. After this they think they have nothing to fear, they ſuppoſe that the Spirits take upon them to be Centinels, and all the Army ſleeps quietly under their ſuppoſed Safeguard. Experience does not undeceive theſe Barbarians, nor bring them out of their preſumptuous Confidence. It has its Source in an Indolence and Lazineſs which nothing can conquer.

Of the meeting of different Parties of War.

Every one is an Enemy in the Way of the Warriors; but nevertheleſs, if they meet any of their Allies, or any Parties nearly equal in Force of People with whom they have no Quarrel, they make Friendſhip with each other. If the Allies they meet are at War with the ſame Enemy, the Chief of the ſtrongeſt Party, or of that which took up Arms firſt, gives ſome Scalps to the other, which they are always provided with for theſe Occaſions, and ſays to him, "*You have done your Buſineſs*; that is to ſay, you have fulfilled your Engagement, your Honour is ſafe, you may return Home." But this is to be underſtood when the Meeting is accidental, when they have not appointed them, and when they have no Occaſion for a Reinforcement. When they are juſt entering upon an Enemy's Country, they ſtop for a Ceremony which is ſomething ſingular. At Night they make a great Feaſt, after which they lay down to ſleep: As ſoon as they are awake, thoſe who have had any Dreams go from Fire to Fire, ſinging their Song of Death, with which they intermix their Dreams in an enigmatical Manner. Every one racks his Brain to gueſs them, and if nobody can do it, thoſe who have dreamt are at Liberty to return Home. This gives a fine Opportunity to Cowards. Then they make new Invocations to the Spirits; they animate each other more than ever to do Wonders; they ſwear to aſſiſt each other, and then they renew their March: And if they came thither by Water, they quit their Canoes, which they hide very carefully. If every Thing was to be obſerved that is preſcribed on theſe Occaſions, it would be difficult to ſurpriſe a Party of War that is entered into an Enemy's Country. They ought to make no more Fires, no more Cries, nor hunt no more, nor even ſpeak to each other but by Signs: But theſe Laws are ill obſerved. Every Savage is born preſumptuous, and incapable of the leaſt Reſtraint. They ſeldom neglect, however, to ſend out every Evening ſome Rangers, who employ two or three Hours in looking round the Country: If they have ſeen nothing, they go to ſleep quietly, and they leave the Guard of the Camp again to the *Manitous*.

Of their Approaches and Attacks.

As ſoon as they have diſcovered the Enemy, they ſend out a Party to reconnoitre them, and on their Report they hold a Council. The Attack is generally made at Day-break. They ſuppoſe the Enemy is at this Time in their deepeſt Sleep, and all Night they lie on their Bellies, without ſtirring. The Approaches are made in the ſame Poſture, crawling on their Feet and Hands till they come to the Place: Then all riſe up, the Chief gives the Signal by a little Cry, to which all the Troop anſwers by real Howlings, and they make at the ſame Time their firſt Diſcharge: Then without giving the Enemy any Time to look about, they fall upon them with their Clubs. In latter Times theſe People have ſubſtituted little Hatchets, in the ſtead of theſe wooden *Head-breakers*, which they call by the ſame Name; ſince which their Engagements are more bloody. When the Battle is over they take the Scalps of the dead and the dying; and they never think of making Priſoners till the Enemy makes no more Reſiſtance.

If they find the Enemy on their Guard, or too well intrenched, they retire if they have Time for it; if not, they take the Reſolution to fight ſtoutly, and there is ſometimes much Blood ſhed on both Sides. The Attack of a Camp is the Image of Fury itſelf; the barbarous Fierceneſs of the Conquerors, and the Deſpair of the Vanquiſhed, who know what they muſt expect if they fall into the Hands of their Enemies, produce on either Side ſuch Efforts as paſs all Deſcription. The Appearance of the Combatants all beſmeared with black and red, ſtill encreases the Horror of the Fight; and from this Pattern one might make a true Picture of Hell. When the Victory is no longer doubtful, they directly dispatch all those whom it would be too troublesome to carry away, and seek only to tire out the rest they intend to make Prisoners.

The Savages are naturally intrepid, and notwithstanding their brutal Fierceness, they yet preserve in the midst of Action much Coolness. Nevertheless they never fight in the Field but when they cannot avoid it. Their Reason is, that a Victory marked with the Blood of the Conquerors, is not properly a Victory, and that the Glory of a Chief consists principally in bringing back all his People safe and sound. I have been told, that when two Enemies that are acquainted meet in the Fight, there sometimes passes between them Dialogues much like that of *Homer*'s Heroes. I do not think this happens in the Height of the Engagement; but it may happen that in little Rencounters, or perhaps before passing a Brook, or forcing an Intrenchment, they say something by Way of Defiance, or to call to Mind some such former Rencounter.

Their Instinct to know the Mark of their Enemies Steps.

War is commonly made by a Surprize, and it generally succeeds; for as the Savages very frequently neglect the Precautions necessary to shun a Surprise, so are they active and skilful in surprising. On the other Hand, these People have a wonderful Talent, I might say an Instinct, to know if any Person has passed through any Place. On the shortest Grass, on the hardest Ground, even upon Stones, they discover some Traces, and by the Way they are turned, by the Shape of their Feet, by the Manner they are separated from each other, they distinguish, as they say, the Footsteps of different Nations, and those of Men from those of Women. I thought a long Time that there was some Exaggeration in this Matter, but the Reports of those who have lived among the Savages are so unanimous herein, that I see no Room to doubt of their Sincerity:

Precautions to secure their Retreat and to keep their Prisoners.

Till the Conquerors are in a Country of Safety, they march forward expeditiously; and lest the Wounded should retard their Retreat, they carry them by turns on Litters, or draw them in Sledges in Winter. When they re-enter their Canoes, they make their Prisoners sing, and they practise the same Thing every Time they meet any Allies; an Honour which costs them a Feast who receive it, and the unfortunate Captives something more than the Trouble of Singing: For they invite the Allies to caress them, and to *caress* a Prisoner is to do him all the Mischief they can devise, or to maim him in such a Manner that he is lamed for ever. But there are

some

ſome Chiefs who take ſome Care of theſe Wretches, and do not ſuffer them to be too much abuſed. But nothing is equal to the Care they take to keep them, by Day they are tied by the Neck, and by the Arms to one of the Bars of the Canoe. When they go by Land there is always one that holds them; and at Night they are ſtretched upon the Earth quite naked; ſome Cords faſtened to Piquets, fixed in the Ground, keep their Legs, Arms, and Necks ſo confined that they cannot ſtir, and ſome long Cords alſo confine their Hands and Feet, in ſuch a Manner that they cannot make the leaſt Motion without waking the Savages, who lye upon theſe Cords.

If among the Priſoners there are found any, who by their Wounds are not in a Condition of being carried away, they burn them directly; and as this is done in the firſt Heat, and when they are often in Haſte to retreat, they are for the moſt Part quit at an eaſier Rate than the others, who are reſerved for a ſlower Puniſhment.

Of the Marks they leave of their Victory.

The Cuſtom among ſome Nations is, that the Chief of the victorious Party leaves on the Field of Battle his Fighting Club, on which he had taken Care to trace the Mark of his Nation, that of his Family, and his Portrait; *that is to ſay*, an Oval, with all the Figures he had in his Face. Others paint all theſe Marks on the Trunk of a Tree, or on a Piece of Bark, with Charcoal pounded and rubbed, mixed with ſome Colours. They add ſome Hieroglyphic Characters, by Means of which thoſe who paſs by may know even the minuteſt Circumſtances, not only of the Action, but alſo of the whole Tranſactions of the Campaign. They know the Chief of the Party by all the Marks I have mentioned: The Number of his Exploits by ſo many Mats, that of his Soldiers by Lines; that of the Priſoners carried away by little *Marmoſets* placed on a Stick, or on a *Chichicoué*; that of the dead by human Figures without Heads, with Differences to diſtinguiſh the Men, the Women, and the Children. But theſe Marks are not always ſet up near the Place where the Action happened, for when a Party is purſued, they place them out of their Route, on Purpoſe to deceive their Purſuers.

How they proclaim their Victory in the Villages.

When the Warriors are arrived at a certain Diſtance from the Village from whence they came, they halt, and the Chief ſends one to give Notice of his Approach. Among ſome Nations, as ſoon as the Meſſenger is within hearing, he makes various Cries, which give a general Idea of the principal Adventures and Succeſs of the Campaign: He marks the Number of Men they have loſt by ſo many Cries of Death. Immediate-

ly

ly the young People come out to hear the Particulars: Sometimes the whole Village comes out, but one alone addresses the Messenger, and learns from him the Detail of the News which he brings: As the Messenger relates a Fact the other repeats it aloud, turning towards those who accompanied him, and they answer him by Acclamations or dismal Cries, according as the News is mournful or pleasing. The Messenger is then conducted to a Cabin, where the Elders put to him the same Questions as before; after which a publick Crier invites all the young People to go to meet the Warriors, and the Women to carry them Refreshments. —— In some Places they only think at first of mourning for those they have lost. The Messenger makes only Cries of Death. They do not go to meet him, but at his entering the Village he finds all the People assembled, he relates in a few Words all that has passed, then retires to his Cabin, where they carry him Food; and for some Time they do nothing but mourn for the dead.

When this Time is expired, they make another Cry to proclaim the Victory. Then every one dries up his Tears, and they think of nothing but rejoicing. Something like this is practised at the Return of the Hunters: The Women who stayed in the Village go to meet them as soon as they are informed of their Approach, and before they enquire of the Success of their Hunting, they inform them by their Tears of the Deaths that have happened since their Departure.—To return to the Warriors, the Moment when the Women join them, is properly speaking the Beginning of the Punishment of the Prisoners: And when some of them are intended to be adopted, which is not allowed to be done by all Nations; their future Parents, whom they take Care to inform of it, go and receive them at a little Distance, and conduct them to their Cabins by some round-about Ways. In general the Captives are a long Time ignorant of their Fate, and there are few who escape the first Fury of the Women.

I am, &c.

LET-

LETTER XV.

The first Reception of the Prisoners. The Triumph of the Warriors. The Distribution of the Captives: How they decide their Fate, and what follows after. With what Inhumanity they treat those who are condemned to die: The Courage they shew. The Negociations of the Savages.

MADAM, *At the Entrance of Lake* ERIE, *May* 27.

I Departed this Morning from the Fall of *Niagara*, I had about seven Leagues to go to the Lake *Erié*, and I did it without any Trouble. We reckoned that we should not lay here this Night; but whilst my People rowed with all their Strength I have pretty well forwarded another Letter, and while they take a little Rest I will finish it to give it to some *Canadians* whom we met here, and who are going to *Montreal*. I take up my Recital where I left off last.

The first Reception of the Prisoners.

All the Prisoners that are destined to Death, and those whose fate is not yet decided, are as I have already told You, Madam, abandoned to the Fury of the Women, who go to meet the Warriors; and it is surprising that they resist all the Evils they make them suffer. If any one, especially, has lost either her Son or her Husband, or any other Person that was dear to her, tho' this Loss had happened thirty Years before, she is a Fury. She attacks the first who falls under her Hand; and one can scarcely imagine how far she is transported with Rage: She has no Regard either to Humanity or Decency, and every Wound she gives him, one would expect him to fall dead at her Feet, if we did not know how ingenious these Barbarians are in prolonging the most unheard of Punishment: All the Night passes in this Manner in the Camp of the Warriors.

The Triumph of Warriors.

The next Day is the Day of the Triumph of the Warriors. The *Iroquois*, and some others, affect a great Modesty and a still greater Disinterestedness on these Occasions. The Chiefs enter alone into the Village, without any Mark of Victory, keeping a profound Silence, and retire to their Cabins, without shewing that they have the least Pretension to the Prisoners. Among other Nations the same Custom is not observed: The Chief marches at the Head of his Troop with the Air of a Conqueror: His Lieutenant comes after him, and a Crier goes before, who is ordered to renew the Death Cries. The Warriors follow by two and two, the Prisoners in the Midst, crowned with Flowers, their Faces and Hair painted, holding a Stick in one Hand, and a *Chichikoue* in the other, their Bodies almost naked, their Arms tied above the Elbow with a Cord, the End of which is held by the Warriors, and they sing without ceasing their Death Song to the Sound of the *Chichikone*.

The Boastings of the Prisoners.

This Song has something mournful and haughty at the same Time; and the Captive has nothing of the Air of a Man who suffers, and that is vanquished. This is pretty near the Sense of these Songs: "*I am brave and intrepid; I do not fear Death, nor any* "*Kind of Tortures: Those who fear them, are Cowards; they are* "*less than Women: Life is nothing to those that have Courage: May* "*my Enemies be confounded with Despair and Rage: Oh! that I* "*could devour them, and drink their Blood to the last Drop.*" From Time to Time they stop them: The People gather round them, and dance, and make the Prisoners dance: They seem to do it with a good Will; they relate the finest Actions of their Lives; they name all those they have killed or burnt; and they make particular Mention of those for whom the People present are most concerned. One would say that they only seek to animate more and more against them the Masters of their Fate. In Fact, these Boastings make those who hear them, quite furious, and they pay dear for their Vanity: But by the Manner in which they receive the most cruel Treatment, one would say that they take a Pleasure in being tormented.

What they make them suffer at their Entrance into the Village.

Sometimes they oblige the Prisoners to run through two Ranks of Savages, armed with Stones and Sticks, who fall upon them as if they would knock them on the Head at the first Blow; yet it never happens that they kill them; so much Care do they take, even when they seem to strike at Random, and that their Hand is guided by Fury alone, not to touch any Part that would endanger Life. In this March every one has a Right to torment them; they are indeed allow'd to defend themselves; but they would, if they were to attempt it, soon be overpower'd. As soon as they are arrived at the Village, they lead them from Cabin to Cabin, and every where they make them pay their Welcome: In one Place they pull off one of their Nails, in another they bite off one of their Fingers, or cut it off with a bad Knife, which cuts like a Saw: An old Man tears their Flesh quite to the Bone: A Child with an Awl wounds them where he can: A Woman whips them without Mercy, till she is so tired that she cannot lift up her Hands: But none of the Warriors lay their Hands upon them, although they are still their Masters; and no one can mutilate the Prisoners without their Leave, which they seldom grant: But this excepted, they have an entire Liberty to make them suffer; and if they lead them through several Villages, either of the same Nation, or their Neighbours or Allies who have desired it, they are received every where in the same Manner.

The Distribution of the Captives.

After these Preludes, they set about the Distribution of the Captives, and their Fate depends on those to whom they are delivered. At the Rising of the Council, where they have consulted of their Fate, a Crier invites all the People to come to an open Place, where the Distribution is made without any Noise or Dispute. The Women who have lost their Children or Husbands in the War, generally receive the first Lot. In the next Place they fulfil the Promises made to those who have given Collars. If there are not Captives enough for this Purpose, they supply the Want of them by Scalps; with which those who receive them, adorn themselves on rejoicing Days; and at other Times they hang them up at the Doors of their Cabins. On the contrary, if the Number of Prisoners exceeds that of the Claimants, they send the Overplus to the Villages of their Allies. A Chief is not replaced, but by a Chief, or by two or three ordinary Persons, who are always burnt, although those whom they replace had died of Diseases. The *Iroquois* never fail to set apart some of their Prisoners for the Publick, and these the Council dispose of as they think proper: But the Mothers of Families may still set aside their Sentence, and are the Mistresses of the Life and Death even of those who have been condemned or absolved by the Council.

How they decide their Fate.

In some Nations the Warriors do not entirely deprive themselves of the Right of disposing of their Captives; and they to whom the Council give them, are obliged to put them again into their Hands, if they require it: But they do it very seldom; and when they do it, they are obliged to return the Pledges or Presents received from those Persons. If, on their Arrival, they have declared their Intentions on this Subject, it is seldom opposed. In general, the greatest Number of the Prisoners of War are condemned to Death, or to very hard Slavery, in which their Lives are never secure. Some are adopted; and from that Time their Condition differs in nothing from that of the Children of the Nation: They enter into all the Rights of those whose Places they supply; and they often acquire so far the Spirit of the Nation of which they are become Members, that they make no Difficulty of going to War against their own Countrymen. The *Iroquois* would have scarcely supported themselves hitherto, but by this Policy. Having been at War many Years against all the other Nations, they would at present have been reduced al-

most

most to nothing, if they had not taken great Care to naturalize a good Part of their Prisoners of War.

It sometimes happens, that instead of sending into the other Villages the Surplus of their Captives, they give them to private Persons, who had not asked for any; and, in this Case, either they are not so far Masters of them, as not to be obliged to consult the Chiefs of the Council how they shall dispose of them; or else they are obliged to adopt them. In the first Case, he to whom they make a Present of a Slave, sends for him by one of his Family; then he fastens him to the Door of his Cabin, and assembles the Chiefs of the Council; to whom he declares his Intentions, and asks their Advice. This Advice is generally agreeable to his Desire. In the second Case, the Council, in giving the Prisoner to the Person they have determined on, say to him, "It is a long Time we have been "deprived of such a one, your Relation, or your Friend, who was a "Support of our Village." Or else, "We regret the Spirit of such "a one whom you have lost; and who, by his Wisdom, maintained "the publick Tranquility: He must appear again this Day; he "was too dear to us, and too precious to defer his Revival any "longer: We place him again on his Mat, in the Person of this "Prisoner."

There are, nevertheless, some private Persons that are in all Appearance more considered than others; to whom they make a Present of a Captive, without any Conditions, and with full Liberty to do what they please with him: And then the Council express themselves in these Terms, when they put him in their Hands, "This is to repair the Loss of such a one, and to cleanse "the Heart of his Father, of his Mother, of his Wife, and of his "Children. If you are either willing to make them drink the "Broth of this Flesh, or that you had rather replace the Deceased "on his Mat, in the Person of this Captive, you may dispose of "him as you please."

Of the Adoption of a Captive.

When a Prisoner is adopted, they lead him to the Cabin where he must live; and the first Thing they do, is to untie him. Then they warm some Water to wash him: They dress his Wounds, if he has any; and if they were even putrified, and full of Worms, he is soon cured: They omit nothing to make him forget his Sufferings, they make him eat, and clothe him decently. In a Word, they would not do more for one of their own Children, nor for him whom *he raises from the Dead*, this is their Expression.------Some Days after, they make a Feast; during which they solemnly give him the Name of the Person whom he replaces, and whose Rights he not only acquires from that Time, but he lays himself also under the same Obligations.

Amongſt the *Hurons*, and the *Iroquois*, thoſe Priſoners they intend to burn, are ſometimes as well treated at firſt, and even till the Moment of their Execution, as thoſe that have been adopted. It appears as if they were Victims which they fattened for the Sacrifice, and they are really a Sacrifice to the God of War. The only Difference they make between theſe and the other, is, that they blacken their Faces all over: After this, they entertain them in the beſt Manner they are able: They always ſpeak kindly to them; they give them the Name of *Sons*, *Brothers*, or *Nephews*, according to the Perſon whoſe Manes they are to appeaſe by their Death: They alſo ſometimes give them young Women, to ſerve them for Wives all the Time they have to live. But when they are informed of their Fate, they muſt be well kept, to prevent their eſcaping. Therefore oftentimes this is concealed from them.

Of thoſe that are to be burnt.

When they have been delivered to a Woman, the Moment they inform her every Thing is ready for Execution, ſhe is no longer a Mother, ſhe is a Fury, who paſſes from the tendereſt Careſſes to the greateſt Exceſs of Rage: She begins by invoking the Spirit of him ſhe deſires to revenge: " Approach, (ſays ſhe) you are going to be appeaſed; I prepare a Feaſt for thee; " drink great Draughts of this Broth which is going to be poured " out for thee; receive the Sacrifice I make to thee in ſacri- " ficing this Warrior; he ſhall be burnt, and put in the Ket- " tle; they ſhall apply red-hot Hatchets to his Fleſh; they ſhall " pull off his Scalp; they ſhall drink in his Skull: Make therefoe " no more Complaints; thou ſhalt be fully ſatisfied."------This Form of Speech, which is properly the Sentence of Death, varies much as to the Terms; but for the Meaning, it is always much the ſame. Then a Cryer makes the Captive come out of the Cabin, and declares in a loud Voice the Intention of him or her to whom he belongs, and finiſhes by exhorting the young People to behave well: Another ſucceeds, who addreſſes him that is to ſuffer, and ſays, " *Brother, take Courage; thou art going to be burnt:* " And he anſwers coolly, " *That is well, I give thee Thanks.*" Immediately there is a Cry made through the whole Village, and the Priſoner is led to the Place of his Puniſhment. For the moſt Part they tie him to a Poſt by the Hands and Feet; but in ſuch a Manner, that he can turn round it: But ſometimes, when the Execution is made in a Cabin from whence there is no Danger of his eſcaping, they let him run from one End to the other. Before they begin to burn him, he ſings for the laſt Time his Death-Song: Then he recites his Atchievements, and almoſt always in a Manner the moſt inſulting to thoſe he perceives around him. Then he exhorts them not to ſpare him, but to remember that he is a Man, and a Warrior.

How they receive their Sentence of Condemnation.

Either

Either I am much mistaken: Or, what ought most to surprise us in these tragical and barbarous Scenes, is not that the Sufferer should sing aloud, that he should insult and defy his Executioners, as they all generally do to the last Moment of their Breath; for there is in this an Haughtiness which elevates the Spirit, which transports it, which takes it off something from the Thoughts of its Sufferings, and which hinders it also from shewing too much Sensibility. ------- Moreover, the Motions they make, divert their Thoughts, take off the Edge of the Pain, and produce the same Effect, and something more, than Cries and Tears. In short, they that there are no Hopes of Mercy, and Despair gives Resolution, and inspires Boldness.

The Principle of the Barbarity they exercise on these Occasions.

But this Kind of Insensibility is not so general as many have thought: It is not unusual to hear these poor Wretches send forth Cries that are capable of piercing the hardest Heart; but which have no other Effect, but to make Sport for the Actors, and the rest that are present.--As to the Causes that should produce in the Savages an Inhumanity, which we could never have believed Men to have been guilty of, I believe they acquired it by Degrees, and have been used to it insensibly by Custom; that a Desire of seeing their Enemy behave meanly, the Insults which the Sufferers do not cease to make to their Tormentors, the Desire of Revenge, which is the reigning Passion of this People, and which they do not think sufficiently glutted whilst the Courage of those who are the Object of it is not subdued, and lastly Superstition, have a great Share in it: For what Excesses are not produced by a false Zeal, guided by so many Passions.

I shall not, Madam, relate the Particulars of all that passes in these horrible Executions: It would carry me too far; because in this there is no Uniformity, nor any Rules but Caprice and Fury. Often there are as many Actors as Spectators; *that is to say*, all the Inhabitants of the Village, Men, Women, and Children, and every one does the worst they can. There are only those of the Cabin to which the Prisoner was delivered, that forbear to torment him; at least, this is the Practice of many Nations. Commonly they begin by burning the Feet, then the Legs; and thus go upwards to the Head: And sometimes they make the Punishment last a whole Week; as it happened to a Gentleman of *Canada* amongst the *Iroquois*. They are the least spared, who having already been taken and adopted, or set at Liberty, are taken a second Time. They look upon them as unnatural Children, or ungrateful Wretches, who have made War with their Parents and Benefactors, and they shew them no Mercy. It happens sometimes that the Sufferer, even when he is not executed in a Cabin, is not tied, and is allowed

to

to defend himself; which he does, much less in Hopes of saving his Life, than to revenge his Death before-hand, and to have the Glory of dying bravely. We have seen, on these Occasions, how much Strength and Courage these Passions can inspire. Here follows an Instance, which is warranted by Eye-Witnesses, who are worthy of Credit.

Courage of an ONNEYOUTH *Captain burnt by the* HURONS.

An *Iroquois*, Captain of the Canton of *Onneyouth*, chose rather to expose himself to every Thing, than to disgrace himself by a Flight, which he judged of dangerous Consequence to the young People that were under his Command. He fought a long Time like a Man who was resolved to die with his Arms in his Hands; but the *Hurons*, who opposed him, were resolved to have him alive, and he was taken. Happily for him, and for those who were taken with him, they were carried to a Village, where some Missionaries resided, who were allowed full Liberty of discoursing with them. These Fathers found them of a Docility which they looked upon as the Beginning of the Grace of their Conversion; they instructed them, and baptized them: They were all burnt a few Days after, and shewed even till Death a Resolution, which the Savages are not yet acquainted with, and which even the Infidels attributed to the Virtue of the Sacraments.

The *Onneyouth* Captain nevertheless believed that he was still allowed to do his Enemies all the Mischief he could, and to put off his Death as much as possible. They made him get upon a Sort of Stage, where they began to burn him all over the Body without any Mercy, and he appeared at first as unconcerned as if he had felt nothing; but as he thought one of his Companions that was tormented near him, shewed some Marks of Weakness, he shewed on this Account a great Uneasiness, and omitted nothing that might encourage him to suffer with Patience, by the Hope of the Happiness they were going to enjoy in Heaven; and he had the Comfort to see him die like a brave Man, and a Christian.

Then all those who had put the other to Death, fell again upon him with so much Fury, that one would have thought they were going to tear him in Pieces. He did not appear to be at all moved at it, and they knew not any longer in what Part they could make him feel Pain; when one of his Tormentors cut the Skin of his Head all round, and pull'd it off with great Violence. The Pain made him drop down senseless: They thought him dead, and all the People went away: A little Time after, he recovered from his Swoon; and seeing no Person near him, but the dead Body of his Companion, he takes a Fire-brand in both his Hands, though they were all overflead and burnt, re-calls his Tormentors, and defies them to approach him. They were affrighted at his Resolution, they sent forth horrid Cries, and armed themselves, some

with

with burning Fire-brands, others with red-hot Irons, and fell upon him all together. He received them bravely, and made them retreat. The Fire with which he was ſurrounded ſerved him for an Intrenchment, and he made another with the Ladders that had been uſed to get upon the Scaffold; and being thus fortified in his own Funeral Pile, now become the Theatre of his Valour, and armed with the Inſtruments of his Puniſhment, he was for ſome Time the Terror of a whole Village, no Body daring to approach a Man that was more than half burnt, and whoſe Blood flowed from all Parts of his Body.

A falſe Step which he made in ſtriving to ſhun a Fire-brand that was thrown at him, left him once more to the Mercy of his Tormentors: And I need not tell you that they made him pay dear for the Fright he had juſt before put them in. After they were tired with tormenting him, they threw him into the Midſt of a great Fire, and left him there, thinking it impoſſible for him ever to riſe up again. They were deceived: When they leaſt thought of it, they ſaw him, arm'd with Fire-brands, run towards the Village, as if he would ſet it on Fire. All the People were ſtruck with Terror, and no Perſon had the Courage to ſtop him: But as he came near the firſt Cabin, a Stick that was thrown between his Legs, threw him down, and they fell upon him before he could riſe: They directly cut off his Hands and Feet, and then rolled him upon ſome burning Coals; and laſtly, they threw him under the Trunk of a Tree that was burning. Then all the Village came round him, to enjoy the Pleaſure of ſeeing him burn. The Blood which flowed from him, almoſt extinguiſhed the Fire; and they were no longer afraid of his Efforts: But yet he made one more, which aſtoniſhed the boldeſt: He crawled out upon his Elbows and Knees with a threatening Look and a Stoutneſs which drove away the neareſt; more indeed from Aſtoniſhment, than Fear; for what Harm could he do them in this maimed Condition? Some Time after, a *Huron* took him at an Advantage, and cut off his Head.

The Skill of theſe People in their Negociations.

Nevertheleſs, Madam, if theſe People make War like Barbarians, we muſt allow that in their Treaties of Peace, and generally in all their Negotiations they diſcover a Dexterity, and a Nobleneſs of Sentiments, which would do Honour to the moſt poliſhed Nations. They have no Notion of making Conqueſts and extending their Dominions. Many Nations have no Domain properly ſo called, and thoſe who have not wandered from their Country, and look upon themſelves as Maſters of their Lands, are not ſo far jealous of them, as to be offended with any one who ſettles upon them, provided they give the Nation no Diſturbance. Therefore, in their Treaties, they conſider nothing but to make themſelves Allies againſt power-

ful

ful Enemies, to put an End to a War that is troublesome to both Parties; or rather, to suspend Hostilities: For I have already observed, that the Wars are perpetual that are between Nation and Nation; so that there is no depending upon a Treaty of Peace, so long as one of the two Parties can give any Jealousy to the other. All the Time they negociate, and before they enter into a Negociation, their principal Care is not to appear to make the first Steps, or at least to persuade their Enemy that it is neither through Fear or Necessity that they do it: And this is managed with the greatest Dexterity. A Plenipotentiary does not abate any Thing of his Stiffness, when the Affairs of his Nation are in the worst Condition; and he often succeeds in persuading those he treats with, that it is their Interest to put an End to Hostilities, though they are Conquerors: He is under the greatest Obligations to employ all his Wit and Eloquence; for if his Proposals are not approved of, he must take great Care to keep upon his Guard. It is not uncommon that the Stroke of a Hatchet is the only Answer they make him: He is not out of Danger, even when he has escaped the first Surprise: He must expect to be pursued, and burnt, if he is taken. And that such a Violence will be coloured with some Pretence as Reprisals. This has happened to some *French* among the *Iroquois*, to whom they were sent by the Governor General: And during many Years, the *Jesuits*, who lived among these Barbarians, tho' they were under the public Protection, and were in some Manner the common Agents of the Colony, found themselves every Day in Danger of being sacrificed to a Revenge, or to be the Victims of an Intrigue of the Governors of *New York*. Lastly, it is surprising that these People, who never make War through Interest, and who carry their Disinterestedness to such a Degree, that the Warriors do never burden themselves with the Spoils of the Conquered, and never touch the Garments of the Dead; and if they bring back any Booty, give it up to the first that will take it; in a Word, who never take up Arms but for Glory, or to be revenged of their Enemies: It is, I say, surprising to see them so well versed as they are in the Arts of the most refined Policy, and to maintain Pensioners among their Enemies. They have also, in Respect to these Sort of Ministers, a Custom which appears at first View odd enough, which may nevertheless be looked upon as the Effect of a great Prudence: Which is, that they never rely upon the Advices they have from their Pensioners, if they do not accompany them with some Presents: They conceive, without Doubt, that to make it prudent to rely on such Advices, it is necessary that not only he who gives them should have nothing to hope for, but also that it should cost him omething to give them, that the ſole Intereſt of the Public good might engage him to it, and that he ſhould not do it too lightly.

I am, &c.

LETTER XVI.

Deſcription of Lake ERIE. *Voyage to* DETROIT *(the* STRAIT*): A Project of a Settlement in this Place: How it failed. The Commandant of the Fort de* PONTCHARTRAIN *holds a Council, and on what Occaſion. The Games of the Savages.*

MADAM, *Fort de Pontchartrain at Detroit, June* 8.

I Departed the 27th from the Entrance of the Lake *Erié*, after I had cloſed my laſt Letter, and though it was very late I went three Leagues that Day by the Favour of a good Wind, and of the fineſt Weather in the World: The Rout is to keep to the North Coaſt, and it is a hundred Leagues. From *Niagara*, taking to the South, it is much more pleaſant, but longer by half. Lake *Erié* is a hundred Leagues long from Eaſt to Weſt: Its Breadth from North to South is thirty, or thereabouts. The Name it bears is that of a Nation of the *Huron* Language ſettled on its Border, and which the *Iroquois* have entirely deſtroyed. *Erié* means *Cat*, and the *Eriés* are named in ſome Relations *the Nation of the Cat*. This Name comes probably from the great Number of theſe Animals that are found in this Country: They are bigger than our's, and their Skins are much valued. Some modern Maps have given Lake *Erié* the Name of *Conti*; but this Name is diſuſed, as well as thoſe of *Condé*, *Tracy*, and *Orleans*, formerly given to Lake *Huron*, the *Upper Lake*, and Lake *Michigan*.

Deſcription of Lake Erié.

The 28th I went nineteen Leagues, and found myſelf over againſt the *Great River*, which comes from the Eaſt, in forty-two Degrees fifteen Minutes. Nevertheleſs, the great Trees were not yet green. This Country appeared to me very fine. We made very little Way the 29th, and none at all the 30th. We embarked the next Day about Sun-riſe, and went forward apace. The firſt of June, being *Whit-Sunday*, after going up a pretty River almoſt an Hour, which comes a great Way, and runs between two fine Meadows, we made a Portage about ſixty Paces, to eſcape going round a Point which advances fifteen Leagues

Of the northern Coaſt.

into

into the Lake; they call it the *Long Point:* It is very ſandy, and produces naturally many Vines. The following Days I ſaw nothing remarkable; but I coaſted a charming Country, that was hid from Time to Time by ſome diſagreeable Skreens, but of little Depth. In every Place where I landed, I was inchanted with the Beauty and Variety of a Landſcape, bounded by the fineſt Foreſts in the World: Beſides this, Water-Fowl ſwarmed every where: I cannot ſay there is ſuch Plenty of Game in the Woods; but I know that on the South Side there are vaſt Herds of wild Cattle.

The Pleaſure of theſe Journeys.

If one always travelled, as I did then, with a clear Sky, and a charming Climate, on a Water as bright as the fineſt Fountain, and were to meet every where with ſafe and pleaſant Encampings, where one might find all Manner of Game at little Coſt, breathing at one's Eaſe a pure Air, and enjoying the Sight of the fineſt Countries, one would be tempted to travel all one's Life. It put me in Mind of thoſe antient Patriarchs who had no fixed Abode, dwelt under Tents, were in ſome Manner Maſters of all the Countries they travelled over, and peaceably enjoyed all their Productions, without having the Trouble which is unavoidable in the Poſſeſſion of a real Domain. How many Oaks repreſented to me that of *Mamré?* How many Fountains made me remember that of *Jacob?* Every Day a new Situation of my own chuſing; a neat and convenient Houſe ſet up and furniſhed with Neceſſaries in a Quarter of an Hour, ſpread with Flowers always freſh, on a fine green Carpet; and on every Side plain and natural Beauties, which Art had not altered, and which it cannot imitate. If theſe Pleaſures ſuffer ſome Interruption, either by bad Weather, or ſome unforeſeen Accident, they are the more reliſhed when they re-appear.

If I had a Mind to moralize I ſhould add, theſe Alternatives of Pleaſures and Diſappointments, which I have ſo often experienced ſince I have been travelling, are very proper to make us ſenſible that there is no Kind of Life more capable of repreſenting to us continually that we are only on the Earth like Pilgrims; and that we can only uſe, as in paſſing, the Goods of this World; that a Man wants but few Things; and that we ought to take with Patience the Misfortunes that happen in our Journey, ſince they paſs away equally, and with the ſame Celerity. In ſhort, how many Things in travelling make us ſenſible of the Dependence in which we live upon Divine Providence, which does not make Uſe of, for this Mixture of good and evil, Mens Paſſions, but the Viciſſitude of the Seaſons which we may foreſee, and of the Caprice of the Elements, which we may expect of Courſe. Of Conſequence how eaſy is it, and how many Opportunities have we

to

to merit by our Dependence on, and Resignation to the Will of God? They say commonly that long Voyages do not make People religious; but nothing one would think should be more capable of making them so, than the Scenes they go through.

Of the white and red Cedars.

The fourth we were stopped a good Part of the Day on a Point which runs three Leagues North and South, and which they call *Pointe Pélée (Bald Point)*: It is, notwithstanding, pretty well wooded on the West Side; but on the East it is only a sandy Soil, with red Cedars, pretty small, and in no great Number. The white Cedar is of more Use than the red, whose Wood is brittle, and of which they can only make small Goods. They say here that Women with Child should not use it for Busks. The Leaves of this Cedar have no Smell, but the Wood has: This is quite the contrary of the white Cedar.----There are many Bears in this Country, and last Winter they killed on the *Point Pélée* alone above four hundred.

Arrival at Detroit.

The fifth, about four o'Clock in the Afternoon, we perceived Land to the South, and two little Islands which are near it: They call them the *Isles des Serpens a Sonnettes (Rattle-Snake Islands)*; and it is said they are so full of them, that they infect the Air. We entered into the Strait an Hour before Sun set, and we passed the Night under a very fine Island, called *Isle des Bois Blanc (of White Wood)*. From the *Long Point* to the Strait, the Course is near West; from the Entrance of the Strait to the Isle *St. Claire*, which is five or six Leagues, and from thence to Lake *Huron*, it is a little East by South: So that all the Strait, which is thirty-two Leagues long, is between forty-two Degrees twelve or fifteen Minutes, and forty-three and half North Latitude. Above the Isle of *St. Claire* the Strait grows wider, and forms a Lake, which has received its Name from the Island, or has given its own to it. It is about six Leagues long, and as many wide in some Places.

The Nature of the Country.

They say this is the finest Part of *Canada*, and indeed to judge of it by Appearances, Nature has denied it nothing that can render a Country beautiful: Hills, Meadows, Fields, fine Woods of Timber Trees, Brooks, Fountains, and Rivers, and all these of such a good Quality, and so happily intermixed, that one could scarce desire any Thing more. The Lands are not equally good for all Sorts of Grain; but the greatest Part are surprisingly fertile, and I have seen some that have produced Wheat eight Years together without being manured. However, they are all good for something. The Isles seem to have been placed on Purpose to please the Eye. The Rivers and the Lakes are full of Fiſh; the Air pure, and the Climate temperate, and very healthy.

Of the Savages ſettled near the Fort.

Before we arrive at the firſt Fort, which is on the left Hand, a League below the Iſle of *St. Claire*, there are on the ſame Side two pretty populous Villages, and which are very near each other. The firſt is inhabited by ſome *Tionnontatez Hurons*, the ſame, who, after having a long Time wandered from Place to Place, fixed themſelves firſt at the Fall of *St. Mary*, and afterwards at *Michillimakinac*. The ſecond is inhabited by ſome *Pouteouatamis*. On the Right, a little higher, there is a third Village of *Outaouais*, the inſeparable Companions of the *Hurons*, ſince the *Iroquois* obliged them both to abandon their Country. There are no *Chriſtians* among them, and if there are any among the *Pouteouatamis*, they are few in Number. The *Hurons* are all *Chriſtians*, but they have no Miſſionaries: They ſay that they chuſe to have none; but this is only the Choice of ſome of the Chiefs, who have not much Religion, and who hinder the others from being heard, who have a long Time deſired to have one. *(a)*

It is a long Time ſince the Situation, ſtill more than the Beauty of the Strait, has made us wiſh for a conſiderable Settlement here: It was pretty well begun fifteen Years ago, but ſome Reaſons, which are kept ſecret, have reduced it very low. Thoſe who did not favour it ſaid, firſt, that it brought the Peltry of the North too near the *Engliſh*, who ſelling their Merchandizes to the Savages cheaper than our's, would draw all the Trade to *New York*. Second, that the Lands of the *Strait* are not good, that the Surface to the Depth of nine or ten Inches is only Sand, and under this Sand there is a Clay ſo ſtiff, that Water cannot penetrate it; whence it happens that the Plains and the inner Parts of the Woods, are always covered with Water, and that you ſee in them only little Oaks badly grown, and hard Walnut-Trees; and that the Trees ſtanding always in the Water, their Fruit ripens very late. But to theſe Reaſons they reply, it is true, that in the Environs of Fort *Pontchartrain* the Lands are mixed with Sand, and that in the neighbouring Foreſts there are ſome Bottoms that are almoſt always full of Water. Nevertheleſs, theſe very Lands have yielded Wheat eighteen Years together without being manured, and one need not go far to find ſome that are excellent. As for the Woods, without going far from the Fort, I have ſeen ſome in my Walks, which are no ways inferior to our fineſt Foreſts.

(a) They have at length given them one for ſome Years paſt.

As

As to what they ſay, that in making a Settlement at the Streight, we ſhould bring the Fur Trade of the. North nearer to the *Engliſh* ; there is no Perſon in *Canada* who does not own that we ſhall never ſucceed in hindering the Savages from carrying their Merchandize to them, in whatſoever Place we make our Settlements, and whatever Precautions we take, if they do not find the ſame Advantages with us as they find at *New York*.—I could ſay many Things to you, Madam, on this Subject ; but theſe Diſcuſſions would carry me too far. We will talk of this ſome Day at our Leiſure.

Council of three Savage Nations at the Fort of Detroit (the *Streight.*)

The 7th of *June*, which was the Day after my Arrival at the Fort, M. *de Tonti*, who is the Commandant, aſſembled the Chiefs of the three Villages I have before mentioned, to communicate to them the Orders he had juſt received from the Marquis *de Vaudreuil*. They heard him patiently, without interrupting him ; and when he had finiſhed, the *Huron* Orator told him in few Words, that they were going to deliberate on what he had propoſed to them, and they would return him an Anſwer in a ſhort Time.—It is the Cuſtom of theſe People, never to give an Anſwer directly, when it concerns a Matter of ſome Importance. Two Days after, they re-aſſembled in a greater Number at the Commandant's, who deſired me to be preſent at this Council with the Officers of the Garriſon. *Saſtaratſi*, who is called by our *French* People, *the King of the Hurons*, and who is actually the hereditary Chief of the *Tionnontatez*, who are the true *Hurons*, was preſent that Day : But as he is ſtill under Age, he only came for Form : His Uncle, who governs for him, and who is called *the Regent*, was Spokeſman, as being the Orator of the Nation : And the Honour of ſpeaking for all, is commonly given by Preference to the *Hurons*, when there are any in a Council. At the firſt Sight of theſe Aſſemblies, one is apt to form a mean Idea of them.—Imagine that you ſee, Madam, a Dozen of Savages almoſt naked, their Hair ſet in as many different Forms, and all ridiculous ; ſome with lac'd Hats on, and every one a Pipe in his Mouth, and looking like People that have no Thought at all. It is much if any one drops a Word in a Quarter of an Hour, and if they anſwer him by ſo much as a Monoſyllable : Neither is there any Marks of Diſtinction, nor Precedency in their Seats. But we are quite of another Opinion, when we ſee the Reſult of their Deliberations.

Two Points were conſidered here, which the Governor had much at Heart. The firſt was, to make the three Villages be contented without any more Brandy, the Sale of which had been entirely prohibited by the Council of the Marine. The ſecond was, to engage all the Nations to unite with the *French* to de-

ſtroy

ſtroy the *Outagamis*, commonly called *les Renards, (the Foxes)*, whom they had pardoned ſome Years before, and who were beginning to commit the ſame Outrages as before. M. *de Tonti* at firſt repeated in few Words, by his Interpreter, what he had more fully explained in the firſt Aſſembly; and the *Huron* Orator replied in the Name of the three Villages: He made no Introduction, but went directly to the Buſineſs in Hand: He ſpoke a long Time, and leiſurely, ſtopping at every Article, to give the Interpreter Time to explain in *French* what he had before ſpoken in his own Language. His Air, the Sound of his Voice, and his Action, though he made no Geſtures, appeared to me to have ſomething noble and engaging; and it is certain that what he ſaid, muſt have been very eloquent; ſince from the Mouth of the Interpreter, who was an ordinary Perſon, deprived of all the Ornaments of the Language, we were all charmed with it. I muſt own alſo, that if he had ſpoken two Hours, I ſhould not have been tired a Moment. Another Proof that the Beauties of his Diſcourſe did not come from the Interpreter, is, that this Man would never have dared to have ſaid of himſelf all he ſaid to us. I was even a little ſurpriſed that he had Courage to repeat ſo faithfully, as he did, certain Matters which muſt be diſpleaſing to the Commandant.—When the *Huron* had done ſpeaking, *Onanguicé* the Chief and Orator of the *Pouteouatamis*, expreſſed in few Words, and very ingeniouſly, all that the firſt had explained more at Length, and ended in the ſame Manner. The *Outaouais* did not ſpeak, and appeared to approve of what the others had ſpoken.

The Reſult of the Council.

The Concluſion was, that the *French*, if they pleaſed, might refuſe to ſell any more Brandy to the Savages; that they would have done very well if they had never ſold them any; and nothing could be imagined more forcible than what the *Huron* Orator ſaid in expoſing the Diſorders occaſioned by this Liquor, and the Injury it has done to all the Savage Nations. The moſt zealous Miſſionary could not have ſaid more. But he added, that they were now ſo accuſtomed to it, that they could not live without it; from whence it was eaſy to judge, that if they could not have it of the *French*, they would apply to the *Engliſh*. As to what concerned the War of the *Outagamis*, he declared, that nothing could be reſolved on but in a general Council of all the Nations who acknowledge *Onontbio (a)* for their Father; that they would, without Doubt, acknowledge the Neceſſity of this War, but they could hardly truſt the *French* a ſecond Time; who having re-united them, to help them to extirpate the common

(a) This is the Name the Savages give the Governor-General.

Enemy, had granted him Peace without consulting their Allies, who could never discover the Reasons of such a Conduct.

The next Day I went to visit the two Savage Villages which are near the Fort; and I went first to the *Hurons*. I found all the Matrons, among whom was the Great Grandmother of *Sasteratsi*, much afflicted to see themselves so long deprived of Spiritual Helps. Many Things which I heard at the same Time, confirmed me in the Opinion I had before entertained, that some private Interests were the only Obstacles to the Desires of these good *Christians*. It is to be hoped that the last Orders of the Council of the Marine will remove these Oppositions. M. *de Tonti* assured me that he was going to labour at it effectually *(b)*.

In what Temper the Author found the Hurons *of* Detroit, (the Streight.)

Those who conducted me to this Village assured me, that without the *Hurons*, the other Savages would be starved. This is certainly not the Fault of the Land they possess: With very little Cultivation it would yield them Necessaries: Fishing alone would supply a good Part, and this requires little Labour. But since they have got a Relish for Brandy, they think of nothing but heaping up Skins, that they may have wherewithal to get drunk. The *Hurons*, more laborious, of more Foresight, and more used to cultivate the Earth, act with greater Prudence, and by their Labour are in a Condition not only to subsist without any Help, but also to feed others; but this indeed they will not do without some Recompence; for amongst their good Qualities we must not reckon Disinterestedness.

I was still better received by the Infidel *Pouteouatamis*, than by the *Christian Hurons*. These Savages are the finest Men of *Canada*: They are moreover of a very mild Disposition, and were always our Friends. Their Chief, *Onanguicé*, treated me with a Politeness which gave me as good an Opinion of his Understanding, as the Speech which he made in the Council: He is really a Man of Merit, and entirely in our Interest.

His Reception by the Pouteouatamis.

As I returned through a Quarter of the *Huron* Village, I saw a Company of these Savages, who appeared very eager at Play. I drew near, and saw they were playing at the Game of *the Dish*. This is the Game of which these People are fondest. At this they sometimes lose their Rest, and in some Measure their Reason. At this Game they hazard all they possess, and many do not leave off till they are almost stripped quite naked, and till they have lost all they have in their Cabins. Some have

(b) The *Hurons* of the Streight have at last obtained a Missionary, who has revived among them their former Fervor.

been

been known to ſtake their Liberty for a Time, which fully proves their Paſſion for this Game; for there are no Men in the World more jealous of their Liberty than the Savages.

The Game of the Diſh, *or of* the little Bones.

The Game of *the Diſh*, which they alſo call the Game of *the little Bones*, is only play'd by two Perſons: Each has ſix or eight little Bones, which at firſt I took for Apricot Stones; they are of that Shape and Bigneſs: But upon viewing them cloſely, I perceived that they had ſix unequal Surfaces, the two principal of which are painted, one Black, and the other White, inclining to Yellow. They make them jump up, by ſtriking the Ground, or the Table, with a round and hollow Diſh, which contains them, and which they twirl round firſt. When they have no Diſh, they throw the Bones up in the Air with their Hands: If in falling they come all of one Colour, he who plays wins five: The Game is forty up, and they ſubtract the Numbers gained by the adverſe Party. Five Bones of the ſame Colour win but one for the firſt Time, but the ſecond Time they win the Game: A leſs Number wins nothing.

He that wins the Game, continues playing: The Loſer gives his Place to another, who is named by the Markers of his Side; for they make Parties at firſt, and often the whole Village is concern'd in the Game: Oftentimes alſo one Village plays againſt another. Each Party chuſes a Marker; but he withdraws when he pleaſes, which never happens, but when his Party loſes. At every Throw, eſpecially if it happens to be deciſive, they make great Shouts. The Players appear like People poſſeſſed, and the Spectators are not more calm. They all make a thouſand Contortions, talk to the Bones, load the Spirits of the adverſe Party with Imprecations, and the whole Village echoes with Howlings. If all this does not recover their Luck, the Loſers may put off the Party till next Day: It coſts them only a ſmall Treat to the Company.

Then they prepare to return to the Engagement. Each invokes his Genius, and throws ſome Tobacco in the Fire to his Honour. They aſk him above all Things for lucky Dreams. As ſoon as Day appears, they go again to Play; but if the Loſers fancy that the Goods in their Cabins made them unlucky, the firſt Thing they do is to change them all. The great Parties commonly laſt five or ſix Days, and often continue all Night. In the mean Time, as all the Perſons preſent, at leaſt thoſe who are concerned in the Game, are in an Agitation that deprives them of Reaſon, as they quarrel and fight, which never happens among the Savages but on theſe Occaſions, and in Drunkenneſs, one may judge, if when they have done playing they do not want Reſt.

It

It happens ſometimes that theſe Parties of Play are made by Order of the Phyſician, or at the Requeſt of the Sick. There needs no more for this Purpoſe than a Dream of one or the other. This Dream is always taken for the Order of ſome Spirit; and then they prepare themſelves for Play with a great deal of Care. They aſſemble for ſeveral Nights to try, and to ſee who has the luckieſt Hand. They conſult their Genii, they faſt, the married Perſons obſerve Continence; and all to obtain a favourable Dream. Every Morning they relate what Dreams they have had, and of all the Things they have dreamt of, which they think lucky; and they make a Collection of all, and put them into little Bags which they carry about with them; and if any one has the Reputation of being lucky, *that is*, in the Opinion of theſe People, of having a familiar Spirit more powerful, or more inclined to do Good, they never fail to make him keep near him who holds the Diſh: They even go a great Way ſometimes to fetch him; and if through Age, or any Infirmity, he cannot walk, they will carry him on their Shoulders.

Superſtitious Uſe of this Game for the Cure of Diſtempers.

They have often preſſed the Miſſionaries to be preſent at theſe Games, as they believe their Guardian Genii are the moſt powerful. It happened one Day in a *Huron* Village, that a ſick Perſon having ſent for a Juggler, this Quack preſcribed the Game of *the Diſh*, and appointed a Village at ſome Diſtance from the ſick Perſon's, to play at. She immediately ſent to aſk Leave of the Chief of the Village: It was granted: They played; and when they had done playing, the ſick Perſon gave a great many Thanks to the Players for having cured her, as ſhe ſaid. But there was nothing of Truth in all this: On the contrary, ſhe was worſe; but one muſt always appear ſatisfied, even when there is the leaſt Cauſe to be ſo.

The ill Humour of this Woman and her Relations fell upon the Miſſionaries, who had refuſed to aſſiſt at the Game, notwithſtanding all the Importunities they uſed to engage them: And in their Anger for the little Complaiſance they ſhewed on this Occaſion, they told them, by Way of Reproach, that ſince their Arrival in this Country, the Genii of the Savages had loſt their Power. These Fathers did not fail to take Advantage of this Confeſſion, to make theſe Infidels ſenſible of the Weakneſs of their Deities, and of the Superiority of the God of the *Chriſtians*. But beſides that on theſe Occaſions it is rare that they are well enough diſpoſed to hear Reaſon, theſe Barbarians reply coldly, "You have your Gods, and we have our's: 'Tis a "Miſfortune for us that they are not ſo powerful as your's."

The Strait is one of the Countries of *Canada* where a Botanist might make the most Discoveries. I have already observed, that all *Canada* produces a great many Simples which have great Virtues. There is no Doubt that the Snow contributes greatly to it: But there is in this Place a Variety of Soil; which, joined to the Mildness of the Climate, and the Liberty which the Sun has to warm the Earth more than in other Places, because the Country is more open, gives Room to believe that the Plants have more Virtue here than in any other Place.

Of the Flea-Plant, *and its Effects.*

One of my Canoe Men lately proved the Force of a Plant, which we meet with every where, and the Knowledge of which is very necessary for Travellers; not for its good Qualities, for I never yet heard it had any, but because we cannot take too much Care to shun it. They call it the *Flea-Plant*; but this Name does not sufficiently express the Effects it produces. Its Effects are more or less sensible, according to the Constitution of those who touch it. There are some Persons on whom it has no Effect at all; but others, only by looking on it, are seized with a violent Fever, which lasts above fifteen Days, and which is accompanied with a very troublesome Itch on the Hands, and a great Itching all over the Body. It has an Effect on others only when they touch it, and then the Party affected appears all over like a Leper. Some have been known to have lost the Use of their Hands by it. We know no other Remedy for it as yet but Patience. After some Time all the Symptoms disappear.

Of the Lemons of the Strait.

There grow also in the Strait Lemon-Trees in the natural Soil, the Fruit of which have the Shape and Colour of those of *Portugal*, but they are smaller, and of a flat Taste. They are excellent in Conserve. The Root of this Tree is a deadly and very subtile Poison, and at the same Time a sovereign Antidote against the Bite of Serpents. It must be pounded, and applied directly to the Wound. This Remedy takes Effect instantly, and never fails. On both Sides the Strait the Country, as they say, preserves all its Beauty for about ten Leagues within Land; after which they find fewer Fruit-Trees, and not so many Meadows. But at the End of five or six Leagues, inclining towards the Lake *Erié* to the South West, one sees vast Meadows which extend above a hundred Leagues every Way, and which feed a prodigious Number of those Cattle which I have already mentioned several Times.

I am, &c.

LETTER

LETTER XVII.

Various Remarks on the Character, Customs, and Government of the Savages.

MADAM, *At* DETROIT (*the* STRAIT), *June* 14.

AFTER I had closed my last Letter, and given it to a Person who was going down to *Quebec*, I prepared myself to continue my Journey, and in Fact, I embarked the next Day, but I did not go far, and by the Want of Precaution in my Conductors, I am returned here to Fort *Pontchartrain*, where I fear I shall be obliged to stay yet several Days. These are Disappointments which we must expect with the *Canadian* Travellers, they are never in Haste, and are very negligent in taking their Measures. But as we must make the best of every Thing, I shall take Advantage of this Delay, to begin to entertain you with the Government of the Savages, and of their Behaviour in public Affairs. By this Knowledge you will be better able to judge of what I shall have Occasion to say to you hereafter; but I shall not speak very largely on this Subject: First, because the Whole is not very interesting: Secondly, because I will write nothing to you but what is supported by good Testimony, and it is not easy to find Persons whose Sincerity is entirely unsuspected, at least of Exaggeration; or who may not be suspected of having given Credit too lightly to all they heard; or who have Discernment enough to take Things in a right View, which requires a long Acquaintance with the Country, and the Inhabitants. I shall say nothing of my own on this Article, and this will prevent me from following a regular Series in what I shall say. But it will not be difficult for you to collect and make a pretty regular Whole of the Remarks which I shall intersperse in my Letters, according as I receive them.

The Savages of Canada *are more easily to be converted than the more civilized Nations.*

It must be acknowledged, Madam, that the nearer View we take of our Savages, the more we discover in them some valuable Qualities. The chief Part of the Principles by which they regulate their Conduct, the general Maxims by which they govern themselves, and the Bottom of their Character, have nothing which appears barbarous. Furthermore, the Ideas, though quite confused, which they have retained of a first Being; the Traces, tho' almost effaced, of a religious Worship, which they appear to have

have rendered formerly to this Supreme Deity; and the faint Marks, which we obſerve, even in their moſt indifferent Actions of the antient Belief, and the primitive Religion, may bring them more eaſily than we think, into the Way of Truth, and make their Converſion to *Chriſtianity* to be more eaſily effected than that of more civilized Nations. In Fact, we learn from Experience, that Policy, Knowledge, and Maxims of State, create in the laſt an Attachment and a Prejudice for their falſe Belief, which all the Skill, and all the Zeal of the Labourers of the Goſpel have much Pains to overcome. So that there is Need of Grace acting more powerfully on enlightened Infidels, who are almoſt always blinded by their Preſumption, than on thoſe who have nothing to oppoſe to it but a very limited Knowledge.

A General Idea of their Government.

The greateſt Part of the People of this Continent have a Kind of Ariſtocratic Government, which varies almoſt to Infinity. For altho' each Village has its Chief, who is independent of all the others of the ſame Nation, and on whom his Subjects depend in very few Things; nevertheleſs, no Affair of any Importance is concluded without the Advice of the Elders. Towards *Acadia* the Sachems were more abſolute, and it does not appear that they were obliged as the Chiefs are in almoſt all other Places, to beſtow Bounties on private Perſons. On the contrary, they received a Kind of Tribute from their Subjects, and by no Means thought it a Part of their Grandeur to reſerve nothing for themſelves. But there is Reaſon to think that the Diſperſion of theſe Savages of *Acadia*, and perhaps alſo their Intercourſe with the *French*, have occaſioned many Changes in their old Form of Government, concerning which *Leſcarbot* and *Champlain* are the only Authors who have given us any Particulars.

The Diviſions of the Nations into Tribes.

Many Nations have each three Families, or principal Tribes, as antient, in all Probability, as their Origin. They are nevertheleſs derived from the ſame Stock, and there is one, who is looked upon as the *firſt*, which has a Sort of Preeminence over the two others, who ſtile thoſe of this Tribe *Brothers*, whereas between themſelves they ſtile each other *Couſins*. Theſe Tribes are mixed, without being confounded, each has its diſtinct Chief in every Village; and in the Affairs which concern the whole Nation, theſe Chiefs aſſemble to deliberate thereon. Each Tribe bears the Name of ſome Animal, and the whole Nation has alſo one, whoſe Name they take, and whoſe Figure is their Mark, or, as one may ſay, their Coat of Arms. They ſign Treaties no otherwiſe than by tracing theſe Figures

on

on it, unleſs ſome particular Reaſons make them ſubſtitute others.

Thus the *Huron* Nation is the Nation of the *Porcupine*. Its firſt Tribe bears the Name of the *Bear*, or of the *Roe-Buck*. Authors differ about this. The two others have taken for their Animals, the *Wolf* and the *Tortoiſe*. In ſhort, each Village has alſo its own Animal; and probably it is this Variety which has occaſioned ſo many Miſtakes in the Authors of Relations. Furthermore, it is proper to obſerve, that beſides theſe Diſtinctions of Nations, Tribes, and Villages, by Animals, there are yet others which are founded upon ſome Cuſtom, or on ſome particular Event. For Inſtance, the *Tionnontatez Hurons*, who are of the firſt Tribe, commonly call themſelves the Nation of *Tobacco*; and we have a Treaty, in which theſe Savages, who were then at *Michillimakinac*, have put for their Mark the Figure of a Beaver.

Obſervation on the Names of the Chiefs.

The *Iroquois* Nation have the ſame Animals as the *Huron*, of which it appears to be a Colony; yet with this Difference, that the Family of the Tortoiſe is divided into two, which they call the *great* and the *little Tortoiſe*. The Chief of each Family bears the Name of it, and in public Tranſactions they never give him any other. It is the ſame in Reſpect to the Chief of the Nation, and of each Village. But beſides this Name, which is, as I may ſay, only a Repreſentation, they have another which diſtinguiſhes them more particularly, and which is, as it were, a Title of Honour. Thus one is called *the moſt noble*, another *the moſt antient*, &c. Laſtly, they have a third Name which is perſonal; but I am apt to think that this is only uſed among the Nations, where the Rank of Chief is hereditary.

The conferring or giving theſe Titles, is always performed with great Ceremony. The new Chief, or if he is too young, he who repreſents him, muſt make a Feaſt and give Preſents, ſpeak the Elogium of his Predeceſſor, and ſing his Song. But there are ſome perſonal Names ſo famous, that no one dares to aſſume them; or which, at leaſt, remain a long Time before they are re-aſſumed: When they do it, they call it, raiſing from the Dead the Perſon who formerly had that Name.

Of the Succeſſion, and of the Election of the Chiefs.

In the North, and in all Places where the *Algonquin* Language prevails, the Dignity of Chief is elective; all the Ceremony of the Election and Inſtallation conſiſts in Feaſts, accompanied with Dances and Songs. The Chief elected never fails to make the Panegyrick of him whoſe Place he takes, and to invoke his Genius. Amongſt the *Hurons*, where this Dignity is hereditary, the Succeſſion is continued

tinued by the Woman's Side ; ſo that at the Death of the Chief, it is not his Son that ſucceeds him, but his Siſter's Son ; or, in Caſe of Failure of ſuch, the neareſt Relation by the Female Line. If a whole Branch happens to be extinct, the nobleſt Matron of a Tribe chuſes the Perſon ſhe likes beſt, and declares him Chief.

Of their Power.

They muſt be of an Age fit to govern ; and if the hereditary Chief is not of Age, they chuſe a Regent, who has all the Authority, but who exerciſes it in the Name of the Minor. In general, theſe Chiefs do not receive any great Marks of Reſpect ; and if they are always obeyed, it is becauſe they know how far their Commands will have Force. It is true alſo, that they entreat or propoſe, rather than command, and that they never exceed the Bounds of the little Authority they have. Thus it is Reaſon that governs ; and the Government is the more effectual, as the Obedience is more voluntary, and that there is no Fear of its degenerating into Tyranny.

Of the Aſſiſtants or Counſellors.

Beſides this, every Family has a Right to chuſe themſelves a Counſellor, or an Aſſiſtant to the Chief, who is to watch over their Intereſts, and without whoſe Advice the Chief can undertake nothing. Theſe Counſellors are eſpecially obliged to take Care of the public Treaſure, and it belongs to them to direct how it is to be employed. The firſt Reception of them into this Office, is in a general Council ; but they do not give Notice of this to their Allies, as they do in the Election or Inſtallation of a Chief.——In the *Huron* Nations, the Women name the Counſellors, and they often chuſe Perſons of their own Sex.

Of the Body of the Elders.

This Body of Counſellors, or Aſſiſtants, is the firſt of all : The ſecond is that of the Elders ; *that is to ſay*, of all who have attained the Age of Maturity. I could never learn exactly what this Age is. The laſt is that of the Warriors : It comprehends all that are able to bear Arms. This Body has often at its Head the Chief of the Nation, or of the Village ; but he muſt have diſtinguiſhed himſelf firſt by ſome brave Action, otherwiſe he is obliged to ſerve as a Subaltern ; *that is to ſay*, as a common Soldier, for there is no other Rank in the Armies of the Savages.

Of the War Chiefs.

A great Party may indeed have ſeveral Chiefs, becauſe they give this Title to all thoſe who have ever commanded ; but they are not the leſs ſubject to the Commander of the Party, a Kind of General without Character, without real Authority, who can neither

neither reward nor punish, whose Soldiers may leave him when they please, without his having a Right to say any Thing to them on that Account, and who nevertheless is scarce ever contradicted. So true is it, that amongst Men who govern themselves by Reason, and are guided by Honour and a Zeal for their Country, Independence does not destroy Subordination, and that a free and voluntary Obedience is generally the most to be depended on. For the rest, the Qualities required in a War Chief, are to be fortunate, brave, and disinterested. It is not strange, that they should obey without Difficulty a Man in whom these three Characters are known to be united.

The Power of the Women in some Nations.

The Women have the principal Authority among all the People of the *Huron* Language, if we except the *Iroquois* Canton of *Onneyouth*, where it is alternate between the Sexes. But if this is their Law, their Practice is seldom conformable to it. In Reality, the Men acquaint the Women only with what they please to let them know, and an important Affair is seldom communicated to them, though all is transacted in their Name, and the Chiefs are only their Lieutenants.

What I told you, Madam, of the Great Grandmother of the hereditary Chief of the *Hurons* of the Strait, who could never obtain a Missionary for her Village, is a good Proof that the real Authority of the Women is confined to very narrow Limits; yet I have been assured, that they deliberate first on what is proposed in the Council, and afterwards they give the Result of their Deliberation to the Chiefs, who make a Report of it to the general Council, composed of the Elders: But it seems very probable, that all this is done for Form, and with the Restrictions I have mentioned. The Warriors consult also among themselves on every Thing in their Department, but they can conclude nothing of Importance, or that concerns the Nation or the Village. Every Thing must be examined and determined in the Council of the Elders, who give the final Decree.

The Wisdom of these Councils.

It must be acknowledged that they proceed in these Assemblies with such Prudence, Maturity, Ability, and I will also say, for the most Part, such Probity, as would have done Honour to the Areopagus of *Athens*, and the Senate of *Rome*, in the most flourishing Times of those Republics. The Reason is, that they conclude nothing hastily, and that the strong Passions which have made such Alterations in the Systems of Policy, even amongst *Christians*, have not yet prevailed in these Savages over the Public Good. The Parties concerned do not fail to employ secret Springs, and such Intrigue to accomplish their Designs, that

one

one would ſcarce believe could enter into the Thoughts of ſuch Barbarians. It is alſo true, that they poſſeſs, in the higheſt Degree, the great Art of concealing their Proceedings. For the moſt Part, the Glory of the Nation, and the Motives of Honour, are the chief Springs of all their Undertakings. What we cannot excuſe in them, is, that generally they place all their Honour in revenging themſelves, and give no Bounds to their Revenge: A Fault which *Chriſtianity* alone can throughly reform, and which all our Politeneſs and our Religion does not always correct.

Of the Orators.

Each Tribe has its Orator in every Village, and there are few but theſe Orators who have a Right to ſpeak in the public Councils, and in the general Aſſemblies. They always ſpeak well, and to the Purpoſe. Beſides that natural Eloquence, which none of thoſe who have been acquainted with them will diſpute, they have a perfect Knowledge of the Intereſts of thoſe who employ them, and a Dexterity in placing their Rights in the faireſt Light, that nothing can exceed. On ſome Occaſions, the Women have an Orator, who ſpeaks in their Name, and as if he was ſolely their Interpreter.

Of the Intereſts of theſe People.

One would think that People, who we may ſay have no Poſſeſſions, either public or private, and who have no Ambition to extend themſelves, ſhould have very few Things to adjuſt with each other. But the Spirit of Man, naturally reſtleſs, cannot remain without Action, and is ingenious in finding itſelf Employment. This is certain, that our Savages negotiate continually, and have always ſome Affair on the Carpet. There are ſome Treaties to conclude, or to renew, Offers of Service, mutual Civilities, Alliances they court, Invitations to join in making War, Condolences on the Death of a Chief, or of ſome conſiderable Perſon. All this is done with a Dignity, an Attention, I will even venture to ſay with an Ability, worthy of the moſt important Affairs: And they are ſometimes more ſo than they ſeem to be; for thoſe they depute for theſe Purpoſes, have almoſt always ſome ſecret Inſtructions, and the apparent Motive of their Deputation is only a Vail that hides another of more Conſequence.

The Policy of the Iroquois.

The *Iroquois* Nation has for the two laſt Ages made the greateſt Figure in *Canada*. By their Succeſſes in War they have gained over the greateſt Part of the other Nations a Superiority, which none of them at preſent are in a Condition to diſpute; and from a peaceable Nation, as they were formerly, they are become very reſtleſs and intriguing. But nothing has contributed more

more to render them formidable, than the Advantage of their Situation; which they soon discovered, and knew very well how to take Advantage of it. Placed between us and the *English*, they soon conceived that both Nations would be obliged to court them; and it is certain that the principal Attention of both Colonies, since their Settlement, has been to gain them, or at least to engage them to remain neuter: Being persuaded on their Part, that if one of these Nations should prevail over the other, they should soon be oppressed, they have found the Secret to balance their Successes; and if we consider that all their Forces joined together have never amounted to more than five or six thousand fighting Men, and that long ago they were diminished above half, one must acknowledge that they could not, with so small a Power, have supported themselves as they have done, but by great Skill and Address.

Of the Government of the Villages.

As to what relates to private Persons, and the particular Concerns of the Villages, these are reduced to a very small Compass, and are soon decided. The Authority of the Chiefs does not extend, or very rarely extends, so far; and generally those who have any Reputation, are employed only for the Public. A single Affair, however trifling it may be, is a long Time under Deliberation. Every Thing is treated of with a great deal Circumspection, and nothing is decided till they have heard every one who desires it. If they have made a Present under Hand to an Elder, to secure his Vote, they are sure to obtain it when the Present is accepted. It was scarce ever heard that a Savage failed in an Engagement of this Kind; but he does not take it easily, and he never receives with both Hands. The young People enter early into the Knowledge of Business, which renders them serious and mature in an Age in which we are yet Children: This interests them in the Public Good from their early Youth, and inspires them with an Emulation, which is cherished with great Care, and from which there is Reason to expect the greatest Things.

The Defects of the Government.

The greatest Defect of this Government, is, that there is no Punishment for Crimes among these People. Indeed this Defect has not the same Consequences here, which it would have with us: The great Spring of our Passions, and the principal Source of the Disorders which most disturb civil Society, *that is to say*, Self-Interest, having scarce any Power over People, who never think of laying up Riches, and who take little Thought for the Morrow.

They may also justly be reproached with their Manner of bringing up their Children. They know not what it is to chastise them: Whilst they are little, they say they have no Reason; and the Savages are not of the Opinion, that Punishment promotes Understanding. When they are old enough to reason, they say that they are Masters of their own Actions, and that they are accountable to no Person for them. They carry these two Maxims so far, as to suffer themselves to be ill used by drunken People, without defending themselves, for Fear of hurting them. If you endeavour to shew them the Folly of this Conduct, they say, *Why should we hurt them? They know not what they do.*

In a Word, these *Americans* are entirely convinced that Man is born free, that no Power on Earth has any Right to make any Attempts against his Liberty, and that nothing can make him Amends for its Loss. We have even had much Pains to undeceive those converted to *Christianity* on this Head, and to make them understand, that in Consequence of the Corruption of our Nature, which is the Effect of Sin, an unrestrained Liberty of doing Evil differs little from a Sort of Necessity of committing it, considering the Strength of the Inclination, which carries us to it; and that the Law which restrains us, brings us nearer to our first Liberty, in seeming to deprive us of it. Happily for them, Experience does not make them feel in many material Articles all the Force of this Bias, which produces in other Countries so many Crimes. Their Knowledge being more confined than our's, their Desires are still more so. Being used only to the simple Necessaries of Life, which Providence has sufficiently provided for them, they have scarce any Idea of Superfluity.

After all, this Toleration, and this Impunity, is a great Disorder. There is also another, in the Defect of Subordination, which appears in the Public, and still more so in Domestic Concerns, where every one does what he pleases; where the Father, Mother, and Children, often live like People met together by Chance, and who are bound by no Obligations to each other; where the young People treat of the Affairs of the Family without communicating any Thing of it to their Parents, no more than if they were Strangers; where the Children are brought up in an entire Independence, and where they accustom themselves early not to hearken either to the Voice of Nature, or the most indispensable Duties of Society.

If in the Nations that are most prudently governed, and which are restrained by the Reins of a most holy Religion, we still see some of those Monsters which are a Disgrace to Human Nature, they at least create Horror, and the Laws suppress them: But what is only the Crime of a private Person, when it is attended with Punishment, becomes the Crime of the Nation that leaves it unpuniſhed, as even Parricide itſelf is among the Savages. Were it ſtill more uncommon than it is, this Impunity is a Blot which nothing can efface, and which appears entirely barbarous. There are, however, in all this, ſome Exceptions, which I ſhall mention preſently; but, in general, ſuch is the Spirit that prevails among our Savages.

The Principles on which the Government is eſtabliſhed.

They are not only perſuaded that a Perſon who is not in his right Senſes is not to be reprehended, or at leaſt not to be puniſhed; but they imagine alſo, that it is unworthy of a Man to defend himſelf againſt a Woman or a Child; but it is always underſtood, where there is no Danger of Life, or of being maimed; yet in this Caſe, if it is poſſible, they get away. But if a Savage kills another belonging to his Cabin, if he is drunk, (and they often counterfeit Drunkenneſs when they intend to commit ſuch Actions) all the Conſequence is, that they pity and weep for the Dead. *It is a Misfortune,* (they ſay) *the Murderer knew not what he did.*

If he did it in cool Blood, they readily conclude that he had good Reaſons for coming to this Extremity: If it is plain he had none, it belongs to thoſe of his Cabin, as the only Perſons concerned, to puniſh him: They may put him to Death, but they ſeldom do it; and if they do, it is without any Form of Juſtice; ſo that his Death has leſs the Appearance of a lawful Puniſhment than the Revenge of a private Perſon. Sometimes a Chief will be glad of the Opportunity to get rid of a bad Subject. In a Word, the Crime is not puniſhed in a Manner that ſatisfies Juſtice, and which eſtabliſhes the public Peace and Safety.

An Aſſaſſination which affects ſeveral Cabins, would alalways have bad Conſequences. Oftentimes there needs no more to ſet a whole Village in a Flame, and even a whole Nation: For which Reaſon, on theſe Occaſions, the Council of the Elders neglect no Means to reconcile the Parties betimes; and if they ſucceed, it is commonly the Public who make the Preſents, and take all the Meaſures to appeaſe the Family offended. The ſpeedy Puniſhment of the Guilty, would at once put an End to the Affair; and if the Relations of the Dead can get the Murderer in their Power, they may puniſh him as they pleaſe; but the People of his Cabin think it is not for their Honour to ſacrifice him; and often the Village, or the Nation, does not think it proper to conſtrain them to do it.

How the Hurons *puniſhed Murder.*

I have read in a Letter of Father *Brebeuf*, who lived amongſt the *Hurons*, that they uſed to puniſh Murder in this Manner. They laid the dead Body upon Poles, at the Top of a Cabin, and the

Murderer was obliged to remain ſeveral Days together, and to receive all that dropt from the Carcaſe, not only on himſelf, but alſo on his Food, which they ſet by him ; unleſs by a conſiderable Preſent to the Cabin of the Deceaſed, he obtained the Favour of having his Food freed from this Poiſon ; but the Miſſionary does not ſay, whether this was done by public Authority, or whether it was only done by Way of Repriſal by the Perſons concerned, when they could get the Murderer in their Power. However this may be, the moſt common Means uſed by the Savages to make Amends to the Relations of a Perſon murdered, is to ſupply his Place by a Priſoner of War ; in this Caſe the Captive is almoſt always adopted : He takes Poſſeſſion of all the Rights of the Deceaſed, and ſoon makes them forget him whoſe Place he ſupplies. But there are ſome odious Crimes which are immediately puniſhed with Death, at leaſt among ſome Nations, amongſt which are Sorceries.

Puniſhment of Magicians.

Whoever is ſuſpected of Sorcery is ſafe no where ; they even make them undergo a Sort of Torture, to oblige them to diſcover their Accomplices, after which they are condemned to the Puniſhment of Priſoners of War ; but the Conſent of his Family is firſt aſked, which they dare not refuſe. Thoſe who are leaſt culpable are knocked on the Head before they are burnt. They treat much in the ſame Manner thoſe that diſhonour their Families, and commonly it is the Family that executes the Delinquent.

Regulation for Things found.

Among the *Hurons*, who were much inclined to ſteal, and who did it ſo dexterouſly, that our moſt ſkillful Pick-pockets would think it an Honour to them, it was allowed when they found out the Thief, not only to take from him again what he had ſtolen, but alſo to carry away every Thing that was in his Cabin, and to ſtrip him, his Wife, and Children, quite naked, without his having the Liberty to make the leaſt Reſiſtance. And to prevent all the Diſputes which might ariſe on this Subject, they agreed on certain Points which they have always obſerved. For Inſtance, every Thing found, tho' it had been loſt but a Moment, belonged to the Perſon that found it, provided the Loſer had not claimed it before. But if they diſcovered the leaſt unfair Dealing on the Part of the Finders, they were obliged to reſtore it, which ſometimes occaſioned Diſputes that were pretty difficult to decide : The following is a ſingular Inſtance of this Kind.

A good

A good old Woman, whose whole Stock consisted in a Collar of Porcelain, or Shells, which was worth about fifty Crowns, carried it always with her in a little Bag. One Day as she was working in the Field, she hung her Bag upon a Tree; another Woman who perceived it, and who longed very much to sharp her out of her Collar, thought it a favourable Opportunity to get it without being accused of Theft: She never lost Sight of it, and in an Hour or two, the old Woman being gone into the next Field, she ran to the Tree and began to cry out, she had made a good Find. The old Woman at this Cry turned her Head, and said the Bag belonged to her; that it was she who had hung it to the Tree, that she had neither lost nor forgot it, and that she intended to take it again when she had done her Work. The other Party replied, that there was no judging of Intentions, and that having quitted the Field without taking again her Bag, one might naturally conclude, she had forgot it.

A singular Instance of a Thing found.

After many Disputes between these two Women, between whom there passed nevertheless not the least disobliging Word, the Affair was carried before an Arbitrator, who was the Chief of the Village, and this was his Decree: "To judge strictly, "says he, the Bag belongs to her that found it; but the Cir-"cumstances are such, that if this Woman will not be taxed "with Avarice, she must restore it to her that claims it, and "be contented with a small Present, which the other is indis-"pensably obliged to make her:" The two Parties submitted to this Decision; and it is proper to observe, that the Fear of being noted for Avarice has as much Influence on the Mind of the Savages, as the Fear of Punishment would have, and that in general these People are governed more by Principles of Honour than by any other Motive. What I have further to add, Madam, will give you another Proof of this: I have said before that to hinder the Consequences of a Murder, the Public takes upon itself to make the Submissions for the Guilty, and to make Amends to the Parties concerned: Would you believe that even this has more Power to prevent these Disorders than the severest Laws? But this is certainly true: For as these Submissions are extremely mortifying to Men whose Pride surpasses all Description, the Criminal is more affected by the Trouble which he sees the Public suffer on his Account, than he would be for himself; and a Zeal for the Honour of the Nation restrains these Barbarians much more powerfully, than the Fear of Death or Punishments.

But it is very certain, that Impunity has not always prevailed amongst them as it has done in these latter Times, and our Missionaries

Missionaries have still found some Traces of the antient Rigour with which they used to suppress Crimes. Theft in particular was looked upon as a Blot which dishonoured a Family, and every one had a Right to wash away the Stain with the Blood of the Delinquent. Father *Brebeuf* one Day saw a young *Huron* who was killing a Woman with a Club, he ran to him to prevent it, and asked him why he committed such Violence, " She is my " Sister, replied the Savage, she is guilty of Theft, and I " will expiate by her Death, the Disgace she has brought upon " me and all my Family." My Letter is just now called for, and I conclude with my Assurances of being,

Your's, &c.

LETTER XVIII.

Voyage from DETROIT *(the* STRAIT) *to* MICHILLIMAKINAC. *Description of the Country.* *Of the* MARRIAGES *of the* SAVAGES.

MADAM, MICHILLIMAKINAC, *June* 30.

IT was the 18th of this Month that I at length departed in good Earnest from the Fort of *Pontchartrain* at *Detroit*, a little before Sun-set. I had scarce gone a League, when a Storm, accompanied with a Deluge of Rain, obliged me to go ashore very wet, and we passed the Night very unpleasantly. The next Day all that I could do was to cross the Lake of *St. Claire*, though this Passage is but four Leagues. The Country appeared to me good on both Sides. At half Way we leave upon the Left Hand a River which is at least seventy Yards wide at its Mouth. They call it the *Huron's River*, because these Savages took Refuge here during the War with the *Iroquois*. On the Right, and almost opposite, there is another, the Entrance of which is twice as wide, and which they go up eighty Leagues without meeting any Fall, which is rare in the Rivers of this Country. I could not learn its Name.

Departure from Detroit.

The Route to Fort *Detroit*, from the End of the Traverse, is East North East; from thence we turn to the North by the East, even to the South for four Leagues, at the End of which on the Right Hand we find a Village of *Missisaguez*, situate on a fruitful Soil at the Entrance of some very fine Meadows, and in the most agreeable

agreeable Situation that can be ſeen. From thence to Lake *Huron* they reckon twelve Leagues, and the Country is all the Way charming. It is a magnificent Canal as ſtrait as a Line, bordered with lofty Woods, divided by fine Meadows, and ſprinkled with Iſlands, ſome of which are pretty large. We ſteer here North North Eaſt, and at the Entrance of Lake *Huron*, the Courſe is North for twelve Leagues further.

The Pains the young Savages take to adorn themſelves.

In croſſing Lake *St. Claire*, I had in my Canoe a young Savage ſtrong and vigorous, and on the Strength of whoſe Arms I much depended, in granting him the Paſſage which he aſked of me; but he gave me little Aſſiſtance. In Recompence he diverted me much, till a Storm which roſe over our Heads, began to make me uneaſy. This young Man had been at his Toilet before he embarked, and he did not give three Strokes with his Oar, but he took his Looking Glaſs to ſee if the Motion of his Arms had not diſordered the dreſſing of his Hair; or if the Sweat had not altered the Figures he had drawn on his Face with Red, and other Colours, with which he had painted himſelf.

I know not whether he did not hope to arrive at the Village of the *Miſſiſaguez* before Night, to be preſent at ſome Feaſt, but we could not go ſo far. The Storm began juſt as we got to an Iſland at the End of the Traverſe of the Lake, and we were forced to ſtay there. The young Savage however did not appear to be much diſconcerted at this Diſappointment, for theſe People are eaſily reconciled to every Accident: Perhaps alſo he only intended to ſhew himſelf to us in all his Finery; but if this was his Deſign he loſt his Labour, I had ſeen him a few Days before in his natural Appearance, and liked him much better than with this odd Mixture of Colours, which had coſt him ſo much Pains. We ſee few Women paint their Faces here, but the Men, and eſpecially the young ones, are very curious in this Ornament: There are ſome who employ half a Day in painting themſelves in this Manner only to go from Door to Door to be looked at, and who return mightily ſatisfied with themſelves, tho' Nobody has ſaid a Word to them.

We entered Lake *Huron* the twentieth, about ten in the Morning. And we preſently had the Diverſion of fiſhing for Sturgeon. The next Day, in Spite of the Thunder, which grumbled all the Day, but which was ſatisfied with threatening us, I advanced near twenty-five Leagues on the Lake, but the twenty-third a thick Fog, which hindered us from ſeeing four Paces before our Canoe, obliged us to go more ſlowly, becauſe we ſailed on a rocky Bottom, which in many Places is not covered with half a Foot Water: It extends a great Way into the Lake,

and

and is ten Leagues long: Our *Canadians* call it *les Pays Plats*, (*the Flat Country.*)

The next Day we gained the Bay of *Saguinam*, which is five or six Leagues wide at the Mouth, and thirty deep. The *Outaouais* have a Village in the Bottom of this Bay, which they say is a very fine Country. From thence to *Michillimakinac* we see nothing fine, no more Vines, bad Woods, and very little Game. Ten Leagues above the Bay of *Saguinam* we see two pretty large Rivers a League distant from each other, and four or five Leagues farther the Bay of *Tonnerre* (*Thunder Bay*), which is three Leagues wide at its Entrance, and has but little Depth.

The Situation of Michillimakinac.

Michillimakinac (*a*) is 43° 30 Minutes North Latitude, and the Course, which is a 100 Leagues from the Mouth of the Strait, coasting the West Side of Lake *Huron*, is almost North. I arrived the twenty-eighth at this Post, which is much declined since *M. de la Motte Cadillac* drew to *Detroit* the greatest Part of the Savages who were settled here, and especially the *Hurons*. Several *Outaouais* have followed them, others have dispersed themselves in the Isles of *Castor*; there is only here a middling Village, where there is still a great Trade for Peltry, because it is the Passage or the Rendezvous of many of the Savage Nations. The Fort is preserved, and the House of the Missionaries, who are not much employed at present, having never found much Docility among the *Outaouais*; but the Court thinks their Presence necessary, in a Place where one must often treat with our Allies, to exercise their Ministry among the *French*, who come hither in great Numbers. I have been assured, that since the Settlement of *Detroit*, and the Dispersion of the Savages occasioned thereby, many Nations of the North who used to bring their Peltries hither, have taken the Route of *Hudson's Bay*, by the River *Bourbon*, and go there to trade with the *English*; but *M. de la Motte* could by no Means foresee this Inconvenience, since we were then in Possession of *Hudson's Bay*.

The Situation of *Michillimakinac* is very advantageous for Trade. This Post is between three great Lakes; Lake *Michigan*, which is three Hundred Leagues in Compass, without mentioning the great Bay that comes into it; Lake *Huron*, which is three Hundred and fifty Leagues in Circumference, and which is triangular; and the Upper *Lake*, which is five Hundred Leagues. All three are navigable for the largest Barks, and the two first are only separated by a little Strait, which has also

(*a*) Some pronounce it *Missillimakinac*, which deceived *M. de la Martiniere*, who has made it two different Places.

Water

Water enough for some Barks which may still sail without any Obstacle through all the Lake *Erié* till they come to *Niagara*. It is true there is no Communication between Lake *Huron*, and the *Upper Lake*, but by a Canal of twenty-two Leagues, much encumbered with Falls or Torrents; but these Torrents do not hinder the Canoes from coming to unload at *Michillimakinac*, every Thing that can be got from the *Upper Lake*.

Description of the Upper Lake.

This Lake is two Hundred Leagues long from East to West, and in many Places eighty wide from North to South, all the Coast is sandy, and pretty strait; it would be dangerous to be surprised here by a North Wind. The North Side is more convenient for sailing, because it is all along lined with Rocks, which form little Harbours, where it is very easy to take Refuge; and nothing is more necessary when we sail in a Canoe on this Lake, in which Travellers have observed a pretty singular Phœnomenon. They say, that when there will be a Storm they have Notice of it two Days before. At first, they perceive a little Trembling on the Surface of the Water, and that lasts all the Day, without any manifest Increase; the next Day the Lake is covered with pretty large Waves, but they do not break all the Day, so that one may sail without Danger, and may also make a great deal of Way if the Wind is fair; but the third Day, when it is least expected, the Lake is all on Fire; the Ocean, in its greatest Fury, is not more agitated, and one must have instantly some Asylum to fly to for Safety; which we are sure to find on the North Side, whereas on the South Coast, one must from the second Day encamp at a good Distance from Shore.

Fable of the Savages of the Upper Lake.

The Savages, by Way of Acknowledgement for the Quantity of Fish this Lake affords them, and through the Respect they are inspired with from its vast Extent, have made it a Kind of Deity, and offer Sacrifices to it after their Manner. But I think that it is not to the Lake itself, but to the Genius which presides over it, that they offer up their Prayers: If we believe them, this Lake has a divine Origin: 'Twas *Michabou*, the God of the Waters, who made it to take Beavers. In the Canal by which it discharges itself into Lake *Huron*, there is a Torrent caused by some great Rocks; our Missionaries who once had here a very flourishing Church called it *the Fall of St. Mary*. These Rocks according to the Tradition of the Barbarians are the Remains of a Causey or Bank, which the God built to stop the Waters of the Rivers, and of the Lake *Alimipegon*, which have filled this Great Lake.

On its Borders, in ſome Places, and about certain Iſlands, they find great Pieces of Copper, which are alſo the Object of the ſuperſtitious Worſhip of the Savages; they look upon them with Veneration, as a Preſent of the Gods who live under the Waters; they gather the ſmalleſt Bits of it, and preſerve them with Care, but make no Uſe of them. They ſay, that formerly there was a great Rock that ſtood high above the Water all of the ſame Matter; and as it does not appear at preſent, they ſay that the Gods have carried it to another Place; but it is very probable, that in Length of Time the Waves of the Lake have covered it with Sand and Mud; and it is certain, that there has been diſcovered in many Places, a pretty large Quantity of this Metal, without being obliged to dig deep for it. At my firſt Journey into this Country, I knew one of our Brethren, who was a Goldſmith by Trade, and who, whilſt he was in the Miſſion of *St. Mary's* Fall, went thither to find Copper, and had made Candleſticks, Croſſes, and Cenſers of it; for this Copper is often almoſt entirely pure.

Copper Mines.

The Savages add, that when *Michabou* made the Upper *Lake*, he dwelt at *Michillimakinac*, where he was born; this Name is properly that of a little Iſland, almoſt round, and very high, ſituate at the Extremity of Lake *Huron*, and by Cuſtom it has given its Name to all the neighbouring Country. The Iſland may be about three or four Miles round, and one may ſee it at the Diſtance of twelve Leagues. There are two Iſlands to the South of it, the fartheſt of which is five or ſix Leagues long, the other is very ſmall, and quite round. They are both well wooded, and the Lands are good; whereas that of *Michillimakinac* is only a barren Rock, and ſcarcely covered with a little Moſs and Herbs. It is nevertheleſs one of the moſt celebrated Places of *Canada*, and was a long Time, according to the antient Tradition of the Savages, the chief Abode of a Nation of the ſame Name, and of which they reckoned thirty Villages in the Environs of the Iſland. They ſay, that the *Iroquois* deſtroyed them, but they do not ſay at what Time, nor on what Occaſion. This is certain, that there are no Marks of them remaining. I have ſomewhere read, that our old Miſſionaries have ſeen ſome Remains of theſe People *(a)*.

Sequel of the Traditions of the Savages.

The *Michillimakinacs* lived almoſt only by Fiſhing, and there is perhaps no Place in the World where there is ſuch Plenty of Fiſh. The moſt common Fiſh in the three Lakes, and in the Rivers that flow into them, are the Herring, the Carp, the Gilt Fiſh, the

Plenty of Fiſh in theſe Parts.

(a) The Word *Michillimakinac* ſignifies a great Number of Tortoiſes; but I never heard they find more here at preſent than in other Places.

Pike,

Pike, the Sturgeon, the *Aſtikamegue*, or white Fiſh, and above all, the Trout. They take three Sorts of the laſt, among which ſome are of a monſtrous Size, and in ſuch Numbers, that a Savage with his Spear will ſometimes ſtrike fifty in three Hours Time. But the moſt famous of all is the White Fiſh: It is about the Bigneſs and Shape of a Mackerel; I know of no Kind of Fiſh that is better eating. The Savages ſay, that it was *Michabou* who taught their Anceſtors to fiſh, that he invented Nets, and that he took the Notion of them from the Spiders Web. Theſe People, as you ſee, Madam, do not give greater Honour to their God than he deſerves, ſince they are not afraid of ſending him to School to a vile Inſect.

Of the Iſles of Caſtor (Beaver), *and of the Nation of the* Caſtor.

Whatever Lands appear in Sight hereabout, do not give an Idea of a good Country; but there is no Need of going far to find Soils fit for every Thing. We may ſay the ſame of the Iſles of *Caſtor*, which we leave on the left Hand, a little after we enter into the Lake *Michigan*. The *Outaouais*, who are retired thither, ſow here Maiz, and they have learnt this good Cuſtom from the *Hurons*, with whom they have lived a long Time in theſe Parts. The *Amikoues* formerly dwelt in theſe Iſlands: This Nation is now reduced to a very ſmall Number of Families, which have paſſed over to the Iſland *Manitoualin*, on the North Side of the Lake *Huron*. It is, nevertheleſs, one of the moſt noble of *Canada*, according to the Savages, who believe it to be deſcended from the *Great Caſtor*, which is, after *Michabou* or the *Great Hare*, their principal Deity, and whoſe Name it bears.

It was He, as they ſay further, that formed the Lake *Nipiſſing*; and all the Falls we meet with in the *Great River* of the *Outaouais*, which goes out of it, are the Remains of Banks he made to compaſs his Deſign. They add, that he died at the ſame Place, and that he is buried on a Mountain, which is ſeen on the North Side of Lake *Nipiſſing*. This Mountain repreſents naturally on one Side the Shape of a Beaver; and this is, no Doubt, what has given Riſe to all theſe Stories: But the Savages maintain, that it was the *Great Caſtor* who gave this Shape to the Mountain, after he had choſen it for his Burial-Place; and they never paſs by this Place without paying their Homage to him, by offering him the Smoke of their Tobacco.

This is, Madam, what I thought worthy of Note in this Poſt, which is ſo famous in the Travels and Accounts of *Canada*.----I return to the Manners and Cuſtoms of the Savages; and after having mentioned what concerned their Wars, I am going to entertain you concerning their Marriages.

A Plurality of Wives is established in many Nations of the *Algonquin* Language, and it is common enough to marry all the Sisters; this Custom is founded on the Notion they have, that Sisters will agree together better than Strangers. In this Case all the Wives are upon an equal Footing; but among the true *Algonquins* they have two Sorts of Wives, and the second are Slaves to the first. Some Nations have Wives in all the Places where they stay any considerable Time for hunting; and I have been assured that this Abuse has been introduced lately among the People of the *Huron* Language, who in all former Times were satisfied with one Wife. But in the *Iroquois* Canton of *Tsonnonthouan* there prevails a much greater Disorder still, which is a Plurality of Husbands.

Of the Plurality of Wives and Husbands.

As to what concerns the Degrees of Kindred, with Respect to Marriage, the *Hurons* and the *Iroquois* are very scrupulous in this Matter: Among them there must be no Manner of Relation between the Parties to be married, and even Adoption is comprehended in this Law. But the Husband, if his Wife dies first, must marry her Sister, or in Default of such, the Woman which his Wife's Family shall chuse for him: The Woman, on her Side, is obliged to the same Thing with Respect to the Brothers, or the Relations of her Husband, if he dies without Children, and she is still of an Age to have any. The Reason they give for it, is the same that is mentioned in the 25th Chapter of *Deuteronomy*, verse 6. The Husband who should refuse to marry the Sister, or the Relation of the deceased Wife, would expose himself to the greatest Outrages that the Person rejected can possibly do him, and would be obliged to suffer them without Complaint or Resistance. When for Want of any Relations, they permit a Widow to provide herself another Way, they are obliged to make her Presents: This is as a Testimony which they give of her good Conduct, and which she has a Right to demand, if she has really behaved well all the Time of her Marriage.

Of the Degrees of Kindred.

There are in all Nations some considerable Families, which cannot marry but among themselves, especially among the *Algonquins*. In general, the Stability of Marriages is sacred in this Country, and for the most Part they consider as a great Disorder those Agreements which some Persons make to live together as long as they like, and to separate when they are tired of each other. A Husband who should forsake his Wife without a lawful Cause, must expect many Insults from her Relations; and a Woman who should leave her Husband without being forced to it by his ill Conduct, would pass her Time still worse.

Particular Laws for Marriages.

Among

Among the *Miamis*, the Husband has a Right to cut off his Wife's Nose if she runs away from him; but among the *Iroquois* and the *Hurons* they may part by Consent. This is done without Noise, and the Parties thus separated may marry again. These Savages cannot even conceive that there can be any Crime in this. "My Wife and I cannot agree together," said one of them to a Missionary, who endeavoured to make him comprehend the Indecency of such a Separation, "my Neighbour's "Case was the same, we changed Wives, and we are all four "happy: What could be more reasonable than to make us "mutually happy, when it is so cheaply done, without wrong- "ing any Body." Nevertheless, this Custom, as I have already observed, is looked upon as an Abuse, and is not antient, at least among the *Iroquois*.

Jealousy of the Savages.

What most commonly disturbs domestic Peace among the People of *Canada*, is Jealousy, which is equal on both Sides. The *Iroquois* boast that they are never troubled with it; but those who are most acquainted with them, affirm, that they are jealous to Excess. When a Woman has discovered that her Husband has a Mistress, her Rival ought to be well on her Guard, inasmuch as the unfaithful Husband cannot defend her, nor in any Manner take her Part. A Man who should use his Wife ill on this Account, would be disgraced.

How they treat of Marriages.

Treaties of Marriage are entirely carried on by the Parents: The Parties interested do not appear at all, and give themselves up entirely to the Will of those on whom they depend. But is it not Matter of Surprise in the Whimsicalness of these Savages, who do not make themselves dependent on their Parents but in that Matter only, where there is the most Reason to use their own Choice. However, the Parents do not conclude any Thing without their Consent; but this is only a Formality. The first Advances must be made by the Matrons, but there are seldom any made on the Woman's Side: Not but if any Girl was to continue too long without being sued for, her Family would act under-hand to find her a Suitor; but this is done with a great deal of Precaution. In some Places the Women are not in Haste to be married, because they are allowed to make what Trials of it they please, and the Ceremony of Marriage only changes their Condition for the worse.

In general, there is observed a great deal of Modesty in the Behaviour of the young People whilst they treat of their Marriage; and they say that it was quite otherwise in the antient Time. But what is almost incredible, and which is nevertheless attested by good Authors, is, that in many Places the new married

ried Couple are together a whole Year, living in a perfect Continence: This is, they say, to shew that they married for Friendship, and not to gratify a sensual Passion. A young Woman would even be pointed at that should happen to be with Child the first Year of her Marriage.

After this it will be easier to believe what is said of the young People's Behaviour, during their Courtship in the Places where they are allowed to see one another in private. For though Custom allows them to have very private Meetings, yet in the greatest Danger that Chastity can be exposed to, and even under the Vail of Night, they say, that nothing passes against the Rules of the strictest Decorum, and that not even a Word is spoken that can give the least Offence to Modesty. I make Account, Madam, that you will approve my not entering into a Detail on this Subject, which some Authors have done; it would make the Thing appear still more improbable.

Of the Ceremonies of Marriage.

I find in all that has been written of the Preliminaries and Ceremonies of the Marriages of these People various Accounts, proceeding either from the different Customs of divers Nations, or from the little Care the Authors of Relations took to be well informed: Furthermore, the whole appeared to me to be so little worthy your Curiosity, that I thought it not worth my while to enquire a great deal about it. The Husband that is to be, must make Presents, and in this, as in every Thing else, nothing can exceed the Discretion with which he behaves, and the respectful Behaviour which he shews to his future Spouse. In some Places the young Man is contented to go and sit by the Side of the young Woman in her Cabin, and if she suffers it, and continues in her Place, it is taken for her Consent, and the Marriage is concluded. But in the midst of all this Deference and Respect, he gives some Tokens that he will soon be Master. In Fact, among the Presents she receives, there are some which ought less to be regarded as Marks of Friendship, than as Symbols and Notices of the Slavery to which she is going to be reduced: Such are the Collar, *(a)* the Kettle, and a Billet, which are carried to her Cabin. This is to let her know, that she is to carry the Burdens, dress the Provisions, and get Wood for Firing. The Custom is also in some Places for her to bring before-hand into the Cabin where she is to dwell after Marriage, all the Wood that will be wanted for the next Winter. And it is to be observed, that in all I have just said, there is no Difference between the Nations, where the

(a) This Collar is that which I have mentioned before; *that is to say,* long and broad Band of Leather which serves to draw Burdens.

Women

Women have all the Authority, and those where they have nothing to do with the Affairs of Government. These same Women, who are in some Degree the Mistresses of the State, at least for Form, and who make the principal Body of it, when they have attained a certain Age, and have Children in a Condition to make them respected, are not at all respected before this, and are in their domestic Affairs the Slaves of the Husbands.

Advantages of the Mothers over the Fathers.

In general there are perhaps no People in the World who more despise the Sex. To call a Savage a Woman, is the greatest Affront that can be given him. Notwithstanding, the Children belong only to the Mother, and acknowledge her alone. The Father is always as a Stranger with Respect to them; in such a Manner, however, that if he is not regarded as a Father, he is always respected as the Master of the Cabin. I know not, however, if all this is universal amongst all the People of *Canada* that we are acquainted with; no more than what I have found in some good Memoirs, that the young Wives, besides what their Husbands have a Right to require of them for the Service of the Cabin, are obliged to supply all the Wants of their own Parents; which probably must be understood of those who have no longer any Person to render them these Services, and who are not, by Reason of their Age or Infirmities, in a Condition to help themselves.

However this may be, the new married Man is not without Employment. Besides Hunting and Fishing, which he is obliged to follow all his Life, he must at first make a Mat for his Wife, build her a Cabin, or repair that they are to live in; and as long as he lives with his Wife's Parents, he must carry to their Cabin all that he gets by Hunting and Fishing. Among the *Iroquois*, the Woman never leaves her Cabin, because she is judged the Mistress, or at least the Heiress of it. Among other Nations, after a Year or two, she goes to live with her Mother-in-law.

Of their Lying-in, and its Consequences.

The Savage Women in general are brought to Bed without any Pain, and without any Assistance; but there are some who are a long Time in Labour, and suffer much. When this happens, they give Notice of it to the young People, who all on a sudden, and when the Patient least expects it, come and make great Noises at the Door of the Cabin, the Surprise of which has such an Effect upon her, as instantly to procure her Delivery. The Women never lay-in in their own Cabins; many are taken suddenly, and bring forth their Children as they are at Work, or on a Journey: For others, when they find them-

themselves near their Time, they make a little Hut without the Village, and they remain there forty Days after they are delivered. But I think I have heard say that this is only done for the first Child.

This Time being expired, they extinguish all the Fires of the Cabin to which she is to return; they shake all the Clothes, and at her Return they light a new Fire: They observe pretty nearly the same Formalities with Regard to all Persons of the Sex in the Time of their Terms, and not only whilst these last, but also whilst a Woman is with Child, or gives Suck, (and they commonly suckle their Children three Years) the Husband never approaches them. Nothing would be more Praise-worthy than this Custom, if both Parties preserved the Fidelity they owe to each other; but there is often a Failure on one Side or other. Such is the Corruption of the human Heart, that the wisest Regulations often produce the greatest Disorders. It is even said, that the Use of some Simples, which have the Power to prevent the Consequences of the Women's Infidelity, is pretty common in this Country.

The Care the Mothers take of their Children.

Nothing can exceed the Care which the Mothers take of their Children while they are in the Cradle; but as soon as they are out of it, they leave them entirely to themselves; not through Want of Affection or Indifference, for they never lose the Tenderness they have for them, but with their Lives; but because they are persuaded it is best to leave Nature to herself, without any Restraint. The Act which terminates the first Stage of Infancy, is giving a Name, which among these People is an Affair of Importance.

Of naming their Children.

This Ceremony is performed in a Feast, where no Persons are present but of the same Sex with the Child that is to be named. While they are eating the Child is upon the Knees of the Father or Mother, who continually recommend it to the Spirits, especially to that which is to be its Guardian Genius; for every Person has their own, but not at their Birth. They never make new Names, each Family has a certain Number, which they take by Turns. Sometimes also they change their Names as they grow up, and there are some Names which they cannot go by after a certain Age; but I do not think this is the Custom every where: And as among some People in taking a Name they take the Place of the Person that bore it last, it sometimes happens that a Child is called Grandfather, and treated as such by one who might really be so to the Child.

They never call a Man by his proper Name, when they talk to him in common Discourse, this would be unpolite; they always give him the Quality he has with Respect to the Person that speaks to him; but when there is between them no Relation or Affinity, they use the Term of Brother, Uncle, Nephew, or Cousin, according to each other's Age, or according to the Value they have for the Person they address.

Remarks on their Names.

Further, it is not so much to render Names immortal, if I may use the Expression, that they revive them, as to engage those to whom they are given either to imitate the brave Actions of their Predecessors, or to revenge them if they have been killed or burnt, or lastly to comfort and help their Families. Thus a Woman who has lost her Husband, or her Son, and finds herself without the Support of any Person, delays as little as she can to transfer the Name of him she mourns for to some Person capable of supplying his Place. They change their Names on many other Occasions, to give the Particulars of which would take up too much Time: There needs no more for this Purpose than a Dream, or the Order of a Physician, or some such trifling Cause. But I have said enough on this Head, and here is a Traveller waiting to know if I have any Commission for him to *Quebec*. I shall therefore close my Letter and give it him.

I am, &c.

LETTER XIX.

Voyage to the Bay. Description of the Route, and of the Bay. Irruption of the SPANIARDS *against the* MISSOURIS, *and their Defeat. The Dances of the* SAVAGES.

MADAM, MICHILLIMAKINAC, *July* 21.

SINCE writing my last Letter, I have made a Voyage to the Bay eighty Leagues distant from this Post. I took Advantage of the Opportunity of going with M. *de Montigny*, Captain of a Company of the Troops which the King maintains in *Canada*, Knt. of St. *Louis*, and whose Name is famous in the Annals of this Colony; but he is at least as valuable for his Probity and his Character full of Equity and Sincerity, as for his Courage and warlike Exploits.

We embarked the second of July in the Afternoon, we coasted for thirty Leagues a Cape which separates Lake *Michigan* from the *Upper Lake*; it is in some Places only a few Leagues wide, and it is scarce possible to see a worse Country; but it is terminated by a pretty River called the *Manistie*, full of Fish, and especially of Sturgeons. A little further, going to the South West, we enter into a great Gulf, the Entrance of which is bordered with Islands; they call it the *Gulf*, or the *Bay of the Noquets*. This is a very small Nation which came from the Borders of the *Upper Lake*, and of which there remains only a few Families dispersed here and there, without any fixed Abode.

Of the Bay of the Noquets.

The *Bay of the Noquets* is separated from the Great Bay only by the Isles of the *Pouteouatamis*, and I have already observed that they were the antient Abode of these Savages. The greatest Part of them are very well wooded; but the only one which is still peopled is not the largest nor the best, there remains in it now only one indifferent Village, where we were obliged to pass the Night, though very much against our Inclinations: We could not refuse the pressing Intreaties of the Inhabitants; and indeed there is no Nation in *Canada* that hath always been more sincerely attached to the *French*.

The Isles of the Pouteouatamis.

The 6th we were stopped almost the whole Day by contrary Winds; but it proving calm at Night, we embarked a little after Sun-set by a fine Moon-light, and we kept going forwards twenty-four Hours together, making only a very short Stop to say Mass, and to dine. The Sun shone so hot, and the Water of the Bay was so warm, that the Gum of our Canoe melted in several Places. To compleat our Misfortune, the Place where we stopped to encamp, was so full of Gnats and Musketoes, that we could not close our Eyes, though we had not slept for two Days before; and as the Weather was fine, and we had Moon-light, we embarked again on our Route at Three o'Clock in the Morning.

After we had gone five or six Leagues, we found ourselves over-against a little Isle, which is not far from the West Side of the Bay, and which hid from us the Entrance of a River, upon which is the Village of the *Malhomines*, which the *French* call *folles Avoines*, (*wild Oats*), probably because they make their common Food of this Grain. The whole Nation consists of no more than this Village, which is not very populous. This is to be regretted, for they are very fine Men, and the best shaped of all *Canada*: They are even taller than the *Pouteouatamis*. I am assured that they have the same Origin, and nearly

Of the Malhomines, *or Nation of* wild Oats.

nearly the ſame Language, as the *Noquets* and the *Saulteurs*, (*Leapers*); but they add, that they have alſo a particular Language which they keep to themſelves. They have likewiſe told me ſome odd Stories of them, as of a Serpent which goes every Year into the Village, and is received by them with great Ceremonies, which makes me believe that they are inclined to Sorcery.

Of the People called Puans, (ſtinking).

A little beyond the Iſland I juſt mentioned, the Country changes its Appearance all at once; and from being wild enough, as it is to this Place, it becomes the moſt charming in the World. It has even ſomething more ſmiling than the Strait; but though it is every where covered with very fine Trees, it is much more ſandy, and not ſo fertile. The *Otchagras*, who are commonly called the *Puans*, dwelt formerly on the Borders of the Bay, in a very delightful Situation. They were attacked here by the *Illinois*, who killed a great Number of them: The Remainder took Refuge in the River of the *Outagamis*, which runs into the Bottom of the Bay. They ſeated themſelves on the Borders of a Kind of Lake; and I judge it was there, that living on Fiſh which they got in the Lake in great Plenty, they gave them the Name of *Puans*; becauſe all along the Shore where their Cabins were built, one ſaw nothing but ſtinking Fiſh, which infected the Air. It appears at leaſt that this is the Origin of the Name which the other Savages had given them before us, and which has communicated itſelf to the Bay, far from which they never removed. Some Time after they had quitted their antient Poſt, they endeavoured to revenge the Blow they had received from the *Illinois*; but this Enterprize cauſed them a new Loſs, which they never recovered. Six hundred of their beſt Men were embarked to go in Search of the Enemy; but as they were croſſing Lake *Michigan*, they were ſurpriſed by a violent Guſt of Wind, which drowned them all.

Of the Fort, and of the Miſſion of the Bay.

We have in the Bay a Fort which ſtands on the Weſt Side of the River of the *Outagamis*, half a League from its Mouth; and before we arrive at it, we leave on the Left Hand a Village of *Sakis*. The *Otchagras* have lately come and ſeated themſelves near us, and have built their Cabins about the Fort. The Miſſionary, who is lodged pretty near the Commandant, hopes, when he has learnt their Language, to find them more docible than the *Sakis*, among whom he labours with very little Succeſs. Both of them appear to be a good Sort of People, eſpecially the firſt; whoſe greateſt Fault is, that they are a little given to thieving. Their Language is very different from all the others, which makes me believe that it is not derived ſrom any of *Canada* ; and indeed they have always had more Intercourſe with the People of the Weſt, than with thoſe we are acquainted with in this Country.

Of the Sakis.

The *Sakis*, though they are but a ſmall Number, are divided into two Factions, one of which ſide with the *Outagamis*, and the other with the *Pouteouatamis*. Thoſe who are ſettled in this Poſt, are for the moſt Part of the laſt Party, and of Conſequence in our Intereſt. They received the new Commandant with great Demonſtrations of Joy. As ſoon as they knew he was near arriving, they ranged themſelves with their Arms on the Bank of the River; and the Moment they ſaw him appear, they ſaluted him with a Diſcharge of their Muſkets, which they accompanied with great Shouts of Joy. Then four of the chief Men went into the River, where they were ſoon up to their Waiſt ; but they waded quite to his Canoe, and took him up in a great Robe made of many Roe-Buck Skins, well ſewed together, of which each of them held a Corner. They carried him thus to his Apartment, where they complimented him, and ſaid many Things to him which were extremely flattering.

The next Day the Chiefs of the two Nations paid me a Viſit, and one of the *Otchagras* ſhewed me a *Catalan* Piſtol, a Pair of *Spaniſh* Shoes, and I know not what Drug, which ſeemed to be a Sort of Ointment. He had received theſe Things from an *Ajouez*, and they came into his Hands by the following Means.

Spaniards *defeated by the Savages of the* Miſſouri.

About two Years ago, ſome *Spaniards*, who came (as they ſay) from *New Mexico*, intending to get into the Country of the *Illinois*, and drive the *French* from thence, whom they ſaw with extreme Jealouſy approach ſo near the *Miſſouri*, came down this River and attacked two Villages of the *Octotatas*, who are Allies of the *Ajouez* ; from whom it is alſo ſaid they are derived. As theſe Savages had no Fire Arms, and were ſurpriſed, the *Spaniards* made an eaſy Conqueſt, and killed a great many of them. A third Village, which was not far off the other two, being informed of what had paſſed, and not doubting but that theſe Conquerors would attack them, laid an Ambuſh, into which the *Spaniards* heedleſsly fell. Others ſay, that the Savages having heard that the Enemy were almoſt all drunk, and faſt aſleep, fell upon them in the Night. However it was, it is certain that they killed the greateſt Part of them.

There was in this Party two *Almoners*, one of whom was kill'd directly, and the other got away to the *Miſſourites*, who took him Priſoner, but he eſcaped from them very dexterouſly : He had a very fine Horſe, and the *Miſſourites* took Pleaſure to ſee him ride

it,

it, which he did very ſkilfully. He took Advantage of their Curioſity to get out of their Hands. One Day, as he was prancing and exerciſing his Horſe before them, he got a little Diſtance from them inſenſibly; then ſuddenly clapping Spurs to his Horſe, he was ſoon out of Sight. As they had taken no other Priſoner, it was not certainly known from what Part of *New Mexico* theſe *Spaniards* came, nor what was their Deſign: For what I have already ſaid of it, is only founded on the Report of the Savages, who perhaps intended to make their Court to us, in publiſhing that by this Defeat they had done us a great Service.

All that they brought me, was of the Spoils of the Almoner that was killed; and they took from him alſo a Book of Prayers, which I did not ſee: It was probably his Breviary. I bought the Piſtol: The Shoes were worth nothing; and the Savage would not part with his Ointment, fancying that it was a Sovereign Remedy for all Diſeaſes. I had the Curioſity to aſk how he intended to uſe it; he replied, it was ſufficient to ſwallow a little; and with what Diſeaſe ſoever one was attacked, it effected an immediate Cure: But he did not tell me that he had as yet made a Trial of it, and I adviſed him to the contrary. We begin here to find the Savages very ignorant; they are far from being ſo ingenious, or at leaſt ſo apt to learn, as thoſe who are more converſant with us.

A Council of the Sakis, *and on what Occaſion.*

The next Day ſeveral *Sakis* came to the Miſſionary, with whom I lodged, and invited me to come to a Kind of Council, which they propoſed to hold. I conſented; and when every one had taken his Place, the Chief laid a Collar on the Ground before me; and the Orator beginning his Speech, prayed me in the Name of all the reſt to engage the King *(a)* to take them under his Protection, and to purify the Air, which for ſome Time they ſaid had been infected, which appeared by the Number of ſick Perſons then in their Villages, and to defend them from their Enemies. I replied, that the King was very powerful, and perhaps more ſo than they imagined; but that his Power did not extend over the Elements; and that when Diſeaſes, and other like fatal Caſualties, afflicted his Provinces, he addreſſed himſelf, that an End might be put to them, to the Great Spirit that created Heaven and Earth, and who is alone the Sovereign Lord of Nature: That they ſhould do the ſame, and they would find the Benefit of it. But to prevail with him to hear their Prayers, they muſt firſt acknowledge him, and ren-

(a) Theſe Savages always ſpeak the Title of the King *(Le Roy)* in *French*.

der

der him the Worship and Homage which he has a Right to expect from all reasonable Creatures: That they could do nothing better, nor more agreeable to the King, than to listen to the Father *(a)* which his Majesty had sent them, and to be docible to his Instructions: That he was a Man beloved by Heaven: That the Manner in which he lived among them, could not fail of making him very much esteemed; and that his Charity towards the Sick, and all those who wanted his Assistance, ought to have convinced them of the tender and sincere Affection he had for them; and lastly, that I would not receive their Collar, till they had promised me to behave with Regard to this Missionary, in quite another Manner than they had done hitherto, and to give him no Cause for the future to complain of their Untowardness.

" As to the Protection of the King, which you ask, and the " Request you make me to engage him to defend you against " your Enemies; this great Prince has prevented your Wishes, " he has given good Orders on this Head to *Onontbio* *(b)*, who " is already inclined to execute them with the Zeal and Affec- " tion of a Father *(c)*. You can make no Doubt of this, if " you consider the Commandant he sends you. You must cer- " tainly know, and you seem in Fact to have been well inform'd, " that among the *French* Captains there are few that equal him " in Valour, and you will soon love him more than you esteem " him already."

They seemed to be satisfied with this Answer, and they promised me much more than they will perform, in all Probability: However, I took their Collar, and the Missionary flattered himself that this Action would have a good Effect.

In the Afternoon of the same Day, the two Nations gave us one after the other, the Diversion of the Dance of the Calumet in a great *Esplanade*, which is before the Lodgings of the Commandant. There was some Difference in their Way of performing this Dance; but it was not considerable. However, I learnt by it that these Feasts vary much; so that it is impossible to give a Description that agrees with them all. The *Otchagras* varied the Dance something more than the other, and shewed an extraordinary Agility; they are also better made, and more active than the *Sakis*.

(a) Father *Peter Chardin*, a *Jesuit*.

(b) This is the Name the Savages give the Governor-General. It means *Great Mountain*, and comes from the Chevalier *de Montmagny*, who was the second Governor of *Canada*.

(c) They always call the Governors, and the Commandants, their Fathers.

This

This Ceremony is properly a military Feast. The Warriors are the Actors, and one would say, that it was instituted only to give them an Opportunity of publishing their great Atchievements in War. I am not the Author of this Opinion, which does not agree well with their's, who have maintained that the Calumet took its Origin from the *Caduceus* of *Mercury*, and that in its Institution it was esteemed as a Symbol of Peace. All those I saw dance, sing, shake the *Chichicoué*, and beat the Drum, were young People equipped, as when they prepare for the March; they had painted their Faces with all Sorts of Colours, their Heads were adorned with Feathers, and they held some in their Hands like Fans. The Calumet was also adorned with Feathers, and was set up in the most conspicuous Place. The Band of Music, and the Dancers were round about it, the Spectators divided here and there in little Companies, the Women separate from the Men, all seated on the Ground, and dressed in their finest Robes, which at some Distance made a pretty Shew.

Description of this Dance.

Between the Music and the Commandant, who sat before the Door of his Lodging, they had set up a Post, on which at the End of every Dance a Warrior came and gave a Stroke with his Hatchet; at this Signal there was a great Silence, and this Man repeated with a loud Voice, some of his great Feats; and then received the Applauses of the Spectators, and after went to to his Place, and the Sport began again. This lasted two Hours for each of the Nations; and I acknowledge to You, Madam, that I took no great Pleasure in it, not only on Account of the same Tone, and the Unpleasantness of the Music, but because all the Dances consisted in Contorsions, which seemed to me to express nothing, and were no Way entertaining.

This Feast was made in Honour of the new Commandant; yet they did him none of the Honours which are mentioned in some Relations. They did not take him and place him on a new Mat; they made him no Present, at least that I know of; they did not pass any Feathers over his Head; I did not see the Calumet presented to him; and there were no Men quite naked, painted all over their Bodies, adorned with Plumes of Feathers, and Beads, and holding a Calumet in their Hands. Perhaps it is not the Custom of these People, or M. *de Montigny* had exempted them from these Ceremonies. I observed only, that from Time to Time all the Assembly set up great Shouts to applaud the Dancers, chiefly during the dancing of the *Otchagras*, who, in the Opinion of the *French*, bore away all the Honour of the Day.

I should

I should probably have had more Pleasure in seeing the Dance of the *Discovery*: It has more Action, and expresses better than the foregoing the Subject it represents. It is a natural Representation of all that passes in an Expedition of War; and, as I have before observed, that the Savages for the greatest Part only endeavour to surprise their Enemies, this is no Doubt the Reason why they have given this Dance the Name of the *Discovery*.

The Dance of the Discovery.

However that may be, only one single Man performs this Dance: At first he advances slowly into the midst of the Place, where he remains for some Time motionless, after which he represents one after another, the Setting out of the Warriors, the March, the Encamping; he goes upon the Discovery, he makes his Approach, he stops as to take Breath, then all on a sudden he grows furious, and one would imagine he was going to kill every Body; then he appears more calm, and takes one of the Company as if he had made him a Prisoner of War; he makes a Shew of knocking another's Brains out; he levels his Gun at another; and lastly, he sets up a running with all his Might; then he stops and recovers himself: This is to represent a Retreat, at first precipitate, and afterwards less so. Then he expresses by different Cries the various Affections of his Mind during his last Campaign, and finishes by reciting all the brave Actions he has performed in the War.

When the Dance of the *Calumet* is intended, as it generally is, to conclude a Peace, or a Treaty of Alliance against a common Enemy, they grave a Serpent on the Tube of the Pipe, and set on one Side of it a Board, on which is represented two Men of the two confederate Nations, with the Enemy under their Feet, distinguished by the Mark of his Nation. Sometimes instead of a Calumet, they set up a Fighting-Club. But if it concerns only a single Alliance, they represent two Men joining one Hand, and holding in the other a Calumet of Peace, and having each at his Side the Mark of his Nation. In all these Treaties they give mutual Pledges, Necklaces, Calumets, Slaves; sometimes Elks, and Deer Skins well dressed, and ornamented with Figures made with Porcupines Hair; and then they represent on these Skins the Things I have mentioned, either with Porcupines Hair, or plain Colours.

Of the Treaties which are made by Means of the Dance of the Calumet.

There are other Dances less compounded, the only Design of which is to give the Warriors an Opportunity of relating all their brave Actions. This is what the Savages are most ready to do, and they are never tired of it. He that gives the Feast invites all the Vil-

Other Dances.

lage by beating a Drum, and they meet in his Cabin, if it can contain all the Guests. The Warriors dance one after another, then striking on a Post, Silence is made: They say what they please, and they stop from Time to Time to receive the Applauses of the Auditors, who are not sparing of them. But if any one boasts falsely, any Person is allowed to take Dirt or Ashes and rub his Head with them, or play him any other Trick he thinks proper. Commonly they black his Face, saying, "What I do is to hide your Shame, for the first Time "you see the Enemy you will turn pale." He who has thus punished the Bragadocio, takes his Place, and if he commits the same Fault, the other never fails to return the Compliment. The greatest Chiefs have no Privilege in this Matter, and they must not be affronted at it.----This Dance is always performed in the Night.

The Dance of the Bull.

In the western Parts there is another Dance used, which is called *the Dance of the Bull.* The Dancers form several Circles or Rings, and the Music, which is always the Drum and the *Chichicoué*, is in the midst of the Place. They never separate those of the same Family: They do not join Hands, and every one carries in his Hand his Arms and his Buckler. All the Circles do not turn the same Way; and tho' they caper much, and very high, they always keep Time and Measure.

From Time to Time a Chief of a Family presents his Shield: They all strike upon it, and at every Stroke he repeats some of his Exploits. Then he goes and cuts a Piece of Tobacco at a Post, where they have fastened a certain Quantity, and gives it to one of his Friends. If any one can prove that he has done greater Exploits, or had a Share in those the other boasts of, he has a Right to take the Piece of Tobacco that was presented, and give it to another. This Dance is followed by a Feast; but I do not well see from whence it derives its Name, unless it be from the Shields, on which they strike, which are covered with Bull's Hides.

Dances ordered by the Physicians.

There are Dances prescribed by their Physicians for the Cure of the Sick, but they are generally very lascivious. There are some that are entirely for Diversion, that have no Relation to any Thing. They are almost always in Circles, to the Sound of the Drum and the *Chichicoué*, the Men apart from the Women. The Men dance with their Arms in their Hands, and tho' they never take hold of each other, they never break the Circle. As to what I said before, that they are always in Time, it is no difficult Thing to believe, because the Music of the Savages has but two or three Notes, which are repeated continually.

This makes their Feasts very tiresome to an *European* after he has seen them once, because they last a long Time, and you hear always the same Thing.

As the Nations near the Bay, if we except the *Pouteoutamis*, are much more rude and ignorant than the others, they are also more given to Superstition. The Sun and Thunder are their principal Deities, and they seem to be more strongly persuaded than those we are conversant with, that every Species of Animals has a Guardian Genius, who watches for its Preservation. A *Frenchman* having one Day thrown away a Mouse he had just catched, a little Girl took it up to eat it: The Father of the Child, who saw it, snatched it from her, and began to make great Caresses to the dead Animal. The *Frenchman* asked him the Reason, he replied, " *It is to appease the Genius* " *of the Mice, that he may not torment my Daughter, after she has* " *eaten this.*" After which he returned the Animal to the Child, who eat it.

They have above all much Veneration for Bears: As soon as they have killed one, they have a Feast, accompanied with some odd Ceremonies. The Head of the Bear, painted with all Sorts of Colours, is placed during the Repast on an elevated Place, and there receives the Homage of all the Guests, who celebrate by Songs the Praises of the Animal, while they cut his Body in Pieces, and feast upon it. These Savages have not only, like the rest, the Custom of preparing themselves for their great Hunting Matches by Fasting, which the *Outagamis* extend even to ten Days together, but also, while the Hunters are in the Field, they often oblige their Children to fast. They observe their Dreams while they fast, and draw from thence good and ill Presages of the Success of the Chace. The Intention of these Fasts is to appease the Guardian Genii of the Animals which they are to hunt; and they pretend that they inform them by Dreams, whether they will hinder or favour the Hunters.

The Nation which for twenty Years last has been the most talked of in these western Parts, is the *Outagamis*. The natural Fierceness of these Savages, sour'd by the ill Treatment they have several Times met with, sometimes without Cause, and their Alliance with the *Iroquois*, who are always disposed to create us new Enemies, have rendered them formidable. They have since made a strict Alliance with the *Sioux*, a numerous Nation, which has inured itself to War by Degrees; and this Union has rendered all the Navigation of the upper Part of the *Mississippi* almost impracticable to us. It is not quite safe to navigate the River of the *Illinois*, unless we are in a Condition to

prevent

prevent a Surprise which is a great Injury to the Trade between the two Colonies.

Various Nations to the North and West of Canada.

I met in the Bay some *Sioux*, of whom I made many Enquiries about the Countries, which are to the West and North West of *Canada*; and tho' I know we must not entirely depend on what the Savages say; yet by comparing what I have heard from them, with that which I have heard from many others, I have great Reason to believe that there are on this Continent some *Spaniards* or other *European* Colonies, much more North than any we know of *New Mexico* and *California*, and that in going up the *Missouri* as far as it is navigable, we come to a great River that runs to the West, and discharges itself into the *South Sea*. Independent of such Discovery, which I believe more easy this Way than by the North, I can make no Doubt, on weighing the Information I have had from many Places, and which agree pretty well together, that by endeavouring to penetrate to the Source of the *Missouri*, one should find wherewithal to make one Amends for the Charges and Fatigues of such an Enterprize.

I am, &c.

LETTER XX.

Departure from MICHILLIMAKINAC. *Remarks on the Currents of the Lake. Portrait of the* SAVAGES *of* CANADA. *Their good and bad Qualities.*

MADAM, LAKE MICHIGAN, *July* 31.

I Departed from *Michillimakinac* the Day before Yesterday at Noon, and I am detained here in a little Island that has no Name; a Canoe that came from the River *St. Joseph*, whither I am going, cannot go out, no more than our's, though they have the Wind favourable for them; but they say it is too stormy, and the Lake too rough, which gives me a fresh Opportunity of writing to you.

Remarks on the Currents of the Lakes.

Though the Wind was against me, when I embarked the 29th, I went eight good Leagues that Day, which proves that I was driven by the Currents. I had already observed the same Thing upon entering the Bay, and was surprised at it. It is certain that this Bay, having no other Outlet, discharges itself into Lake *Michigan*; and Lake *Michigan*, for the

the ſame Reaſon, muſt diſcharge its Waters into Lake *Huron*, and the rather, becauſe both the Bay and Lake *Michigan* receive ſeveral Rivers; Lake *Michigan* eſpecially, which receives a great Number, ſome of which are little inferior to the *Seine*; theſe great Currents are not perceivable but in the midſt of the Channel, and produce Eddies or counter Currents, of which we take Advantage when we go along Shore, as they are obliged to do who go in Canoes of Bark.

I went at firſt five Leagues to the Weſt, to get into Lake *Michigan*, I then turned to the South, and this is the only Route we have to take for a hundred Leagues to the River *St. Joſeph*. Nothing is finer than the Country which ſeparates the Lakes *Michigan* and *Huron*: Yeſterday I went three Leagues further, and a high Wind obliged me to ſtop at this Iſland. I ſhall ſhun the Irkſomeneſs of waiting here, by employing myſelf in finiſhing my Account of the natural Inhabitants of this vaſt Country, a great Part of which I have already travelled over.

Portrait of the Savages.

The Savages of *Canada* are generally well made, and of a lofty Stature; but it is not unuſual in ſome Nations to ſee ſome of only a middle Stature; but it is very uncommon to ſee any that are deformed, or that have any outward Blemiſh. They are robuſt, and of a healthy Conſtitution: They would be very long lived, if they ſpared themſelves a little more; but the greateſt Part ruin their Conſtitutions by forced Marches, by deſperate Faſtings, and by great Exceſſes in eating: Beſides that, during their Childhood, they have often their naked Feet in the Water, on the Snow and Ice. The Brandy which the *Europeans* have ſupplied them with, and for which they have ſuch a ſtrong Inclination that exceeds all that can be ſaid of it, and which they always drink till they are drunk, has compleated their Ruin, and has not a little contributed to the Deſtruction of all theſe Nations, which are at preſent reduced to leſs than the twentieth Part of what they were a hundred and fifty Years ago. If this continues they will become entirely extinct.

Their Strength.

Their Bodies are not confined in their Infancy like our's, and nothing is more proper to make their Joints free, and to give them that Suppleneſs in all their Limbs, which we ſo much admire in them, than this Liberty, and the Exerciſes to which the Children there are accuſtomed very early. The Mothers ſuckle them a long Time, and there are ſome that at ſix or ſeven years old ſtill take the Breaſt. Nevertheleſs, this does not hinder them from taking all Kinds of Food the firſt Year: In ſhort, the open Air to which they are expoſed, the Fatigues they make them ſuffer, but by little and little, and in a Manner proportioned to their

Age.

Age, with plain and natural Food; all this forms Bodies capable of performing and of suffering incredible Things; the Excess of which, as I have already observed, destroys many before they arrive at an Age of Maturity. We have seen some, after their Stomachs were swelled four Inches, still continue eating as heartily as if they had just begun: When they find themselves overcharged they smoke, then they sleep, and when they wake the Digestion is generally perfected. Sometimes they take an Emetic, after which they begin to eat again.

Their Vices.

In the Southern Countries they have but little Restraint in the Article of Women; who, on their Side, are very lascivious. From hence arises the Corruption of Manners, which for some Years past has infected the Northern Nations. The *Iroquois* in particular were chaste enough, till they were conversant with the *Illinois*, and other neighbouring People of *Louisiana:* They have gained nothing by their Acquaintance with them, but adopting their Vices. It is certain that Effeminacy and Lust were carried in these Parts to the greatest Excess. There were amongst them some Men who were not ashamed to dress themselves like Women, and to submit to all the Employments that belonged to the Women; from whence there followed a Corruption that cannot be expressed. Some have pretended, that this Custom came from I know not what Principle of Religion: But this Religion, like many others, has taken its Rise from the Depravation of the Heart; or if this Custom took its Rise from the Spirit, it ended in the Flesh. These effeminate Persons never marry, and abandon themselves to the most infamous Passions; they are also treated with the greatest Contempt.

Why the Country is not better peopled.

On the other Hand, though the Women are strong and lusty, they are unfruitful. Besides the Reasons I have already mentioned, *that is to say*, the Time they take to suckle their Children, their Custom of Continence all this Time, and the excessive Labours they are obliged to undergo, in whatsoever Condition they find themselves, this Barrenness proceeds also from the Custom established in many Places, which permits young Women to prostitute themselves before they are married; add to this, the extreme Necessity to which these People are often reduced, and which takes away their Desire of having Children.

The Advantages they have over us.

For the rest, it is certain, that they have great Advantages over us; and I consider, as the chief of all, the Perfectness of their Senses, either internal or external. In Spite of the Snow, which dazzles their Eyes, and the Smoke, which almost smothers them for six Months in the Year, their Sight never decays: Their

Hearing

Hearing is extremely quick, and their Smelling ſo exquiſite, that they ſmell Fire a long Time before they can diſcover it. On Account of the Exquiſiteneſs of their Smell, they can't bear the Scent of Muſk, nor any ſtrong Smell. They ſay alſo, that they like no Odours, but thoſe of Eatables.

Their Apprehenſion is very wonderful: It is enough for them to have been but once in a Place, to have an exact Idea of it, which is never effaced. If a Foreſt is ever ſo large and pathleſs, they croſs it without wandering, when they have well conſidered certain Marks, by which they guide themſelves.

The Inhabitants of *Acadia*, and of the Environs of the Gulf of *St. Laurence*, in their Canoes of Bark (to paſs over to *Terre de Labrador (New Britain)* to ſeek out the *Eſkimaux*, with whom they were at War) would go thirty or forty Leagues on the main Sea without Compaſs, and make the Land exactly at the Place they propoſed. In the moſt cloudy Weather they will follow the Sun many Days, without making any Miſtake: The beſt Clock cannot give us better Information of the Progreſs of the Sun, than they can, only by viewing the Sky; ſo that do what you can to put them out of their Way, 'tis very rare that they loſe their Route. They are born with this Talent: It is not the Fruit of their Obſervations, nor of long Cuſtom: Youth, who never before went out of their Village, travel as ſecurely as thoſe who have been moſt uſed to range the Country.

Their Eloquence.

The Beauty of their Imagination is equal to its Vivacity, and this appears in all their Diſcourſe. They are quick at Repartee, and their Speeches are full of ſhining Paſſages, that would have been applauded in the public Aſſemblies at *Rome* and *Athens*. Their Eloquence has ſomething in it ſo ſtrong, ſo natural, ſo pathetic, that Art cannot attain, and which the *Greeks* admired in the Barbarians: And though it does not appear to be ſupported by Action, though they make no Geſtures, and do not raiſe their Voice, we feel that they are thoroughly affected with what they ſay, and their Eloquence is perſuaſive.

Their Memory, their Penetration, their Judgment.

It would be ſtrange, that with ſuch a fine Imagination, they ſhould not have an excellent Memory. They are deſtitute of all the Helps we have invented to aſſiſt our's, or to ſupply its Defect. Nevertheleſs, it is ſcarcely credible of how many Matters, with what particular Circumſtances, and with how much Order, they treat in their Councils. On ſome Occaſions, however, they uſe little Sticks, to recollect the Articles they are to diſcuſs; and by this they form a Sort of local Memory ſo certain, that they will ſpeak four or five Hours together, will diſplay twenty Preſents, each of which requires an en-

tire

the Discourse, without forgetting any Thing, or even without Hesitation. Their Narration is clear and exact; and though they use many Allegories, and other Figures, it is animated, and has all the pleasing Turns which their Language affords.

They have a true and solid Judgment, and go directly to the Mark in View, without stopping, without wandering, and without being put on a wrong Scent. They readily conceive all that is within the Compass of their Knowledge; but to put them in a Way of succeeding in the Arts, without which they have lived hitherto, as they have not the least Idea of them, it would require a great deal of Labour; and the more so, as they have the highest Contempt for every Thing which they do not find necessary, *that is to say*, for what we value most. It would also be no small Difficulty to make them capable of Restraint and Application in Things merely speculative, or which they should look upon as useless. As to what relates to their own Concerns, they neglect nothing, nor do any Thing precipitately: And though they are so slow in taking their Resolutions, yet they are as warm and active in putting them in Execution. This is observed especially of the *Hurons* and the *Iroquois*. They are not only ready at Repartee, but also witty.

An *Outaouais*, named *John le Blanc*, a bad *Christian*, and a great Drunkard, being asked by *Comte de Frontenac*, what he thought Brandy was made of, which he loved so well, said it was an Extract of Tongues and Hearts; for (added he) when I have drank it, I fear nothing, and I talk to Admiration.

Their Greatness of Soul.

The greatest Part of them have truly a Nobleness and an Equality of Soul, to which we seldom arrive, with all the Helps we can obtain from Philosophy and Religion. Always Masters of themselves, in the most sudden Misfortunes, we can't perceive the least Alteration in their Countenances. A Prisoner, who knows in what his Captivity will end, or, which is perhaps more surprising, who is still uncertain of his Fate, does not lose on this Account a Quarter of an Hour's Sleep: Even the first Emotions do not find them at a Fault.

A *Huron* Captain was one Day insulted and struck by a young Man. Those who were present, would have punished this Audaciousness on the Spot. "*Let him alone*, (said the Captain) "*Did not you feel the Earth tremble? He is sufficiently informed of* "*his Folly.*"

Their Constancy in suffering Pain.

Their Constancy in suffering Pain, is beyond all Expression. A young Woman shall be a whole Day in Labour, without making one Cry: If she shewed the least Weakness, they would esteem her unworthy to be a Mother; because, as they say, she could only

only breed Cowards. Nothing is more common, than to see Persons of all Ages, and of both Sexes, suffer for many Hours, and sometimes many Days together, the sharpest Effects of Fire, and all that the most industrious Fury can invent to make it most painful, without letting a Sigh escape. They are employed for the most Part, during their Sufferings, in encouraging their Tormenters by the most insulting Reproaches.

An *Outagami*, who was burnt by the *Illinois* with the utmost Cruelty, perceiving a *Frenchman* among the Spectators, begged of him that he would help his Enemies to torment him; and upon his asking why he made this Request, he replied, " *Because I should have the Comfort of dying by the Hands of a Man.* " *My greatest Grief* (adds he) *is, that I never killed a Man.*" " *But* (said an ILLINOIS) *you have killed such and such a Person.*" " *As for the* ILLINOIS, (replied the Prisoner) *I have killed enough* " *of them, but they are no Men.*"

What I have observed in another Place, Madam, to lessen the Astonishment which such an Insensibility fills one with, does not hinder us from allowing that such a Behaviour shews a great deal of Bravery. There must always be, to elevate the Soul above the Sense of Pain to such a Degree, an Effort which common Souls are not capable of. The Savages exercise themselves in this all their Lives, and accustom their Children to it from their tenderest Years. We have seen little Boys and Girls tie themselves together by one Arm, and put a lighted Coal between them, to see which would shake it off first. In short, we must also allow, that according to *Cicero*'s Remark, an Habit of Labour makes us bear Pain more easily *(a)*. But there are perhaps no Men in the World who fatigue themselves more than the Savages, either in their Huntings, or in their Journies. Lastly, what proves that this Kind of Insensibility is in these Barbarians the Effect of a true Courage, is, that it is not found in all of them.

It is not surprising that with this Greatness of Soul, and these elevated Sentiments, the Savages should be intrepid in Danger, and of a Courage, Proof against every Thing. It is true, that in their Wars they expose themselves as little as may be, because they make it their chief Glory never to buy the Victory at a dear Rate; and because of their Nations not being numerous, they have made it a Maxim not to weaken them: But when they must fight, they do it like Lions, and the Sight of their Blood does but encrease their Strength and Courage. They have been in many Actions with our brave Men, who have seen them perform Things almost incredible.

(a) Consuetudo enim laborum perpessionem dolorum efficit faciliorem. 2 *Tusc.* 15.

A Miſſionary having accompanied ſome *Abenakis* in an Expedition againſt *New England*, and knowing that a great Party of the *Engliſh* were purſuing them in their Retreat, endeavoured all he could to make them make Haſte forward, but without Effect. All the Anſwer he received, was, that they were not afraid of thoſe People. At laſt all the *Engliſh* came in Sight, and they were at leaſt twenty to one. The Savages, without ſeeming at all ſurpriſed, firſt conducted the Father to a Place of Safety, then went and waited boldly for the Enemy in a Place where there was only ſome Stumps of Trees. The Engagement laſted almoſt the whole Day. The *Abenakis* did not loſe a Man, and put the *Engliſh* to Flight, after having covered the Field of Battle with the Dead.——I had this Account from the Miſſionary himſelf *(a)*.

Their Kindneſs to each other.

But what ſurpriſes infinitely in Men whoſe whole outward Appearance proclaims nothing but Barbarity, is to ſee them behave to each other with ſuch Kindneſs and Regard, that are not to be found amongſt the moſt civilized Nations. Doubtleſs this proceeds in ſome Meaſure from the Words MINE and THINE being as yet unknown to theſe Savages. Thoſe cold Words, as *St. Chryſoſtom* calls them, which extinguiſhing in our Hearts the Fire of Charity, lights up that of Covetouſneſs. We are equally charmed with that natural and unaffected Gravity which reigns in all their Behaviour, in all their Actions, and in the greateſt Part of their Diverſions; as likewiſe with the Civility and Deference they ſhew to their Equals, and the Reſpect of young People to the Aged; and laſtly, never to ſee them quarrel among themſelves with thoſe indecent Expreſſions, and the Oaths and Curſes, ſo common amongſt us. All which are Proofs of good Senſe, and a great Command of Temper.

I have already ſaid, that one of their Principles, and that of which they are the moſt jealous, is, that one Man owes nothing to another: But from this bad Maxim they draw a good Inference, *that is to ſay*, that we muſt never do an Injury to any Perſon, from whom we have received no Wrong. There is nothing wanting to their Happineſs, but to behave between Nation and Nation, as they do between private Perſons, and never to attack any People of whom they have no Cauſe to complain, and not to carry their Revenge ſo far.

Their Pride, and their other Failings.

On the other Hand, we muſt allow that what we moſt admire in the Savages, is not always pure Virtue; that Conſtitution and Vanity have a great Share in it, and that their beſt Qualities are

(a) Father *Vincent Bigot*.——This ſeems to be Apocrypha.

tarnished by great Vices. These Men, who at first View appear to us so contemptible, of all Mankind have the greatest Contempt for all others, and the highest Opinion of themselves. The proudest of all were the *Hurons*, before Successes had lifted up the Hearts of the *Iroquois*, and grafted in them a Haughtiness, which nothing can yet suppress, on a fierce Rudeness, which before was their distinguishing Character.

On the other Side, these People, so proud and jealous of their Liberty, are beyond all Imagination Slaves to Human Respect: They are accused of being light and inconstant; but they are so, rather through a Spirit of Independence, than by Character, as I have observed of the *Canadians*. They are distrustful and suspicious, especially towards us; treacherous, when their Interest is concerned; Dissemblers, and revengeful to Excess. Time does not abate in them their Desire of Revenge: It is the most precious Inheritance which they leave to their Children, and which is transmitted from Generation to Generation, till they find an Opportunity to execute it.

Qualities of the Heart.

As to what we call more particularly the Qualities of the Heart, the Savages do not value themselves much on them; or, to speak more properly, they are not Virtues in them. Friendship, Compassion, Gratitude, Attachment, they have something of all this, but it is not in the Heart; and in them it is less the Effect of a good Disposition, than of Reflexion, or Instinct. The Care they take of Orphans, Widows, and the Infirm, and the Hospitality they exercise in such an admirable Manner, are to them only the Consequence of their Persuasion, that all Things ought to be in common among Men. Fathers and Mothers have a Fondness for their Children, which rises even to Weakness; but which does not incline them to make them virtuous, and which appears to be purely Animal. Children, on their Side, have no natural Gratitude for their Parents, and they even treat them sometimes with Indignity, especially their Fathers. I have heard some Examples of this Sort, that are horrible, and which cannot be related: But here follows one Instance that was public.

Example of the little Affection of Children for their Parents.

An *Iroquois*, who served a long Time in our Troops against his own Nation, and even as an Officer, met his Father in an Engagement, and was going to kill him. When he discovered who he was, he held his Hand, and said to him, "*You have once given me Life, and now I give it to you. Let me meet with you no more; for I have paid the Debt I ow'd you.*" Nothing can better prove the Necessity of Education, and that Nature alone does not sufficiently instruct us in

our

our most essential Duties. And what demonstrates more evidently the Advantages of the *Christian* Religion, is, that it has produced in the Hearts of these Barbarians, in all these Respects, a Change which appears wonderful.

Particular Friendships among the Savages.

But if the Savages know not how to taste the Sweets of Friendship, they have at least discovered its Usefulness. Every one amongst them has a Friend nearly of his own Age, between whom there is a mutual Engagement, which is indissoluble. Two Men thus united for their common Interest, are obliged to do every Thing, and to run all Hazards to assist and succour each other. Death itself, as they believe, separates them only for a Time: They depend on meeting again in the other World, never to part more, being persuaded that they shall still want each other's Assistance.

I have heard it reported, on this Occasion, that a *Christian* Savage, but one who did not pursue the Maxims of the Gospel, being threatened with Hell by a *Jesuit*, asked this Missionary, if he thought his Friend, who was lately dead, was gone to that Place of Punishment? The Father replied, that he had Reason to judge that he had found Mercy with God. "*I won't go to* "*Hell neither*," said the Savage; and this Motive engaged him to do all we required, *that is to say*, that he was as willing to go to Hell as to Heaven, to meet with his Companion: But God makes Use of all Means to save his Elect. They add, that these Friends, when they are at a Distance from each other, use mutual Invocations in any Dangers they meet with; which is to be understood, without Doubt, of their Guardian Deities. These Associations are bound by Presents, and strengthened by Interest and Necessity. This is a Support on which they can almost always depend. Some report, that there is something unnatural in these Associations; but I have Reason to believe at least it is not general.

The Colour of the Savages.

The Colour of the Savages does not prove a third Species between the White and the Black, as some People have imagined. They are very swarthy, and of a dirty dark Red, which appears more in *Florida*, of which *Louisiana* is a Part: But this is not their natural Complexion. The frequent Frictions they use, gives them this Red; and it is surprising that they are not blacker, being continually exposed to the Smoke in Winter, to the great Heats of the Sun in Summer, and in all Seasons to all the Inclemencies of the Air.

It is not so easy to give a Reason why they have not a Hair on their whole Body, excepting the Hairs of their Head, which they have all very black, the Eye Lashes, and Eyebrows, which some also pluck off; and 'tis the same Case with almost all the *Americans*. What makes it still more surprising, is, that their Children are born with a thin Hair, and pretty long, all over their Bodies, but which disappears after eight Days. The old Men have also some Hairs on the Chin, as we see some old Women have with us. I have known some who attribute this Singularity to the constant Custom the *Americans* have of smoking, and which is common to both Sexes. Others think it more natural to say, that this proceeds from the Quality of their Blood; which being more pure, because of the Plainness of their Aliments, produces less of those Superfluities, which our's, being more gross, supplies so plentifully; or that having fewer Salts, it is less fit for these Sort of Productions. There is no Doubt that it is at least this Plainness of Food which renders the Savages so swift of Foot. I have seen a Man who came from an Island not far from *Japan*, who, before he had eat any Bread, assured me that he could travel on Foot thirty Leagues a Day, commonly without Fatigue; but since he had been used to Bread, he could not travel with the same Ease.

Why they have no Beards.

This is certain, that our Savages think it a very great Beauty to have no Hair but on the Head; that if they have any grow on their Chin, they pluck it off directly; that the *Europeans*, the first Time they saw them, appeared frightful to them with their long Beards, as was then the Fashion; that they do not think our white Colour handsome; and that they found the Flesh of the *English* and *French*, when they eat it, of a bad Taste, because it was salt.

Thus, Madam, the Idea which we formerly had in *Europe* of Savages, which were represented as hairy Men, is not only entirely the Reverse of the *Americans*, but it is exactly that which they at first had of us, because they thought all our Bodies were like our Breasts and Chins.

I am, &c.

LETTER

LETTER XXI.

Journey to the River ST. JOSEPH. *Remarks on the Rivers which run into Lake* MICHIGAN *from the East Of Father* MARQUETTE's *River, aud the Origin of its Name. Two Games of the* SAVAGES. *Some Remarks on the Character of these People.*

MADAM, ST. JOSEPH, *August* 16.

IT is eight Days since I arrived at this Post, where we have a Mission, and where there is a Commandant with a small Garrison. The House of the Commandant, which is a trifling Thing, is called the Fort, because it is surrounded with a poor Palisade, and it is much the same Thing in all other Places, excepting the Forts of *Chambly* and *Cataracoui*, which are real Fortresses. There are however in all of them some Pieces of Cannon or Pattereroes, which, in Case of Need, are sufficient to prevent a *Coup de Main*, and to keep the Savages in Awe.

Danger of the Navigation of Lake Michigan.

We have here two Villages of Savages, one of *Miamis* and the other of *Pouteouatamies*, they are both for the most Part *Christians*, but they have been a long Time without Pastors, and the Missionary that was lately sent hither will have no little Trouble to restore the Exercise of Religion. The River *St. Joseph* comes from the South East to discharge itself into the Bottom of Lake *Michigan*, the East Coast of which we must range, which is a hundred Leagues long, before we enter this River. Then we go up it two hundred Leagues to arrive at the Fort: This Navigation requires much Care, because when the Wind comes from the open Lake, *that is*, the West, the Waves are the whole length of the Lake; and the West Winds are very common here. It is also very probable that the Number of Rivers, which run into the Lake on the West Side, contribute by the Shock of their Currents with the Waves, to render the Navigation more dangerous: It is certain that there are few Places in *Canada* where there are more Wrecks.----But I take up my Journal again where I left off.

The

The first of *August*, after having failed cross a Bay that is thirty Leagues deep, I left on the Right the Isles of *Castor*, which appeared to be very well wooded; and some Leagues further, on the Left, I perceived on an Eminence of Sand a Kind of Bush, which, when we are over against it has the Shape of an Animal lying down. The *French* call it *L'ours qui dort (the sleeping Bear)*, and the Savages the *Bear lying down*. I went twenty Leagues that Day, and encamped in a little Island, 44° 30′ North Latitude; this is nearly the Latitude of *Montreal*. From the Entrance of Lake *Michigan* to this Island, the Coast is very sandy, but if we go a little Way into the Country it appears to be very good, at least to judge of it by the fine Forests with which it is covered. On the other Hand, it is well watered, for we went not a League without discovering either some large Brook, or some pretty River, and the farther we go South, the Rivers grow larger, and have a longer Course, the *Peninsula*, which separates Lake *Michigan* from Lake *Huron*, growing wider as it advances to the South. Nevertheless, the greatest Part of these Rivers are but narrow, and shallow at their Mouths; but they have this Singularity, that they form Lakes near their Entrance of two, three, or four Leagues round. This proceeds, no Doubt, from the Quantity of Sand which they bring down: These Sands being driven back by the Waves of the Lake, which almost always come from the West, gather at the Mouths of the Rivers, whose Waters being stopt by these Banks, which they pass over with Difficulty, have made themselves by Degrees these Lakes, or Ponds, which prevent the Inundation of the whole Country when the Snows melt.

Remarks on the Rivers we meet with in this Route.

On the third I entered Father *Marquette's* River to examine if what I had heard of it was true. It is at first only a Brook, but fifteen Paces higher, which is near two Leagues round, to make a Passage for it into the *Michigan*, one would think they had dug away with Pickaxes, a great Hill, which we leave to the Left at the Entrance, and on the Right the Coast is very low for the length of a good Musket-Shot; then all at once it rises very high. It had been thus represented to me; concerning which, this is the constant Tradition of all our Travellers, and what I have heard from some antient Missionaries.

Father Marquette's *River*.

Father *Joseph Marquette*, a Native of *Laon* in *Picardy*, where his Family still holds a distinguished Rank, was one of the most illustrious Missionaries of *New France*; he travelled over almost all Parts of it, and made many Discoveries; the last of which was the *Mississippi*, which he entered with the Sieur *Joliet* in 1673. Two Years after this Discovery, of which he published an Account, as he was going from *Chicagou*, which is at the Bottom of Lake *Michigan*, to *Michillimakinac*, he entered the River I am ſpeaking of; the Entrance of which was then at the Extremity of the low Land, which I have ſaid we leave to the Right at entering it. He ſet up his Altar here, and ſaid Maſs. After this, he went a little Diſtance to return Thanks, and prayed the two Men who managed his Canoe, to leave him alone for half an Hour. This Time being expired, they went to ſeek him, and were greatly ſurpriſed to find him dead; but they recollected, that upon entering the River, he had ſaid that he ſhould finiſh his Journey there. Nevertheleſs, as it was too far from thence to *Michillimakinac*, to carry his Body thither, they buried him pretty near the Side of the River; which from that Time has retired, as out of Reſpect, to the Cape, at the Foot of which it now runs, and where it has made a new Paſſage. The Year following, one of the two Men who had performed the laſt Duties to this Servant of GOD, returned to the Place where he had buried him, took up his Remains, and carried them to *Michillimakinac*. I could not learn, or I have forgot, what Name this River had before; but at preſent the Savages always call it the River of the *Black Gown (a)*. The *French* have given it the Name of *Father Marquette*; and never fail to invoke him, when they find themſelves in any Danger on the Lake *Michigan*. Many have affirmed, that they believe it was owing to his Interceſſion, that they have eſcaped very great Dangers.

Of the red and the white Pines.

I went three Leagues further that Day, and encamped at the Entrance of the River *St. Nicolas*, on the Side of a pretty Lake, that is longer, but not ſo wide as the former. I found here a great Number of red and white Pines, the laſt have the hardeſt Bark, but the beſt Wood, and ſhed a Gum which is pretty fine; the firſt have the ſofteſt Bark, but the Wood is heavier. They draw from theſe the Tar of which the beſt Pitch is made. I ſailed thus pleaſantly to the River *St. Joſeph*, which I entered the 6th, very late, or the 7th very early in the Morning, for it was about Midnight when we arrived here, having reſted ourſelves two good Hours at the Side of the Lake of *La Riviere Noire (the Black River)*, which is eight Leagues diſtant, and where there is a great deal of *Gin-ſeng*.

An Adventure of the Author's in the River St. Joſeph.

The River *St. Joſeph* is above a hundred Leagues long, and its Source is not far from Lake *Eriè*: It is navigable eighty Leagues, and in the twenty-five Leagues which I went up to arrive at the Fort, I ſaw none but good Lands, covered with Trees of a prodigious Height, under which there

(a) Thus the Savages call the Jeſuits. They call the Prieſts, the *White Caps*; and the Recollets, the *Grey Gowns*.

grows

grows in ſome Places very fine *Capillaire, (Maiden Hair)*. I was two Days making this Way, but the Night of the firſt was very near putting an End to my Journey. I was taken for a Bear, and I was within a Hair's Breadth of being killed under this Denomination, by one of my Canoe Men in the following Manner.

After Supper and Prayer, as it was very hot, I went to take a Walk, keeping always by the Side of the River. A Spaniel that followed me every where, took a Fancy to jump into the River, to fetch I know not what, which I had thrown in without Thought. My People, who thought I was gone to Reſt, eſpecially as it was late, and the Night dark, hearing the Noiſe this Creature made, thought it was a Roe-Buck that was croſſing the River; and two of them immediately ſet out with their Guns charged. Luckily for me, one of the two, who was a blundering Fellow, was called back by the reſt, for Fear he ſhould occaſion the Loſs of their Game; otherwiſe it might have happened, that by his blundering I ſhould have been ſhot.

The other advancing ſlowly, perceived me about twenty Paces from him, and made no Doubt that it was a Bear ſtanding upon his hind Feet, as theſe Animals always do when they hear a Noiſe. At this Sight he cocks his Gun, which he had loaded with three Balls; and crouching down almoſt to the Ground, made his Approaches as ſilently as poſſible. He was going to fire, when on my Side I thought I ſaw ſomething, without being able to diſtinguiſh what it was; but as I could not doubt but that it was one of my People, I thought proper to aſk him if by Chance he did not take me for a Bear: He made me no Anſwer, and when I came up to him, I found him like one Thunder-ſtruck, and as it were ſeized with Horror at the Blow he was juſt going to give. It was his Comrades who told me what had paſſed.

The River *St. Joſeph* is ſo convenient for the Trade of all Parts of *Canada*, that it is no Wonder it has always been much frequented by the Savages. Furthermore, it waters a very fertile Country: But this is not what theſe People value moſt. It is even a great Loſs to give them good Lands: Either they make no Uſe of them, or they ſoon make them poor by ſowing their Maiz.

The *Maſcoutins* had, not long ſince, a Settlement on this River; but they are returned to their own Country, which is, as they ſay, ſtill finer. The *Poutewatamies* have ſucceſſively occupied here ſeveral Poſts, and remain here ſtill. Their Village is on the ſame Side as the Fort, a little lower, and on a very fine Spot. The Village of the *Miamies* is on the other Side of the River.

The

These Savages who have at all Times applied themselves more than the others to Physic, set a high Value on *Gin-seng*, and are persuaded that this Plant has the Virtue to render Women fruitful. But I do not think that it was for this Reason they called it *Abesoutchenza*, which means a Child: It owes this Name to the Shape of its Root, at least among the *Iroquois*. You have seen without Doubt, Madam, what Father *Laffitau*, who brought it first to *France*, has wrote of it under the Name of *Aurelia Canadensis*: It is at least for Shape absolutely the same as that which comes to us from *China*, and which the *Chinese* get from *Corea* and *Tartary*. The Name they give it, which signifies *the Likeness of a Man*; the Virtues they attribute to it, and which have been experienced in *Canada* by those who have used it, and the Conformity of the Climate *(a)*, are great Reasons to think, that if we took it as coming from *China*, it would be as much esteemed as that the *Chinese* sell us; perhaps it is so little esteemed by us, because it grows in a Country that belongs to us, and that it has not the Recommendation of being entirely Foreign.

Of the Gin-seng *of* Canada.

In going up the River *St. Joseph*, I observed several Trees, which I had not seen in any other Place. The most remarkable, and which I took at first for an Ash by its Leaves, grows very large, and bears Beans which appear very good to the Eye; but the more they are boiled the harder they grow, so that they could never be used. The Fields which surround the Fort are so full of Sassafras, that it perfumes the Air; but it is not a great Tree as in *Carolina*: They are little Shrubs which grow near the Ground; perhaps also they are but Shoots of the Trees that were cut down to clear the Environs of the Fort, and of the Savage Villages.

Of the Bean-Tree, and the Sassafras.

There are here many Simples, which they say the Savages make Use of a little at a Venture, without any other Principle than a slight Experiment made by Chance, and which sometimes deceives them; for the same Remedies do not act equally on all Sorts of Subjects, attacked with the same Distempers; but these People know not how to make all these Distinctions. One Thing which much surprises me, is the impenetrable Secrecy they keep con-

Secrecy of the Savages concerning their Simples, and the Mines of their Country.

(a) The *Black River (la Riviere Noire)* is in 41 Deg. 50 Min. it is in the same Latitude they get the *Gin-seng* of *Corea* for the Emperor of *China*. Some of our's has been carried to *China*, and being prepared by the *Chinese*, they have sold it as coming from *Corea* or *Tartary*. For the rest, this Preparation adds nothing to it.

cerning their Simples, or the little Curiosity of the *French* to get the Knowledge of them. If the last are not in Fault, nothing makes it appear more, in my Opinion, that the Savages are not pleased to see us in their Country: And we have other Proofs, which are as clear as this. It is very likely also that they are of the same Opinion with Regard to their Simples, as they are about their Mines; *that is to say,* that they would soon die, if they discovered any of them to Strangers.

Of the Miamis.

The Savages of these Parts are naturally Thieves, and think all good Prizes that they can catch. It is true, that if we soon discover that we have lost any Thing, it is sufficient to inform the Chief of it, and we are sure to recover it; but we must give the Chief more than the Value of the Thing, and he requires further some Trifle for the Person that found it, and who is probably the Thief himself: I happened to be in this Case the Day after my Arrival, and they shewed me no Favour. These Barbarians would sooner engage in a War than make the least Concessions on this Point.

Some Days after I paid a Visit to the Chief of the *Miamies,* who had got the Start of me: He is a tall Man, well shaped, but much disfigured, for he has no Nose: I was told that this Misfortune happened to him in a drunken-bout. When he heard I was coming to see him, he went and placed himself at the Bottom of his Cabin, on a Sort of an Alcove, where I found him sitting with his Legs across, after the Eastern Manner. He said very little to me, and seemed to assume a proud Gravity, which he did not maintain well: This is the first Savage Chief that I saw, who observed this Ceremony; but I was told beforehand that he must be treated in the same Way, if you would not be despised by him.

The Game of Straws.

That Day the *Poutcouatamis* were come to play at *the Game of Straws* with the *Miamis:* They played in the the Cabin of the Chief, and on an open Place before the Cabin. These Straws are small Reeds about the Bigness of a Wheat Straw, and about six Inches long. They take a Parcel, which are commonly two hundred and one, and always an odd Number. After having shuffled them well together, making a thousand Contorsions, and invoking the Genii, they separate them with a Kind of an Awl, or a pointed Bone, into Parcels of ten each: Every one takes his own at a Venture, and he that happens to get the Parcel with eleven, gains a certain Number of Points that are agreed on. The whole Game is sixty or eighty.

There are other Ways of playing this Game, and they would have explained them to me, but I did not comprehend it, only

that

that ſometimes the Number Nine wins the Game. They added, that there was as much Skill as Hazard in this Game, and that the Savages are great Sharpers in this as well as in all other Games; and that they are ſo eager at it, that they play whole Days and Nights, and ſometimes do not leave off playing till they are quite naked, and have nothing more to loſe. They have another Game, at which they do not play for any Thing, but merely for Diverſion; but it has almoſt always ſome bad Conſequences with Reſpect to their Manners.

Another Game.

As ſoon as it is Night, they ſet up in the Middle of a great Cabin ſeveral Poſts in a Ring, in the Midſt are their Inſtruments of Muſic: They place on each Poſt a Packet of Down, and which muſt be each of a different Colour. The young People of both Sexes, mingled together, dance round about theſe Poſts: The young Women have alſo Down of the Colour they like. From Time to Time a young Man ſteps out of the Ring, and goes to take from a Poſt ſome Down of the Colour which he knows his Miſtreſs likes, and putting it upon his Head, he dances round her, and by a Sign appoints her a Place of Rendezvous. When the Dance is over, the Feaſt begins, and laſts all Day: At Night every one retires, and the young Women manage Matters ſo well, that in Spite of the Vigilance of their Mothers, they go to the Place of Aſſignation.

The *Miamis* have two Games more, the firſt of which is called the *Game of the Bat*. They play at it with a Ball, and Sticks bent and ending in a Kind of Racket. They ſet up two Poſts, which ſerve for Bounds, and which are diſtant from each other according to the Number of Players. For Inſtance, if they are eighty, there is half a League Diſtance between the Poſts. The Players are divided into two Bands, which have each their Poſt: Their Buſineſs is to ſtrike the Ball to the Poſt of the adverſe Party without letting it fall to the Ground, and without touching it with the Hand, for in either of theſe Caſes they loſe the Game, unleſs he who makes the Fault repairs it by ſtriking the Ball at one Blow to the Poſt, which is often impoſſible. Theſe Savages are ſo dexterous at catching the Ball with their Bats, that ſometimes one Game will laſt many Days together.

The ſecond Game is much like the former, but is not ſo dangerous. They mark out two Bounds, as in the firſt, and the Players occupy all the Space between. He that is to begin, throws a Ball up in the Air as perpendicularly as poſſible, that he may catch it the better, and throw it towards the Bounds. All the others have their Hands lifted up, and he that catches the Ball repeats the ſame, or throws the Ball to one of his Band

 that

that he judges more nimble and dexterous than himself; for to win the Game, the Ball must never have been in the Hands of the adverse Party before it comes to the Bound. The Women also play at this Game, but it is but seldom: Their Bands consist of four or five, and the first that lets the Ball fall, loses the Game.

Of the Chief, and the Orator of the Pouteouatamis.

The *Pouteouatamis* have here a Chief, and an Orator, who are Persons of Merit. The first, named *Piremon*, is a Man upwards of sixty, very sober and prudent: The second, named *Ouilamek*, is younger: He is a *Christian*, and well instructed, but he makes no Exercise of his Religion. One Day as I was making him some Reproaches on this Account, he left me suddenly, went into the Chapel, and said his Prayers aloud, so that we heard him at the Missionary's Lodging. It is difficult to find a Man that speaks better, and who has more Sense. On the other Hand, he is of a very amiable Character, and sincerely attached to the *French*. *Piremon* is not inferior in any Respect, and I have heard them both in a Council at the Commandant's, where they spoke with a great deal of Eloquence.

The sad Consequences of Drunkenness.

Many Savages of the two Nations which are settled on this River, are just returned from the *English* Colonies, whither they went to sell their Peltry, and from whence they have brought back a great deal of Brandy. It has been divided according to Custom; *that is to say*, every Day they distribute to a certain Number of Persons as much as is necessary for each to get drunk, and the whole was drank in eight Days. They began to drink in the two Villages as soon as the Sun was set, and every Night the Country resounded with frightful Cries and Howlings. One would have said that a Flight of Devils had escaped from Hell, or that the two Villages were cutting one another's Throats. Two Men were lamed: I met one of them who broke his Arm with a Fall, and I said to him, that certainly another Time he would be wiser: He replied, that this Accident was nothing, that he should soon be cured, and that he would begin to drink again as soon as he had got a fresh Stock of Brandy.

Judge, Madam, what a Missionary can do in the midst of such a Disorder, and how greatly it must affect an honest Man, who has quitted his own Country to gain Souls to God, to be obliged to be a Witness of it, without having it in his Power to remedy it. These Barbarians are sensible that Drunkenness ruins and destroys them; but when one strives to persuade them that they should be the first to ask that we should hinder them of a Liquor that

that is attended with ſuch fatal Conſequences, they are ſatisfied with replying, " It is you that have accuſtomed us to it, we can " no longer do without it, and if you refuſe to ſupply us, we " will get it of the *Engliſh*. This Liquor ſtrips us naked, and " kills us, it is true, but it is you who have done the Miſchief, " and there is now no Remedy." Nevertheleſs, they are in the wrong to blame us alone; had it not been for the *Engliſh* I believe we could have put a Stop to this Trade in the Colony, or reduced it within proper Bounds.—But we ſhall perhaps be ſoon obliged to give Permiſſion to ſupply them with it from *France*, taking Meaſures to prevent its Abuſe, inaſmuch as the *Engliſh* Brandy is more hurtful than our's.

A Diſorder that corrupts the Manners of a People never comes alone; it is always the Principle, or the Riſe of many others. The Savages, before they fell into this I am ſpeaking of, excepting War, which they always made in a barbarous and inhuman Manner, had nothing to diſturb their Happineſs: Drunkenneſs hath rendered them intereſted, and has diſturbed the Peace they enjoyed in their Families, and in the Commerce of Life. Notwithſtanding, as they are only ſtruck with the preſent Object, the Evils, which this Paſſion has cauſed them, have not yet become a Habit: They are Storms which paſs over, and which they almoſt forget when they are paſt, thro' the Goodneſs of their Character, and the great Fund of Calmneſs of Soul, which they have received from Nature.

Happineſs of the Savages.

We muſt acknowledge that at firſt Sight, the Life they lead appears very hard; but beſides that in this nothing gives Uneaſineſs but by Compariſon, and that Cuſtom is a ſecond Nature, the Liberty they enjoy, ſufficiently compenſates the Loſs of thoſe Conveniencies they are deprived of. What we ſee every Day in ſome Beggars by Profeſſion, and in ſeveral Perſons in the Country, gives us a ſenſible Proof that we may be happy in the midſt of Indigence. But the Savages are ſtill more happy: Firſt, becauſe they think themſelves ſo: Secondly, becauſe they are in the peaceable Poſſeſſion of the moſt precious of all the Gifts of Nature: And laſtly, becauſe they are entirely ignorant of, and have not even a Deſire to know thoſe falſe Advantages which we ſo much eſteem, and which we purchaſe at the Expence of real Good; and of which we have ſo little Enjoyment.

In Fact, what they are moſt valuable for, and for which they ought to be looked upon as true Philoſophers, is, that the Sight of our Conveniencies, our Riches, our Magnificence, have little moved them, and that they are pleaſed with themſelves that they can do without them. Some *Iroquois*, who went to *Paris* in 1666, and who were ſhewed all the Royal Houſes, and all the Beauties of of that great City, admired nothing in it, and would have preferred their Villages to the Capital of the most flourishing Kingdom of *Europe*, if they had not seen the Street of *la Huchette*, where the Shops of the roasting Cooks, which they always found furnished with all Kinds of Meat, charmed them greatly.

The Contempt they have for our Way of living.

We cannot even say that they are so highly delighted with their Way of living, only because they are not acquainted with the Sweetness of our's. A good Number of the *French* have lived like them, and have been so well pleased with it, that many Persons could never prevail with them to return, though they might have been very much at their Ease in the Colony. On the contrary, it was never possible for a single Savage to conform to our Way of living. We have taken Children from the Cradle, and brought them up with much Care, and omitted nothing to hinder their knowing any Thing of what passed amongst their Parents. All these Precautions were useless: The Force of Blood prevailed over Education. As soon as they found themselves at Liberty, they have torn their Garments to Pieces, and went through the Woods to seek their Countrymen, whose Way of Life appeared to them more pleasing than that they led with us.

An *Iroquois*, named *la Plaque*, lived many Years with the *French*; the same who, as I have told you, Madam, in saving his Father's Life in an Engagement, thought he had fully satisfied all the Debt he owed him: He was also made a Lieutenant in our Troops to fix him, because he was a very brave Man; but he could not continue in our Way of living: He returned to his Nation, only carrying from us our Vices, without correcting any of those he brought with him. He loved Women to Excess: He was well shaped: His Valour and his brave Actions gave him a great Reputation: He had a great deal of Wit, and very amiable Manners: He had many Intrigues with other Men's Wives; and his Disorders went so far, that it was debated in the Council of his Canton, whether they should not take him off. It was however concluded, by the Majority of Votes, to spare his Life; because, as he was extremely courageous, he would people the Country with good Warriors.

The Care which the Mothers take of their Children.

The Care which the Mothers take of their Children, whilst they are yet in the Cradle, is beyond all Expression, and proves very clearly that we often spoil all, when we exceed the Limits which Nature has taught us. They never leave them: They carry them every where with them; and when they seem ready to sink under the Burdens they load themselves with, the Cradle of their Child is reckoned as nothing. One would even ſay, that this additional Weight is an Eaſement that renders the reſt lighter.

Nothing can be neater than theſe Cradles: The Child lies very conveniently, and very eaſy in them; but it is bound only as high as the Waiſt; ſo that when the Cradle is upright, theſe little Creatures have their Heads and half their Bodies hanging down. In *Europe* they would fancy that a Child that was left in this Condition, would grow quite deformed; but it happens directly contrary: This renders their Bodies ſupple; and they are all, in Fact, of a Stature and Port, that the beſt ſhaped among us would envy. What can we ſay againſt ſuch a general Experience? But what I am going to mention, cannot be ſo eaſily juſtified.

The ridiculous Shapes which ſome give to their Children.

There are on this Continent ſome Nations which they call *flat Heads*, which have in Fact their Foreheads very flat, and the Top of their Heads ſomething lengthened. This Shape is not the Work of Nature; it is the Mothers who give it their Children as ſoon as they are born. For this End, they apply to their Foreheads, and the back Part of their Heads, two Maſſes of Clay, or of ſome other heavy Matter, which they bind by little and little, till the Skull has taken the Shape they deſire to give it. It appears that this Operation is very painful to the Children, whoſe Noſtrils ſhed a whitiſh Matter, pretty thick. But neither this Circumſtance, nor the Cries of theſe little Innocents, alarm their Mothers, jealous of procuring them a handſome Appearance, without which they can't conceive how others can be ſatisfied. It is quite the reverſe with certain *Algonquins* amongſt us, named *Round Heads*, or *Bowl Heads*, whom I have mentioned before; for they make their Beauty conſiſt in having their Heads perfectly round, and Mothers take Care alſo very early to give them this Shape.

I would willingly, Madam, take Advantage of the Leiſure I have in this Place, and which perhaps will be longer than I deſire, to finiſh what I have to ſay to you on this Subject; but ſome Troubles which have happened to me, and the approaching Departure of a Traveller, who is returning to the Colony, oblige me to interrupt this Recital, which I ſhall reſume the firſt Opportunity.

I am, &c.

LETTER

LETTER XXVI.

Sequel of the Character of the Savages, and their Way of living.

MADAM, ST. JOSEPH'S RIVER, *August* 8.

I Resume the Course of my Memoirs, where I broke it off. You will think, perhaps, that I do not observe a sufficient Regularity: But we excuse, at least in a Relation, what we admire in an Ode: What in a *Lyrick* Poet is an Effect of Art, is a Matter of Necessity in a Traveller, who cannot relate Things but as he gets Information, and who is obliged to write what he sees, for Fear of forgetting it.

What it is that strengthens the Savages, and makes them so well shap'd.

The Children of the Savages, when they leave the Cradle, are not confined in any Manner; and as soon as they can crawl upon their Hands and Feet, they let them go where they will quite naked, into the Water, into the Woods, into the Dirt, and into the Snow, which makes their Bodies strong, their Limbs very supple, and hardens them against the Injuries of the Air; but also, as I observed before, it makes them subject to Distempers of the Stomach and Lungs, which destroys them early. In Summer they run, as soon as they are up, to the River, or into the Lakes, and continue there a Part of the Day, playing like Fish when it is fine Weather at the Surface of the Water *(a)*. It is certain that nothing is better than this Exercise to make their Joints free, and to render them nimble.

Their first Exercises, and their Emulation.

They put a Bow and Arrows into their Hands betimes, and to excite in them that Emulation, which is the best Teacher of the Arts, there is no Need to set their Breakfast on the Top of a Tree, as they did by the young *Lacedemonians*: They are all born with that Passion for Glory, that has no Need of a Spur; and indeed they shoot with a surprizing Exactness, and with a little Practice, they acquire the same Dexterity in the Use of our Fire Arms. They make them also wrestle, and they pursue this Exercise so eagerly, that they would often kill one another, if they were not parted: Those who are worsted are so en-

(a) It is very probable that this is the Reason why the Small-Pox is so fatal among the Savages. Much Bathing hardens the Skin, and prevents the Eruption of the Pustules.

raged

raged at it, that they do not take the leaſt Repoſe, till they have their Revenge.

In what their Education conſiſts.

In general one may ſay, that the Fathers and Mothers neglect nothing to inſpire their Children with certain Principles of Honour, which they preſerve all their Lives, but of which they often make a bad Application; and in this their whole Education conſiſts. When they give them Inſtructions on this Head, it is always in an indirect Way; the moſt common is to relate to them the brave Actions of their Anceſtors, or of their Countrymen. Theſe young People are fired at theſe Stories, and are never eaſy till they find an Opportunity of imitating the Examples they have made them admire. Sometimes, to correct them for their Faults, they uſe Prayers and Tears, but never Menaces. They would make no Impreſſion on Spirits, prepoſſeſſed with an Opinion that no Perſon has a Right to uſe Compulſion.

A Mother, who ſees her Daughter behave ill, falls a crying: On the Daughter's aſking the Cauſe, ſhe is ſatisfied with ſaying, *You diſgrace me.* It ſeldom happens that this Way of reproving is not effectual: Nevertheleſs, ſince they have converſed more with the *French*, ſome of them begin to chaſtiſe their Children; but this is ſcarcely amongſt any but the *Chriſtians*, or thoſe that are ſettled in the Colony. Generally the greateſt Puniſhment they uſe to correct their Children, is to throw a little Water in their Faces. The Children are much affected by it, and by every Thing that ſavours of Reproof; the Cauſe of which is, that Reſentment is their ſtrongeſt Paſſion, even at that Age.

Of the Paſſions of the Savages.

We have known ſome Girls hang themſelves, for having only received a ſlight Reprimand from their Mothers, or a few Drops of Water in their Faces; and who have given Notice of it, by ſaying, *You ſhall loſe your Daughter.* The greateſt Misfortune is, that it is not to Virtue that they exhort theſe young People; or, which is the ſame Thing, that they do not always give them true Notions of Virtue. In Reality, they recommend nothing to them ſo much as Revenge, and 'tis THIS of which they ſhew them the moſt frequent Examples.

One would expect, Madam, that a Childhood ſo badly diſciplined, ſhould be followed by a Youth of Turbulence and Corruption: But on one Hand, the Savages are naturally calm, and early Maſters of themſelves; Reaſon alſo guides them rather more than other Men: And on the other Hand, their Conſtitution, eſpecially in the Northern Countries, does not incline them to Debauchery; yet we find ſome Cuſtoms among them, in which Chaſtity is entirely diſregarded; but it appears that this proceeds more from Superstition, than the Depravation of the Heart.

The *Hurons*, when we first began to converse with them, were more lascivious, and very brutal in their Pleasures. The young Persons of both Sexes abandoned themselves without Shame to all Manner of Dissoluteness; and it was chiefly among them, that it was not esteemed a Crime for a Girl to prostitute herself. Their Parents were the first to engage them in this Way, and many did the same by their Wives, for a base Interest. Many never married, but took young Women to serve them, as they said, for Companions; and all the Difference they made between these Concubines and their lawful Wives, was, that with the first there was no Agreement made: For the rest, their Children were on the same Foot as the others; which produced no Inconvenience, in a Country where there are no Estates to inherit.

One does not distinguish Nations here by their Dress. The Men, when it is hot, have often only something of an Apron to cover their Nakedness. In Winter they clothe themselves more or less, according to the Climate. They wear on their Feet a Sort of Sandals, made of Roe-Buck Skins smoked: Their Stockings are also Skins, or Bits of Stuffs, which they wrap round their Legs. A Waistcoat, made of Skin, covers them to the Waist, and they wear over that a Rug or Blanket, when they can have it; if not, they make themselves a Robe with a Bear's Skin, or of several Beaver or other like Skins, or Furs, with the Hair inwards. The Women's Waistcoats reach just below their Knees; and when it is very cold, or when they travel, they cover their Heads with their Blanket, or their Robe. I have seen several who had little Caps, like Skull Caps; others have a Sort of Capuchin, fastened to their Waistcoats; and they have besides a Piece of Stuff which serves them for a Petticoat, which covers them from the Waist down to the Middle of the Leg.

They are all very desirous of having Shirts and Shifts; but they never put them under their Waistcoats, till they are dirty, and then they wear them till they drop to Pieces, for they never take the Trouble to wash them. Their Waistcoats are generally dressed in the Smoke, like their Sandals; *that is to say*, after they have hung a proper Time in it, they rub them a little, and then they may be washed like Linen: They prepare them also by soaking them in Water, then rubbing them with their Hands till they are dry and pliable; but the Savages think our Stuffs and Blankets are much more convenient.

How they prick themselves all over the Body.

Many make various Figures all over their Bodies by pricking themselves, others only in some Parts. They don't do this merely for Ornament: They find also, as it is said, great Advantages by this Custom. It serves greatly to defend them

them from the Cold, renders them less sensible of the other Injuries of the Air, and frees them from the Persecution of the Gnats. But it is only in the Countries possessed by the *English*, especially in *Virginia*, that the Custom of pricking themselves all over the Body is very common. In *New France* the greatest Part are satisfied with some Figures of Birds, Serpents, or other Animals, and even of Leaves, and such-like Figures, without Order or Symmetry, but according to every one's Fancy, often in the Face, and sometimes even on the Eye-lids. Many Women are marked in the Parts of the Face that answer to the Jaw Bones, to prevent the Tooth-ach.

This Operation is not painful in itself. It is performed in this Manner: They begin by tracing on the Skin, drawn very tight, the Figure they intend to make; then they prick little Holes close together with the Fins of a Fish, or with Needles, all over these Traces, so as to draw Blood: Then they rub them over with Charcoal Dust, and other Colours well ground and powdered. These Powders sink into the Skin, and the Colours are never effaced: But soon after the Skin swells, and forms a Kind of Scab, accompanied with Inflammation. It commonly excites a Fever; and if the Weather is too hot, or the Operation has been carried too far, there is Hazard of Life.

How, and why they paint their Faces.

The Colours with which they paint their Faces, and the Grease they rub themselves with all over their Bodies, produce the same Advantages, and, as these People fancy, give the same good Appearance, as pricking. The Warriors paint themselves, when they take the Field, to intimidate their Enemies, perhaps also to hide their Fear; for we must not think they are all exempt from it. The young People do it to conceal an Air of Youth, which would make them less taken for old Soldiers, or a Paleness remaining after some Distemper, and which they are apprehensive might be taken for the Effect of Want of Courage: They do it also to make them look handsome; but then the Colours are more lively, and more varied. They paint the Prisoners that are going to die; but I don't know why: Perhaps it is to adorn the Victim, who is to be sacrificed to the God of War. Lastly, they paint the Dead, to expose them dressed in their finest Robes; and this is, without Doubt, to hide the Paleness of Death, which disfigures them.

The Ornaments of the Men.

The Colours they use on these Occasions are the same they employ to dye Skins, and they make them from certain Earths, and the Bark of some Trees. They are not very lively, but they do not very easily wear out. The Men add to this Ornament the Down of Swans or other Birds, which they strew upon their Hair after it has been greaſed, like Powder. They add to this Feathers of all Colours, and Bunches of the Hair of divers Animals, all placed in an odd Manner. The Placing of their Hair, ſometimes ſtanding up like Briſtles on one Side, and flatted on the other, or dreſſed in a thouſand different Faſhions, Pendants in their Ears, and ſometimes in their Noſtrils, a great Shell of Porcelain hanging about their Neck, or on their Breaſt, ſome Crowns made of the Plumage of ſcarce Birds, the Claws, Feet, or Heads of Birds of Prey, little Horns of Roe-Bucks, all theſe Things make up their Finery. But whatever they have moſt precious is always employed to adorn the Captives when theſe Wretches make their firſt Entry into the Village of their Conquerors.

The Ornaments of the Women.

It is obſervable that the Men take very little Pains to adorn any Part but their Heads. It is juſt the Reverſe with the Women: They wear ſcarcely any Thing on it, they are only fond of their Hair, and they would think themſelves diſgraced if it was cut off; therefore, when at the Death of a Relation they cut off Part of it, they pretend by this to ſhew the greateſt Grief for their Loſs. To preſerve their Hair they greaſe it often, and powder it with the Duſt of Spruce Bark, and ſometimes with Vermilion, then they wrap it up in the Skin of an Eel or a Serpent, in the Faſhion of Whiſkers, which hang down to their Waiſt. As to their Faces, they are ſatisfied with tracing ſome Lines on them with Vermilion, or other Colours.

Their Noſtrils are never bored, and it is only among ſome Nations that they bore their Ears; then they wear in them Pendants, as do alſo the Men, made of Beads of Porcelain. When they are dreſſed in their greateſt Finery, they have Robes painted with all Sorts of Figures, with little Collars of Porcelain ſet on them without much Order or Symmetry, with a Kind of Border tolerably worked with Porcupine's Hair, which they paint alſo of various Colours. They adorn in the ſame Manner the Cradles of their Children, and they load them with all Sorts of Trinkets. Theſe Cradles are made of light Wood, and have at the upper End one or two Semicircles of Cedar, that they may cover them without touching the Head of the Child.

Beſides the Houſhold Work, and providing Wood for Fuel, the Women have almoſt always the ſole Trouble of cultivating the Lands: As ſoon as the Snow is melted, and the Waters ſufficiently drained, they begin to prepare the Earth, which conſiſts in ſtirring it lightly with a Piece of Wood bent, the Handle of which is very long, having firſt ſet Fire to the dry Stalks of the Maiz and other Herbs that remained after the laſt Harveſt. Beſides that the Grain theſe People make Uſe of is

Summer

Summer Grain, they pretend that the Nature of the Soil of this Country will not allow of sowing any Thing before Winter. But I believe the true Reason why Seeds would not grow if they were sowed in Autumn is, that they would be destroyed by the Winter, or rot at the melting of the Snow. It may also be, and this is the Opinion of many Persons, that the Wheat they cultivate in *Canada*, though originally brought from *France*, has in Process of Time contracted the Property of Summer Seeds, which have not Strength enough to shoot several Times, as those do which we sow in *September* and *October*.

Of their Sowing and Harvest.

Beans, or rather Kidney-Beans, are sowed along with the Maiz, the Stalks of which serve to support them: I think I have heard that the Savages received this Seed from us, on which they set a high Value, and it differs nothing from our's. But I was surprised that they make little or no Use of our Peas, which have acquired in the Soil of *Canada*, a Degree of Goodness much superior to what they have in *Europe*. Sun-Flowers, Water-Melons, and Pomkins are set by themselves; and before they sow the Seed, they make it shoot in Smoke, in light and black Earth.

For the most Part the Women help one another in the Work of the Field, and when it is Time to gather the Harvest, they have sometimes Recourse to the Men, who do not disdain to assist in it. It ends in a Festival and Feast, which is made in the Night: Grain, and other Fruits of the Earth, are kept in Holes, which they dig in the Earth, and which are lined with large Pieces of Bark. Many leave the Maiz in the Ear as it grows, made up in Ropes as we do Onions, and spread them on great Poles over the Entrance of the Cabins. Others get out the Grain, and fill great Baskets with it made of Bark, full of Holes to hinder it from heating. But when they are obliged to be absent some Time, or are afraid of some Irruption of an Enemy, they make great Holes in the Earth to hide it, where this Grain keeps very well.

Of the Maiz.

In the northern Parts they sow little, and in many Places none at all; but they purchase the Maiz by Exchange. This Grain is very wholesome, it is nourishing, and light of Digestion. The most common Way of preparing it among our *French* Travellers is by Lixivating, *that is to say*, by boiling it some Time in a Sort of Lie. This Way keeps it a long Time; they make Provision of it for long Journeys, and as they want it, they boil it again in Water, or in Broth, if they have any Thing to make it of, and they put a little Salt to it.

It

It is not an unpleaſant Food, but many People are perſuaded that too frequent Uſe of it is prejudicial to Health, becauſe the Lye gives it a corroſive Quality, the Effects of which are felt in Time. When the Maiz is in the Ear, and ſtill green, ſome broil it on the Coals, and it has a very good Taſte. Our *Canadians* call it *Bled groule*. There is a particular Sort that opens as ſoon as it is laid on the Fire, they call it *Bled fleuri*, and it is very delicate. This is what they treat Strangers with. They carry it in ſome Places to Perſons of Diſtinction, who arrive in a Village, much in the ſame Manner as they do in *France* the Preſent of a Town.

Of the Sagamitty.

Laſtly, it is of this Grain they make the *Sagamitty*, which is the moſt common Food of the Savages. For this Purpoſe they begin by broiling it, then they pound it, and take off the Huſk, then they make a Sort of Broth with it, which is inſipid enough when they have no Meat, or Prunes to give it a Reliſh. They ſometimes reduce it to Flour, which they call here *Farine froide (cold Flour)*, and this is the beſt Proviſion that can be made for Travellers. Thoſe who travel on Foot cannot carry any other. They alſo boil the Maiz in the Ear, while it is ſtill ſoft, then they broil it a little, they get out the Grain, and dry it in the Sun; this they keep a long Time, and the Sagamitty they make of it has a very good Taſte.

You will perceive, Madam, by the Detail of theſe Meſſes, that the Savages are not nice in their eating. We ſhould think that they have a very depraved Taſte, if it was poſſible to make a fixed Rule for Taſte. They love Greaſe, and it predominates in all their Diſhes, if they can get it. A few Pounds of Candles in a Kettle of Sagamitty makes them think it excellent. They even ſometimes put Things into it which cannot be mentioned, and they are ſurpriſed to ſee our Stomachs turn at them.

The Nations of the South had only Veſſels of baked Earth to dreſs their Meat. In the North they uſed Kettles of Wood, and they made the Water boil by throwing in Flints made red hot. They found our Iron and Tin Kettles much more convenient, and this is the Merchandize which we are ſure to find a Vent for when we trade with them. In the Nations of the Weſt, the wild Oats ſupply the Want of Maiz: It is quite as wholeſome, and if it is not ſo nouriſhing, the Fleſh of the Buffalo, which abounds in theſe Parts, makes Amends for it.

Of the Rock Tripe, and rotten Wheat.

Among the wandering Savages, who never cultivate the Earth, when the Chace and the Fiſhery fail, their only Reſource is a Kind of Moſs, which grows on certain Rocks, and which our *French* People call *Tripe of the Rocks*. Nothing is more inſipid than this Moſs, which has but little Subſtance;

ſtance: This is being reduced to what is juſt ſufficient to keep them from ſtarving. I ſtill find it harder to conceive, which yet I have heard affirmed by Perſons of Credit, that ſome Savages eat by Way of Dainty a Sort of Maiz, which they leave to rot in a ſtanding Water, as we do Hemp, and they take it out all black and ſtinking. They add alſo, that thoſe who have a Liking to ſuch a ſtrange Meſs as this is, will not loſe any of the Water, or rather Mud, that drops from it, the Smell of which alone would make the Heart heave of any other People. It was probably Neceſſity that diſcovered this Secret, and if this does not give it all its Reliſh, nothing proves more clearly that there is no diſputing about Taſtes.

Of the Bread of the Maiz.

The Savage Women make Bread of Maiz, and tho' it is only a Meſs of Paſte ill wrought, without Leaven, and baked under the Aſhes, theſe People find it very good, and treat their Friends with it; but it muſt not be eaten hot: It will not keep when it is cold. Sometimes they mix with it Beans, various Fruits, Oil, and Greaſe. They muſt have good Stomachs that can digeſt ſuch Hotch-potch.

Various Roots, &c. and their Uſe.

The Sun-Flowers only ſerve the Savages for an Oil, which they rub themſelves with. They get it more commonly from the Seed than from the Root of this Plant. This Root differs but little from a Sort of Potatoes, which we call in *France Topinambours*. The Potatoes which are ſo common in the *Weſt-Indian* Iſlands, and in the Continent of *South America*, have been planted with Succeſs in *Louiſiana*. The continual Uſe which all the Nations of *Canada* made of a Sort of *Petun*, or wild Tobacco, which grows every where in this Country, have made ſome Travellers ſay that they ſwallowed the Smoke, and that it ſerved them for Food; but this is not found true, and was founded only on obſerving them often remain a long Time without eating. Since they have taſted our Tobacco, they can ſcarcely bear their *Petun*, and it is very eaſy to ſatisfy them on this Head, for Tobacco grows very well here; and they ſay alſo, that by chuſing proper Soils, we might have a moſt excellent Sort.

Works of the Women.

The little Works of the Women, and which are their common Employment in the Cabins, are to make Thread of the inner Membranes of the Bark of a Tree, which they call the *white Wood*, and they work it pretty nearly as we do Hemp. The Women alſo dye every Thing: They make alſo ſeveral Works with Bark, on which they work ſmall Figures with Porcupines Hair: They make little Cups, or other Utenſils of Wood; they paint and

and embroider Roe-Buck Skins; they knit Girdles and Garters with the Wool of the Buffaloes.

As for the Men, they glory in their Idleneſs, and in Reality they paſs above half their Lives in doing nothing, in the Perſuaſion that daily Labour diſgraces a Man, and is only the Duty of the Women. Man, they ſay, is only made for War, Hunting, and Fiſhing. Nevertheleſs, it belongs to them to make all Things neceſſary for theſe three Exerciſes: Therefore, making Arms, Nets, and all the Equipage of the Hunters and Fiſhers, chiefly belong to them, as well as the Canoes, and their Rigging, the Raquets, or Snow Shoes, the building and repairing the Cabins, but they often oblige the Women to aſſiſt them. The *Chriſtians* employ themſelves ſomething more, but they only do it by Way of Penance.

Works of the Men.

Theſe People, before we had furniſhed them with Hatchets, and other Tools, were greatly embarraſſed to cut down their Trees, and fit them for Uſe. They burnt them at the Foot, and to ſplit and cut them, they uſed Hatchets made of Flints, which did not break, but took up a great deal of Time to ſharpen. To fix them in the Handle, they cut off the Head of a young Tree, and as if they would have grafted it, they made a Notch in it, in which they thruſt the Head of the Hatchet. After ſome Time, the Tree, by growing together, kept the Hatchet ſo fixed that it could not come out; then they cut the Tree to ſuch a Length as they would have the Handle.

Their Tools.

Their Villages have generally no regular Form. The greateſt Part of our antient Relations repreſent them of a round Form, and perhaps their Authors had not ſeen but of this Sort. For the reſt, imagine you ſee, Madam, a Heap of Cabins without Order, or being ſet on a Line: Some like Cart-Houſes, others like Tunnels built of Bark, ſupported by ſome Poſts, ſometimes plaiſtered on the Outſide with Mud, in a coarſe Manner: In a Word, built with leſs Art, Neatneſs, and Solidity, than the Cabins of the Beavers. Theſe Cabins are about fifteen or twenty Feet in Breadth, and ſometimes a hundred in Length: Then they contain ſeveral Fires, for a Fire never takes up more than 30 Feet.

The Form of the Villages.

When the Floor is not ſufficient for all the Inhabitants to ſleep on, the young People lay on a wide Bench, or a Kind of Stage, about five or ſix Feet high, that runs the whole Length of the Cabin. The Furniture and the Proviſions are over this, placed on Pieces of Wood put acroſs under the Roof. For the moſt Part, there is before the Door a Sort of Porch, where the young People ſleep in the Summer, and which ſerves for a Wood-Houſe in the Winter. The Doors are nothing but

Bark,

Bark, fixed up like the Umbrello of a Window, and they never ſhut cloſe. Theſe Cabins have neither Chimnies nor Windows, but they leave an Opening in the Middle of the Roof, by which Part of the Smoke goes out, which they are obliged to ſhut when it rains or ſnows; and then they muſt put out the Fire, if they will not be blinded with the Smoke.

The Manner of fortifying themſelves.

The Savages fortify themſelves better than they lodge: We ſee ſome Villages pretty well paliſſadoed with Redoubts, where they always take Care to make a good Proviſion of Water and Stones. The Paliſſadoes are even double, and ſometimes treble, and have commonly Battlements at the laſt Encloſure. The Poſts they are compoſed of are interwoven with Branches of Trees, that leave no Place open. This was ſufficient to ſupport a long Siege, before theſe People knew the Uſe of Fire Arms. Every Village has a pretty large open Place, but it is ſeldom of a regular Figure.

Formerly the *Iroquois* built their Cabins much better than the other Nations, and than they do themſelves at preſent: They ſometimes wrought Figures in Relievo on their Cabins, tho' the Work was very rude; but ſince in ſeveral Incurſions their Enemies have burnt almoſt all their Villages, they have not taken the Pains to re-eſtabliſh them in their firſt State. But if theſe People take ſo little Pains to procure the Conveniencies of Life in the Places of their ordinary Reſidence, what can we think of their Encampings in their Travels, and their Winter Quarters. An antient Miſſionary *(a)*, who to lay himſelf under a Neceſſity of learning the Language of the *Montagnais*, would accompany them in their Hunting during the Winter, has given us an Account of it, which I ſhall tranſcribe almoſt Word for Word.

Of their Winter Camps.

Theſe Savages inhabit a Country very wild and uncultivated, but not ſo much as THAT which they chuſe for their Hunting. You muſt march a long Time before you come to it, and you muſt carry on your Back all you want for five or ſix Months, through Ways ſometimes ſo frightful, that one can't conceive how the wild Creatures can come here. If they had not the Precaution to furniſh themſelves with the Bark of Trees, they would have nothing to defend them from the Snow and Rain during the Journey. As ſoon as they arrive at the Place propoſed, they accommodate themſelves a little better; but this conſiſts only in not being expoſed continually to all the Injuries of the Air.

Every Body is employed for this End; and the Miſſionaries, who at firſt had no Body to ſerve them, and for whom

(a) Father *Paul le Jeune.*

the Savages had no Regard, were not spared any more than the rest; they did not even allow them a separate Cabin, and they were obliged to lodge in the first that would receive them. These Cabins, among the greatest Part of the *Algonquin* Nations, are much in the Shape of our Ice-Houses, round, and ending in a Cone: They have no other Support but Poles, fixed in the Snow, tied together at the Ends, and covered with Pieces of Bark ill joined together, and not well fastened to the Poles; so that the Wind comes through on every Side.

The setting up these Cabins is but the Work of half an Hour at most. Some Branches of Pine serve for Mats, and there are no other Beds. The only Convenience attending this is, that they may be changed every Day. The Snow, which is heaped up round about them, forms a Sort of a Parapet, which has its Use, for the Winds do not pierce through it. By the Side, and under the Shelter of this Parapet, they sleep as quietly on these Branches, covered with a poor Skin, as on the softest Bed. The Missionaries have some Difficulty to accustom themselves to this Lodging, but Fatigue and Necessity soon reconcile them to it. They cannot so well reconcile themselves to the Smoke, which almost always fills the Top of the Cabin in such a Manner, that one cannot stand upright in them without having one's Head in a Sort of a Cloud. This is no Trouble to the Savages, accustomed from their Childhood to sit or lie on the Ground all the Time they are in their Cabins: But it is a great Punishment to the *French*, who can't reconcile themselves to this Inaction.

On the other Hand, the Wind, which enters as I before observed, on all Sides, blows in a Cold that chills one Part, whilst one is smothered and broil'd on the other. Often one cannot distinguish any Thing at two or three Feet Distance; and our Eyes water so, that we are blinded: Sometimes, to get a little Breath, we are forced to lie on our Bellies, with our Mouths almost close to the Ground. The shortest Way would be to go out; but the greatest Part of the Time this is not to be done; sometimes because of a Snow so thick, that it darkens the Day, and sometimes because there blows a dry Wind, that cuts the Face, and even shivers the Trees in the Forests. Nevertheless, a Missionary is obliged to say his Office, to sing Mass, and to perform all the other Duties of his Ministry.

To all these Inconveniencies we must add another, which at first will seem a Trifle to you, but which is really very considerable; it is the Troublesomeness of the Dogs. The Savages have always a great Number that follow them every where, and which are very much attached to them; they are not fawning, because they are never fondled, but they are bold and skilful Hunters.

I have already said that the Savages break their Dogs very early to that Sort of Hunting they are intended for; I add, that every Man must have many, because a great Number are destroyed by the Teeth or the Horns of the wild Creatures, which they attack with a Courage that nothing can daunt. Their Masters take little Care to feed them: They live by what they can catch, and this is not much, so they are always very lean: On the other Hand, they have little Hair, which makes them very sensible of the Cold. To keep themselves warm, if they can't come to the Fire, where it would be difficult for them all to find Room, though there should be no Person in the Cabin, they go and lie down on the first they meet with; and often one wakes in the Night in a Surprize, almost stifled by two or three Dogs. If they were a little more discreet in placing themselves, their Company would not be very troublesome; one could put up with it well enough; but they lie where they can: Drive them away as often as you please, they return directly. 'Tis much worse in the Day-time; as soon as any Meat appears, you are incommoded with the Bustle they make to have their Share.

A poor Missionary is lying on the Ground leaning on his Elbow near the Fire, to say his Breviary, or to read a Book, striving as well as he can to endure the Smoke; and he must also bear the Persecution of a Dozen Dogs, which do nothing but run over him backwards and forwards after a Piece of Meat they have discovered. If he has Need of a little Rest, it is hard for him to find a little Nook, where he may be free from this Vexation. If they bring him any Thing to eat, the Dogs get their Noses in his Dish before he can have his Hand in it; and often while he is employed in defending his Portion against those that attack him in Front, there comes one behind that carries off half of it, or by running against him, beats the Dish out of his Hands, and spills the Sagamitty in the Ashes.

Oftentimes the Evils I have mentioned, are effaced by a greater; in Comparison of which the others are nothing, viz. Hunger. The Provisions they carry with them do not last long: They depend on the Chace, and that fails sometimes. It is true, that the Savages can bear Hunger with as much Patience as they take little Precaution to prevent it; but they are sometimes reduced to such Extremity, that they sink under it.

The Missionary, from whom I took this Account, was obliged, in his first Winter encamping, to eat the Eel Skins and Elk Skins, with which he had patched his Cassock; after which he was forced to eat young Branches, and the softest Bark of Trees. Nevertheless, he stood this Trial, without losing his Health; but all Persons have not his Strength.

The Nastiness of the Savages.

The Nastiness alone of the Cabins, and the Stench which naturally arises from it, is a real Punishment to any one but a Savage. It is easy to judge how far both must go among People who never change their Linen or Clothes but when they drop to Pieces, and who take no Care to wash them. In Summer they bathe every Day; but they rub themselves directly with Oil or Grease of a strong Scent. In Winter they continue in their Filth, and in all Seasons one cannot enter into their Cabins without being almost poisoned.

All they eat is not only without any Seasoning, and commonly very insipid, but there reigns in their Meals a Slovenliness which exceeds all Description. What I have seen, and what I have heard, would frighten you. There are few Animals who do not feed cleaner. And after we have seen what passes among these People in this Article, one can no longer doubt that Fancy has a great Share in our Antipathies; and that many Messes, which really hurt our Health, do not produce this Effect but by the Power of these Antipathies, and by the little Courage we have to conquer them.

We must nevertheless acknowledge, that Things are a little changed in all these Articles since our Arrival in this Country. I have seen some who have endeavoured to procure themselves some Conveniencies, which perhaps they will soon find it hard to be deprived of. Some begin also to take a little more Precaution not to find themselves unprovided, when the Chace fails; and among those who dwell in the Colony, there is little to add to make them arrive at the Point of having tolerable Necessaries: But it is to be feared, when they are got so far, they will soon go further, and seek for Superfluities, which will make them more unhappy still, than they are at present in the midst of the greatest Indigence.

However, it will not be the Missionaries who will expose them to this Danger. Being persuaded that it is morally impossible to take the exact Medium, and keep within it, they much rather chuse to partake with these People of what is most troublesome in their Way of living, than to open their Eyes on the Means of finding out Conveniencies: And indeed those who are Witnesses of their Sufferings, can hardly conceive how they can support them; and the rather, because they have no Relaxation, and that all the Seasons have their particular Inconveniencies.

The Inconveniencies of the Summer for the Savages.

As their Villages are always situated near Woods, or on the Side of some Water, and often between both. As soon as the Air begins to grow warm, the Musketoes, and an infinite Number of other small Flies, begin a Persecution more grievous than the Smoke, which we are often obliged

to

to call to our Aſſiſtance; for there is ſcarce any other Remedy againſt the Stings of theſe little Inſects, which ſet all Parts of the Body in a Flame, and do not ſuffer you to ſleep in Quiet. Add to this, the frequent forced Marches, and always very fatiguing ones, which one muſt make to follow theſe Barbarians; ſometimes in Water up to the Waiſt, and ſometimes in Mud up to the Knees; in the Woods, thro' Brambles and Thorns, in Danger of being blinded; in the open Country, where there is no Shelter from the Heat of the Sun, which is as violent in Summer as the Wind is piercing in Winter.

If one travels in Canoes, the confined Poſture which one muſt keep, and the Apprehenſions we are under at firſt from the extreme Weakneſs of theſe Vehicles, the Inaction which can't be avoided, the ſlow Progreſs they make, which is retarded by the leaſt Rain, or a little too much Wind, the little Society one can have with People who know nothing, and who never ſpeak when they are about any Thing, who offend you with their ill Smell, and who fill you with Filth and Vermin; the Caprices and rough Behaviour which muſt be borne with from theſe People; the Affronts to which one is expoſed from a Drunkard, or a Man who is put out of Humour by an unforeſeen Accident, a Dream, or the Remembrance of ſome Misfortune; the Coveting, which is eaſily produced in the Hearts of theſe Barbarians, at the Sight of an Object capable of tempting them, and which has coſt the Lives of ſeveral Miſſionaries; and if War is declared between the Nations where they happen to be, the continual Danger they run, of being ſuddenly reduced either to the hardeſt Servitude, or to periſh in the moſt horrible Torments: This is, Madam, the Life which the Miſſionaries (eſpecially the firſt) have led. If for ſome Time paſt it has been leſs ſevere in ſome Reſpects, it has had for the Labourers of the Goſpel other inward Troubles, and of Conſequence more grievous; which, far from being leſſened by Time, encreaſe in the ſame Meaſure as the Colony encreaſes, and as the natural Inhabitants of the Country have more Communication with all Sorts of People.

A ſhort Portrait of the Savages.

In ſhort, to make a brief Portrait of theſe People: With a ſavage Appearance, and Manners and Cuſtoms which are entirely barbarous, there is obſervable amongſt them a ſocial Kindneſs, free from almoſt all the Imperfections which ſo often diſturb the Peace of Society among us. They appear to be without Paſſion; but they do that in cold Blood, and ſometimes through Principle, which the moſt violent and unbridled Paſſion produces in thoſe who give no Ear to Reaſon. They ſeem to lead the moſt wretched Life in the World; and they were perhaps the only happy People on Earth, before the Knowledge

Knowledge of the Objects, which so much work upon and seduce us, had excited in them Desires which Ignorance kept in Supineness; and which have not as yet made any great Ravages among them. We discover in them a Mixture of the fiercest and the most gentle Manners, the Imperfections of wild Beasts, and Virtues and Qualities of the Heart and Mind, which do the greatest Honour to Human Nature. One would think at first that they have no Form of Government, that they acknowledge neither Laws nor Subordination; and that living in an entire Independence, they suffer themselves to be solely guided by Chance, and the wildest Caprice: Nevertheless, they enjoy almost all the Advantages that a well regulated Authority can procure for the best governed Nations. Born free and independent, they look with Horror even on the Shadow of a despotic Power; but they seldom depart from certain Principles and Customs, founded on good Sense, which are to them instead of Laws, and which in some Measure supply the Place of a lawful Authority. They will not bear the least Restraint; but Reason alone keeps them in a Kind of Subordination; which, for being voluntary, is not the less effectual to obtain the End intended.

A Man who should be highly esteemed by them, would find them docible enough, and would make them do almost what he pleased; but it is not easy to obtain their Esteem to such a Degree: They never give it but to Merit, and to superior Merit; of which they are as good Judges as those amongst us, who think they have the most Discernment.

They rely much on Physiognomy, and perhaps there are no Men in the World who are better Judges of it. The Reason is, that they have none of that Respect for any Person whatsoever, which seduces us: And studying only pure Nature, they have a perfect Knowledge of it. As they are not Slaves to Ambition and Interest, and that there is scarce any Thing but these two Passions which has weakened in us that Sense of Humanity which the Author of Nature had graved in our Hearts, the Inequality of Conditions is no Way necessary to them for the Support of Society.

Therefore, Madam, we do not see here, at least we seldom meet with those haughty Spirits, who, full of their own Grandeur, or their Merit, almost fancy they are a different Species, disdaining the rest of Mankind, by whom of Consequence they are never trusted nor beloved; who think none like themselves, because the Jealousy which reigns among the Great, does not permit them to see each other near enough; who do not know themselves, because they never study their own Hearts, but always flatter themselves; who do not consider that to win the Hearts of Men, we must in some Measure make ourselves their Equals: So that with this pretended Superiority of Knowledge, which

 they

they look upon as the essential Property of the eminent Rank they possess, the greatest Part of them live in a proud and incurable Ignorance of what concerns them the most to know, and never enjoy the true Pleasures of Life.

In this Country all Men think themselves equally Men; and in Man what they esteem most, is the Man. Here is no Distinction of Birth; no Prerogative allowed to Rank, which hurts the Rights of private Persons; no Preheminence given to Merit, that inspires Pride, and which makes other People feel too much their Inferiority. There is perhaps less Delicacy of Sentiments than among us, but more Justness; less of Ceremonies, and of what may render them equivocal; less of Consideration to ourselves.

Religion alone can bring to Perfection the good Qualities of these People, and correct their evil ones; this is common to them with others, but what is peculiar in them is, that they start fewer Obstacles when they begin to believe, which can only be the Work of special Grace. It is also true, that to establish perfectly the Empire of Religion over them, they ought to see it practised in all its Purity by those who profess it; they are very apt to be scandalized at the Behaviour of bad *Christians*, as all those are, who are instructed for the first Time in the Principles of the Gospel Morality.

You will ask me, Madam, if they have any Religion? to this I reply, that we cannot say they have none, but that it is pretty hard to define what they have. I will entertain you more fully on this Article, at my first Leisure; for though I am not much employed here, I am so often interrupted, that I scarce get two Hours in the Day to myself. This Letter, as well as most of the preceeding, will inform you, that I do not write regularly. I content myself at present with adding, to finish the Portrait of the Savages, that even in the most indifferent Actions, we find some Traces of the primitive Religion, but which escape the Observation of those, who do not consider them with Attention, because they are still more effaced through the Want of Instruction, than altered by the Mixture of a superstitious Worship, or fabulous Traditions.

I am, &c.

LETTER

LETTER XXIII.

Of the Traditions, and of the Religion of the SAVAGE *of* CANADA.

MADAM, *At the Fort of the River* ST. JOSEPH, *Sept.* 8.

THIS Letter will be very long, if some unforeseen Accident does not oblige me to put off to another Opportunity, what I have to entertain you with concerning the Belief, the Traditions, and the Religion of our Savages.

The Notion of the Savages of the Origin of Man.

Nothing is more certain, than that the Savages of this Continent have an Idea of a first Being, but at the same Time nothing is more obscure. They agree, in general, in making him the first Spirit, the Lord and Creator of the World; but when we press them a little on this Article, to know what they mean by the FIRST SPITIT, we find nothing but odd Fancies. Fables so ill conceived, Systems so little digested, and so little Uniformity, that one can say nothing regular on this Subject. They say that the *Sioux* come much nearer than the rest to what we ought to think of this first Principle. But the little Intercourse we have had with them hitherto, has not afforded me an Opportunity of learning their Traditions, as far as I could have wished, to speak of them with any Certainty.

Almost all the *Algonquin* Nations have given the Name of the *Great Hare* to the first Spirit; some call him *Michabou*, others *Atahocan*. The greatest Part say, that being supported on the Waters with all his Court, all composed of four-footed Creatures like himself, he formed the Earth out of a Grain of Sand, taken from the Bottom of the Ocean; and created Men of the dead Bodies of Animals. There are some also that speak of a God of the Waters who opposed the Design of the *Great Hare*, or at least refused to favour it. This God is, according to some, the great Tiger, but it is to be observed, that there are no true Tigers in *Canada*; therefore this Tradition might probably be derived from some other Country. Lastly, they have a third God named *Matcomek*, whom they invoke during the Winter, and of whom I could learn nothing particular.

The *Areskoui* of the *Hurons*, and the *Agreskoué* of the *Iroquois*, is in the Opinion of these People the Supreme Being, and the God of War. These People do not give the same Origin to Men as the *Algonquins*, and they do not go so far back as the Creation of the World.

World. They say there were six Men in the World at first; and when we ask them who placed them there, they answer, that they know not. They add, that one of these Men went up into Heaven, to seek a Woman there named *Atahentsic*, with whom he lived, and who soon appeared to be with Child; that the Lord of Heaven perceiving it, threw her down from the highest Part of Heaven, and she was received on the Back of a Tortoise. That she brought forth two Children, one of which killed the other.

They have no Tradition after this, either of the other five Men, or even of the Husband of *Atahentsic*, who according to some had but one Daughter, who was Mother of *Thaouitsaron*, and of *Jouskeka*. The latter who was the Eldest killed his Brother, and soon after his Grandmother left the Care of governing the World to him. They say farther, that *Atahentsic* is the Moon, and *Jouskeka* is the Sun. There is, as you see, Madam, nothing regular in all this; for the Sun is often taken for *Areskoui*, as being a great Spirit: But is there less Contradiction in the Theology of the *Egyptians* and the *Greeks*, who are the first Sages of the *Pagan* Antiquity? It is the Nature of Falsehood to contradict itself, and to have no Principle.

Their Notion of Spirits.

The Gods of the Savages have, according to their Notions, Bodies, and live much in the same Manner as we do, but without any of the Inconveniencies which we are subject to. The Term *Spirit* signifies among them only a Being of a more excellent Nature than the rest. They have no Terms to express what exceeds the Limits of their Understanding, which is extremely confined in every Thing that is not the Object of their Senses, or in common Use: But they give nevertheless to their pretended Spirits a Kind of Immensity, which renders them present in all Places; for wherever they happen to be, they invoke them, they speak to them, and they suppose that the Spirits hear what they say to them, and that they act in Consequence thereof. To all the Questions we ask these Barbarians, to know more, they answer this is all they have been taught; and it is only some old Men who have been initiated in their Mysteries who know so much.

According to the *Iroquois*, the Posterity of *Jouskeka* went no farther than the third Generation; there came then a Deluge, from which no Person escaped, and to re-people the Earth Beasts were changed to Men. For the rest, Madam, the Notion of a universal Deluge is generally received among the *Americans* but one can scarce doubt; but that there has been one of a much fresher Date, which was confined to *America*. I should never make an End, was I to mention all the Stories the Savages tell about their principal Deities, and the Origin of the World:

But besides the first Being, or the Great Spirit, and the other Gods which are confounded with him, they have an infinite Number of Genii, or Subaltern Spirits, good and evil, which have their particular Worship.

Of the Good and evil Genii.

The *Iroquois* place *Atahentsic* at the Head of the evil Spirits, and make *Jouskeka* the Chief of the Good. They even confound him sometimes with the God who expelled his Grandmother from Heaven, for suffering herself to be seduced by a Man. They address themselves to the evil Genii, only to beg that they would do them no Harm; but they suppose that the others watch over Men for their Good, and that every Man has his own Genius. In the *Huron* Language they call them OKKIS, and in the *Algonquin*, MANITOUS. They have Recourse to them when they are in any Danger, when they go on any Enterprize, and when they would obtain some extraordinary Favour. They think they may ask any Thing of them, however unreasonable it may be, or however contrary even to good Behaviour and Honesty. But Children, they suppose are not born under their Protection. They must first know how to handle a Bow and Arrows, to merit this Favour. There must also be some Preparations to receive it. This is the most important Affair of Life. These are its principal Ceremonies:

The necessary Preparations to obtain a Guardian Genius.

They begin by blacking the Face of the Child; then it must fast for eight Days, without having the least Nourishment; and during this Time his future Guardian Genius must appear to him in his Dreams. The empty Brain of a poor Child, just entering on the first Stage of Youth, can't fail of furnishing him with Dreams; and every Morning they take great Care to make him relate them. However, the Fasting often ends before the Time appointed, as few Children have Strength to bear it so long; but that creates no Difficulty. They are acquainted here, as in other Places, with the convenient Use of Dispensations. The Thing which the Child dreams of most frequently, is supposed to be his Genius; but no doubt this Thing was considered at first only as a Symbol, or Shape under which the Spirit manifests himself: But the same has happened to these People, as to all those who have erred from the primitive Religion: They have attached themselves to the Representation, and have lost Sight of the Reality.

Nevertheless, these Symbols signify nothing of themselves: Sometimes it is the Head of a Bird, sometimes the Foot of an Animal, or a Piece of Wood: In a Word, the most ordinary Things, and the least valued. They preserve them, however, with as much Care as the Antients did their *Penates*. There is even

even nothing in Nature that hath not its Spirit, if we believe the Savages; but they are of all Degrees, and have not the same Power. When they do not comprehend a Thing, they assign to it a superior Genius, and their Way of Expression in this Case is to say, *It is a Spirit*. It is the same for stronger Reasons with Respect to Men, those who have singular Talents, or who do extraordinary Things, they say are Spirits; *that is to say*, they have a Guardian Genius of a more exalted Degree than Men in general.

Some, especially the Jugglers, endeavour to persuade the Multitude that they are sometimes in a Trance. This Madness has existed at all Times, and among all Nations, and has given Birth to all the false Religions. The Vanity, which is so natural to Mankind, has never imagined a more effectual Method to rule over the Weak: The Multitude at last draw after them those who pride themselves most in their Wisdom. The *American* Impostors are not behind-hand with any in this Point, and they know how to obtain all the Advantages from it which they propose. The Jugglers never fail to publish, that during their pretended Extacies, their Genii give them great Informations of Things done at the greatest Distance, and of future Events; and as by Chance, if we will not allow the Devil any Share in it, they sometimes happen to divine or guess pretty right, they acquire by this a great Reputation: They are reckoned Genii of the first Order.

Sometimes they change their Genii, and why.

As soon as they have declared to a Child what he must for the Time to come look upon as his Guardian Genius, they instruct him carefully of the Obligation he is under to honour him, to follow the Council he shall receive from him in his Sleep, to merit his Favours, to put all his Trust in him, and to dread the Effects of his Anger if he neglects his Duty towards him. The Festival terminates in a Feast, and the Custom is also to prick on the Body of the Child, the Figure of his *Okki*, or his *Manitou*. One would imagine that such a solemn Engagement, the Mark of which can never be effaced, should be inviolable; nevertheless, there needs only a Trifle to break it.

The Savages do not easily acknowledge themselves in the Wrong, even with their Gods, and make no Difficulty to justify themselves at their Expence: Therefore, the first Time they have Occasion to condemn themselves, or to lay the Blame on their Guardian Genius, the Fault always falls on the latter. They seek another without any Ceremony, and this is done with the same Precautions as at first. The Women have also their *Manitous*, or their *Okkis*, but they do not so much regard them as the

Men; perhaps, because they do not find them so much Employment.

They make to all these Spirits different Sorts of Offerings, which you may call, if you please, Sacrifices. They throw into the Rivers and the Lakes *Petun*, Tobacco, or Birds that have had their Throats cut, to render the God of the Waters propitious to them. In Honour of the Sun, and sometimes also of the inferior Spirits, they throw into the Fire Part of every Thing they use, and which they acknowledge to hold from them. It is sometimes out of Gratitude, but oftener through Interest: Their Acknowledgment also is interested; for these People have no Sentiments of the Heart towards their Deities. We have observed also on some Occasions a Kind of Libations, and all this is accompanied with Invocations in mysterious Terms, which the Savages could never explain to the *Europeans*, either that in Fact they have no Meaning, or that the Sense of them has not been transmitted by Tradition with the Words; perhaps also they keep it as a Secret from us.

Sacrifices of the Savages.

We find also Collars of Porcelain, Tobacco, Ears of Maiz, Skins, and whole Animals, especially Dogs, on the Sides of difficult and dangerous Ways, on Rocks, or by the Side of the Falls; and these are so many Offerings made to the Spirits which preside in these Places. I have already said that a Dog is the most common Victim that they sacrifice to them: Sometimes they hang him up alive on a Tree by the hind Feet, and let him die there raving mad. The War Feast, which is always of Dogs, may very well also pass for a Sacrifice. In short, they render much the same Honours to the mischievous Spirits, as to those that are beneficent, when they have any Thing to fear from their Malice.

Thus, Madam, among these People, whom some have represented as having no Idea of Religion, or a Deity, almost every Thing appears to be the Object of a Religious Worship, or at least to have some Relation to it. Some have fancied that their Fasts were only intended to accustom them to bear Hunger, and I agree that they may be partly designed for this End; but all the Circumstances which accompany them, leave no Room to doubt that Religion is the principal Motive; was it only their Attention, which I have spoken of, to observe their Dreams during that Time; for it is certain that these Dreams are esteemed as real Oracles, and Notices from Heaven.

Of the Fasts.

There is still less Room to doubt that Vows are among these People pure Acts of Religion, and the Custom of them is absolutely the same as with us. For Instance, when they are out of Provisions, as it often happens in their

Of Vows.

their Journies and in their Huntings, they promiſe their Genii to give in Honour of them, a Portion of the firſt Beaſt they ſhall kill to one of their Chiefs, and not to eat till they have perform-ed their Promiſe. If the Thing becomes impoſſible, becauſe the Chief is at a great Diſtance, they burn what was deſigned for him, and make a Sort of Sacrifice.

Formerly the Savages in the Neighbourhood of *Acadia* had in their Country, on the Side of the Sea, a very old Tree, of which they uſed to tell many wonderful Stories, and which was always loaded with Offerings. The Sea having laid all its Roots bare, it ſupported itſelf ſtill a long Time againſt the Violence of the Winds and Waves, which confirmed the Savages in their Notion, that it was the Seat of ſome great Spirit: Its Fall was not even capable of undeceiving them, and as long as there appeared ſome Ends of the Branches out of the Water, they paid it the ſame Honours as the whole Tree had re-ceived while it was ſtanding.

The Affinity of the Savages with the Jews.

The greateſt Part of their Feaſts, their Songs, and their Dances appear to me to have had their Riſe from Religion, and ſtill to preſerve ſome Traces of it; but one muſt have good Eyes, or ra-ther a very lively Imagination, to perceive in them all that ſome Travellers have pretended to diſcover. I have met with ſome who could not help thinking that our Sa-vages were deſcended from the *Jews*, and found in every Thing ſome Affinity between theſe Barbarians and the People of God. There is indeed a Reſemblance in ſome Things, as not to uſe Knives in certain Meals, & not to break the Bones of the Beaſt they eat at thoſe Times, and the Separation of the Women during the Time of their uſual Infirmities. Some Perſons, they ſay, have heard them, or thought they heard them, pronounce the Word *Hallelujah* in their Songs: But who can believe, that when they pierce their Ears and Noſes, they do it in Purſuance of the Law of Circumciſion? On the other Hand, don't we know that the Cuſtom of Circumciſion is more antient than the Law that was given to *Abraham* and his Poſterity? The Feaſt they make at the Return of the Hunters, and of which they muſt leave no-thing, has alſo been taken for a Kind of Burnt-Offering, or for a Remain of the Paſſover of the *Iſraelites*; and the rather, they ſay, becauſe when any one cannot compaſs his Portion, he may get the Aſſiſtance of his Neighbours, as was practiſed by the People of God, when a Family was not ſufficient to eat the whole Paſchal Lamb.

Their Prieſts.

An antient Miſſionary *(a)*, who lived a long Time with the *Outaouais*, has written, that among theſe Savages an old Man performs the Office of a Prieſt at

(a) Father *Claude Allouez*, a *Jeſuit*.

the

the Feasts, which I have just mentioned; that they begin by giving Thanks to the Spirits for the Success of the Chace; afterwards another takes a Loaf of *Petun*, breaks it in two, and throws it into the Fire. This is certain, that those who have mentioned them as a Proof of the Possibility of *Atheism*, properly so called, are not acquainted with them. It's true that they never discourse about Religion, and that their extreme Indolence on this Point has always been the greatest Obstacle we have met with in converting them to *Christianity*. But however little they discourse about it, we should do wrong to conclude from thence that they have no Idea of God.

Indolence is their prevailing Character: It appears even in the Affairs which concern them most: But in Spite of this Fault, in Spite even of that Spirit of Independence in which they are bred, no People in the World have a greater Dependence on the confused Ideas they have preserved of the Deity; even to that Degree, that they attribute nothing to Chance, and that they draw Omens from every Thing; which they believe, as I have said before, are Notices from Heaven.

Vestals among the Savages.

I have read in some Memoirs, that many Nations of this Continent have formerly had young Maids, who never had any Conversation with Man, and never married. I can neither warrant, nor contradict this Fact. Virginity is of itself a State so perfect, that it is no Wonder it has been respected in all the Countries of the World: But our oldest Missionaries have said nothing, that I know of, of these Vestals; though many agree concerning the Esteem they had for Celibacy in some Countries. I find also, that among the *Hurons* and the *Iroquois* there were, not long since, a Kind of Hermits, who observed Continence; and they shew us some very salutary Plants, which the Savages say have no Virtue, if they are not administered by Virgin Hands.

Their Thoughts of the Immortality of the Soul.

The Belief the best established amongst our *Americans*, is that of the Immortality of the Soul. Nevertheless, they do not believe it purely spiritual, no more than their Genii; and to speak the Truth, they cannot well define either one or the other. When we ask what they think of their Souls, they answer, they are as it were the Shadows, and the animated Images of the Body: And 'tis in Consequence of this Principle, that they believe every Thing is animated in the Universe. Therefore it is entirely by Tradition that they hold that our Souls do not die. In the different Expressions they use to explain themselves on this Subject, they often confound the Soul with its Faculties, and the Faculties with their Operations,

though

though they know very well how to make the Diſtinction, when they chuſe to ſpeak correctly.

Their Notion of what becomes of the Soul, when ſeparated from the Body.

They ſay alſo that the Soul, ſeparated from the Body, has ſtill the ſame Inclinations it had before; and this is the Reaſon why they bury with the Dead every Thing they uſed when living. They are alſo perſuaded, that the Soul remains near the Corpſe till the Feſtival of the Dead, which I ſhall preſently mention; that afterwards it goes into the Country of Souls, where, according to ſome, it is transformed into a Dove.

Why they carry Proviſions to the Tombs.

Others think there are two Souls in every Man: They attribute to one all I have juſt mentioned: They ſay that the other never leaves the Body, but to go into another; which nevertheleſs ſeldom happens, they ſay, but to the Souls of Children; which having little enjoyed Life, are allowed to begin a new one. For this Reaſon, they bury Children by the Sides of Highways, that the Women, as they paſs by, may gather their Souls. Now theſe Souls, which ſo faithfully keep Company with their Bodies, muſt be fed; and it is to fulfil this Duty, that they carry Proviſions to the Tombs: But this does not laſt long, and theſe Souls muſt accuſtom themſelves in Time to faſt. It is hard enough ſometimes to get a Subſiſtence for the Living, without burthening themſelves farther with providing Food for the Dead.

The Preſents they make to the Dead.

But one Thing which theſe People never fail to perform, in whatſoever Extremity they find themſelves, is, that as among us the Spoils of the Dead enrich the Living, among them they not only carry to the Grave all that the Deceaſed poſſeſſed, but alſo Preſents from their Friends and Relations.——They were highly provoked, when they ſaw ſome *French* open the Graves, to get the Gowns of Beaver Skins in which the Dead were buried. The Graves are ſo ſacred in this Country, that to profane them is the greateſt Hoſtility that can be committed againſt a Nation, and the greateſt Sign that they will come to no Terms with them.

Of the Country of Souls.

I have mentioned that the Souls, when the Time is come that they are to part for ever from their Bodies, go to a Region which is appointed to be their everlaſting Abode. This Country, ſay the Savages, is very far to the Weſt, and the Souls are ſeveral Months travelling thither. They have alſo great Difficulties to ſurmount, and they run through great Dangers before they arrive there. They ſpeak eſpecially of a River they have to paſs, where many have been wrecked; of a Dog, from which they find it hard to defend themselves; of a Place of Torment, where they expiate their Faults; of another, where the Souls are tormented of the Prisoners of War that have been burnt.

This Notion is the Reason why, after the Death of these Wretches, for Fear their Souls should stay about the Cabins, to revenge their Sufferings, they very carefully visit all Places, striking continually with a Stick, and sending forth hideous Cries, to drive away these Souls.

The *Iroquois* say, that ATAHENTSIC makes her ordinary Residence in this *Tartarus*, and that she is solely employed in deceiving Souls, to destroy them. But JOUSKEKA omits nothing to defend them against the evil Designs of his Grandmother. Among the fabulous Stories which they tell of what passes in this Hell, which so much resembles those of *Homer* and *Virgil*, there is one that seems to be copied from the Adventure of *Orpheus* and *Eurydice*. There is scarce any Thing in it to change but the Names.

How they pretend to merit eternal Happiness.

For the rest, Madam, the Happiness which the Savages hope to enjoy in their fancied *Elisium*, they do not regard precisely as the Reward of Virtue. To have been a good Hunter, a gallant Warrior, fortunate in all his Enterprizes, to have killed and burnt a great Number of Enemies; these are the only Titles which give them a Right to their Paradise: All the Happiness of which consists in finding a hunting and fishing Place that never fails, an eternal Spring, great Plenty of all Things, without being obliged to labour, and all the Pleasures of Sense: And this is all they ask of their Gods in their Life. All their Songs, which are originally their Prayers, run only on the present Good. There is no Mention made, no more than in their Vows, of a future Life. They think themselves sure of being happy in the other World, in Proportion to what they have been in this.

Of the Souls of Beasts.

The Souls of Beasts have also their Place in the Country of Souls; for, according to the Savages, they are no less immortal than our's. They also allow them a Sort of Reason; and not only each Species, but also each Animal, if we may believe them, has also its Guardian Genius. In a Word, they make no Difference between us and Brutes, but that our Souls are something of a better Sort. Man, they say, is the King of Animals, which have all the same Attributes; but Man possesses them in a much higher Degree. They believe also that in the other World there are Models of all Sorts of Souls; but they don't trouble themselves

ſelves much to explain the Idea; and in general they are little concerned about thoſe that are purely ſpeculative. And have the wiſeſt Philoſophers of *Pagan* Antiquity, who have taken ſuch immenſe Pains to explain them, have they made a much greater Progreſs than the Savages? We muſt always loſe ourſelves in theſe dark Ways, unleſs we are guided by the Light of Faith.

The Nature of Dreams, according to the Savages.

There is nothing in which the Savages have ſhewn more Superſtition and Extravagance, than in what regards their Dreams; but they differ much in the Manner of explaining their Thoughts on this Matter. Sometimes it is the reaſonable Soul that wanders out, while the ſenſitive Soul continues to animate the Body. Sometimes it is the familiar Genius that gives good Advice about future Events. Sometimes it is a Viſit they receive from the Soul of the Object they dream of. But in whatſoever Manner they conceive of a Dream, it is always regarded as a ſacred Thing, and as the Means which the Gods moſt uſually employ to declare their Will to Men.

Prepoſſeſſed with this Idea, they can't conceive that we ſhould take no Notice of them. For the moſt Part they look upon them as Deſires of the Soul, inſpired by ſome Spirit, or an Order from it. And in Conſequence of this Principle, they make it a Duty of Religion to obey theſe Commands.--------A Savage having dreamt that his Finger was cut off, really had it cut off when he awoke, after he had prepared himſelf for this important Action by a Feaſt. Another dreaming that he was a Priſoner in the Hands of his Enemies, was greatly embarraſſed. He conſulted the Jugglers, and by their Advice he got himſelf tied to a Poſt, and burnt in ſeveral Parts of the Body.

There are ſome Dreams lucky, and ſome unfortunate: For Inſtance, to dream they ſee many Elks, is, they ſay, a Sign of Life: To dream of Bears, is a Sign they will die ſoon. I have obſerved before, that we muſt except thoſe Times when they prepare for hunting thoſe Animals. But to let you ſee, Madam, to what an Extravagance theſe Savages carry this Matter of Dreams, I will relate to you a Fact atteſted by two undeniable Witneſſes, who ſaw the Thing with their own Eyes.

A Story on this Subject.

Two Miſſionaries were travelling with ſome Savages; and one Night, when all their Conductors were faſt aſleep, one of them ſtarted up in a Fright quite out of Breath, trembling, ſtriving to cry out, and beating himſelf as if he had been poſſeſſed with a Devil. At the Noiſe he made, every Body were ſoon up. At firſt they thought the Man was ſeized with a Fit of Madneſs: They took hold of him, and did all they could to quiet him, but to no Purpoſe: His Fury ſtill encreaſed; and as they could not hold him any longer, they hid all the Arms for Fear of some Accident. Some thought it proper to prepare a Draught for him, made of certain Herbs of great Virtue; but, when they least expected it, the pretended Madman jump'd into the River.

He was taken out immediately, and he complained of Cold; yet he would not come near a good Fire that was presently made: He sat down at the Foot of a Tree; and as he seemed more calm, they brought him the Drink they had prepared for him. "*You must give it to this Child,*" (said he) and what he called a Child, was the Skin of a Bear stuffed with Straw: He was obeyed, and they poured all the Drink into the Jaws of this Figure: Then they ask'd him, what it was that troubled him? "*I have dreamt* (replied he) *that a* Huart (a Kind of Cormorant) *is got into my Stomach.*" Then they all fell a laughing: But something was to be done to cure his Imagination; and the Method they took for it, was as follows:

They all began to counterfeit themselves mad, and to cry out as loud as they could, that they had also an Animal in their Stomachs; but they did not chuse to jump into the River to drive them out, as it was very cold; they had rather sweat themselves. The whimsical Person liked this Advice very well. They presently made a Stove, and they entered into it, crying out as loud as they could bawl: Then they all began to counterfeit the Cry of the Animal, which they pretended was in their Stomachs; one a Goose, another a Duck, another a Bustard, another a Frog: The Dreamer also counterfeited his *Huart*. But the Joke was, that all the rest beat Time, by striking upon him with all their Strength, with Design to tire him and make him sleep. For any but a Savage, there was Beating enough to hinder him from closing his Eyes for many Days; nevertheless, they obtained what they desired. The Patient slept a long Time, and when he awoke he was cured; feeling no Effects of the Sweating, which was enough to have weakened him greatly, nor of the Blows with which he was bruised all over; having lost even the Remembrance of a Dream, for which he had paid so dear.

How they are satisfied about a Dream, when it is too hard to accomplish its Instructions.

But it is not the Person alone, who has had a Dream, that must satisfy the Obligations that he imagines are imposed on him by it; but it would also be a Crime in any Person that he addresses himself to, to refuse him any Thing he desired in dreaming. And you must perceive, Madam, that this may have disagreeable Consequences. But as the Savages are not Self-interested, they abuse this Principle much less than they would in other Places. If the Thing desired is of such a Nature that it cannot be supplied by a private Person, the Public takes Care of of the Matter; and if it must be sought for five hundred Leagues off, it must be found at any Rate; and it is not to expressed with how much Care, they keep it when they have got it. If it is an inanimate Thing, they are more easy, but if it is an Animal, its Death causes surprizing Uneasiness.

The Affair is more serious still, if any one takes it into his Head to dream that he knocks another's Brains out, for he does it in Fact if he can; but he must expect the same if any other takes a Fancy in his Turn to dream that he revenges the dead. On the other Hand, with a little Presence of Mind, it is easy to get out of this Trouble: It is only knowing how to oppose immediately such a Dream with another that contradicts it. "Then says the the first Dreamer, I see plainly that your "Spirit is stronger than mine, therefore let us talk no more "about it." Nevertheless, they are not all so easily quieted; but there are few that are not satisfied, or whose Genius is not appeased by some Present.

Of the Festival of Dreams.

I know not if Religion has ever had any Share in what they generally call *the Festival of Dreams*, and which the *Iroquois*, and some others, have more properly called *the turning of the Brain*. This is a Kind of *Bacchanal*, which commonly lasts fifteen Days, and is celebrated about the End of Winter.

They act at this Time all Kinds of Fooleries, and every one runs from Cabin to Cabin, disguised in a thousand ridiculous Ways: They break and overset every Thing, and no Body dares to contradict it. Whoever chuses not to be present in such a Confusion, nor to be exposed to all the Tricks they play, must keep out of the Way. If they meet any one, they desire him to guess their Dream, and if they guess, it is at their Expence, he must give the Thing they dreamt of. When it ends, they return every Thing, they make a great Feast, and they only think how to repair the sad Effects of the Masquerade, for most commonly it is no trifling Business: For this is also one of those Opportunities which they wait for, without saying any Thing, to give those a good Drubbing who they think have done them any Wrong. But when the Festival is over, every Thing must be forgot.

A Description of one of these Festivals.

I find the Description of one of these Festivals in the Journal of a Missionary *(a)*, who was forced to be a Spectator of it much against his Will, at *Onnontague*. It was thus observed: It was proclaimed the 22d of *February*, and it was done by the Elders, with as much Gravity as if it had been a

(a) Father *Claude Dablon.*

weighty Affair of State. They had no sooner re-entered their Cabins, but instantly there came forth Men, Women, and Children, almost quite naked, though the Weather was excessive cold. They entered directly into all the Cabins, then they went raving about on every Side, without knowing whither they went, or what they would have: One would have taken them for People drunk, or stark mad.

Many carried their mad Freaks no further and appeared no more: Others were resolved to make Use of the Privilege of the Festival, during which they are reputed to be out of their Senses, and of Consequence not responsible for what they do, and so revenge their private Quarrels. They did so to some Purpose: On some they threw whole Pails full of Water, and this Water, which froze immediately, was enough to chill them with Cold who were thus used. Others they covered with hot Ashes, or all Sorts of Filth: Others took lighted Coals, or Fire-brands, and threw them at the Head of the first they met: Others broke every Thing in the Cabins, falling upon those they bore a Grudge to, and beating them unmercifully. To be freed from this Persecution, one must guess Dreams, which often one can form no Conception of.

The Missionary and his Companion were often on the Point of being more than Witnesses of these Extravagancies: One of these Madmen went into a Cabin, where he had seen them take Shelter at the first. Happy for them, they were just gone out; for there was great Reason to think this furious Fellow intended them some Harm. Being disappointed by their Flight, he cried out, that they must guess his Dream, and satisfy it immediately: As they were too long about it, he said, *I must kill a* FRENCHMAN: Immediately the Master of the Cabin threw him a *French* Coat, to which this Madman gave several Stabs.

Then he that had thrown the Coat, growing furious in his Turn, said he would revenge the *Frenchman*, and burn the whole Village to the Ground. He began in Fact by setting Fire to his own Cabin, where the Scene was first acted; and when all the rest were gone out, he shut himself up in it. The Fire, which he had lighted in several Places, did not yet appear on the Outside, when one of the Missionaries came to the Door: He was told what had happened, and was afraid that his Host could not get out, tho' he might be willing: He broke open the Door, laid hold of the Savage, turned him out, put out the Fire, and shut himself up in the Cabin. His Host nevertheless ran through the Village, crying out that he would burn it: They threw a Dog to him, in Hopes that he would glut his Fury on that Animal; he said it was not enough to repair the

Affront he had received by the killing of a *Frenchman* in his Cabin: They threw him a ſecond Dog, he cut it in Pieces, and inſtantly all his Fury was over.

This Man had a Brother, who would alſo play his Part: He dreſſed himſelf up, nearly as Painters repreſent the *Satyrs*, covering himſelf from Head to Foot with the Leaves of Maiz: He equipped two Women like real *Megaras*, their Faces blacked, their Hair diſhevelled, a Wolf Skin over their Bodies, and a Club in their Hands. Thus attended, he goes into all the Cabins, yelling and howling with all his Strength: He climbs upon the Roof, and plays as many Tricks there as the moſt ſkilful Rope-Dancer could perform; then he made moſt terrible Outcries, as if he had got ſome great Hurt; then he came, down, and marched on gravely, preceded by his two *Bacchantes*, who growing furious in their Turn, overſet with their Clubs every Thing they met in their Way. They were no ſooner out of this Frenzy, or tired with acting their Parts, than another Woman took their Place, entered the Cabin, in which were the two *Jeſuits*, and armed with a Blunderbuſs, which ſhe had juſt before got by having her Dream gueſſed, ſhe ſung the War-Song, making a thouſand Imprecations on herſelf if ſhe did not bring home ſome Priſoners.

A Warrior followed cloſe after this *Amazon*, with a Bow and Arrows in one Hand, and a Bayonet in the other. After he had made himſelf hoarſe with bawling, he threw himſelf all at once on a Woman, who was ſtanding quietly by, not expecting it, and lifting up his Bayonet to her Throat, took her by the Hair, cut off a Handful, and went away. Then a Juggler appeared, holding a Stick in his Hand adorned with Feathers, by Means of which he boaſted that he could reveal the moſt ſecret Things. A Savage accompanied him, carrying a Veſſel full of I know not what Liquor, which from Time to Time he gave him to drink: The Juggler had no ſooner taken it in his Mouth, than he ſpit it out again, blowing upon his Hands, and on his Stick, and at every Time he explained all the Enigmas that were propoſed to him.

Two Women came afterwards, and gave to underſtand that they had ſome Deſires: One directly ſpread a Mat on the Ground: They gueſſed that ſhe deſired ſome Fiſh, which was given her. The other had a Hoe in her Hand, and they judged that ſhe deſired to have a Field to cultivate: They carried her out of the Village, and ſet her to Work. A Chief had dreamt, as he ſaid, that he ſaw two human Hearts: They could not explain his Dream, and at this every Body was greatly concerned. It made a great Noiſe, they even prolonged the Feſtival for a Day, but all was in vain, and he was obliged to make himſelf

himself easy without. Sometimes there were Troops of People that made Sham-Fights; sometimes Companies of Dancers, who acted all Sorts of Farces. This Madness lasted four Days, and it appeared that it was out of Respect to the two *Jesuits* that they had thus shortened the Time: But there were as many Disorders committed in this Space of Time, as they used to do in fifteen Days. Nevertheless, they had this further Regard for the Missionaries, that they did not disturb them in their Functions, and did not hinder the *Christians* from acquitting themselves of their religious Duties. But I have said enough on this Article. I close my Letter to give it to a Traveller, who is returning to the Colony, assuring you that

I am, &c.

LETTER XXIV.

Sequel of the Traditions of the SAVAGES.

MADAM, *At the Fort of the River* ST. JOSEPH, *Sept.* 14.

THREE Days ago I left this Place, to go to *Chicagou*, by coasting the South shore of Lake *Michigan*; but we found the Lake so rough, that we thought it betterto return hither; and take another Route to get to *Louisiana*. Our Departure it fixed for the 16th, and I shall take Advantage of these two Days Delay, to proceed in my Account of the Customs and Traditions of our *Americans*.

Of the evil Genii, and of the Wizards.

The Savages, in what I said to you in my former Letter, acknowledge only the Operations of the Good Genii. The Wizards alone, and those who use Enchantments, are reputed to hold any Correspondence with the Evil; and 'tis Women most commonly that follow this detestable Trade. The Jugglers by Profession not only forbear it, at least openly, but they make it a particular Study, to know how to discover Enchantments, and to hinder their pernicious Effects. At the Bottom, in all the Stories I have heard on this Matter, there is scarce any Thing but juggling. They use on these Occasions either Serpents, out of which they take the Venom; or Herbs, gathered at certain Seasons; or pronounce certain Words; or use Animals whose Throats they have cut, and some Parts of which are thrown into the Fire.

Among the *Illinois*, and ſome other Nations, they make little *Marmoſets* to repreſent thoſe whoſe Days they would ſhorten, and which they ſtab to the Heart. At other Times they take a Stone, and by the Means of ſome Invocations they pretend to form one like it, in the Heart of their Enemy. I am perſuaded this ſeldom happens, unleſs the Devil is concerned in it; however, they are ſo afraid of Magicians, that the leaſt Suſpicion is enough to cauſe whoever is the leaſt ſuſpected of being ſuch, to be cut to Pieces. Yet though this Profeſſion is ſo dangerous, there are People to be found every where, who have no other. It is alſo true that the moſt ſenſible, and the leaſt credulous of thoſe who have been moſt converſant with the Savages; do allow that there is ſometimes ſome Reality in their Magic.

Why ſhould theſe Infidels, Madam, be the only People in whom we ſhould not diſcover the Operation of the Devil? and what other Maſter but this miſchievous Spirit, *who was a Murderer from the Beginning (a)*, could have taught ſo many People, who have had no Correſpondence with each other, an Art, which we cannot look upon as abſolutely trifling, without contradicting the ſacred Writings? We muſt therefore acknowledge, that the Infernal Powers have ſome Agents upon Earth, but that God has confined their Malignity within very narrow Limits; and permits but ſeldom, that we ſhould feel the Effects of the Power he has thought fit to leave to them only to make it ſubſerve, ſometimes to his Juſtice, and ſometimes to his Mercy.

Of the Jugglers.

We may ſay much the ſame of the Jugglers of *Canada*, who make a Profeſſion of correſponding only with what they call the beneficial Genii, and who boaſt of knowing by their Means whatever paſſes in the moſt diſtant Countries, and whatever ſhall come to paſs in the moſt diſtant Ages; and who pretend to diſcover the Riſe and Nature of the moſt hidden Diſeaſes, and to have the Secret of curing them; to diſcern in the moſt intricate Affairs what Reſolution it is beſt to take; to explain the moſt obſcure Dreams, to obtain Succeſs to the moſt difficult Undertakings; to render the Gods propitious to Warriors and Hunters. Theſe pretended good Genii, are like all the *Pagan* Deities, real Devils, who receive Homages that are due only to the true God, and whoſe Deceits are ſtill more dangerous than thoſe of the evil Genii, becauſe they contribute more to keep their Worſhippers in Blindneſs.

It is certain, that amongſt their Agents the boldeſt are the moſt reſpected; and with a little Artifice, they eaſily perſuade People who are brought up in Superſtition. Tho' they have ſeen

(a) *John* viii. 44.

the

the Birth of theſe Impoſtors, if they take a Fancy to give themſelves a ſupernatural Birth, they find People, who believe them on their Word, as much as if they had ſeen them come down from Heaven, and who take it for a Kind of Enchantment and Illuſion, that they thought them born at firſt like other Men: Their Artifices are nevertheleſs, in general, ſo groſs, and ſo common, that there are none but Fools, and Children, that are impoſed upon by them; unleſs it is when they act as Phyſicians: For every one knows, that in what concerns the Recovery of Health, the greateſt Credulity is to be found in all Countries, as well among thoſe who value themſelves moſt on their Wiſdom, as among the Weaker Sort.

After all, Madam, I repeat it, it is difficult not to acknowledge that among theſe Infidels there ſometimes paſs Things that are very capable of deceiving, at leaſt the Multitude, not to ſay more. I have heard ſome Perſons ſay, whoſe Truth and Judgment I could no Way ſuſpect, that when theſe Impoſtors ſhut themſelves up in their Stoves to ſweat, and this is one of their moſt common Preparations to perform their Tricks, they differ in nothing from the *Pythoniſſæs*, as the Poets have repreſented them on the *Tripod:* That they are ſeen to become convulſed, and poſſeſſed with Enthuſiaſm, to acquire Tones of the Voice, and to do Actions which appear to be beyond the Strength of Nature, and which ſeize the moſt unprejudiced Spectators with a Horror, and a Diſorder of Spirits, that they cannot overcome.

It is alſo aſſerted, that they ſuffer much on theſe Occaſions; and that there are ſome who do not readily engage, even when they are well paid, to give themſelves up in this Manner to the Spirit that agitates them. But we need not believe that there is any Thing ſupernatural in this, that after coming out of theſe violent Sweats they go and throw themſelves into cold Water, and ſometimes when it is frozen, without receiving any Damage. This is common to them with the other Savages, and even with other People of the North *(a)*. This is a Matter which Phyſic cannot eaſily account for, but in which 'tis certain the Devil has no Share.

It is alſo true, that the Jugglers are too often right in their Predictions, to make it believed that they always gueſs by Chance; and that there paſſes on theſe Occaſions Things that it is ſcarce poſſible to attribute to any natural Secret. Some Perſons have ſeen the Poſts which encloſed theſe Stoves, bend down quite to the Earth, whilſt the Juggler was very tranquil,

(a) The Poet *Regnard* aſſures us, in his Voyage to *Lapland*, that he ſaw the ſame Thing done in *Eſtonia*.

without any Motion, and without touching them, singing and foretelling Things that should come to pass. The Letters of the antient Missionaries are full of Facts, which leave no Room to doubt that these Seducers have a real Correspondence with the Father of Deceit and Lies. Many of the *French* have talked to me in the same Manner. I will only relate to you one Story which I have from its Source.

You have seen at *Paris* Madam *de Marson*, and she is there still. This is what the Marquis *de Vaudreuil*, her Son-in-Law, at present our Governor-General, told me this Winter, and which he learnt of this Lady, who is very far from being suspected of Weakness and Credulity. She was one Day very uneasy about her Husband, M. *de Marson*, who was Commandant of a Post which we have in *Acadia:* He was absent, and the Time was past which he had set for his Return. A Woman Savage, who saw Madam *de Marson* was troubled, asked her the Cause of it; and being told it, she said, after pausing a little on the Matter, "*Don't trouble yourself any longer; your Husband will come back on* "*such a Day, and at such an Hour,* (which she named) *wearing a* "*grey Hat.*" As she perceived that the Lady gave no Heed to her Prediction, on the Day and at the Hour she had foretold, she came again to the Lady, and asked her if she would come and see her Husband arrive, and pressed her in such a Manner to follow her, that she drew her to the Side of the River. They had hardly got thither, when M. *de Marson* appeared in a Canoe, wearing a grey Hat; and being informed of what had passed, he declared that he could not conceive how the Savage could have foreknown the Hour and the Day of his Arrival.

Of Pyromancy.

This Example, Madam, and many others that I know, which are equally certain, prove that the Devil is sometimes concerned in the Magic of the Savages; but it belongs only, they say, to the Jugglers to raise up Spirits, when public Affairs are concerned. It is said that all the *Algonquins* and *Abenaquis* formerly practised a Kind of Pyromancy, of which this was the whole Mystery: They reduced to a very fine Powder some Coals of Cedar Wood; they placed this Powder after a particular Manner, then they set Fire to it, and by the Turn the Fire took in running on this Powder, they discovered, as it is said, what they sought for. They add, that the *Abenaquis*, on their Conversion to *Christianity*, could hardly be brought to forsake a Custom, which they looked upon as a very innocent Means of knowing what passed at a Distance from them.

Installation of the Jugglers.

I never heard that private Persons, who desired to be acquainted with these Secrets, were obliged, for that Purpose, to go thro' any Ceremony; but the Jugglers by Profession are never invested with this Character, which makes them contract a Kind of League with the Genii, and which procures them Respect, till they have prepared themselves for it by Fastings, which they carry to an uncommon Length; and during which they do nothing but beat a Drum, cry, howl, sing, and smoke. The Instalment is afterwards made in a Kind of *Bacchanal*, with Ceremonies so extravagant, and accompanied with so many furious Actions, that one would say that the Devil then takes Possession of their Persons.

Of the Priests.

But they are not, nevertheless, the Ministers of these pretended Deities, but only to declare their Will to Men, and to be their Interpreters; for if we may give the Name of Sacrifices to the Offerings which these People make to their Deities, the Jugglers are never their Priests. In the public Ceremonies, they are the Chiefs; and in private Ceremonies it is generally the Father of the Family, or the chief Person of the Cabin. The chief Employment of the Jugglers, or at least that by which they get most, is Physick: They practise this Art on Principles founded on the Knowledge of Simples, on Experience, and on Circumstances, as they do in other Places; but they most commonly also join with these Principles, Superstition and Imposture, of which the Vulgar are always the Dupes.

The common Distempers of the Savages.

There are perhaps no Men in the World who are more the Dupes of such Impostors than the Savages, tho' there are few who have less Need of Physick. They are not only almost all of a healthy and strong Constitution, but they have never known the greatest Part of the Distempers which we are subject to, but since they conversed with us. They knew not what the Small-Pox was, when they took it from us; and we must attribute the great Ravages it has made amongst them to this Ignorance. The Gout, the Gravel, the Stone, the Apoplexy, and many other Diseases, so common in *Europe*, have not yet reached this Part of the New World, among the natural Inhabitants of the Country.

'Tis true, that their Excesses in their Feasts, and their immoderate Fasts, make them subject to Pains and Weaknesses of the Stomach and Breast, which destroy a great Number of them: Also, many young Persons die of the Phthisick; and they say that this is the Effect of the great Fatigues and violent Exercises to which they expose themselves from their Childhood, before they are strong enough to support them. 'Tis a Folly to believe, as some do, that their Blood is colder than our's, and to attribute to this Cause their Insensibility in Torments; but their Blood is extremely balsamic; and this arises, without Doubt,

Doubt, from their uſing no Salt nor any of thoſe Things we uſe, to give a higher Reliſh to our Meats.

The Uſe the Savages make of their Simples.

They ſeldom look upon a Diſeaſe as merely natural, or among the common Remedies they uſe, allow any to have in themſelves the Virtue of healing. The great Uſe they make of their Simples, is for Wounds, Fractures, Diſlocations, Luxations, and Ruptures. They blame the great Inciſions which our Surgeons make to cleanſe Wounds: They ſqueeze out the Juice of many Plants, and with this Compoſition they draw out all the Corruption, and even the Splinters of broken Bones, Stones, Iron, and in general all the foreign Matter that remains in the wounded Part. Theſe ſame Juices are all the Food of the Patient, till the Wound is cloſed. The Perſon that dreſſes the Wound, takes alſo ſome of theſe Juices before he ſucks it, if he finds it neceſſary to uſe that Method. But there is ſeldom a Neceſſity to do this; moſt commonly they find it ſufficient to ſyringe the Wound with theſe Juices.

All this is according to Rule; but as theſe People muſt have ſomething ſupernatural in all their Tranſactions, the Juggler often tears the Wound with his Teeth, and afterwards ſhewing a Bit of Wood, or ſome ſuch Thing, that he had the Precaution to put before-hand in his Mouth, he makes the Patient believe that he drew it out of the Wound, and that this was the Charm which cauſed all the Danger of his Malady. This is certain, that they have wonderful Secrets and Remedies. A broken Bone is well united, and grows ſolid in eight Days. A *French* Soldier, who was in Garriſon in a Fort of *Acadia*, was troubled with the falling Sickneſs; and his Fits were grown ſo frequent, as to attack him almoſt every Day with great Violence. A Woman Savage, who happened to be preſent at one of his Fits, went and made him two Boluſſes of a powdered Root, the Name of which ſhe concealed, and deſired that he would take one at the End of his next Fit, giving Notice that he would ſweat much, and have great Evacuations both upwards and downwards; and added, that if the firſt Bolus did not carry off all the Complaint, the ſecond would entirely cure it. The Thing happened as the Woman had ſaid: The Patient had another Fit after the firſt Doſe, but it was the laſt. He enjoyed afterwards a perfect State of Health.

Divers other Remedies.

Theſe People have alſo quick and ſovereign Remedies againſt the Palſy, the Dropſy, and the Venereal Diſeaſe. The Shavings of Guiacum Wood, and of Saſſafras, are their common Specifics in the two laſt Diſeaſes: They make a Drink of theſe Woods,

 which

which cures and prevents these Diseases, if it is constantly used *(a)*.

In acute Diseases, as in the Pleurisy, they work on the Side opposite the Pain: They apply Cataplasms, which draw, and prevent the Humours from settling. In the Fever they use cold Lotions, with a Decoction of Herbs, and by this prevent Inflammations and Delirium. They boast especially of the Effects of Diet, but they make it consist only in abstaining from certain Aliments, which they esteem hurtful.

Formerly, they had not the Use of Blood-letting, and instead of it, they used Scarifications in the Places where they felt Pain: Then they applied a Sort of Cupping Vessel made of Gourds, which they filled with combustible Matter, which they set on Fire. They very commonly used several Kinds of real Caustics; but as they were not acquainted with the *Lapis Infernalis (the Blue Stone)*, they used instead of it rotten Wood. At present Bleeding supplies the Place of these Operations. In the northern Parts, they frequently use Clysters; a Bladder serves them for a Syringe. They have a Remedy against the Dysentery, which is almost always effectual: This is a Juice they squeeze out of the Extremities of the Branches of the Cedar-Tree, after they have been well boiled.

Of Sweating.

But their great Remedy, and their great Preservative against all Diseases, is Sweating. I have before told you, Madam, that at their coming out of the Stove, and while the Sweat runs down from all Parts of their Bodies, they go and plunge into a River; if there is not any near enough, they get some Body to throw the coldest Water over them. They frequently sweat only to recover the Fatigue of a Journey, to calm their Spirits, and to enable them the better to discourse on Affairs. As soon as a Stranger comes into a Cabin, they make a Fire for him, they rub his Feet with Oil, and then they conduct him to a Stove, where his Host keeps him Company. They have also another Manner of promoting Sweats, which they use in certain Distempers: It consists in laying the Patient along upon a Kind of Couch, a little elevated, under which they boil, in a Kettle, some Wood of *Epinette*, and Branches of Pine. The Vapour which arises from it, causes a most plentiful Sweat *(b)*: They say also that the Smell is very wholesome. The Sweat of the Stoves, that is procured only by the Vapour of Water poured upon hot Flints, has not this Advantage.

(a) They have since talked of a Powder, composed of three Simples, which a Savage gave to one of our Missionaries, and which radically cures in a few Days, the most inveterate *French* Disease.

(b) This seems to deserve the Attention of the *European* Physicians.

In

In *Acadia*, a Distemper was never considered to be of much Consequence, but when the Patient refused all Kind of Nourishment, and many Nations are still in the same Error: Let a Person have any Kind of Fever, if they can eat, they eat of every Thing like other People. But as soon as the Distemper appears dangerous, *that is to say*, when the Patient refuses all Kinds of Food, they employ all their Attention. It is true that the Principles on which all the Physic of the Savages is founded, are very extraordinary: They refuse the Patient nothing that he asks, because, say they, his Desires in this State are the Orders of the Genius, that presides over his Preservation *(a)*: And when they call in the Jugglers, 'tis less on Account of their Skill, than because they suppose they are better informed by the Genii of the Cause of the Distemper, and of the Remedies for the Cure.

The Principles on which the whole Practice of Physic is founded among the Savages.

Furthermore, they will have nothing to reproach themselves with: One would imagine that Death loses something of its Terror, when it follows after a Course of Physic, though this Physic might be the Cause of it. Our Savages are with Regard to this Notion under the general Law, and the common Prejudice of all Nations, and all Ages; and they are the more excusable for carrying their Credulity so far, as they acknowledge something supernatural in all Distempers; and as they make Religion share in the Art of healing them, they think themselves the less obliged to be guided by Reason, and make it a Duty to suffer themselves to be led blindfold.

Oftentimes the Patient takes it into his Head that his Distemper is the Effect of Witchcraft: Then all their Care is to discover it, and this is the Duty of the Juggler. He begins by sweating himself, and when he has throroughly tired himself with bawling, beating himself, and invoking his Genius, the first extraordinary Thing that comes into his Thought, he ascribes as the Cause of the Distemper. Many, before they enter into the Stove, take a compound Potion, very proper, as they say, to make them receive the heavenly Impression; and they pretend that the Presence of the Spirit is manifested by a strong Wind that rises on a sudden, or by a Bellowing which they hear under Ground, or by the Agitation or shaking of the Stove. Then full of his pretended Deity, and more like one possessed with the Devil, than a Man inspired by Heaven, he pronounces his Decision in a magisterial Tone on the State of the Patient, and sometimes hits pretty right.

Their extravagant Notion of Distempers.

(a) This seems to deserve to be attended to, as Experience has often proved that the Indulgence of the Desires of the Sick has been salutary.

But

But these Quacks have found out a pretty singular Way of not being answerable for Events. As soon as they perceive a Patient has the Symptoms of Death, they never fail to give Orders, that are so difficult to be put in Execution, that they are always sure of an Excuse, on Account of their Orders not having been punctually followed. It is not to be conceived to what Extravagancies they go on these Occasions: They order some Patients to counterfeit themselves mad: In some Distempers they order Dances, which are generally very laborious. One would think for the most Part, that they have the Cure of the Patient less in View, than to hasten his Death. But what shews the Force of Imagination is, that these Doctors, with all their Follies, perform as many Cures as ours.

Impostures of the Jugglers.

In some Nations, when the Distemper is desperate, they kill the Patients to put them out of their Pain. In the Country of [illegible], they destroy young Children that lose their Mothers at their Birth, or bury them alive with them, because they are persuaded that another Woman cannot nurse them, and that they would pine to Death. But I think however that lately they have laid aside this barbarous Custom. Some others forsake the Diseased when the Doctors give them over, and let them die with Hunger and Thirst. There are some, who to hinder the Difference of the Features in dying Persons, close their Eyes and Mouth, when they see them in the Agony of Death.

Their Cruelty to the Sick

In *Acadia*, the Jugglers are called *Autmoins*, and it is generally the Chief of the Village who is invested with this Dignity; therefore they have more Authority than the other Jugglers, though they have not more Skill, nor less of Imposture. When they are called to a Patient, the first Thing they do is to view him attentively for some Time, then they blow upon him: If this has no Effect, "The Reason is, that the Devil is "within him, say they, but however he must come out; yet "let every one be upon his Guard, for this evil Spirit out of "Spite may fall upon one of the Company." Then they enter into a Kind of Madness, they make strange Postures, they cry out, they threaten the pretended Devil, they speak to him as if they saw him, and they make Passes at him: But all this is only a Farce to hide their Imposture.

Of the Autmoins of Acadia.

When they enter the Cabin, they always have the Precaution to thrust into the Earth a Piece of Wood, fastened to a String: Afterwards they offer the End of the String to all the

[illegible]

I am, &c.

LETTER

LETTER XXV.

Departure from the Fort of the River ST. JOSEPH. *The Sources of the* THEAKIKI. *What passes at the Death of the Savages: Of their Funerals; of their Tombs; of their Mourning; of Widowhood; of the Festival of the Dead.*

MADAM, *From the Source of the* THEAKIKI, *Sept.* 17.

I Did not expect to take up my Pen to write to you so soon; but my Conductors have just now broke their Canoe, and here I am detained the whole Day in a Place where I can find nothing that can excite the Curiosity of a Traveller; therefore I can do nothing better than employ my Time in entertaining you.

I think I informed you in my last, that I had the Choice of two Ways to go to the *Illinois*: The first was to return to Lake *Michigan*, to coast all the South Shore, and to enter into the little River *Chicagou*. After going up it five or six Leagues, they pass into that of the *Illinois*, by the Means of two Portages, the longest of which is but a League and a Quarter. But as this River is but a Brook in this Place, I was informed that at that Time of the Year I should not find Water enough for my Canoe; therefore I took the other Route, which has also its Inconveniencies, and is not near so pleasant, but it is the surest.

Departure from Fort St. Joseph.

I departed Yesterday from the Fort of the River *St. Joseph*, and I went up that River about six Leagues. I landed on the Right, and I walked a League and a Quarter; at first by the Bank of the River, then cross the Country in a vast Meadow, interspersed all over with little Clusters of Trees, that have a very fine Effect. They call it the Meadow *de la Tête de Bœuf, (the Buffalo's Head)* because they found here a Buffalo's Head of a monstrous Size. Why should there not be Giants among these Animals?——I encamped in a very fine Place, which they call the Fort *des Renards, (of the Foxes)*, because the *Renards*, THAT IS TO SAY, the *Outagamis*, had here, and not long since, a Village fortified after their Manner.

This Morning I walked a League further in the Meadow, having almost all the Way my Feet in Water. Then I met with a little Pool, which communicates with several others of different Bigness, the largest of which is not one hundred Paces in Compass. These are the Sources of a River called *Theakiki*, and which

which our *Canadians* by Corruption call *Kiakiki*. *Theak* signifies a Wolf, I forget in what Language; but this River is so call'd, because the *Mahingans*, which are also called *the Wolves*, formerly took Refuge here.

We put our Canoe, which was brought hither by two Men, into the second of these Springs, or Pools, and we embarked; but we found scarce Water enough to keep it afloat: Ten Men, in two Days, might make a strait and navigable Canal, which would save much Trouble, and ten or twelve Leagues Way; for the River, at the first coming out from its Spring, is so narrow, and we are continually obliged to turn so short, that every Moment one is in Danger of breaking the Canoe, as it has just now happened to us.———But let us return to the Savages; and after having seen in what Manner they are treated in their Distempers, let us see them die, and what passes after their Death.

What passes at the Death of a Savage.

In general, when they think themselves past Recovery, they meet their Fate with a Resolution truly *stoical*, and they often see their Days shortened by the Persons that are most dear to them, without shewing the least Chagrin. The Declaration of the Sentence of the Doctor is scarcely finished to a dying Man, before he makes an Effort to harangue these that are about him. If it is the Chief of a Family, he first makes his Funeral Oration, which he finishes by giving very good Counsel to his Children. After this, he takes Leave of every Body, gives Orders for a Feast, in which they must use all the Provisions that remain in the Cabin, and then he receives the Presents of his Family.

During this Time they cut the Throats of all the Dogs they can catch, that the Souls of these Animals may go into the other World, and give Notice that such a Person will arrive there soon; and all the Bodies are put into the Kettle, to enlarge the Feast. After the Feast is over, they begin to weep: Their Tears are interrupted to bid the last Farewel to the dying Person, to wish him a good Journey, to comfort him on his being separated from his Relations and Friends, and to assure him that his Children will maintain all the Glory he has acquired.

We must acknowledge, Madam, that the Calmness with which these People look Death in the Face, has something in it very admirable; and this is so universal, that perhaps there never was an Instance of a Savage shewing any Concern upon hearing that he had but a few Hours to live. The same Principle, and the same Spirit, prevails every where, though the Customs vary much in all that I have just mentioned, according to the different Nations. In most Places there are Dances, Songs, Invocations, and Feasts ordered by the Doctors, which are almost always Remedies more fit, according to our Notions, to kill a Man that was well, than to cure a ſick Perſon. In ſome Places they uſe no Means at all: They are ſatisfied with having Recourſe to the Spirits; and if the ſick Perſon recovers his Health, they have all the Honour: But the dying Perſon is always the leaſt concerned about his Fate.

Their Generoſity to the Dead.

It may further be added, that if theſe People ſhew ſo little Judgment in their Manner of treating the Sick, we muſt acknowledge that they behave towards the Dead with a Generoſity and an Affection that cannot be too much admired. Some Mothers have been known to have kept the dead Bodies of their Children whole Years, and could never go from them; others draw Milk from their Breaſts, and pour it upon the Tombs of theſe little Creatures. If a Village happens to take Fire, in which there are any dead Bodies, this is the firſt Thing they take Care to preſerve: They ſtrip themſelves of every Thing that is moſt valuable, to adorn the Dead: From Time to Time they open their Coffins to change their Dreſs; and they deprive themſelves of Food to carry it to the Sepulchres, and to the Places where they fancy their Souls walk. In a Word, they are at much greater Expences for the Dead, than for the Living.

Of their Funerals.

As ſoon as the ſick Perſon expires, the Place is filled with mournful Cries; and this laſts as long as the Family is able to defray the Expence, for they muſt keep open Table all this Time. The dead Body, dreſſed in the fineſt Robe, with the Face painted, the Arms and all that belonged to the Deceaſed by his Side, is expoſed at the Door of the Cabin in the Poſture it is to be laid in the Tomb; and this Poſture is the ſame, in many Places, as that of the Child in the Mother's Womb. The Cuſtom of ſome Nations is for the Relations of the Deceaſed to faſt to the End of the Funeral; and all this Interval is paſſed in Tears and Cries, in treating their Viſitors, in praiſing the Dead, and in mutual Compliments. In other Places they hire Women to weep, who perform their Duty punctually: They ſing, they dance, they weep without ceaſing, always keeping Time: But theſe Demonſtrations of a borrowed Sorrow do not prevent what Nature requires from the Relations of the Deceaſed.

Of the Tombs.

It appears to me, that they carry the Body without Ceremony to the Place of Interment; at leaſt I find no Mention about it in any Relation: But when it is in the Grave, they take Care to cover it in ſuch a Manner, that the Earth does not touch it: It lies as in a little Cave lined with Skin, much richer and better adorned than their Cabins. Then they ſet up a Poſt on the Grave, and fix on it every

Thing that may ſhew the Eſteem they had for the Deceaſed. They ſometimes put on it his Portrait, and every Thing that may ſerve to ſhew to Paſſengers who he was, and the fineſt Actions of his Life. They carry freſh Proviſions to the Tomb every Morning; and as the Dogs and other Beaſts do not fail to reap the Benefit of it, they are willing to perſuade themſelves that theſe Things have been eaten by the Souls of the Dead.

Of Apparitions.

It is not ſtrange, after this, that the Savages believe in Apparitions: And in Fact they tell Stories of this Sort all Manner of Ways. I knew a poor Man, who, by continually hearing theſe Stories, fancied that he had always a Troop of Ghoſts at his Heels; and as People took a Pleaſure to encreaſe his Fears, it made him grow fooliſh.--Nevertheleſs, at the End of a certain Number of Years, they take as much Care to efface out of their Minds the Remembrance of thoſe they have loſt, as they did before to preſerve it; and this ſolely to put an End to the Grief they felt for their Loſs.

Some Miſſionaries one Day aſking their new Converts, why they deprived themſelves of their moſt neceſſary Things in Favour of the Dead? they replied, "It is not only to ſhew the "Love we bore to our Relations, but alſo that we may not "have before our Eyes, in the Things they uſed, Objects which "would continually renew our Grief." It is alſo for this Reaſon that they forbear, for ſome Time, to pronounce their Names; and if any other of the Family bears the ſame Name, he quits it all the Time of Mourning. This is probably alſo the Reaſon why the greateſt Outrage you can do to any Perſon, is to ſay to them, *Your Father is dead*, or, *Your Mother is dead.*

Various Practices about the Dead.

When any one dies in the Time of Hunting, they expoſe his Body on a very high Scaffold, and it remains there till the Departure of the Troop, who carry it with them to the Village. There are ſome Nations who practiſe the ſame with Regard to all their Dead; and I have ſeen it practiſed by the *Miſſiſaguez* of *Detroit.* The Bodies of thoſe who die in War are burnt, and their Aſhes brought back to be laid in the Burying-Place of their Fathers. Theſe Burying-Places, among the moſt ſettled Nations, are Places like our Church-yards, near the Village. Others bury their Dead in the Woods, at the Foot of a Tree; or dry them, and keep them in Cheſts till the Feſtival of the Dead, which I ſhall preſently deſcribe: But in ſome Places they obſerve an odd Ceremony for thoſe that are drowned, or are frozen to Death.

Before I deſcribe it, it is proper, Madam, to tell you that the Savages believe, when theſe Accidents happen, that the Spirits are incenſed, and that their Anger is not appeaſed till the Body is found. Then the Preliminaries of Tears, Dances, Songs, and Feasts, being ended, they carry the Body to the usual Burying-Place; or, if they are too far off, to the Place where it is to remain till the Festival of the Dead. They dig there a very large Pit, and they make a Fire in it: Then some young Persons approach the Corpse, cut out the Flesh in the Parts which had been marked out by a Master of the Ceremonies, and throw them into the Fire with the Bowels: Then they place the Corpse, thus mangled, in the Place destined for it. During the whole Operation, the Women, especially the Relations of the Deceased, go continually round those that are at it, exhorting them to acquit themselves well of their Employment, and put Beads of Porcelain in their Mouths, as we would give Sugar-Plumbs to Children to entice them to do what we desire.

What passes after the Interment.

The Interment is followed by Presents, which they make to the afflicted Family; and this is called *covering the Dead*. These Presents are made in the Name of the Village, and sometimes in the Name of the Nation. Allies also make some Presents at the Death of considerable Persons: But first the Family of the Deceased makes a great Feast in his Name, and this Feast is accompanied with Games, for which they propose Prizes, which are performed in this Manner: A Chief throws on the Tomb three Sticks about a Foot long: A young Man, a Woman, and a Maiden, take each of them one; and those of their Age, their Sex, and their Condition, strive to wrest them out of their Hands. Those with whom the Sticks remain, are Conquerors. There are also Races, and they sometimes shoot at a Mark. In short, by a Custom which we find established in all the Times of *Pagan* Antiquity, a Ceremony entirely mournful is terminated by Songs, and Shouts of Victory.

Of Mourning.

It is true, that the Family of the Deceased take no Part in these Rejoicings: They observe even in his Cabin, after the Obsequies, a Mourning, the Laws of which are very severe: They must have their Hair cut off, and their Faces blacked: They must stand with their Heads wrapped in a Blanket: They must not look at any Person, nor make any Visit, nor eat any Thing hot: They must deprive themselves of all Pleasures, wear scarce any Thing on their Bodies, and never warm themselves at the Fire, even in the Depth of Winter.

After this deep Mourning, which lasts two Years, they begin a second more moderate, which lasts two or three Years longer, and which may be softened by little and little; but they dispense with nothing that is prescribed, without the Consent of the Cabin

Cabin to which the Widower or the Widow belongs. These Permissions, as well as the End of the Mourning, always cost a Feast.

Of Widowhood and second Marriages.

Widows cannot contract a second Marriage without the Consent of those on whom they depend, in Virtue of the Laws of Widowhood. If they can find no Husband for the Widow, she finds herself under no Difficulties: If she has any Sons of an Age to support her, she may continue in a State of Widowhood, without Danger of ever wanting any Thing: If she is willing to marry again, she may chuse, and the Man she marries becomes the Father of her Children: He enters into all the Rights, and all the Obligations of the first Husband.

The Husband does not weep for his Wife; because, according to the Savages, Tears do not become Men; but this is not general among all Nations. The Women weep for their Husbands a Year: They call him without ceasing, and fill their Village with Cries and Lamentations, especially at the rising and setting of the Sun, at Noon, and in some Places when they go out to Work, and when they return. Mothers do much the same for their Children. The Chiefs mourn only six Months, and may afterwards marry again.

The Notion of the Savages about those who die violent Deaths.

The first, and often the only Compliment they make to a Friend, and even to a Stranger they receive in their Cabins, is to weep for those of his near Relations, whom he has lost since they saw him last. They put their Hands on his Head, and they give him to understand who it is they weep for, without mentioning his Name. All this is founded in Nature, and has nothing in it of Barbarity. But what I am going to speak of, does not appear to be any Way excusable; *that is*, the Behaviour of these People towards those who die by a violent Death, even though it is in War, and for the Service of their Country.

They have got a Notion that their Souls, in the other World, have no Communication with the others; and on this Principle they burn them, or bury them directly, sometimes even before they expire. They never lay them in the common Burying-Place, and they give them no Part in the great Ceremony, which is renewed every eight Years among some Nations, and every ten Years among the *Hurons* and the *Iroquois*.

They call it the *Festival of the Dead*, or the *Feast of Souls*: And here follows what I could collect that was most uniform and remarkable concerning this Ceremony, which is the most singular and the most celebrated of the Religion of the Savages. They begin by fixing a Place for the Assembly to meet in: Then they chuse

chuſe the King of the Feaſt, whoſe Duty it is to give Orders for every Thing, and to invite the neighbouring Villages. The Day appointed being come, all the Savages aſſemble, and go in Proceſſion two and two to the Burying-Place. There every one labours to uncover the Bodies; then they continue ſome Time contemplating in Silence a Spectacle ſo capable of exciting the moſt ſerious Reflexions. The Women firſt interrupt this religious Silence, by ſending forth mournful Cries, which encreaſe the Horror with which every one is filled.

This firſt Act being ended, they take up the Carcaſſes, and pick up the dry and ſeparated Bones, and put them in Parcels; and thoſe who are ordered to carry them, take them on their Shoulders. If there are any Bodies not entirely decayed, they waſh them; they clean away the corrupted Fleſh, and all the Filth, and wrap them in new Robes of Beaver Skins: Then they return in the ſame Order as they came; and when the Proceſſion is come into the Village, every one lays in his Cabin the Burden he was charged with. During the March, the Women continue their Lamentations, and the Men ſhew the ſame Signs of Grief as they did on the Day of the Death of thoſe whoſe Remains they have been taking up. And this ſecond Act is followed by a Feaſt in each Cabin, in Honour of the Dead of the Family.

The following Days they make public Feaſts; and they are accompanied, as on the Day of the Funeral, with Dances, Games, and Combats, for which there are alſo Prizes propoſed. From Time to Time they make certain Cries, which they call *the Cries of the Souls*. They make Preſents to Strangers, among whom there are ſometimes ſome who come an hundred and fifty Leagues, and they receive Preſents from them. They alſo take Advantage of theſe Opportunities to treat of common Affairs, or for the Election of a Chief. Every Thing paſſes with a great deal of Order, Decency, and Modeſty; and every one appears to entertain Sentiments ſuitable to the principal Action. Every Thing, even in the Dances and Songs, carries an Air of Sadneſs and Mourning; and one can ſee in all, Hearts pierced with the ſharpeſt Sorrow. The moſt Inſenſible would be affected at the Sight of this Spectacle. After ſome Days are paſt, they go again in Proceſſion to a great Council-Room built for the Purpoſe: They hang up againſt the Walls the Bones and the Carcaſſes in the ſame Condition they took them from the Burying-Place, and they lay forth the Preſents deſigned for the Dead. If among theſe ſad Remains there happens to be thoſe of a Chief, his Succeſſor gives a great Feaſt in his Name, and ſings his Song. In many Places the Bones are carried from Village to Village, are received every where with great Demonſtrations of Grief and Tenderneſs, and every where they make them

them Presents: Lastly, they carry them to the Place where they are to remain always. But I had forgot to tell you, that all these Marches are made to the Sound of their Instruments, accompanied with their best Voices, and that every one in these Marches keeps Time to the Music.

This last and common Burial-Place is a great Pit, which they line with their finest Furs, and the best Things they have. The Presents designed for the Dead, are set by themselves. By Degrees, as the Procession arrives, each Family range themselves on a Kind of Scaffolds set up round the Pit; and the Moment the Bones are laid in, the Women renew their weeping and wailing. Then all present go down into the Pit, and every one takes a little of the Earth, which they keep carefully. They fancy it procures Luck at Play. The Bodies and the Bones, ranged in Order, are covered with entire new Furs, and over that with Bark, on which they throw Stones, Wood, and Earth. Every one returns to his own Cabin; but the Women come for several Days after, and pour *Sagamitty* on the Place.

I am, &c.

LETTER XXVI.

Journey to PIMITEOUY. *Of the River of the* ILLINOIS. *Reception of the Prisoners among these People. Their Manner of burning them. Some Things peculiar in their Way of living.*

MADAM, PIMITEOUY, *October* 5.

THE Night of the 17th of this Month, the Frost, which for eight Days past was perceivable every Morning, encreased considerably. This was early for this Climate, for we were in 41° 40′ Lat. The following Days we went forward from Morning to Night, favoured by the Current, which is pretty strong, and sometimes by the Wind: In Fact, we made a great deal of Way, but we advanced very little on our Journey: After having gone 10 or 12 Leagues, we found ourselves so near our last Encampment, that Persons in both Places might have seen each other, and even have talked together, at least with a Speaking-Trumpet. But it was some Consolation to us, that the River and its Borders were covered with Wild-Fowl, fattened with wild Oats, which were then ripe. I also gathered some ripe Grapes, which were of the Shape and Bigness of a Musket-Ball, and soft enough, but of

A Description of the Theakiki.

of a bad Taste. This is probably the same that they call in LOUISIANA *Raisin Prune (the Plumb Grape).* The River by Degrees grows less winding; but its Borders are not pleasant till we are fifty Leagues from its Source. It is also for all this Space very narrow, and as it is bordered with Trees, whose Roots are in the Water, when one falls it bars up the whole River, and it takes a great deal of Time to clear a Passage for a Canoe.

Having got over these Difficulties, the River, about fifty Leagues from its Source, forms a small Lake, and afterwards grows considerably wider. The Country begins to be fine: The Meadows here extend beyond the Sight, in which the Buffaloes go in Herds of 2 or 3 hundred: But one must keep a good Look-out, not to be surprised by the Parties of *Sioux* and *Outagamis*, which are drawn hither by the Neighbourhood of the *Illinois*, their mortal Enemies, and who give no Quarter to the *French* they meet on their Route. The Misfortune is, that the *Theakiki* loses its Depth as it grows wider, so that we are often obliged to unlade the Canoes and walk, which is always attended with some Danger, and I should have been greatly perplexed, if they had not given me an Escort at the River *St. Joseph*.

What surprised me at seeing so little Water in the *Theakiki* was, that from Time to Time it receives some pretty Rivers. I saw one among the rest, above sixty Yards wide as it's Mouth, which they have named the *Irequois River*, because these gallant Men suffered themselves to be surprised here by the *Illinois*, who killed a great Number of them. This Blow humbled them the more, as they greatly despised the *Illinois*, who for the most Part can never face them.

Of the River of the ILLINOIS.

The 27th of *September* we arrived *la Fourche (at the Fork;)* this is the Name the *Canadians* give the Place where the *Theakiki* and the River of the *Illinois* join. The last, after a Course of sixty Leagues, is still so shallow, that I saw a Buffalo cross it, and the Water did not come above the Middle of his Legs. On the contrary, the *Theakiki*, besides bringing it's Waters a hundred Leagues, is a fine River. Nevertheless it loses it's Name here, without doubt because the *Illinois* being settled in many Places of the other have given it their Name. Being enriched all at once by this Junction, it yields to none that we have in *France*; and I dare assure you, Madam, that it is not possible to see a better nor a finer Country than that it waters; at least up to this Place, from whence I write. But it is fifteen Leagues below the *Fork* before it acquires a Depth answerable to its Breadth, although in this Interval it receives many other Rivers.

The largeſt is called *Piſtìcoui*, and comes from the fine Country of the *Maſcoutins*. It has a Fall at its Mouth, which they call *la Charboniere (the Coal Fall)* becauſe they find many Coals in its Environs. In this Route we ſee only vaſt Meadows, with little Cluſters of Trees here and there, which ſeem to have been planted by the Hand; the Graſs grows ſo high in them, that one might loſe one's ſelf amongſt it; but every where we meet with Paths that are as beaten as they can be in the moſt populous Countries; yet nothing paſſes through them but Buffaloes, and from Time to Time ſome Herds of Deer, and ſome Roe-Bucks.

A League below the Coal-Fall we ſee on the Right a Rock quite round, and very high, the Top of which is like a Terraſs; they call it the *Fort of the Miamis*, becauſe theſe Savages had formerly a Village here. A League farther on the left, we ſee another juſt like it, which they call only *Le Rocher (the Rock.)* It is the Point of a very high level Place, that runs for the Length of two hundred Paces, always following the Side of the River, which widens very much in this Place. It is perpendicular on every Side, and at a Diſtance one would take it for a Fortreſs. Here are ſtill ſome Remains of Paliſadoes, becauſe the *Illinois* formerly made an Intrenchment here, which they can eaſily repair in Caſe of any Irruption of their Enemies.

The Village is at the Foot of the Rock in an Iſland, which with ſeveral others, all wonderfully fruitful, divide the River in this Place into two pretty large Channels. I landed the 29th about four in the Afternoon, and I found ſome *French* here, who were trading with the Savages. As ſoon almoſt as I had ſet my Foot on Shore, I was viſited by the Chief of the Village. He is a Man about forty, well ſhaped, mild, of a very pleaſing Countenance, and the *French* ſaid many Things in his Praiſe.

Then I went up the Rock by a tolerably eaſy Way, but very narrow. I found a very ſmooth Terraſs, of a great Extent; and where all the Savages of *Canada* could not force two hundred Men, who had Fire Arms, if they could have Water, which they can get only from the River; and to do this they muſt expoſe themſelves. All the Recourſe of thoſe who ſhould happen to be beſieged here, would be the natural Impatience of theſe Barbarians. In ſmall Parties they will wait without Uneaſineſs eight or ten Days behind a Buſh, in Hopes that ſome Body will paſs by, whom they may kill or take Priſoner: But when they are a numerous Body of Warriors, if they do not preſently ſucceed, they ſoon grow weary, and take the firſt Excuſe to retreat. This they never want; for there needs only for this Purpoſe a Dream, real or feigned.

The Rain, and ſtill more a Spectacle, which filled me with Horror, hindered me from making the Tour of theſe Rocks, from whence I hoped to diſcover a great Country. I perceived at the End, and juſt above the Village, the Bodies of two Savages that had been burnt a few Days before, and which were abandoned according to Cuſtom, to the Birds of Prey, in the ſame Poſture, in which they were executed. The Way of burning the Priſoners among theſe ſouthern Nations, is ſomething ſingular; and they have alſo ſome Cuſtoms different from the others in their Manner of behaving towards theſe unhappy Wretches.

Reception of the Priſoners among the ILLINOIS.

When they have made a military Expedition, which has ſucceeded, the Warriors order their March ſo, that they never arrive at the Village till Night. As ſoon as they are near it, they halt; and when it is Night, they depute two or three young People to the Chief, to acquaint him with the principal Adventures of the Campaign. Next Day, at the Appearance of the Dawn they dreſs their Priſoners in new Robes, adorn their Hair with Down, paint their Faces with various Colours, and put a white Stick in their Hands, which is ſet round with the Tails of Roe-Bucks. At the ſame Time the War-Chief makes a Cry, and all the Village aſſembles at the Water-ſide, if they are near a River.

As ſoon as the Warriors appear, four young Men in their fineſt Dreſs embark in a *Pettiaugre (a)*, the two firſt carry a Calumet, and go ſinging all the Way, to fetch the Priſoners, which they bring as in Triumph to the Cabin, where they are to be ſentenced. The Maſter of the Cabin, to whom it belongs to decide their Fate, firſt gives them ſomething to eat, and during this Meal he holds a Council. If they give his Life to any one, two young Men go and untie him, take him each by one Hand and make him run full Speed to the River, where they throw him in Headforemoſt. They throw themſelves in after him, waſh him well, and lead him to the Perſon whoſe Slave he is to be.

As to thoſe who are condemned to die, as ſoon as the Sentence is pronounced, the Cry is made to aſſemble the Village; and the Execution is deferred, only juſt Time enough to make the Preparations for it. They begin by ſtripping the Sufferer quite naked: They fix in the Earth two Poſts, to which they faſten two croſs Pieces, one about two Feet from the Ground, and the other ſix or ſeven Feet higher, and this is what they call a Frame. They

Their Manner of burning them.

(a) This is a long Boat, made of the ſingle Trunk of a Tree. They uſe but few Canoes of Bark in theſe Parts.

make the Sufferer get upon the firſt croſs Piece, to which they faſten his Feet, at a little Diſtance from each other: Then they tie his Hands to the upper Angles of the Frame; and in this Poſture they burn him in all Parts of the Body.

All the Village, Men, Women, and Children, gather round him; and every one has a Right to torture him as they pleaſe. If no one preſent has any particular Reaſon to prolong his Sufferings, his Puniſhment his ſoon over; and commonly they diſpatch him with their Arrows, or elſe they cover him with the Bark of Trees, which they ſet on Fire. Then they leave him in his Frame, and towards Night they run through all the Cabins, ſtriking with little Sticks on the Furniture, on the Walls, and on the Roofs, to hinder his Soul from ſtaying there to revenge the Injuries they have done to his Body. The reſt of the Night is paſſed in Rejoicings.

Some Particularities concerning their Parties of War.

If the Party has met no Enemy, or if it has been obliged to fly, it enters the Village by Day, keeping a profound Silence; but if it has been beaten, it enters by Night, after having given Notice of their Return by a Cry of Death, and named all thoſe they have loſt, either by Diſtempers, or by the Sword of the Enemy. Sometimes the Priſoners are condemned and executed before they arrive at the Village; eſpecially when they have any Room to fear they will be reſcued. Some Time ſince a *Frenchman* being taken by the *Outagamis*, theſe Barbarians held a Council on their Route, to know how they ſhould diſpoſe of him. The Reſult of the Deliberation was to throw a Stick up in the Tree, and if it lodged there, to burn their Priſoner; but to throw it only a certain Number of Times. By good Fortune for the Priſoner, though the Tree was very thick of Branches, the Stick always fell to the Ground.

The doleful Songs of the Illinois.

I ſtayed twenty-four Hours at the Rock, and to pleaſe the Savages, and to ſhew my entire Confidence in them, though all my Conductors were encamped on the other Side of the River, I lay in a Cabin in the midſt of the Village. I paſt the Night quiet enough; but I was waked very early by a Woman, who lived in the next Cabin; when ſhe awoke, the Remembrance of her Son, whom ſhe had loſt ſome Years before, came into her Mind, and immediately ſhe began to weep, and to ſing in a very doleful Tone.

The *Illinois* have the Character of being cunning Thieves, for this Reaſon I cauſed all my Baggage to be carried over to the other Side; but in ſpite of this Precaution, and the Vigilance of my People, at our Departure we miſſed a Gun, and ſome

Trifles, which we could never recover. The ſame Evening we paſſed the laſt Place of the River, where one is obliged to drag the Canoe; afterwards the River has every where a Breadth and Depth, that makes it equal to moſt of the largeſt Rivers of *Europe*.

Of the Parrots of Louiſiana.

I ſaw alſo this Day, for the firſt Time, ſome Parrots: There are ſome on the Sides of the *Theakiki*, but in Summer only. Theſe were ſome Stagglers that were going to the *Miſſiſſipi*, where there are ſome in all Seaſons: They are but little bigger than a Black-bird, their Head is yellow, with a red Spot in the Middle, Green prevails in all the reſt of their Plumage. The two following Days we traverſed a charming Country, and the third of *October* about Noon we found ourſelves at the Entrance of the Lake *Pimitcouy*; it is the River which grows wider here, and which for three Leagues is one League in Breadth. At the End of theſe three Leagues, we find on the Right a ſecond Village of *Illinois*, diſtant about fifteen Leagues from that of the Rock.

Of the Village of Pimiteouy.

Nothing can be more pleaſant than the Situation; it has over againſt it, as in Perſpective, a very fine Foreſt, which was then of all Colours, and behind it a Plain of an immenſe Extent, bordered with Woods. The Lake and the River ſwarm with Fiſh, and their Sides with Wild-Fowl. I met alſo in this Village four *French Canadians*, who informed me that I was between four Parties of Enemies, and that it was not ſafe for me either to go forward, or to return; they told me further, that on the Route which I had travelled, there were thirty *Outagamis* in Ambuſh; that the like Number of the ſame Savages were ranging round the Village of *Pimiteouy*, and others to the Number of eighty kept at the Bottom of the River, divided into two Bands.

This Account made me recollect what had happened to us the Evening before; we had ſtopt at the End of the Iſland, to look for ſome Buſtards, at which ſome of my People had fired; and we heard ſomebody cutting of Wood in the Middle of the Iſland. The Nearneſs of the Village of *Pimiteouy*, made us judge that it was ſome *Illinois*, and we held in that Opinion; but it is very likely that they were *Outagamis*, who having diſcovered us, and not daring to attack us, becauſe I had twelve Men well armed, thought to draw ſome of us into the Woods, judging that they ſhould have an eaſy Conqueſt of the reſt; but our little Curioſity kept us from this Misfortune, which I ſhould certainly not have eſcaped, if I had not had an Eſcort commanded by a Man, who was not of a Humour to ſtop where there was no real Occaſion.

What

What further confirmed the Account of the four *Frenchmen* was, that thirty Warriors of *Pimiteouy*, commanded by the Chief of the Village, were in the Field, to endeavour to get more certain News of the Enemy; and that a few Days before their Departure, there had been an Action in the Neighbourhood, in which the two Parties had each made one Prisoner: The *Outagami* had been burnt about a Musket-Shot from the Village, and he was still in his Frame. The *Canadians*, who assisted in his Punishment, told me that it lasted five Hours, and that this unfortunate Wretch had maintained till his Death that he was an *Illinois*, and that he had been taken in his Childhood by the *Outagamis*, who had adopted him.

However, he had fought very well, and had it not been for a Wound received in the Leg, he had not been taken. But as he could give no Proofs of what he had alledged, and had been very near making his Escape, they would not believe him on his Word. He made it appear in the midst of his Torments, that Bravery, and Courage in bearing Pain, are very different Virtues, and that they do not always go together, for he made most lamentable Cries, which only served to animate his Executioners. It is true that an old Woman, whose Son had been formerly killed by the *Outagamis*, made him suffer all the Pains that Fury inspired by Revenge could invent. However, at last they took Pity on his Cries, they covered him with Straw, which they set on Fire; and as he had still some Life in him after it was burnt out, the Children killed him with their Arrows. Generally, when a Sufferer does not die bravely, it is a Woman, or Children, that give him his Death's Wound: He does not deserve, they say, to die by the Hand of a Man.

I found myself, Madam, greatly embarrassed. On one Side, my Conductors did not think it prudent to go forward; on the other, it was very inconvenient for my Affairs to winter at *Pimiteouy*: I should then have even been obliged to follow the Savages in their Winter-Quarters, and this would have made me lose a whole Year. At last the two *Canadians*, of the four which I found at *Pimiteouy*, offered to encrea.e my Escort, and they all took Heart. I would have departed the next Day, the fourth of *October*, but the Rain, and some other Difficulties which we met with, stopt me the whole Day.

The Difficulties in which I found myself.

The Warriors, who had been out on the Discovery, came back in the Afternoon, without making any Cry, because they had seen nothing. They all filed off before me with a proud Sort of an Air: They were only armed with Arrows, and a round Shield of Buffalo's Hides, and they did not

seem

ſeem to take any Notice of me. It is the Cuſtom of the Warriors to ſalute no Perſon when they are in a Body for War: But almoſt as ſoon as they had got into their Cabins, the Chief having dreſſed himſelf, came and paid me a Viſit of Ceremony. He is about forty Years old, pretty tall, and ſomething lean, of a mild Character, and very rational. He is alſo the braveſt Soldier of his Nation, and there is no *Illinois* that deſerves better than he the Sirname *(a)* that *Homer* gives by Way of Preference to the Hero of his *Iliad.* This is ſaying a great deal, for the *Illinois* are perhaps the ſwifteſt Runners in the World: The *Miſſourites* are the only People that can diſpute this Glory with them.

A remarkable Story of the Chief of Pimiteouy.

As I perceived a Croſs of Copper, and a little Figure of the Virgin hanging about the Neck of this Savage, I thought he had been a *Chriſtian,* but they aſſured me that he had only put himſelf in this Equipage out of Reſpect to me. They told me farther what I am going to relate, without requiring you to believe more of it, than the Credit of my Authors deſerve: They are *Canadian* Travellers, who certainly did not invent what they told me, but who heard it reported as a certain Fact. This is the Story.

The Image of the Virgin, which the Chief wore, having fallen into his Hands, I know not how, he was curious to know who it repreſented: They told him it was the Mother of God, and that the Child which ſhe held in her Arms, was God himſelf, who made himſelf Man for the Salvation of Mankind. They explained to him in few Words the Myſtery of this ineffable Incarnation; and farther told him, that the *Chriſtians* always addreſſed themſelves to this divine Mother when they were in any Danger, and that they ſeldom did it in vain. The Savage liſtened to this Diſcourſe with much Attention; and ſome Time after, as he was hunting alone in the Woods, an *Outagami,* who had laid in Ambuſh, ſhewed himſelf the Moment after he had diſcharged his Gun at ſome Game, and took Aim at him. Then he remembered what had been told him of the Mother of God: He invoked her, and the *Outagami* attempting to ſhoot, his Gun miſſed Fire: He cocked it again, and the ſame Thing happened five Times together. During this Time, the *Illinois* charged his own, and in his Turn took Aim at his Enemy, who choſe rather to ſurrender than be ſhot. Since this Adventure, the Chief never goes out of the Village without carrying his Safeguard with him, with which he thinks himſelf invulnerable. If the Story is true, it is very probable that it was the Fault of the Miſſionary

(a) Swift-footed.

alone

alone that has hindered him from becoming a *Chriſtian*, and that the Mother of God, after having preſerved him from a temporal Death, will obtain for him the Grace of a ſincere Converſion *(a)*.

The Manner of Mourning for the Dead among the Illinois.

As ſoon as the Chief had left me, I went out to viſit the Environs of the Village, and I perceived two Savages, who went from Cabin to Cabin, wailing much in the ſame Tone as the Woman of the *Rock*, I mentioned before. One had loſt his Friend in the laſt Battle, the other was the Father of him that had been ſlain. They walked a great Pace, and put their Hands on the Heads of all they met; probably to invite them to ſhare in their Grief. Thoſe who have ſought Reſemblances between the *Hebrews* and the *Americans*, would not have failed to have taken particular Notice of this Manner of Mourning, which ſome Expreſſions of Scripture might give Room to theſe Conjecturers to judge might have been in Uſe among the People of God.

The Care of the Chief for my Safety.

About Evening, the Chief deſired me to come to a Houſe where one of our Miſſionaries had lodged ſome Years before, and where probably they uſed to hold the Council: I went thither, and found him there with two or three Elders. He began by ſaying that he was deſirous of informing me of the great Danger to which I was going to expoſe myſelf, by continuing my Route: That upon thoroughly conſidering all Circumſtances, he adviſed me to put off my Departure till the Seaſon was a little more advanced; that he hoped then the Enemy's Parties would be retired, and leave me a free Paſſage. As he might have his Views in detaining me at *Pimiteouy*, I let him know that I was not much affected with his Reaſons, and added, that I had ſome more prevailing ones to haſten my Departure. He ſeemed to be concerned at my Anſwer, and I ſoon found that it proceeded from his Affection for me, and his Zeal for our Nation.

" Since your Reſolution is taken, ſaid he, I am of Opinion, " that all the *French* who are here, ſhould join themſelves to " you to ſtrengthen your Eſcort: I have alſo already declared " my Thoughts to them on this Matter, and have ſtrongly re- " preſented to them, that they would be for ever loſt to all Ho- " nour, if they ſhould leave their Father in Danger, without " ſharing it with him. I ſhould be very glad to accompany " you myſelf at the Head of all my Soldiers, but you know " my Village is in Danger of being attacked every Day, and

(a) He is in Fact converted ſince.

" it

" it is not proper for me to be absent, and to leave it un-
" guarded in such Circumstances. As for the *French*, nothing
" can detain them here, but an Interest which they ought to
" sacrifice to your Preservation. This is what I have given
" them to understand, and have farther told them, that if any one
" of them fell into the Hands of the Enemy, it would only be
" the Loss of a Man, whereas a Father was alone to be esteem-
" ed as many, and that they ought to run all Hazards, to pre-
" vent so great a Misfortune."

I was charmed, Madam, with the Wisdom of this Man, and more still with his Generosity, which inclined him, out of his Regard for me, to deprive himself of four Men, whose Assistance was a Matter of Consequence, in his present Situation. I made no Doubt before, that in his Willingness to detain me, he had a View of making Use of my Escort in Case of Need. I gave him many Thanks for his Good-will and his Care, and I assured him that I was very well satisfied with the *French*, that I would divide them with him, and leave him two for his Defence, in Case he should be attacked; that the other two should accompany me till I was in a Place of Safety, and with this Reinforcement I should think myself in a Condition to go any where without Fear. He pressed me no further to stay, and I retired.

He causes his Daughter to be baptized.

This Morning he came to pay me a second Visit, accompanied with his Mother-in-Law, who carried a young Child in her Arms: " You see, said he, ad-
" dressing himself to me, a Father in great
" Affliction. This is my Daughter, who is
" dying, her Mother died in bringing her into the World, and
" no Woman could succeed in nursing her. She brings up all
" she takes, and has perhaps but a few Hours to live: You
" will do me a Pleasure to baptize her, that she may go to see
" God after her Death." The Child was really very ill, and past all Hopes of Recovery, so I made no Scruple to baptize it.

Should my Travels have been useless in all other Respects, I acknowledge to you, Madam, I should not regret all the Fatigues and Dangers of them, since, in all Probability, if I had not come to *Pimiteouy*, this Child had never gone to Heaven, where I make no Doubt she will soon arrive. I hope also, that this little Angel will obtain for her Father the same Grace he has procured for her. I depart an Hour hence, and I trust this Letter with the two *Frenchmen* I leave here, and who intend to take the first Opportunity to return to *Canada*.

I am, &c.

LETTER XXVII.

Journey from PIMITEOUY *to the* KASKASQUIAS. *Of the Course of the River of the* ILLINOIS. *Of the Copper Mines. Of the* MISSOURI. *Of the Mines of the River* MARAMEG. *Description of Fort* DE CHARTRES, *and of the Mission of the* KASKASQUIAS. *Of the Fruit-Trees of* LOUISIANA. *Description of the* MISSISSIPPI *above the* ILLINOIS. *Different Tribes of that Nation. Some Traditions of the Savages. Their Notions of the Stars and Planets, Eclipses, and Thunder: Their Manner of computing Time.*

MADAM, KASKASQUIAS, *October* 20:

I Confess very sincerely, that I was not so easy at leaving *Pimitcouy*, as I feigned myself to be, as well for my own Credit, as not entirely to discourage those who accompanied me, some of whom concealed their Fear but very indifferently. The Alarms in which I had found the *Illinois*, their doleful Songs, the Sight of the Carcasses exposed in their Frames, horrible Objects, which continually represented to me what I was to expect, if I should have the Misfortune to fall into the Hands of these Barbarians: All this made an Impression upon me which I could not overcome, and for seven or eight Days I could not sleep very sound.

I was not apprehensive indeed that the Enemy would attack us openly, because I had fourteen Men well armed, and well commanded *(a)*; but we had every Thing to fear from Surprises, as the Savages use all Manner of Artifices to draw their Enemies into the Snares they lay for them. One of the most common is to counterfeit the Cry of some Animal, or the Note of a Bird, which they imitate so perfectly, that every Day some are brought into an Ambush by it. One happens to be encamped at the Entrance of a Wood, we think we hear a Buffalo, a Deer, or a Duck, two or three Men run that Way in Hopes of getting something, and frequently they never return.

M. *de St. Ange*, who has since very much distinguished himself against the *Renards*, commanded my Escort.

They reckon 70 Leagues from *Pimiteouy* to the *Mississippi:* I have already said that it was 15 from the Rock to *Pimeteouy*; the first of these two Villages is in 41 Degrees Lat. the Entrance of the River of the *Illinois* is in 40 Degrees; so that from the Rock this River runs West, inclining a little to the South, but it makes many Windings. From Time to Time we meet with Islands, some of which are pretty large: Its Banks are but low in many Places: In the Spring it overflows the greatest Part of the Meadows, which are on the Right and Left, and which are afterwards covered with Grass and Herbs, that grow very high. They say it abounds with Fish every where, but we had no Time to fish, nor any Nets that were fit for its Depth. Our Business was sooner done by killing a Buffalo, or a Roe-Buck, and of these we had the Choice.

The Course of the River of the Illinois.

The 6th we saw a great Number of Buffaloes crossing the River in a great Hurry, and we scarce doubted but that they were hunted by one of the Parties of the Enemy, which they had spoken of: This obliged us to sail all Night, to get out of such a dangerous Neighbourhood. The next Day before it was light we passed the *Saguimont*, a great River that comes from the South: Five or six Leagues lower we left on the same Hand another smaller, called the River of the *Maccopines:* These are great Roots, which eaten raw, are Poison, but being roasted by a small Fire for five or six Days or more, have no longer any hurtful Quality. Between these two Rivers, at an equal Distance from both we find a Marsh called *Machoutin*, which is exactly half-way from *Pimiteouy* to the *Mississippi*.

Soon after we had passed the River of the *Maccopines*, we perceived the Banks of the *Mississippi*, which are very high. We rowed however above twenty-four Hours longer, and often with our Sail up, before we entered it; because the River of the *Illinois* changes its Course in this Place from the West to the South and by East. One might say, that out of Resentment at being obliged to pay the Homage of its Waters to another River, it sought to return back to its Spring.

Its Entrance into the *Mississippi* is East South East. It was the 10th, about half past Two in the Morning, that we found ourselves in this River, which at that Time made so much Noise in *France*, leaving on the Right Hand a great Meadow, out of which there rises a little River, in which there is a great deal of Copper. Nothing can be more charming than all this Side; but it is not quite the same on the Left Hand. We see there only very high Mountains interspersed with Rocks, between which there grows some Cedars;

Copper.

dars; but this is only a Skreen that has little Depth, and which hides some very fine Meadows.

The Confluence of the Missouri *&* *the* Mississippi.

The 10th, about Nine in the Morning, after we had gone five Leagues on the *Mississippi*, we arrived at the Mouth of the *Missouri*, which is North North West, and South South East. I believe this is the finest Confluence in the World. The two Rivers are much of the same Breadth, each about half a League; but the *Missouri* is by far the most rapid, and seems to enter the *Mississippi* like a Conqueror, through which it carries its white Waters to the opposite Shore, without mixing them; afterwards it gives its Colour to the *Mississippi*, which it never loses again, but carries it quite down to the Sea.

The same Day we went to lay in a Village of the *Caoquias*, and the *Tamarouas*: These are two Nations of *Illinois*, which are united, and who do not together make a very numerous Village. It is situated on a little River, which comes from the East, and which has no Water but in the Spring Season; so that we were forced to walk a good half League to the Cabins. I was surprised that they had chosen such an inconvenient Situation, as they might have found a much better; but they told me that the *Mississippi* washed the Foot of the Village when it was built, and that in three Years it had lost half a League of Ground, and that they were thinking of looking out for another Settlement.

I passed the Night in the House of the Missionaries, which are two Ecclesiastics of the Seminary of *Quebec*, formerly my Disciples, but who might be now my Masters. The oldest of the two (*a*) was absent; I found the youngest (*b*) such as he had been reported to me, severe to himself, full of Charity for others, and making Virtue amiable in his own Person. But he has so little Health, that I think he cannot long support the Way of Life, which they are obliged to lead in these Missions.

Of the Mines of the River Marameg.

The eleventh, after having gone five Leagues, we left on our Right the River of *Marameg*, where some Persons are actually employed in seeking Silver Mines. Perhaps you will be pleased, Madam, to know what Success there is to be expected from these Searches. This is what I have heard concerning them, from an intelligent Person, who has been here many Years. In 1719 the Sieur *de Lochon*, sent by the Western Company in the Capacity of a Founder, having dug in a Place that was shewed him, took up a pretty large Quantity of the Mineral, a Pound of which, that took up four Days to melt,

(*a*) M. *Taumur*. (*b*) M. *Le Mercier*.

produced, as they say, two Drachms of Silver; but some Persons suspect he put in the Silver. Some Months after he returned again, and without thinking any more of Silver, from two or three thousand Weight of the Mineral he extracted fourteen Pounds of very bad Lead, which cost him 1400 Livres: Being disheartened with this bad Success, he returned to *France*.

The Company, being persuaded of the Certainty of the Signs which had been reported to them, thought the Unskilfulness of the Founder was the only Cause of this ill Success, and sent in his Stead a *Spaniard*, named *Anthony*, taken at the Siege of *Pensacola*, and who had been a Slave in the Gallies, but who boasted of having worked at a Mine in *Mexico*. He was allowed a considerable Salary, but he succeeded little better than the Sieur *de Lochon*. He was not disheartened however, and People were willing to believe he failed only through Want of Skill to build Furnaces. He gave up the Lead, and undertook to get Silver, he found Means to open the Rock, which was eight or ten Feet thick, and he blew up several Pieces of it, which he put into melting Pots; 'twas reported, that he got two or three Drachms of Silver, but many Persons still doubt of it.

During these Transactions, there arrived a Company of the King's Miners, the Chief which was one *Renaudiere*, who determining to begin with the Lead Mine, did nothing at all, because neither he nor any of his Company understood the Construction of Furnaces. 'Twas very surprising, to see the Easiness of the Company in advancing large Sums, and the little Precaution they took to be assured of the Capacity of those they employed. *La Renaudiere* and his Miners not being able to accomplish the making of Lead, a particular Company undertook the Mines of *Marameg*, and the Sieur *Renaud*, one of the Directors, surveyed them very carefully. He found here in the Month of *June* last a Bed of Lead at only the Depth of two Feet through the whole Length of a Mountain, which extends a great Way, and he is actually at Work upon it. He flatters himself also that there is Silver under the Lead; but every Body is not of his Opinion: Time will discover what there is in it.

Description of the Kaskasquias.

I arrived the next Day at the *Kaskasquias* at Nine in the Morning. The *Jesuits* had here a very flourishing Mission, which has lately been divided into two, because it was thought proper to form two Villages of Savages instead of one. The most populous is on the Side of the *Mississippi*; two *Jesuits* (a) have the Government of it in Spiritual Affairs. Half a League

(a) Father *Le Boulanger*, and Father *de Kereben*.

lower

lower is the Fort *de Chartres*, about a Musket Shot from the River. M. *Dugué de Boisbrilland*, a *Canadian* Gentleman, commands here for the Company, to which this Place belongs; and all the Space between these two Places begins to be peopled with *French*. Four Leagues farther, and a League from the River, there is a large Village of *French*, almost all *Canadians*, who have a *Jesuit* for their Priest *(b)*. The second Village of the *Illinois* is two Leagues distant from it, and farther up in the Country. A fourth Jesuit has the Care of it *(c)*.

The *French* are here pretty much at their Ease. A *Fleming*, a Servant of the *Jesuits*, has taught them how to sow Wheat, and it thrives very well. They have some Horned Cattle and Fowls. The *Illinois*, on their Side, cultivate the Lands after their Manner, and are very laborious. They also breed Fowls, which they sell to the *French*. Their Wives are sufficiently dexterous: They spin the Buffalo's Wool, and make it as fine as that of the *English* Sheep. Sometimes one would even take it for Silk. They make Stuffs of it, which they dye black, yellow, and a dark red. They make Gowns of it, which they sew with the Thread made of the Sinews of Roe-Bucks. Their Method of making this Thread is very easy. When the Sinew is well cleaned from the Flesh, they expose it in the Sun two Days: When it is dry, they beat it, and get out of it, without any Trouble, a Thread as white and as fine as that of *Malines*, and much stronger.

The *French* Village is bounded on the North by a River; the Banks of which are so high, that although the Waters sometimes rise twenty-five Feet, it seldom runs out of its Bed. All this Country is open: It consists of vast Meadows, which extend for twenty-five Leagues, and which are separated only by little Groves, which are all of good Wood. There are especially some white Mulberry-Trees; but I was surprized that they suffer the Inhabitants to cut them down to build their Houses; and the rather, because they do not want other Trees fit for that Use.

Fruit-Trees of Louisiana.

Among the Fruit-Trees, which are peculiar to this Country, the most remarkable are those which bear the Fruits called the *Pacane*, the *Acimine*, and the *Piakimine*. The *Pacane* is a Nut of the Length and Shape of a large Acorn. There are some which have a very thin Shell, some have a harder and thicker one, and this is so much taken from the Fruit: They are also something smaller. They are all of a very fine and delicate Taste. The Tree that bears them grows very high: Its Wood and Bark, its

(b) Father *Deheauleis*. *(c)* Father. *Guymorneau*.

Smell, and the Shape of its Leaves, appeared to me to be much like the Walnut-Trees of *Europe*.

The *Acimine* is a Fruit of the Length of three or four Inches, and an Inch Diameter: Its Pulp is tender, something sweetish, and full of a Seed like that of the Water Melon. The *Acimine* Tree does not grow large, nor very high. All those I have seen, are little more than Shrubs of a brittle Wood. Its Bark is thin: The Leaves are as long and large as those of the Chesnut-Tree, but of a darker Green.

The *Piakimine* is of the Shape, and a little bigger than a Damson: Its Skin is tender, its Substance watery, its Colour red; and it has a very delicate Taste. It has Seeds which differ in nothing from those of the *Acimine*, but in being smaller. The Savages make a Paste of this Fruit, and form little Loaves of it about an Inch thick, and of the Consistence of a dry'd Pear. The Taste at first seems a little insipid, but one grows easily us'd to it. They are very nourishing, and a sovereign Remedy, it is said, against a Looseness and the Bloody-Flux. The *Piakimine* Tree is a fine Tree, as high as our common Plumb-Trees: Its Leaves have five Points: Its Wood is tolerably hard, and its Bark very rough.

Various People which are settled on the Missouri, *and its Environs.*

The *Osages*, a pretty numerous Nation, settled on the Side of a River that bears their Name, and which runs into the *Missouri*, about forty Leagues from its Junction with the *Mississippi*, send once or twice a Year to sing the Calumet amongst the *Kaskasquias*, and are actually there at present. I have also just now seen a *Missourite* Woman, who told me that her Nation is the first we meet with going up the *Missouri*, from which she has the Name we have given her, for Want of knowing her true Name. It is situated 80 Leagues from the Confluence of that River with the *Mississippi*.

Higher up we find the *Cansez*; then the *Octotatas*, which some call *Mactotatas*; then the *Ajouez*, and then the *Panis*, a very populous Nation, divided into several Cantons, which have Names very different from each other. This Woman has confirmed to me what I had heard from the *Sioux*, that the *Missouri* rises out of some naked Mountains, very high, behind which there is a great River, which probably rises from them also, and which runs to the West. This Testimony carries some Weight, because of all the Savages which we know, none travel farther than the *Missourites*.

Description of the Mississippi, *above the* Illinois.

All the People I have mentioned, inhabit the West Side of the *Missouri*, except the *Ajouez*, which are on the East Side, Neighbours of the *Sioux*, and their Allies. Among the Rivers which run into the *Mississippi*, above the River of the *Illinois*, one of the most considerable is the Ri-

ver

ver of *Bulls*, which is twenty Leagues diſtant from the River of the *Illinois*, and which comes from the Weſt. They have diſcovered in its Neighbourhood a very fine Salt-Pit. They have alſo found ſeveral ſuch on the Sides of the *Marameg*, about twenty Leagues from hence. About forty Leagues further, we leave the *Aſſeneſipi*, or the *River of the Rock*; ſo called, becauſe it is over-againſt a Mountain which is in the Bed of the *Miſſiſſippi*, and where ſome Travellers have affirmed there was Rock Chryſtal.

Twenty-five Leagues higher, we find the River *Ouiſconſing*, on the Right Hand, by which Father *Marquette*, and the Sieur *Jolict*, entered the *Miſſiſſippi*, when they firſt diſcovered it. The *Ajouez*, who are in this Latitude, *that is to ſay*, in about 43°. 30'. who travel much, and who go, we are aſſured, from twenty-five to thirty Leagues a Day, when they have not their Families with them, ſay that ſetting out from their Habitations, they come in three Days to a People called *Omans*; who are of a fair Complexion, with light Hair, eſpecially the Women. They add, that this Nation is continually at War with the *Panis*, and other Savages further to the Weſt; and that they havè heard them ſpeak of a great Lake, very diſtant from them, in the Environs of which there are People like the *French*, who have Buttons to their Clothes, who build Towns, who uſe Horſes for hunting the Buffaloes, which they cover with Buffaloes Skins; but who have no Arms but Bows and Arrows.

On the Left, about ſixty Leagues above the River of *Bulls*, we ſee the *Moingona* come out of the Midſt of an immenſe and magnificent Meadow, which is quite covered with Buffaloes and other wild Creatures. At its Entrance into the *Miſſiſſippi*, it has little Water, and it is alſo but narrow: It has nevertheleſs a Courſe, as they ſay, of two hundred and fifty Leagues, winding from the North to the Weſt. They add, that its Source is in a Lake, and that it forms a ſecond fifty Leagues from the firſt.

From this ſecond Lake it inclines to the Left, and enters the *Blue River*; thus named, becauſe of its Bottom, which is an Earth of this Colour. It diſcharges itſelf into the River *St. Peter*. In going up the *Moingona*, they find a great deal of Coal; and when they have gone up it one hundred and fifty Leagues, they perceive a great Cape, which makes the River wind; the Water of which, in this Part, is red and ſtinking. It is aſſured, that many Mineral Stones have been gathered on this Cape, and that Antimony has been brought hither from thence.

A League above the Mouth of the *Moingona*, there are two Falls in the *Miſſiſſippi*, which are pretty long, where they are obliged to unload and tow the Pettiaugre: And above the ſecond Fall, *that is to ſay*, twenty-one Leagues from the *Moingona*, they

they find on both Sides the River Lead Mines, discovered formerly by a famous Traveller of *Canada*, named *Nicolas Perrot*, and which bear his Name. Ten Leagues above the *Ouisconsing*, on the same Side, begins a Meadow sixty Leagues long, bordered by Mountains, which make a charming Prospect. There is another Meadow on the West Side, but not so long. Twenty Leagues higher than the Extremity of the first, the River grows wider, and they have named the Place the Lake *de bon Secours*, *(of good Succour)*. It is a League wide, and seven Leagues in Compass, and it is also environed with Meadows. *Nicolas Perrot* built a Fort on the Right.

At coming out of the Lake, we meet with *L'Isle Pelée*, *(the bald Island)*; so called, because there is not one Tree in it; but it is a very fine Meadow. The *French* of *Canada* have often made it the Centre of their Trade in these Western Parts; and many have wintered here, because all the Country is very fit for Hunting. Three Leagues below *L'Isle Pelée*, we leave on the Right Hand the River of *St. Croix*, *(the Holy Cross)*, which comes from the Environs of the *Upper Lake*. They say that Copper has been found pretty near its Mouth. Some Leagues further, we leave on the Left Hand the River of *St. Pierre*, *(St. Peter)*, the Sides of which are peopled with *Sioux*, and the Mouth of which is not far from the Fall of *St. Anthony*. The *Mississippi* is little known above this great Cascade.

To return to the *Illinois*.---If it is true which I have been assured of in many Places, and which the *Missourite* Woman I mentioned before confirmed to me, that they and the *Miamis* come from the Borders of a Sea very distant to the West *(a)*, it appears that their first Station, when they came down into this Country, was the *Moingona*: At least it is certain that one of their Tribes bears that Name. The others are known by the Names of the *Peorias*, the *Tamarouas*, the *Caoquias*, and the *Kaskasquias*: But these Tribes are now much intermixed, and reduced to be very inconsiderable. There remains at present but very few of the *Kaskasquias*; and the two Villages that bear their Name, are almost wholly composed of *Tamarouas*, and of *Metchigamias*, a strange Nation, who came from the Borders of a little River, which we shall meet with going down the *Mississippi*, and whom the *Kaskasquias* have adopted.

This is, Madam, all that I can at present inform you of, concerning *Louisiana*, into which I am but newly come. But before I finish this Letter, I must communicate to you some Ac-

(a) A Woman of the *Miamis*, Prisoner of the *Sioux*, assured Father *St. Pe*, at present Superior of the Missions of *New France*, that she was carried by the *Sioux* to a Village of her own Nation, that was very near the Sea.

counts

counts, which will ſerve as a Supplement to what I have already ſaid of the Savages in general, and which I learnt on my Route from the River *St. Joſeph* to this Place.

Traditions of the Sin of the firſt Woman, and of the Deluge.

You may have obſerved in the Fable of *Atahentſic* driven from Heaven, ſome Traces of the Story of the firſt Woman, baniſhed from the terreſtrial Paradiſe, in Puniſhment of her Diſobedience; and the Tradition of the Deluge, as well as of the Ark, in which *Noah* ſaved himſelf with his Family. This Circumſtance does not hinder me from adhering to the Opinion of *F. de Acoſta*, who thinks that this Tradition does not relate to the univerſal Deluge, but a particular Deluge in *America*. In Fact, the *Algonquins*, and almoſt all the People who ſpeak their Language, taking for granted the Creation of the firſt Man, ſay that his Poſterity being almoſt all entirely deſtroyed by a general Inundation, one named *Meſſou*, others call him *Saketchak*, who ſaw all the Earth deeply covered with Waters by the overflowing of a Lake, ſent a Raven to the Bottom of this Abyſs, to fetch him ſome Earth: That this Raven not having well executed his Commiſſion, he ſent a Muſk Rat on the ſame Errand, who ſucceeded better: That out of this little Earth, which the Animal brought him, he reſtored the World to its firſt State: That he ſhot Arrows into the Trunks of the Trees which ſtill appeared, and that theſe Arrows turned into Branches: That he wrought many other Miracles; and that, in Acknowledgment of the Service which the Muſk Rat had done him, he married a Female of that Species, by which he had Children, which re-peopled the World: That he communicated his Immortality to a certain Savage, and gave it him in a little Pacquet, with Orders not to open it, on the Penalty of loſing ſuch a precious Gift.

The *Hurons* and the *Iroquois* ſay that *Taronhiacuagon*, the King of Heaven, gave his Wife a Kick, ſo violent, that it threw her from Heaven to the Earth: That this Woman fell upon the Back of a Tortoiſe; which beating off the Waters of the Deluge with his Feet, he at laſt diſcovered the Earth, and carried the Woman to the Foot of a Tree, where ſhe lay-in of Twins; and that the Elder killed the Younger.

Their Notions of the Stars and Planets.

It is not ſurprizing that theſe People, who are ſo indifferent about Things paſt, and who are very little concerned about Things to come, ſhould have no Knowledge of the Heavens, and ſhould make no Difference between the Planets and fixed Stars; unleſs it be that they divide the laſt, as we do, into Conſtellations. They call the *Pleiades*, the *Male* and *Female Dancers*. They give the Name of the *Bear* to the four first of those we call the *Great Bear*; the three others, which make its Tail, are, according to them, three Hunters, who pursue the Bear; and the little Star that accompanies the middle one, is the Kettle, which the second carries with him. The Savages of *Acadia* call this Constellation and the following, simply the *Great* and the *Little Bear*: But may we not judge, that when they talked in this Manner to the Sieur *Lescarbot*, they only repeated what they had heard from several of the *French*?

The greatest Part of the Savages call the Pole Star, the Star that never moves. It is this that guides them in their Travels by Night, as the Sun serves them for a Compass in the Day. They have also other Marks to distinguish the North. They pretend to have observed that the Tops of the Trees always lean a little that Way, and that the inward Skin of their Bark is always thicker on that Side: But they do not trust so entirely to these Observations, as not to take other Precautions not to go wrong, and to find their Way back when they return.

How they know the North when the Sky is cloudy.

As to what regards the Course of the Stars and Planets, the Causes of the Celestial Phœnomenons, the Nature of Meteors, and such-like Things, they are in all these Respects, as in every Thing else that does not affect them sensibly, in a most profound Ignorance, and a perfect Indifference. If an Eclipse happens, they imagine there is some great Combat in the Heavens; and they shoot many Arrows into the Air, to drive away the pretended Enemies of the Sun and Moon. The *Hurons*, when the Moon is eclipsed, fancy that she is sick; and to recover her from this Sickness, they make a great Noise, and accompany this Noise with many Ceremonies and Prayers; and they never fail to fall upon the Dogs with Sticks and Stones, to set them a yelping, because they believe the Moon loves these Animals.

These Savages, and many others, could never be brought to believe that an Eclipse is an indifferent Thing, and purely natural. They expect Good or Evil from it, according to the Place of the Heavens where the Planet is darkened. Nothing surprized them more, than to see how exactly the Missionaries foretold these Phœnomenons; and they concluded that they must also foresee their Consequences.

These People are not better acquainted with the Nature of Thunder: Some take it for a Voice of a particular Species of Men, who fly in the Air. Others say, the Noise comes from certain Birds, that are unknown to them. According to the *Montagnais*, it is the Effort which a Genius makes to bring up a Snake which he hath swallowed, and they found this Notion on

2 observing,

observing, that when the Thunder falls upon a Tree, it leaves a Mark something like the Shape of a Snake.

Their Manner of dividing Time.

They all reckon the Months by the Moons; the greatest Number reckon but twelve in the Year, and some thirteen. The Inconveniencies, which may arise from this Diversity, are not of any great Consequence among People, who have no Annals, and whose Affairs do not depend on Annual Epochas. There is also among them a great Variety in the Names of the Seasons and of the Moons, because in all the different Nations, these are distinguished or marked out by their Hunting and Fishing, their Sowing and Harvest, the first Appearance and the Fall of the Leaves, the Passage of certain Beasts and Birds, the Time when the Roe-Bucks shed their Hair, and the Rutting Time of various Animals; and these Things vary much according to the different Cantons.

There are some Nations, where they reckon the Years by the twelve Signs, unless when they speak of their Age, and on some other Occasions, in Regard to which they use the Lunar Years. They have not among any of them any Distinction of Weeks, and the Days have no particular Names in any of their Languages. They have four fixed Points in the Day, *viz.* the rising and setting of the Sun, Noon and Midnight, and whatever Weather they happen to have, they are never mistaken in these. For the rest, that astronomical Exactness in adjusting the Lunar with the Solar Years, Baron *la Hontan* does them the Honour of attributing to them, is a meer Invention of this Writer.

They have no chronological Computation, and if they preserve the Epochas of certain remarkable Events, they do not comprehend exactly the Time that is past since: They are satisfied with remembering the Facts, and they have invented several Ways of preserving the Remembrance of them. For Instance, the *Hurons* and the *Iroquois* have in their public Treasuries Belts of Procelain, in which are wrought Figures, that revive the Memory of Transactions. Others make use of Knots of a particular Form, and if in these Things their Imagination labours, yet it always leads them to the Point proposed. Lastly, they all reckon from one to ten, the tens by ten to a hundred, the hundreds by ten to a thousand, and they go no farther in their Calculations.

I am, &c.

LETTER XXVIII.

Of the Colony of the ILLINOIS. *Journey to the* AKANSAS. *Deſcription of the Country.*

MADAM, KASKASQUIAS, *Nov.* 8.

MY laſt Letter is gone for *Canada*, from whence I am aſſured that it will go ſooner to *France* by *L'Iſle Royal.* And indeed, if it ſhould happen to miſcarry by the Way, the Loſs would not be great. I begin this again at the *Kaſkaſquias*, but, according to all Appearances, I ſhall not finiſh it here. I have been here above a Month, and I am haſtening my Departure as much as poſſible.

The Uſefulneſs of the Poſt of the Illinois.

As I have as yet ſeen in *Louiſiana* only this Poſt, the firſt of all by Right of Antiquity, I cannot judge of it by Compariſon with others. But it appears certain to me, that it has two Advantages, one of which can never be diſputed, and the other renders it at preſent neceſſary to the whole Province. The firſt ariſes from its Situation, which is near *Canada*, with which it will always have a Communication equally uſeful to the two Colonies. The ſecond is, that it may be made the Granary of *Louiſiana*, which it can ſupply with Plenty of Wheat, though it ſhould be quite peopled down to the Sea.

The Land is not only fit to bear Wheat, but has hitherto refuſed nothing that is neceſſary for the Food of Man. The Climate is very mild, in thirty-eight Degrees, thirty-nine Minutes North Latitude: It would be very eaſy to encreaſe Flocks here. They might alſo tame the wild Buffaloes, from which they would obtain a great Benefit in the Trade of their Wool and Hides, and for the Suſtenance of the Inhabitants.

The Air is good here, and if we ſee ſome Diſtempers, we may attribute them only to Poverty and Diſſoluteneſs, and perhaps in ſome ſmall Degree to the Lands newly turned up; but this laſt Inconvenience will not continue always, and the Climate will not at all affect thoſe who hereafter ſhall be born here. Laſtly we are aſſured of the *Illinois*, more than of any Nation of Savages in *Canada*, if we except the *Abenaquis*. They are almoſt all *Chriſtians*, of a mild Diſpoſition, and at all Times very affectionate to the *French*.

I am

I am here, Madam, one hundred and fifty Leagues from the Place where I began this Letter: I am going to finish it here, and trust it with a Traveller, who reckons to be at *New Orleans* much sooner than I, because he will stop no where, and I must make some Stay at the *Natchez*. I had depended on two Things on leaving the *Illinois*; the first, that as I was going down a very rapid River, and on which I was in no Danger of being stopt by those Falls and Torrents so frequent in the Rivers of *Canada*, I should not be long in my Journey, though I had near four hundred Leagues to go, because of the Windings which the River makes. The second was, that my Route being all the Way to the South, it would be quite unnecessary to take any Precautions against the Cold; but I was mistaken in both. I found myself obliged to sail still slower than I had done on the Lakes, which I was obliged to cross, and I suffer'd a Cold as piercing as any I had ever felt at *Quebec*.

Extreme Cold.

It is true, that it was still quite another Thing at the *Kaskasquias*, which I had left a few Days before; for the River, as I heard on my Route, was soon frozen in such a Manner that they went upon it in Carriages. It is notwithstanding a good half League wide at that Place, and more rapid than the *Rhone*. This is the more surprizing, as generally excepting some slight Frosts, caused by the North and North West Winds, the Winter in this Country is scarcely perceivable. The River was not frozen where I was, but I was all Day in an open Pettiaugre, and by Consequence exposed to all the Injuries of the Air, and as I had taken no Precaution against the Cold which I did not expect, I found it very severe *(a)*.

If I could have made more Way, I should have found every Day a sensible Decrease of the Cold; but we must navigate the *Mississippi* with Prudence. We do not readily hazard ourselves upon it in Canoes of Bark, because the River always bringing down a great Number of Trees, which fall from it's Sides, or which are brought into it by the Rivers it receives; many of these Trees are stopt in passing by a Point, or on a Shoal; so that every Moment one is exposed to run upon a Branch or against a Root hidden under the Water, and there needs no more to spilt these brittle Carriages; especially when to shun an Enemy's Party, or for any other Reason, we proceed in the Night, or set out before Day.

The Manner of navigating the Mississippi.

Therefore one is obliged to use Pettiaugres instead of Canoes of Bark, *that is to say*, Trunks of Trees made hollow, which are

(a) This lasted two Months.

not ſubject to the ſame Inconveniences, but which are very clumſy, and are not managed as we pleaſe. I am in one which is made of a Walnut-Trée, ſo narrow that it will not bear a Sail; and my Conductors accuſtomed, to the little Paddles, which they uſe in the Canoes, find it difficult to manage the Oars. Add to this, if the Wind is a little freſh, the Water comes into the Pettiaugre, and this frequently happens at this Seaſon of the Year.

Why the Leaves fall ſo ſoon, and appear ſo late on the Trees of Louiſiana.

It was the tenth of *November*, at Sun-ſet, that I embarked on the little River of *Kaſkaſquias*; I had but two Leagues to the *Miſſiſſippi*, nevertheleſs I was obliged to encamp at about half Way, and the next Day I could make but ſix Leagues on the River. The Leaves fall ſooner in this Country than in *France*, and new ones do not appear till the End of *May*; and yet it very ſeldom ſnows here, and I have already obſerved that the Winters here are generally very mild. What then can be the Reaſon of this Backwardneſs? I can ſee no other than the Thickneſs of the Foreſts, which hinders the Earth from being ſo ſoon warmed, to make the Sap riſe.

Of the Reeds.

The 12th, after having gone two Leagues, I left Cape *St. Anthony* on the left Hand. It is here that we begin to ſee Canes or Reeds: They are much like thoſe which grow in many Places of *Europe*, but they are higher and ſtronger. It is ſaid that they are never ſeen but in a good Soil; but the Lands where they grow muſt be moiſt, and of Conſequence fitter for Rice than Wheat. They do not take the Pains to pull them up, when they would clear the Land where they grow; and indeed it would not be very eaſy to do it, their knotty Roots being very long, and joined together by a great Number of Filaments, which extend a great Way. Theſe Roots have naturally a pretty fine Poliſh, and come near to thoſe of the Bamboos of *Japan*; of which they make the fine Canes which the *Dutch* ſell by the Name of *Rottangs*.

Why Wheat has not ſucceeded in Louiſiana.

They content themſelves therefore when they would cultivate a Field covered with theſe Reeds, to cut them down at the Foot; and then leave them to dry, and afterwards burn them: The Aſhes ſerve them for Manure, and the Fire opens the Pores of the Earth, which they ſtir lightly, and then ſow what they pleaſe; Rice, Maiz, Water Melons, in a Word all Sorts of Grain and Pulſe, except Wheat, which in theſe rich Soils ſhoots into Straw and produces no Ears. This Defect might be remedied by throwing Sand on this Soil, and by ſowing Maiz on it for ſome Years.

As for the high Grounds, and others, which are not expoſed to the Inundations of the River, they are very fit at preſent to bear Wheat, and if the Trials which they have made in ſome Places have not ſucceeded, becauſe the Grain grew ſmutty, it was becauſe the Country not being open enough, the Air is too much confined to diſperſe the Miſts that breed the Smut. The Proof of this is, that among the *Illinois*, where there are more Meadows than Woods, Wheat grows up and ripens as well as in *France*.

The 13th, after a very hot Night, we went about three Leagues in Spite of a South Wind, which was continually blowing ſtronger and ſtronger, and which became at laſt ſo violent, that it obliged us to ſtop. A great Rain made it fall in the Evening, and about Midnight there aroſe a North Weſt Wind, which began the extreme Cold I have mentioned. To compleat our ill Luck, an Accident ſtopt us all the next Day, tho' it was not ſafe for us to remain where we were. It is not long ſince that the *Cherokees* killed forty *Frenchmen* here, at whoſe Head was a Son of M. *de Ramezai*, Governor of *Montreal*, and one of the Baron *de Longueuil*'s, the King's Lieutenant for the ſame Town. Beſides theſe Savages, who are not yet reconciled to us, the *Outagamis*, the *Sioux*, and the *Chicachas*, kept us in great Uneaſineſs, and I had with me only three Men.

The 15th, the Wind changed to the North, and the Cold encreaſed. We went four Leagues to the South, then we found that the River turned four Leagues to the North. Immediately after this Reach, we paſſed on the Left by the fine River *Ouabache (Wabache)*, by which one may go quite up to the *Iroquois*, when the Waters are high. Its Entrance into the *Miſſiſſippi* is little leſs than a Quarter of a League wide. There is no Place in *Louiſiana* more fit, in my Opinion, for a Settlement than this, nor where it is of more Conſequence to have one. All the Country that is watered by the *Ouabache*, and by the *Ohio* that runs into it, is very fruitful: It conſiſts of vaſt Meadows, well watered, where the wild Buffaloes feed by Thouſands. Furthermore, the Communication with *Canada* is as eaſy as by the River of the *Illinois*, and the Way much ſhorter. A Fort, with a good Garriſon, would keep the Savages in Awe, eſpecially the *Cherokees*, who are at preſent the moſt numerous Nation of this Continent.

River Ouabache (Wabache).

Six Leagues below the Mouth of the *Ouabache*, we find on the ſame Side a very high Coaſt, on which they ſay there are Iron Mines. We went a great Way this Day, which was the 16th; but we ſuffered much

Iron Mines.

much by the Cold: It ſtill encreaſed the following Days, tho' the Wind was changed to South South Weſt. We were alſo obliged to break the Ice, tho' it was indeed but thin, to get forward. The 19th, we went four Leagues, after which a South Wind ſtopt us ſhort. I never felt a North Eaſt Wind ſharper than this from the South. It is very probable, that is was ſtill the North Eaſt Wind that blew, but which the Land reflected ſometimes one Way, and ſometimes another, as we turned with the River.

Wild Cats. Walnut Trees, and their Properties.

We meet on this Route with a Kind of wild Cats, called *Pijoux*, which are very much like our's, but larger. I obſerved ſome that had ſhorter Tails, and others that had much longer, and bigger: They alſo look very wild, and they aſſured me, that they are very carnivorous and good Hunters. The Foreſts are full of Walnut-Trees, like thoſe of *Canada*, and their Roots have ſeveral Properties, which I have not heard remarked of the others. They are very ſoft, and their Bark dyes a black Colour; but their principal Uſe is for Phyſic. They ſtop the Flux of the Belly, and are an excellent Emetic.

The twentieth it ſnowed all Day, and we never ſtirred: The Weather grew milder, but the next Night the South Weſt Wind cleared the Sky, and the Cold began again with the greateſt Severity. The next Morning ſome Brandy, which we had left all Night in the Pettiaugre was found thick like frozen Oil; and ſome Spaniſh Wine which I had for the Maſs was frozen. The farther we went down it, the more we found that the River winded; the Wind followed all theſe Turnings, and which Way ſoever it came, theCold was ſtill exceſſive. They had never known any Thing like it in this Country in the Memory of Man.

Marks of the Warriors.

The ſame Day we perceived on the right Side of the River a Poſt ſet up: We went near it, and we found it was a Monument ſet up by the *Illinois*, for an Expedition they had lately made againſt the *Chicachas*. There were two Figures of Men without Heads, and ſome entire. The firſt denoted the Dead, and the ſecond the Priſoners. One of my Conductors told me on this Occaſion, that when there are any *French* among either, they ſet their Arms a-kimbo, or their Hands upon their Hips, to diſtinguiſh them from the Savages, whom they repreſent with their Arms hanging down. This Diſtinction is not purely arbitrary; it proceeds from theſe People having obſerved that the *French* often put themſelves in this Poſture, which is not uſed among them.

Garcilaſſo

Of the Chicachas.

Garcilasso de la Vega speaks of the *Chicachas* in his History of the Conquest of *Florida*, and places them nearly in the same Place where they are at present. He reckons them among the People of *Florida* who submitted to the *Spaniards:* But this pretended Submission lasted no longer than the *Spaniards* continued in their Neighbourhood; and it is certain that the *Spaniards* bought the Victory dear which they gained over them. They are still the bravest Soldiers of *Louisiana*. They were much more numerous in the Time of *Ferdinand de Soto* than they are at present; but for the Riches, which this Historian gives them, I do not easily conceive neither from where they could get them, nor what could dry up the Source from whence they derived them; for they are now neither more wealthy, nor less savage, than their Neighbour Nations.

It was our Alliance with the *Illinois*, which set us at War with the *Chicachas*, and the *English* of *Carolina* blow up the Fire. Our Settlement in *Louisiana* makes them very uneasy: It is a Barrier, which we set between their powerful Colonies of *North America*, and *Mexico*, and we must expect they will employ all Sorts of Means to break it. The *Spaniards*, who are so jealous of seeing us fortify ourselves in this Country, are not yet sensible of the Importance of the Service we do them.——A few Days after I had passed by the Place where we saw the Post of the *Illinois*, the *Chicachas* had their Revenge on two *Frenchmen*, who followed me in a *Pettiaugre*. These Savages lay in Ambush in the Reeds, by the Side of the River, and when they saw the *Frenchmen* over-against them, they moved the Reeds, withour discovering themselves; the *Frenchmen* thought that it was a Bear, or some other Beast, and they approached, thinking to kill it; but the Moment they prepared to land, the *Chicachas* fired upon them, and laid them dead in their Pettiaugre. I was very fortunate in not being seen by them, for my People would lose no Opportunity of going after Game.

River of the Chicachas.

The 23d, after a very cold Night, we had a very fine Day; for though the Earth was covered with Snow, the Cold was to be borne. The next Day we passed before the Mouth of the River of the *Chicachas*, which is but narrow, but it comes a great Way. Its Mouth is North and South. They reckon from thence to the *Kaskasquias* eighty six Leagues; but the Way would not be half so much by Land. Nothing would be more pleasant than this Navigation, if the Season was milder: The Country is charming, and in the Forests there are a Number of Trees always green; the few Meadows we meet with, also preserve their Verdure, and a considerable Number of

Islands well wooded, some of which are pretty large, form very agreeable Canals, where the largest Ships may pass: For they say, that at above a hundred and fifty Leagues from the Sea, they find in this River even to sixty Fathom Water.

The Forests of Louisiana.

As to what concerns the Forests, which cover almost all this great Country, there are perhaps none in the World that are comparable to them, if we consider either the Bigness and Height of the Trees, or the Variety, and the Uses that may be made of them; for excepting Woods for dying, which require a warmer Sun, and which are found only between the Tropicks, we cannot say that there is any Kind of Wood wanting here. There are Woods of Cypress that extend eight or ten Leagues. All the Cypress Trees here are of a Bigness proportionable to their Height, which exceeds that of the highest Trees in *France*. We begin to be acquainted in *Europe* with that Species of Ever-Green Laurel, which we call the *Tulip Tree*, from the Shape of its Flowers. It grows higher than our Horse-Chesnut Trees, and has a finer Leaf. The *Copalme* is still bigger and higher, and there distills from it a Balsam, which perhaps is not much inferior to that of *Peru*. All the known Species of Walnuts are here very numerous, and also all the Woods that are fit for Building, and the Carpenters Use, that can be desired: But in using them, Care must be taken not to fix upon those which grow on the Side of the River, nor where the Inundation of the River reaches, because having their Roots continually in the Water, they will be too heavy, and will soon rot.

At length, I arrived Yesterday, *December* the 2d, at the first Village of the *Akansas*, or *Akanseas*, about ten in the Morning. This Village is built in a little Meadow, on the West Side of the *Mississippi*. There are three others in the Space of eight Leagues, and each makes a Nation, or particular Tribe: There is also one of the four which unites two Tribes; but they are all comprised under the Name of *Akansas*. They call the Savages which inhabit the Village from whence I write, *Ouyapes*. The Western Company have a Magazine here which expects some Merchandizes, and a Clerk, who fares but poorly in the mean Time, and who is heartily weary of living here.

Description of the River of the Akansas.

The River of the *Akansas*, which they say comes a great Way, runs into the *Mississippi* by two Channels, four Leagues distant from each other. The first is eight Leagues from hence. This River comes, as they say, from the Country of certain Savages, whom they call the *Black Panis*, and I think they are the same which are more commonly known by the Name of *Panis Ricaras*. I have with me a Slave of this Nation. One

goes

goes up the River of the *Akansas* with Difficulty, because there are many Falls or Torrents in it, and in many Places the Waters are often so low, that there is a Necessity to tow the Petiaugres.

Different Tribes of the Akansas.

The Separation of its two Branches is made at seven Leagues above the second, and the smallest of its two Mouths, but only at two Leagues above the first. It receives a fine River that comes from the Country of the *Osages*, and which they call *La Riviere blanche (the White River)*. Two Leagues higher are the *Torimas*, and the *Topingas*, who make but one Village. Two Leagues higher are the *Sothouis*. The *Kappas* are a little farther. This Nation was very numerous in the Time of *Ferdinand de Soto*, and even when M. *de la Sale* finished the Discovery of the *Mississippi*. Over against their Village, we see the sad Ruins of Mr. *Law*'s Grant, of which the Company remains the Proprietors.

Mr. Law's *Grant.*

It was here that the nine Thousand *Germans* were to be sent, which were raised in the *Palatinate*, and 'tis great Pity they never came here. There is not perhaps in all *Louisiana* a Country more fit, after that of the *Illinois*, to produce all Sorts of Grain, and to feed Cattle. But Mr. *Law* was ill used, as well as the greatest Part of the other Grantees. It is very probable, that in a long Time they will not again make the like Levies of Men; they have Need of them in the Kingdom, and indeed it is pretty common among us to square our Measures according to the Success of such Enterprizes, instead of observing what their Miscarriage was owing to, in order to correct what was before done amiss.

Mortality among the Akansas.

I found the Village of the *Ouyapes* in the greatest Desolation. Not long since, a *Frenchman* passing this Way was attacked with the Small-Pox: The Distemper was communicated presently to some Savages, and soon after to the whole Village. The Burying-Place appears like a Forest of Poles and Posts newly set up, and on which there hangs all Manner of Things: There is every Thing which the Savages use.

I had set up my Tent pretty near the Village, and all the Night I heard weeping; the Men do this as well as the Women: They repeated without ceasing *Nihahani*, as the *Illinois* do, and in the same Tone. I also saw in the Evening a Woman, who wept over the Grave of her Son, and who poured upon it a great Quantity of Sagamitty. Another had made a Fire by a neighbouring Tomb, in all Appearence to warm the Dead. The *Akansas* are reckoned to be the tallest and best shaped of all the Savages of this Continent, and they are called by Way of Distinction *the fine Men.* It is thought, and perhaps for this Reason, that they have the same Origin as the *Cansez* of the *Missouri*, and the *Poutewatamis* of *Canada*. But my Pettiaugre is loaded, and I have only Time to close my Letter, after having assured you, that

I am, &c.

LETTER XXIX.

Journey from the AKANSAS *to the* NATCHEZ. *Description of the Country: Of the River of the* YASOUS: *Of the Manners, Customs, and Religion of the* NATCHEZ.

MADAM, *At the* NATCHEZ, *Dec.* 25. 1721

I Departed the 3d of *December* something late from the Village of the *Ouyapes*; nevertheless I went to encamp a little below the first Mouth of the River of the *Akansas*, which appeared to me to be at most but five hundred Paces wide. The next Day I passed by the second, which is very narrow, and the 5th we pushed on to *La Point coupée (the Point cut off)*. This was a pretty high Point, which advanced into the River on the West Side: The River has cut it off, and made it an Island, but the new Channel is not yet passable, but in the Time of the Floods. They reckon from this Place to the principal Branch of the River of the *Akansas* twenty-two Leagues, but it is not perhaps ten in a strait Line, for the River winds much in the seventy Leagues we make to go from the Village of the *Ouyapes* to the River of the *Yasous* or *Yachoux*, which I entered the 9th in the Afternoon. It has not snowed here, as in the Country of the *Illinois*, and at the River *Ouabache*, but there has fallen a hoar Frost, which has broke all the tender Trees, with which the low Points and the wet Lands are covered; one would think that some one had broken all their Branches with a Stick.

River of the Yasous.

The Entrance of the River of the *Yasous* is North West, and South West, and is about a hundred Perches wide: Its Waters are reddish, and they say, they give the Bloody-Flux to those who drink them: And besides this, the Air is very unwholsome. I was obliged to go up it 3 Leagues to get to the Fort, which I found all in Mourning for the Death of M. *Bizart*, who commanded here. Every where that I met with any *Frenchmen* in *Louisiana*, I had

I had heard very high Elogiums of this Officer, who was born in *Canada:* His Father was a *Swiss*, and a Major at *Montreal.* At the *Yasous* they told me extraordinary Things of his Religion, his Piety, and his Zeal, of which he was the Victim. Every Body regretted him as their Father, and every one agrees, that this Colony in losing him has had an irreparable Loss.

Of the Fort of the Yasous.

He had chosen a bad Situation for his Fort, and he was preparing, when he died, to remove it a League higher in a very fine Meadow, where the Air is more healthy, and where there is a Village of *Yasous*, mixed with *Couroas* and *Ofogoulas*, which all together may have at most two hundred Men fit to bear Arms. We live pretty well with them, but do not put too much Confidence in them, on Account of the Connections which the *Yasous* have always had with the *English*.

Of the Caimans or Crocodiles.

There are many Caimans in this River, and I saw two, which were at least from twelve to fifteen Feet long. We hear them seldom but in the Night, and their Cry so much resembles the Bellowing of Bulls, that it deceives one. Our *French* People nevertheless bathe in it as freely as they would in the *Seine*. As I declared my Surprise at it, they replied, that there was no Cause to fear; that indeed when they were in the Water, they saw themselves almost always surrounded with Caimans, but they never came near them, that they seemed only to watch to seize upon them at the Moment of their coming out of the River; and that then to drive them away, they stirred the Water with a Stick, which they always had the Precaution to carry with them, and that this made these Animals run away far enough to give them Time to get out of Danger.

A Grant badly situated.

The Company has in this Post a Magazine of Expectation, as at the *Akansas*; but the Fort and the Land belongs to a Society composed of M. *le Blanc*, Secretary of State, of M. *le Comte de Belle-Isle*, of M. le Marquis *d'Asfeld*, and M. *le Blond*, Brigadier Engineer. The last is in the Colony with the Title of Director General of the Company. I can see no Reason why they chose the River of the *Yasous* for the Place of their Grant. There was certainly Choice of better Lands, and a better Situation. It is true, that it is of Importance to secure this River, the Source of which is not far from *Carolina*; but a Fort with a good Garrison to keep under the *Yasous*, who are Allies to the *Chicachas*, would be sufficient for that Purpose. It is not the Way to settle a Colony on a solid Foundation, to be obliged always to be on their Guard against the Savages who are Neighbours of the *English*.

I de-

I departed from the *Yasous* the 10th; and the 13th, had it not been for a *Natché* Savage, who had asked his Passage of me to return home, I had been lost in a Gulf, which none of my Conductors knew, and which one does not discover till one is so far engaged in it, that it is impossible to get out. It is on the Left Hand, at the Foot of a great Cape, where they affirm there is a Quarry of very good Stone: This is what they are most afraid of wanting in this Colony; but in Recompence, they may make as many Brick as they please.

Gulf and Quarry.

The 15th we arrived at the *Natchez.* This Canton, the finest, the most fertile, and the most populous of all *Louisiana*, is forty Leagues distant from the *Yasous*, and on the same Hand. The Landing-Place is over-against a pretty high Hill, and very steep; at the Foot of which runs a little Brook, that can receive only Boats and Pettiaugres. From this first Hill we ascend a second smaller one, and not so steep, at the Top of which they have built a Kind of Redoubt, inclosed with a single Palisade. They have given this Intrenchment the Name of a Fort.

Description of the Country of the Natchez.

Several little Hills rise above this Hill, and when we have passed them, we see on every Side great Meadows, divided by little Clumps of Trees, which have a very fine Effect. The Trees most common in these Woods are the Walnut and the Oak; and all about the Lands are excellent. The late M. *d'Iberville*, who was the first that entered the *Mississippi* by its Mouth, being come as high as the *Natchez*, found this Country so charming, and so advantageously situated, that he thought he could find no better Situation for the Metropolis of the new Colony. He traced out the Plan of it, and intended to call it *Rosalie*, which was the Name of Madam, the Chancellor's Lady of *Pontchartrain.* But this Project is not likely to be soon executed, though our Geographers have always roundly set down in their Maps, the Town of *Rosalie* at the *Natchez.*

It is certain that we must begin by a Settlement nearer the Sea: But if *Louisiana* ever becomes a flourishing Colony, as may very well happen, I am of Opinion that they cannot find a better Situation for the Capital than in this Place. It is not subject to the Inundation of the River, the Air is pure, and the Country very extensive, the Soil is fit for every Thing, and well watered, it is not too far from the Sea, and nothing hinders Ships from coming hither. Lastly, it is near all the Places where, according as appears, there is any Design to make Settlements. The Company have a Ware-house, and keep a Clerk here, who has not as yet much Employment.

Among

Among a great Number of particular Grants, which are already in a Condition of producing ſomething, there are two of the firſt Magnitude; *that is to ſay*, four Leagues ſquare: One belongs to a Society of *St. Malo*, who bought it of M. *Hubert*, governing Commiſſary, and Preſident of the Council of *Louiſiana*: The other belongs to the Company, who have ſent hither ſome Workmen from *Clerac* to make Tobacco here. Theſe two Grants are ſo ſituated, that they make an exact Triangle with the Fort, and the Diſtance of one Angle from the other is a League. Half Way between the two Grants, is the great Village of the *Natchez*. I have carefully viſited all theſe Places: And here follows an Account of what I found moſt remarkable.

The Grant of the *Maloins* is well ſituated; it wants nothing to make an Improvement of the Land but Negroes, or hired Servants. I ſhould prefer the laſt: When the Time of their Service is expired, they become Inhabitants, and encreaſe the Number of the King's natural Subjects; whereas the firſt are always Strangers: And who can be aſſured, that by continually encreaſing in our Colonies, they will not one Day become formidable Enemies! Can we depend upon Slaves, who are only attached to us by Fear, and for whom the very Land where they are born has not the dear Name of *Mother Country*?

The firſt Night I lay in this Habitation, there was a great Alarm about Nine at Night. I enquired the Cauſe of it, and they told me that there was in the Neighbourhood a Beaſt of an unknown Species, of a monſtrous Size, and the Cry of which reſembled no Animal that we knew. However, no Perſon affirmed that he had ſeen it, and they only gueſſed at its Size by its Strength. It had already carried off ſome Sheep and Calves, and killed ſome Cows. I ſaid to thoſe who told me this Story, that a mad Wolf might have done all this; and as to the Cry, People were miſtaken every Day. I could bring no Body to be of my Opinion; they would have it, that it was a monſtrous Beaſt: They had juſt then heard it, and they ran out armed with the firſt Thing they could find, but all to no Purpoſe.

Succeſs of Tobacco in this Canton.

The Grant of the Company is ſtill more advantageouſly ſituated than that of the *Maloins*. The ſame River waters both, and afterwards diſcharges itſelf into the *Miſſiſſippi*, two Leagues from the Grant of the *Maloins*, to which a magnificent Cypreſs Wood, of ſix Leagues Extent, makes a Screen, that covers all the back Parts. Tobacco has ſucceeded very well here, but the Workmen of *Clerac* are almoſt all returned to *France*.

I saw in the Garden of the Sieur *le Noir*, chief Clerk, very fine Cotton on the Tree, and a little lower we begin to see some wild Indigo. They have not yet made a Trial of it; but it is very likely that it will turn out as well as that they found in the Island of *St. Domingo*, which is as much esteemed there as that which is brought from other Places. And furthermore, Experience teaches us that the Soil which naturally produces Indigo, is very fit to bear any foreign Sort that one chuses to sow in it.

Cotton, Indigo.

The great Village of the *Natchez* is at present reduced to a very few Cabins. The Reason which I heard for it is, that the Savages, from whom the Great Chief has a Right to take all they have, get as far from him as they can; and therefore many Villages of this Nation have been formed at some Distance from this. The *Tioux*, their Allies and our's, have also settled a Village in their Neighbourhood.

Description of the great Village and the Temple of the Natchez.

The Cabins of the great Village of the *Natchez*, the only one I saw, are in the Shape of a square Pavillion, very low, and without Windows; the Top is rounded much like an Oven: The greatest Part are covered with the Leaves and Stalks of Maiz; some are built of Clay mixed with cut Straw, which seemed to me to be tolerably strong, and which were covered within and without with very thin Mats. That of the Great Chief is very neatly plaistered in the Inside: It is also larger and higher than the rest, placed on a Spot something elevated, and stands alone, no other Building adjoining to it on any Side. It fronts the North, with a large open Place before it, which is not of the most regular Figure. All the Furniture I found in it was a narrow Couch of Boards, raised about two or three Feet from the Ground. Probably when the Great Chief wants to lie down, he spreads a Mat upon it, or some Skin.

There was not a Soul in the Village: All the People were gone to a neighbouring Village, where there was a Feast, and all the Doors were open; but there was nothing to fear from Thieves, for there was nothing to be seen any where but the bare Walls. These Cabins have no Vent for the Smoke, nevertheless, all those which I entered, were white enough. The Temple is very near the Great Chief's Cabin, turned towards the East, and at the End of the open Place. It is composed of the same Materials as the Cabins, but its Shape is different; it is a long Square, about forty Feet by twenty wide, with a common Roof, in Shape like our's. At the two Ends there is to Appearance like two Weather-cocks of Wood, which represent very indifferently two Eagles.

The

The Door is in the midſt of the Length of the Building, which has no other Opening: On each Side there are Benches of Stones. The Inſide anſwers perfectly this ruſtick Outſide. Three Pieces of Wood, which touch at the Ends, and which are placed in a Triangle, or rather equally diſtant from each other, take up almoſt all the Midſt of the Temple. Theſe Pieces are on Fire, and burn ſlowly. A Savage, whom they call the Keeper of the Temple, is obliged to tend the Fire, and prevent its going out. If it is cold, he may have his Fire apart, but he is not allowed to warm himſelf at that which burns in Honour of the *Sun*. This Keeper was alſo at the Feaſt, at leaſt I ſaw him not; and his Brands made ſuch a Smoke that it blinded us.

As to Ornaments, I ſaw none, nor abſolutely any Thing that could make me know that I was in a Temple. I ſaw only three or four Cheſts placed irregularly, in which there was ſome dry Bones, and upon the Ground ſome wooden Heads, a little better wrought than the two Eagles on the Roof. In ſhort, if I had not found a Fire here, I ſhould have thought that this Temple had been a long Time abandoned, or that it had been plundered. Thoſe Cones wrapped up in Skins, which ſome Relations ſpeak of; thoſe Bodies of the Chiefs ranged in a Circle in a round Temple, terminating in a Kind of Dome; that Altar, &c. I ſaw nothing of all this. If Things were thus in Times paſt, they are very much changed ſince.

Perhaps alſo, for we ought to condemn no Body, but when there is no Way to excuſe them; perhaps, I ſay, that the Neighbourhood of the *French* made the *Natchez* fear that the Bodies of their Chiefs, and every Thing that was moſt precious in their Temple, were in ſome Danger, if they did not convey them to another Place; and that the little Attention they have at preſent to guard this Temple, proceeds from its being deprived of what it contained moſt ſacred in the Opinion of theſe People. It is true, notwithſtanding, that againſt the Wall, over-againſt the Door, there was a Table, the Dimenſions of which I did not take the Pains to meaſure, becauſe I did not ſuſpect it to be an Altar. I have been aſſured ſince, that it is three Feet high, five long, and four wide.

I have been further informed that they make a little Fire on it with the Bark of Oak, and that it never goes out; which is falſe, for there was then no Fire on it, nor any Appearance of there ever having been any made. They ſay alſo, that four old Men lay by Turns in the Temple, to keep in this Fire; that he who is on Duty, muſt not go out for the eight Days of his Watch; that they carefully take the burning Aſhes of the Pieces that burn in the midſt of the Temple, to put upon the Altar;

 that

that twelve Men are kept to furnish the Bark; that there are Marmosets of Wood, and a Figure of a Rattle-Snake likewise of Wood, which they set upon the Altar, and to which they pay great Honours. That when the Chief dies, they bury him directly; that when they judge his Flesh is consumed, the Keeper of the Temple takes the Bones up, washes them clean, wraps them in whatever they have most valuable, and puts them in great Baskets made of Canes, which shut very close; that he covers these Baskets with Skins of Roe-Bucks very neatly, and places them before the Altar, where they remain till the Death of the reigning Chief; that then he encloses these Bones in the Altar itself, to make Room for the last dead.

I can say nothing on this last Article, only that I saw some Bones in one or two Chests, but they made not half a Human Body; that they appeared to be very old, and that they were not on the Table which they say is the Altar. As to the other Articles, 1st. As I was in the Temple only by Day, I know not what passes in it at Night. 2d. There was no Keeper in the Temple when I visited it. I very well saw, as I said before, that there were some Marmosets, or grotesque Figures; but I observed no Figure of a Serpent.

As to what I have seen in some Relations, that this Temple is hung with Tapestry, and the Floor covered with Cane Mats; that they put in it whatever they have that is handsomest, and that they bring every Year hither the first Fruits of their Harvest, we must certainly abate a great deal of all this. I never saw any Thing more slovenly and dirty, nor more in Disorder. The Billets burnt upon the bare Ground; and I saw no Mats on it, no more than on the Walls. M. *le Noir*, who was with me, only told me that every Day they put a new Billet on the Fire, and that at the Beginning of every Moon they made a Provision for the whole Month. But he knew this only by Report; for it was the first Time he had seen this Temple, as well as myself.

Of the Nation of the Natchez,

As to what regards the Nation of the *Natchez* in general, here follows what I could learn of it. We see nothing in their outward Appearance that distinguishes them from the other Savages of *Canada* and *Louisiana*. They seldom make War, not placing their Glory in destroying Men. What distinguishes them more particularly, is the Form of their Government, entirely despotic; a great Dependence, which extends even to a Kind of Slavery, in the Subjects; more Pride and Grandeur in the Chiefs, and their pacific Spirit, which, however, they have not entirely preserved for some Years past.

The *Hurons* believe, as well as they, that their hereditary Chiefs are descended from the Sun; but there is not one that would be his Servant, nor follow him into the other World for the Honour of ſerving him there, as it often happens among the *Natchez*.

Garcilaſſo de la Vega ſpeaks of this Nation as of a powerful People, and about ſix Years ago they reckoned among them four thouſand Warriors. It appears that they were more numerous in the Time of M. *de la Sale*, and even when M. *d'Iberville* diſcovered the Mouth of the *Miſſiſſippi*. At preſent the *Natchez* cannot raiſe two thouſand fighting Men. They attribute this Decreaſe to ſome contagious Diſeaſes, which in theſe laſt Years have made a great Ravage among them.

Of the Great Chief, and the Woman-Chief.

The Great Chief of the *Natchez* bears the Name of THE SUN; and it is always, as among the *Hurons*, the Son of the Woman who is neareſt related to him, that ſucceeds him. They give this Woman the Title of *Woman Chief*; and though in general ſhe does not meddle with the Government, they pay her great Honours. She has alſo, as well as the Great Chief, the Power of Life and Death. As ſoon as any one has had the Misfortune to diſpleaſe either of them, they order their Guards, whom they call *Allouez*, to kill him. "*Go and rid me* "*of that Dog*," ſay they; and they are immediately obeyed. Their Subjects, and even the Chiefs of the Villages, never approach them, but they ſalute them three Times, ſetting up a Cry, which is a Kind of Howling. They do the ſame when they retire, and they retire walking backwards. When they meet them, they muſt ſtop, and range themſelves on both Sides of the Way, and make the ſame Cries till they are gone paſt. Their Subjects are alſo obliged to carry them the beſt of their Harveſt, and of their Hunting and Fiſhing. Laſtly, no Perſon, not even their neareſt Relations, and thoſe who are of noble Families, when they have the Honour to eat with them, have a Right to put their Hand to the ſame Diſh, or to drink out of the ſame Veſſel.

Every Morning, as ſoon as the Sun appears, the Great Chief comes to the Door of his Cabin, turns himſelf to the Eaſt, and howls three Times, bowing down to the Earth. Then they bring him a Calumet, which ſerves only for this Purpoſe, he ſmokes, and blows the Smoke of his Tobacco towards the Sun; then he does the ſame Thing towards the other three Parts of the World. He acknowledges no Superior but the Sun, from which he pretends to derive his Origin. He exerciſes an unlimited Power over his Subjects, can diſpoſe of their Goods and Lives, and for whatever Labours he requires of them, they cannot demand any Recompence.

When this Great Chief, or the Woman Chief dies, all their *Allouez*, or Guards, are obliged to follow them into the other World: But they are not the only Perſons who have this Honour; for ſo it is reckoned among them, and is greatly ſought after.-------The Death of a Chief ſometimes coſts the Lives of more than a hundred Perſons; and I have been aſſured that very few principal Perſons of the *Natchez* die, without being eſcorted to the Country of Souls by ſome of their Relations, their Friends, or their Servants. It appears by the various Relations which I have ſeen of theſe horrible Ceremonies, that they differ greatly.---I ſhall here deſcribe the Obſequies of a Woman-Chief, as I had it from a Traveller, who was a Witneſs of them, and on whoſe Sincerity I have good Reaſon to depend.

What happens at the Death of the Great Chief, or the Woman-Chief.

The Huſband of this Woman not being noble, *that is to ſay*, of the Family of the Great Chief, his eldeſt Son ſtrangled him, according to Cuſtom: Then they cleared the Cabin of all it contained, and they erected in it a Kind of Triumphal Car, in which the Body of the deceaſed Woman, and that of her Huſband, were placed. A Moment after they ranged round theſe Carcaſſes twelve little Children, which their Parents had ſtrangled by Order of the eldeſt Daughter of the Woman-Chief, and who ſucceeded to the Dignity of her Mother. This being done, they erected in the public Place fourteen Scaffolds, adorned with Branches of Trees, and Cloths on which they had painted various Figures. Theſe Scaffolds were deſigned for as many Perſons, who were to accompany the Woman-Chief into the other World. Their Relations were all round them, and eſteemed as a great Honour for their Families the Permiſſion that they had obtained to ſacrifice themſelves in this Manner. They apply ſometimes ten Years before-hand to obtain this Favour; and the Perſons that have obtained it, muſt themſelves make the Cord with which they are to be ſtrangled.

They appear on their Scaffolds dreſſed in their richeſt Habits, holding in their Right Hand a great Shell. Their neareſt Relation is on their Right Hand, having under their Left Arm the Cord which is to ſerve for the Execution, and in their Right Hand a fighting Club. From Time to Time their neareſt Relation makes the Cry of Death; and at this Cry the fourteen Victims deſcend from their Scaffolds, and go and dance all together in the Middle of the open Place that is before the Temple, and before the Cabin of the Woman-Chief.

That Day and the following ones they ſhew them great Reſpect: They have each five Servants, and their Faces are painted red. Some add, that during the eight Days that precede their Death, they

they wear a red Ribbon round one of their Legs; and that during this Time, every Body ſtrives who ſhall be the firſt to feaſt them. However that may be, on the Occaſion I am ſpeaking of, the Fathers and Mothers who had ſtrangled their Children, took them up in their Hands and ranged themſelves on both Sides the Cabin: The fourteen Perſons, who were alſo deſtined to die, placed themſelves in the ſame Manner, and were followed by the Relations and Friends of the Deceaſed, all in Mourning; *that is to ſay*, their Hair cut off: They all made the Air reſound with ſuch frightful Cries, that one would have ſaid that all the Devils in Hell were come to howl in the Place. This was followed by the Dances of thoſe who were to die, and by the Songs of the Relations of the Woman-Chief.

At laſt they began the Proceſſion. The Fathers and Mothers, who carried the dead Children, appeared the firſt, marching two and two, and came immediately before the Bier on which was the Body of the Woman-Chief, which four Men carried on their Shoulders. All the others came after in the ſame Order as the firſt. At every ten Paces, the Fathers and Mothers let their Children fall upon the Ground: Thoſe who carried the Bier, walked upon them, then turned quite round them; ſo that when the Proceſſion arrived at the Temple, theſe little Bodies were all in Pieces.

While they buried the Body of the Woman-Chief in the Temple, they undreſſed the fourteen Perſons who were to die: They made them ſit on the Ground before the Door, each having two Savages by him; one of whom ſat on his Knees, and the other held his Arms behind. Then they put a Cord about his Neck, and covered his Head with a Roe-Buck's Skin: They made him ſwallow three Pills of Tobacco, and drink a Glaſs of Water; and the Relations of the Woman-Chief drew the two Ends of the Cord, ſinging, till he was ſtrangled. After which, they threw all the Carcaſſes into the ſame Pit, which they covered with Earth.

When the Great Chief dies, if his Nurſe is living, ſhe muſt die alſo.——The *French* not being able to hinder this Barbarity, have often obtained Leave to baptize the young Children that were to be ſtrangled; and who of Conſequence did not accompany thoſe, in whoſe Honour they were ſacrificed, in their pretended Paradiſe.

Manners of the Natchez.

We know no Nation on this Continent, where the Female Sex are more irregular, than in this. They are even forced by the Great Chief and his Subalterns to proſtitute themſelves to all Comers: And a Woman, for being common, is not the leſs eſteemed. Although Polygamy is permitted, and the Number of Women they

they may have is unlimited, commonly each has only one, but he may put her away when he pleases; a Licence which few but the Chiefs make Use of.---The Women are pretty well shaped for Savages, and neat enough in their Dress, and in every Thing they do. The Daughters of the Noble Families can marry none but obscure Persons; but they have a Right to turn away their Husbands when they please, and to take another, provided there is no Relationship between them.

If their Husbands are unfaithful to them, they can order them to be knocked on the Head, but they are not subject to the same Law themselves. They may also have as many Gallants as they think fit, and the Husband is not to take it amiss. This is a Privilege belonging to the Blood of the Great Chief. The Husband of any one of these must stand in the Presence of his Wife in a respectful Posture; he does not eat with her; he salutes her in the same Tone as her Domesticks. The only Privilege which such a burthensome Alliance procures him, is to be exempt from Labour, and to have Authority over those who serve his Wife.

Various Customs of the Natchez.

The *Natchez* have two War Chiefs, two Masters of the Ceremonies for the Temple, two Officers to regulate what is done in Treaties of Peace or War, one that has the Inspection of Works, and four others who are employed to order every Thing in the public Feasts. It is the Great Chief who appoints Persons to these Offices, and those who hold them are respected and obeyed as he would be himself.---The Harvest among the *Natchez* is in common. The Great Chief sets the Day for it, and calls the Village together. Towards the End of *July* he appoints another Day for the Beginning of a Festival, which lasts three Days, which are spent in Sports and Feasting.

Description of a Festival.

Each private Person contributes something of his Hunting, his Fishing, and his other Provisions, which consist in Maiz, Beans, and Melons. The Great Chief and the Woman-Chief preside at the Feast, sitting in a Cabin raised above the Ground, and covered with Boughs: They are carried to it in a Litter, and the Great Chief holds in his Hand a Kind of Sceptre, adorned with Feathers of various Colours. All the Nobles are round him in a respectful Posture. The last Day the Great Chief makes a Speech to the Assembly: He exhorts every Body to be exact in the Performance of their Duties, especially to have a great Veneration for the Spirits which reside in the Temple, and to be careful in instructing their Children. If any one has distinguished himself by some Action of Note, he makes his Elogium. Twenty Years ago, the Temple was reduced to Ashes by Lightning.

ning. Seven or eight Women threw their Children into the midſt of the Flames to appeaſe the Genii. The Great Chief immediately ſent for theſe Heroines, gave them publicly great Praiſes, and finiſhed his Diſcourſe by exhorting the other Women to follow their great Example on a like Occaſion.

The firſt Fruits offered in the Temple.

The Fathers of Families never fail to bring to the Temple the firſt Fruits of every Thing they gather; and they do the ſame by all the Preſents that are made to the Nation. They expoſe them at the Door of the Temple, the Keeper of which, after having preſented them to the Spirits, carries them to the Great Chief, who diſtributes them to whom he pleaſes. The Seeds are in like Manner offered before the Temple with great Ceremony: But the Offerings which are made there of Bread and Flour every new Moon, are for the Uſe of the Keepers of the Temple.

Of their Marriages.

The Marriages of the *Natchez*, are very little different from thoſe of the Savages of *Canada:* The principal Difference we find in them conſiſts in that here the future Spouſe begins by making, to the Relations of the Woman, ſuch Preſents as have been agreed upon; and that the Wedding is followed by a great Feaſt. The Reaſon why there are few but the Chiefs who have ſeveral Wives, is, that as they can get their Fields cultivated by the People without any Charge, their Wives are no Burthen to them. The Chiefs marry with leſs Ceremony ſtill than the others. It is enough for them to give Notice to the Relations of the Woman on whom they have caſt their Eyes, that they place her in the Number of their Wives. But they keep but one or two in their Cabins; the others remain with their Relations, where their Huſbands viſit them when they pleaſe. No Jealouſy reigns in theſe Marriages: The *Natchez* lend one another their Wives without any Difficulty; and 'tis probably from hence that proceeds the Readineſs with which they part with them to take others.

Of levying Soldiers.

When a War Chief wants to levy a Party of Soldiers, he plants, in a Place marked out for that Purpoſe, two Trees adorned with Feathers, Arrows, and Fighting-Clubs, all painted red, as well as the Trees, which are alſo pricked on that Side which is towards the Place whither they intend to carry the War. Thoſe who would enliſt, preſent themſelves to the Chief, well dreſſed, their Faces ſmeared with various Colours, and declare to him the Deſire they have to learn the Art of War under his Orders; that they are diſpoſed to endure all the Fatigues of War, and ready to die, if needful, for their Country.

When

When the Chief has got the Number of Soldiers that the Expedition requires, which he intends to make, he causes a Drink to be prepared at his Cabin, which is called *the Medicine of War*. This is a Vomit made with a Root boiled in Water: They give to each Man two Pots of it, which they must drink all at once, and which they throw up again almost as soon as they have drank it, with most violent Reachings. Afterwards they labour in making the necessary Preparations; and till the Day settled for their Departure, the Warriors meet every Evening and Morning in an open Place, where after much dancing, and telling their great Feats of War, every one sings his Song of Death.------These People are not less superstitious about their Dreams, than the Savages of *Canada:* There needs only a bad Omen to cause them to return when they are on a March.

Of the Provisions for War.

The Warriors march with a great deal of Order, and take great Precautions to encamp, and to rally. They often send out Scouts, but they never set Centinels at Night: They put out all the Fires, they recommend themselves to the Spirits, and they sleep in Security, after the Chief has exhorted every one not to snore too loud, and to keep always their Arms near them in good Condition. Their Idols are exposed on a Pole leaning towards the Enemy, and all the Warriors, before they lay down, pass one after another, with their Fighting-Clubs in their Hands, before these pretended Deities: Then they turn towards the Enemy's Country, and make great Threatnings, which the Wind often carries another Way.

Of their Marches and Encampments.

It does not appear that the *Natchez* exercise on their Prisoners, during the March, the Cruelties which are used in *Canada*. When these Wretches are arrived at the Great Village, they make them sing and dance several Days together before the Temple. After which, they are delivered to the Relations of those who have been killed during the Campaign. They, on receiving them, burst into Tears, then after having wiped their Eyes with the Scalps which the Warriors have brought home, they join together to reward those who have made them the Present of their Captives, whose Fate is always to be burnt.

Of the Prisoners.

The Warriors change their Names as often as they perform new Exploits: They receive them from the antient War Chief, and these Names have always some Relation to the Action by which they have merited this Distinction. Those who for the first Time have made a Prisoner, or taken off a Scalp, must, for a Month,

Names of the Warriors.

Month, abſtain from ſeeing their Wives, and from eating Fleſh. They imagine, that if they ſhould fail in this, that the Souls of thoſe whom they have killed or burnt, would effect their Death, or that the firſt Wound they ſhould receive would be mortal; or at leaſt, that they ſhould never after gain any Advantage over their Enemies. If the Great Chief, called THE SUN, commands his Subjects in Perſon, they take great Care that he ſhould not expoſe himſelf too much; leſs perhaps through Zeal for his Preſervation, than becauſe the other War Chiefs, and the Heads of the Party, would be put to Death for their Want of Care in guarding him.

Of the Jugglers.

The Jugglers, or Doctors of the *Natchez*, pretty much reſemble thoſe of *Canada*, and treat their Patients much after the ſame Manner. They are well paid when the Patient recovers; but if he happens to die, it often coſts them their Lives. There is in this Nation another Set of Jugglers, who run no leſs Riſque than theſe Doctors. They are certain lazy old Fellows, who, to maintain their Families without being obliged to work, undertake to procure Rain, or fine Weather, according as they are wanted. About the Spring Time they make a Collection to buy of theſe pretended Magicians a favourable Seaſon for the Fruits of the Earth. If it is Rain they require, they fill their Mouths with Water, and with a Reed, the End of which is pierced with ſeveral Holes, like a Funnel, they blow into the Air, towards the Side where they perceive ſome Clouds, whilſt holding their *Chichicoué* in one Hand, and their *Manitou* in the other, they play upon one, and hold the other up in the Air, inviting, by frightful Cries, the Clouds to water the Fields of thoſe who have ſet them to Work.

If the Buſineſs is to obtain fine Weather, they mount on the Roof of their Cabins, make Signs to the Clouds to paſs away; and if the Clouds paſs away, and are diſperſed, they dance and ſing round about their Idols; then they ſwallow the Smoke of Tobacco, and preſent their Calumets to the Sky. All the Time theſe Operations laſt, they obſerve a ſtrict Faſt, and do nothing but dance and ſing. If they obtain what they have promiſed, they are well rewarded; if they do not ſucceed, they are put to Death without Mercy. But they are not the ſame who undertake to procure Rain and fine Weather: The Genius of one Perſon cannot, as they ſay, give both.

Of Mourning.

Mourning among theſe Savages conſiſts in cutting off their Hair, and in not painting their Faces, and in abſenting themſelves from public Aſſemblies: But I know not how long it laſts. I know not neither, whither they celebrate the grand Feſtival of the Dead, which I have before deſcribed. It appears as if in this Nation, where every

Body is in some Sort the Slave of those who command, all the Honours of the Dead are for those who do so, especially for the Great Chief, and the Woman Chief.

Of Treaties.

Treaties of Peace and Alliances are made with great Pomp, and the Great Chief on these Occasions always supports his Dignity like a true Sovereign. As soon as he is informed of the Day of the Arrival of the Ambassadors, he gives his Orders to the Masters of the Ceremonies, for the Preparations for their Reception, and names those who are by Turns to maintain these Envoys; for it is at the Cost of his Subjects, that he defrays the Expences of the Embassage. The Day of the Entry of the Ambassadors, every one has his Place assigned him according to his Rank; and when the Ambassadors are come within five hundred Paces of the Great Chief, they stop, and sing the Song of Peace.

Commonly the Embassy is composed of thirty Men and six Women. Six of the best Voices march at the Head of this Train and sing aloud, the rest follow, and the *Chichicoué* serves to regulate the Time. When the Great Chief makes Signs to the Ambassadors to approach, they renew their March: Those who carry the Calumet, dance as they sing, and turn themselves on every Side, with many Motions, and make a great many Grimaces and Contorsions. They renew the same Tricks round about the Great Chief when they are come near him; then they rub him with their Calumet from Head to Foot, and afterwards go and rejoin their Company.

How the Great Chief gives Audience to Ambassadors.

Then they fill a Calumet with Tobacco, and holding Fire in one Hand, they advance all together towards the Great Chief, and present him the Calumet lighted. They smoke with him, and blow towards the Sky the first Whiff of their Tobacco, the second towards the Earth, and the third round about the Horizon. When they have done this, they present their Calumets to the Relations of the Great Chief, and the Subaltern Chiefs. Then they go and rub with their Hands the Stomach of the Great Chief, after which they rub themselves all over the Body; and lastly, they lay their Calumets on Forks over-against the Great Chief, and the Orator of the Embassy begins his Speech, which lasts an Hour.

When he has finished, they make Signs to the Ambassadors, who till now were standing, to sit down on Benches placed for them near the Great Chief, who answers their Discourse, and speaks also a whole Hour. Then a Master of the Ceremonies lights a great Calumet of Peace, and makes the Ambassadors smoke in it, who swallow the first Mouthful. Then the Great Chief enquires after their Health, and all those who are present

at

at the Audience make them the ſame Compliment; then they conduct them to the Cabin that is appointed for them, and where they give him a great Feaſt. The Evening of the ſame Day the Great Chief makes them a Viſit; but when they know he is ready to do them this Honour, they go to ſeek him, and carry him on their Shoulders to their Lodging, and make him ſit on a great Skin. One of them places himſelf behind him, leans his Hands on his Shoulders, and ſhakes him a pretty long Time, whilſt the reſt, ſitting round on the Earth, ſing their great Actions in the Wars.

Theſe Viſits are renewed every Morning and Evening; but in the laſt the Ceremonial varies. The Ambaſſadors ſet up a Poſt in the midſt of their Cabin, and ſit all round it: The Warriors who accompany the Great Chief, or as they call him, *the Sun*, dreſſed in their fineſt Robes, dance, and one by one ſtrike the Poſt, and relate their braveſt Feats of Arms; after which they make Preſents to the Ambaſſadors. The next Day they are permitted for the firſt Time to walk about the Village, and every Night they make them Entertainments, which conſiſt only in Dances. When they are on their Departure, the Maſter of the Ceremonies ſupplies them with all the Proviſions they may want for their Journey, and this is always at the Expence of private Perſons.

Religion of Fire in Florida.

The greateſt Part of the Nations of *Louiſiana* had formerly their Temples, as well as the *Natchez*, and in all theſe Temples there was a perpetual Fire. It ſeems alſo probable, that the *Maubiliens* had over all the People of this Part of *Florida*, a Kind of Primacy of Religion; for it was at their Fire they were obliged to kindle THAT, which by Negligence or Accident had been ſuffered to go out. But at preſent the Temple of the *Natchez* is the only one that ſubſiſts, and it is held in great Veneration among all the Savages which inhabit this vaſt Continent, the Decreaſe of which Nation is as conſiderable, and has been ſtill more ſudden, than that of the Savages of *Canada*, without its being poſſible to diſcover the true Cauſe of it. Whole Nations have entirely diſappeared within forty Years at moſt. Thoſe which are ſtill ſubſiſting, are but the Shadow of what they were when M. *de la Sale* diſcovered this Country. I take my Leave of you, Madam, for Reaſons which I ſhall have the Honour to explain to you ſoon.

I am, &c.

LETTER XXX.

Journey from the NATCHEZ *to* NEW ORLEANS. *Deſcription of the Country, and of ſeveral Villages of the* SAVAGES, *and of the Capital of* LOUISIANA.

MADAM, NEW ORLEANS, *January* 10.

I Am at length arrived in this famous City, which they have called *la nouvelle Orleans*. Thoſe who have given it this Name, thought that *Orleans* was of the feminine Gender: But what ſignifies that? Cuſtom has eſtabliſhed it, and that is above the Rules of Grammar.

This City is the firſt, which one of the greateſt Rivers in the World has ſeen raiſed on its Banks. If the eight Hundred fine Houſes, and the five Pariſhes, which the News-Papers gave it ſome two Years ago, are reduced at preſent to a hundred Barracks, placed in no very great Order; to a great Store-Houſe, built of Wood; to two or three Houſes, which would be no Ornament to a Village of *France*; and to the half of a ſorry Store-Houſe, which they agreed to lend to the Lord of the Place, and which he had no ſooner taken Poſſeſſion of, but they turned him out to dwell under a Tent; what Pleaſure, on the other Side, to ſee inſenſibly encreaſing this future Capital of a fine and vaſt Country, and to be able to ſay, not with a Sigh, like the Hero of *Virgil*, ſpeaking of his dear native Place conſumed by the Flames, and the Fields where *Troy* Town had been *(a)*, but full of a well grounded Hope, this wild and deſart Place, which the Reeds and Trees do yet almoſt wholly cover, will be one Day, and perhaps that Day is not far off, an opulent City, and the Metropolis of a great and rich Colony.

You will aſk me, Madam, on what I found this Hope? I found it on the Situation of this City, at thirty-three Leagues from the Sea, and on the Side of a navigable River, that one may come up to this Place in twenty-four Hours: On the Fruitfulneſs of the Soil; on the Mildneſs and Goodneſs of its Climate, in 30° North Latitude; on the Induſtry of its Inhabitants; on the Neighbourhood of *Mexico*, to which we may go in fifteen Days by Sea; on that of the *Havannah*, which is ſtill nearer; and of

(a) Et Campos, ubi Troja fuit.

the fineſt Iſlands of *America*, and of the *Engliſh* Colonies. Need there any Thing more to render a City flouriſhing? *Rome* and *Paris* had not ſuch conſiderable Beginnings, were not built under ſuch happy Auſpices, and their Founders did not find on the *Siene* and the *Tyber* the Advantages we have found on the *Miſſiſſippi*, in Compariſon of which, thoſe two Rivers are but little Brooks. ——— But before I undertake to mention what there is here worthy your Curioſity, that I may proceed according to Order, I ſhall take up my Journal again where I broke it off.

Miſſionaries of the Natchez *without Succeſs.*

I ſtayed at the *Natchez* much longer than I expected, and it was the abandoned Condition in which I found the *French*, with Reſpect to ſpiritual Aids, that kept me there till after *Chriſtmas.* The Dew of Heaven hath not yet fallen on this fine Country, which above all others may boaſt of its Portion of the Fatneſs of the Earth. The late M. *d'Iberville* had deſtined a *Jeſuit (a)* for this Purpoſe, who accompanied him in the ſecond Voyage he made to *Louiſiana*, with a Deſign to eſtabliſh *Chriſtianity* in a Nation, whoſe Converſion, he made no Doubt, would be followed by that of all the reſt. But this Miſſionary paſſing by the Village of the *Bayagoulas*, thought he found there more favourable Diſpoſitions for Religion, and while he was thinking to fix his Abode amongſt them, he was called to *France* by ſuperior Orders.

After this, an Eccleſiaſtic of *Canada (b)* was ſent to the *Natchez*, and remained there a pretty long Time, but he made no Proſelytes, tho' he had gained the good Graces of the Woman Chief, who out of Reſpect to him, gave his Name to one of her Sons. This Miſſionary having been obliged to make a Journey to *Maubile*, was killed on the Way by Savages, who probably only wanted his Baggage, as it had happened before to another Prieſt *(c)* on the Side of the *Akanſas.* Since that Time all *Louiſiana*, above the *Illinois*, has remained without any Prieſt, except the *Tonicas*, who have had for ſeveral Years an Eccleſiaſtic *(d)*, whom they loved and eſteemed, and whom they would have made their Chief, and who, notwithſtanding, could never perſuade one of them to embrace *Chriſtianity*.

The French *deprived of ſpiritual Aids.*

But it is ſomething prepoſterous to think of taking Meaſures for the Converſion of Infidels, whilſt the Houſhold even of the Faith are almoſt all without Paſtors. I have already had the Honour of telling you, Madam, that the

(a) Father *Paul Du Ru.* *(b)* M. *de S. Coſme.* *(c)* M. *Foucault.* *(d)* M. *Davion.*

Canton

Canton of the *Natchez* is the most populous of the Colony ; nevertheless, it is five Years since any *Frenchman* has heard Mass here, or even seen a Priest. I soon saw that the Privation of the Sacraments had produced in the greatest Part of them that Indifference for the Exercises of Religion, which is the common Effect of such Privation : Yet many shewed a great Desire to take Advantage of my Presence, for regulating the Affairs of their Consciences; and I thought it was my Duty to help them to this Comfort without much Sollicitation.

The first Proposal that they made to me was, that I would agree to marry, in the Presence of the Church, some Inhabitants, who by Virtue of a civil Contract, drawn up in the Presence of the Commandant and the principal Clerk, lived together without any Scruple, alledging, as well as they who had authorized this Concubinage, the Necessity of peopling the Country, and the Impossibility of having a Priest. I represented to them, that there was one at the *Yasous*, and at *New Orleans*, and that the Matter was worth the Pains of taking the Journey: They replied, that the contracting Parties were not in a Condition to take long Journies, nor to be at the Expence of bringing a Priest hither. In short, the Evil was done, and there remained nothing but to remedy it, which I did. Then I confessed all who presented themselves, but the Number of these was not so great as I had hoped.

Departure from the Natchez.

Nothing more detaining me at the *Natchez*, I departed from thence the 26th of *December*, pretty late, accompanied by M. *de Pauger*, the King's Engineer, who was visiting the Colony, to examine the Places where it was fit to build Forts. We went four Leagues, and encamped at the Side of a little River, which we found on the Left. We re-embarked the next Day two Hours before it was light, with the Wind pretty high, and against us. The River in this Place makes a Circuit of fourteen Leagues; and as we turned, the Wind turned with us, being beaten back by the Land, and by the Islands, which we found in great Numbers, so that it was always in our Faces. Notwithstanding which, we went ten Leagues farther, and entered into another little River on the Left Hand. All Night we heard a great Noise, and I thought it was the Effect of the Wind, that was grown stronger, but they assured me that the River had been very quiet, and that the Noise which had waked me, was made by the Fish, that dashed about the Water with their Tails.

The

The 28th, after having gone two Leagues, we arrived at the River of the *Tonicas*, which appeared to me at first to be but a Brook; but at a Musket-Shot Distance from its Mouth, it forms a very pretty Lake. If the *Mississippi* continues to throw itself as it does on the other Side, all this Place will become inaccessible. The River of the *Tonicas* has its Source in the Country of the *Tchactas*, and its Course is very much obstructed with Falls. The Village is beyond the Lake, on a pretty high Ground; yet they say that the Air here is bad, which they attribute to the Quality of the Waters of the River; but I should rather judge that it proceeds from the Stagnation of the Waters in the Lake.---This Village is built in a Circle, round a very large open Space, without any Inclosure, and moderately peopled.

Description of the Village of the Tonicas.

The Cabin of the Chief is very much adorned on the Outside for the Cabin of a Savage. We see on it some Figures in Relievo, which are not so ill done as one expects to find them. The Inside is dark, and I observed nothing in it but some Boxes, which they assured me were full of Clothes and Money. The Chief received us very politely; he was dressed in the *French* Fashion, and seemed to be not at all uneasy in that Habit. Of all the Savages of *Canada*, there is none so much depended on by our Commandants as this Chief. He loves our Nation, and has no Cause to repent of the Services he has rendered it. He trades with the *French*, whom he supplies with Horses and Fowls, and he understands his Trade very well. He has learnt of us to hoard up Money, and he is reckoned very rich. He has a long Time left off the Dress of a Savage, and he takes a Pride in appearing always well dressed, according to our Mode.

Of the Chief of the Tonicas.

The other Cabins of the Village are partly square, as that of the Chief, and partly round, like those of the *Natchez*. The Place round which they all stand, is about a hundred Paces Diameter; and notwithstanding the Heat of the Weather was that Day suffocating, the young People were diverting themselves at a Kind of *Truck*, much like our's.

The State of this Nation.

There are two other Villages of this Nation at a little Distance from this; and this is all that remains of a People formerly very numerous.---I said before, that they had a Missionary whom they greatly loved: I have learnt that they drove him away not long since, because he had burnt their Temple; which nevertheless they have not rebuilt, nor lighted their Fire again; a certain Proof of their little Attachment to their false Religion! They even soon recalled the Missionary; but they

they heard all he could ſay to them with an Indifference, which he could never conquer, and he has forſaken them in his Turn.

A Deſcription of the Red River.

From the Bottom of the Lake, or the Bay of the *Tenicas*, if we uſed Canoes of Bark, we might make a Portage of two Leagues, which would ſave ten on the *Miſſiſſipi*; but this is not practicable with Pettiaugres. Two Leagues lower than the River of the *Tenicas*, we leave on the Right Hand the *Red River*, or *Rio Colorado*; at the Entrance of which, the famous *Ferdinand de Soto*, the Conqueror of *Florida*, ended his Days and his Exploits, or rather his Rambles. This River runs Eaſt and Weſt ſome Time, then turns to the South. It is ſcarcely navigable for Pettiaugres, and that for no more than forty Leagues; after which we meet with unpaſſable Marſhes. Its Mouth appeared to me to be about two hundred Fathom wide. Ten Leagues higher, it receives on the Right Hand the *Black River*, otherwiſe called the River of the *Ouachitas*; which comes from the North, and has Water only for ſeven Months in the Year.

Grants ill ſituated.

Nevertheleſs, there are ſeveral Grants ſituated here, which in all Appearance will not grow very rich. The Motive of this Settlement is the Neighbourhood of the *Spaniards*, which at all Times has been a fatal Enticement to this Colony. In Hopes of trading with them, they leave the beſt Lands in the World uncultivated. The *Natchitoches* are ſettled on the *Red River*, and we have judged it convenient to build a Fort among them, to hinder the *Spaniards* from ſettling nearer us. We encamped the twenty-ninth, a little below the Mouth of the *Red River*, in a very fine Bay.

The Point cut off.

The 30th, after having gone five Leagues, we paſſed a ſecond Point cut off. The *Miſſiſſipi*, in this Place, makes a great Winding. Some *Canadians*, by Dint of hollowing a little Brook, which was behind the Point, brought the Waters of the River into it; which ſpreading themſelves impetuouſly in this new Channel, compleatly cut off the Point, and hath ſaved Travellers fourteen Leagues of Way. The old Bed of the River is actually dry, and has no Water in it but in the Seaſon of the Floods; an evident Proof that the *Miſſiſſipi* caſts itſelf here towards the Eaſt; and this deſerves to be conſidered with the greateſt Attention, in making Settlements on either Side of the River. The Depth of this new Channel has been lately ſounded, and they have let out a Line in it of thirty Fathom long, without finding any Bottom.

Just below, and on the same Hand, we saw the weak Beginnings of a Grant, which bears the Name of *St. Reyne*, and at the Head of which are Messrs. *de Coetlogon* and *Kolly*. It is situated on a very fertile Soil, and there is nothing to fear from the overflowing of the River: But with Nothing, Nothing can be done, especially when they want Men for Labour, and Men want an Inclination for Labour; and this seemed to us to be the Condition of this Grant. We went a League farther this Day, and came to the Grant of Madam *de Mezieres*, where the Rain stopped us all the next Day. Some Huts, covered with the Leaves of the *Latanier* and a great Tent of Cloth at present form all this Grant. They wait for Men and Goods from the *Black River*, where the Magazines are, and which they are not willing to leave. I am afraid that by endeavouring to make two Settlements at once, both will fail.

The Grant of St. Reyne, *and that of Madam* de Mezieres.

The Soil on which they have begun this, is very good; but they must build a Quarter of a League from the River, behind a Cypress Wood, which is a marshy Ground, and of which they might make Advantage in sowing Rice and making Gardens. Two Leagues farther in the Wood, there is a Lake two Leagues in Compass, the Sides of which are covered with wild Fowl, and which perhaps may supply them with Fish, when they have destroyed the *Caimans*, which swarm in it. I have learnt in this Place some Secrets; which you shall have, Madam, at the same Rate they cost me; for I have no Time to make Trial of them.

The Male Cypress bears in this Country a Pod; which must be gathered green, and then they find it a sovereign Balm for Cuts. That which is distilled from the *Copalme*, has, among other Virtues, that of curing the Dropsy. The Root of those great Cotton-Trees I mentioned in another Place, and which we find continually on all the Route which I have made from the Lake *Ontario*, is a certain Remedy against all Hurts of the Skin. You must take the Inside of the Bark, boil it in Water, bathe the Wound with this Water, and then lay on the Ashes of the Bark itself.

On *New-Year's-Day* we went to say Mass three Leagues from Madam *de Mezieres*, in a Grant very well situated, and which belongs to M. *Diron d'Artaguette*, Inspector General of the Troops of *Louisiana* (a). They brought us here a monstrous Tortoise, and they assured us that these Animals were capable of breaking a

The Grant of M. Diron.

(a) He died lately the King's Lieutenant at Cape *François*, in *St. Domingo*.

large Iron Bar. If the Fact is true, for I should be willing to see it before I believe it, the Saliva of these Animals must be a very powerful Dissolvent. As for the Leg of a Man, I would not trust it in their Jaws. This is certain, that the Meat of that which I saw, was enough to satisfy ten Persons who had good Stomachs. We staid all the Day in this Grant, which is not much forwarder than the rest, and which they call *le Bâton rouge, (the red Stick).*

Description of the Bayagoulas.

The next Day we made eleven Leagues, and we encamped a little below the *Bayagoulas*, which we had left on the Right Hand, after having visited here the Ruins of the antient Village I mentioned before. It was very populous about twenty Years since. The Small-Pox has destroyed a Part of its Inhabitants, the rest are gone away and dispersed: They have not so much as even heard any News of them for several Years, and 'tis a Doubt whether there is a single Family remaining. The Land they possessed is very rich. Messrs. *Paris* have a Grant here, where they have planted in Rows a great Number of white Mulberry-Trees, and they make very fine Silk here already. They also begin to cultivate here, with much Success, Indigo and Tobacco. If they laboured the same in all other Places, the Proprietors of Grants would soon be indemnified for all their Expences.

An Account of the Oumas *and the* Chetimachas.

The 3d of *January* we arrived about Ten o'Clock in the Morning at the little Village of the *Oumas*, which is on the Left, and where there are some *French* Houses. A Quarter of a League higher up in the Country, is the great Village. This Nation is very well affected to us. The *Mississippi* begins to fork, or to divide into two Branches, two Leagues higher. It has hollowed itself on the Right, to which it always inclines, a Channel, which they call the *Fork* of the *Chetimachas*, or *Sitimachas*; and which, before it carries its Waters to the Sea, forms a pretty large Lake. The Nation of the *Chetimachas*, is almost entirely destroyed; the few that remain are Slaves in the Colony.

We went that Day six Leagues beyond the *Oumas*, and we passed the Night on the fine Spot where they had settled the Grant of M. *le Marquis D'Ancenis*, at present Duke *de Bethune*; which, by a Fire happening in the great Magazine, and by several other Accidents one after another, is reduced to nothing. The *Colapissas* had here formed a little Village, which did not subsist long.

The 4th we arrived before Noon at the great Village of the *Colapissas*. It is the finest Village of *Louisiana*, yet they reckon in it but two hundred Warriors, who have the Character of being very brave. Their Cabins are in the Shape of a Pavilion, like those of the *Sioux*, and they seldom make any Fire in them. They have a double Roof; that in the Inside is made of the Leaves of the *Lattanier*, interwoven together, that in the Outside is made of Mats.

The Cabin of the Chief is thirty-six Feet Diameter: I had not before seen one so large; for that of the Great Chief of the *Natchez* is but thirty Feet. As soon as we appeared in Sight of this Village, they beat a Drum; and we were scarcely landed, before the Chief sent his Compliments to me. I was surprised, in advancing towards the Village, to see the Drummer dressed in a long Gown, half white and half red, with white Sleeves on the red Side, and red Sleeves on the white. I enquired into the Origin of this Custom, and they told me it was not antient; that a Governor of *Louisiana* had made a Present of a Drum to these Savages, who have always been our faithful Allies, and that this Kind of Beadle's Habit was their own Invention.———The Women are better shaped here than in *Canada*, and their Way of dressing themselves is also something more becoming.

The Grant of M. le Comte D'Artagnan.

After Dinner, we went five Leagues further, and we stopped at *Cannes brulées, (the burnt Reeds)*, where the Grant of M. *le Comte D'Artagnan* has an Habitation on it, which is also to serve him for a Store-House, if it has not the Fate of almost all the rest. This House is on the Left; and the first Object that presented itself to my Sight, was a great Cross set up on the Bank of the River, about which they actually sing Vespers. This is the first Place of the Colony, from the *Illinois*, where I found this Mark of our Religion. Two Mousquetaires, M. *D'Artiguiere*, and *de Benac (a)*, are the Directors of this Grant; and it was M. *de Benac* who had the Direction of the House of *Cannes brulées*, together with M. *Chevalier*, Nephew to the Master of the Mathematics to the King's Pages. They have no Priest, but it is not their Fault: They had one whom they were obliged to get rid of, because he was a Drunkard; and they judged rightly, that a bad Priest is likely to do more Harm in a new Settlement, where he has no Superior that watches over his Conduct, than his Services are worth.

Description of the Taensas.

Between the *Colapissas* and the *Cannes brulées*, we leave on the Right Hand the Spot which was formerly possessed by the *Taensas*; who, in the Time of M. *de la Sale*, made a great Figure in this

(a) The last is now Captain in the Troops of *Louisiana*.

Country, but who have entirely disappeared for some Years. This is the finest Place, and the best Soil of *Louisiana*. M. *de Meuse*, to whom it was granted, has done nothing here yet: Nevertheless he keeps here a Director, who has neither Men nor Merchandize.

Description of the Chapitoulas.

The 5th we stopped to dine at a Place which they call the *Chapitoulas*, and which is but three Leagues distant from *New Orleans*, where we arrived at Five in the Evening. The *Chapitoulas*, and some neighbouring Habitations, are in very good Condition. The Soil is fruitful, and it is fallen into the Hands of People that are skilful and laborious. They are the *Sieur du Breuil* and three *Canadian* Brothers, named *Chauvins*. The last have contributed nothing but their Industry, which was perfected by the Necessity of labouring for a Subsistence. They have lost no Time, they have spared no Pains, and their Example is a Lesson for those lazy People, whose Poverty very unjustly disparages a Country which will render a hundred-fold of whatever is sowed in it.

I am, &c.

LETTER XXXI.

Journey from NEW ORLEANS *to the Mouth of the* MISSISSIPPI: *Description of this River quite to the Sea. Reflexions on the Grants.*

TOULOUSE ISLAND, *or* LA BALISE *(the* BUOY, *or* SEA MARK) *January* 26.

MADAM,

THE Environs of *New Orleans* have nothing very remarkable. I did not find this City so well situated as I had been told. Others are not of the same Opinion. These are the Reasons on which their Opinion is founded: I will afterwards explain mine. The first is, that about a League from hence, inclining to the North East, they have found a little River, which they have called the *Bayouc of St. John* (a), which at the End of two Leagues discharges itself into the Lake *Pontchartrain*, which communicates with the Sea: By this Means, they say, it

(a) *Bayouc* in the Savage Language signifies a Rivulet.

is

is eaſy to keep up a certain Commerce between the Capital and *la Maubile*, *Biloxi*, and all the other Poſts which we poſſeſs near the Sea. The ſecond is, that below this City, the River makes a great Turn, which they have called *le Detour aux Anglois, (the Engliſh Reach)*, which may cauſe a Retardment, which they judge very advantageous to prevent a Surpriſe. Theſe Reaſons are ſpecious, but they don't appear to me to be ſolid; for in the firſt Place, thoſe who have reaſoned in this Manner, have ſuppoſed that the Entrance of the River could receive none but ſmall Veſſels; therefore in this Caſe, what is there to be feared from a Surpriſe, if the Town is ever ſo little fortified, as I ſuppoſe in my Turn it will be ſoon? Will they come to attack it with Boats, or with Veſſels which cannot carry Guns? On the other Hand, in whatever Place the City is ſituated, muſt not the Mouth of the River be defended by good Batteries, and by a Fort, which will at leaſt give Time to receive Intelligence, and to keep themſelves ready to receive the Enemy? In the ſecond Place, what Neceſſity is there for this Communication, which cannot be carried on but by Boats, and with Poſts, which they cannot ſuccour if they were attacked; and from which conſequently they can receive but weak Succours, which for the moſt Part are good for nothing: I add, that when a Veſſel muſt go up the *Engliſh Reach*, they muſt change their Wind every Moment, which may detain them whole Weeks to make ſeven or eight Leagues.

Little Depth of the Country below New Orleans.

A little below *New Orleans*, the Land begins to have but little Depth on both Sides of the *Miſſiſſippi*, and this goes on diminiſhing quite to the Sea. It is a Point of Land, which does not appear very antient; for if we dig ever ſo little in it, we find Water; and the Number of Shoals and little Iſlands, which we have ſeen formed within twenty years paſt in all the Mouths of the River, leave no Room to doubt that this Slip of Land was formed in the ſame Manner. It appears certain, that when M. *de la Sale* came down the *Miſſiſſippi* quite to the Sea, the Mouth of this River was not the ſame as it is at preſent.

Changes that have happened in the Mouth of the River.

The more we approach the Sea, the more what I ſay appears evident: The Bar has ſcarce any Water in the greateſt Part of thoſe little Outlets, which the River has opened for itſelf, and which are ſo much encreaſed only by the Means of the Trees, which are brought down with the Current, one of which being ſtopt by its Branches, or by its Roots, in a Place where there is little Depth, ſtops a thouſand others. I have ſeen Heaps of theſe 200 Leagues from

from hence, one of which alone would have filled all the Wood-Yards of *Paris*. Nothing is capable of removing them, the Mud which the River brings down serves them for a Cement, and covers them by Degrees; every Inundation leaves a new Layer, and in ten Years at most the Reeds and Shrubs begin to grow upon them. Thus have been formed the greatest Part of the Points and Islands, which make the River so often change its Course.

Departure from New Orleans.

I have nothing to add to what I said in the Beginning of the former Letter concerning the present State of *New Orleans*. The truest Idea that you can form of it, is to represent to yourself two hundred Persons that are sent to build a City, and who are encamped on the Side of a great River, where they have thought of nothing but to shelter themselves from the Injuries of the Air, whilst they wait for a Plan, and have built themselves Houses. M. *de Pauger*, whom I have still the Honour to accompany, has just now shewed me one of his drawing. It is very fine and very regular; but it will not be so easy to execute it, as it was to trace it on Paper. We set out the 22d of *July* for *Biloxi*, which is the Head-Quarters. Between *New Orleans* and the Sea there are no Grants; they would have too little Depth; there are only some small private Habitations, and some Magazines for the great Grants.

Of the Chaouachas.

Behind one of these Habitations, which is on the Right, immediately below the *English* Reach, there was not long since a Village of the *Chaouachas*, the Ruins of which I visited. I found nothing entire but the Cabin of the Chief, which was pretty much like the House of one of our Peasants in *France*, only with this Difference, that it had no Windows. It was built of Branches of Trees, the Vacancies between which were filled up with the Leaves of *Lattanier*; the Roof was of the same Structure. This Chief is very absolute, as are all those of *Florida*; he never hunts or shoots but for his Diversion, for his Subjects are obliged to give him Part of their Game. His Village is at present on the other Side of the River, half a League lower, and the Savages have transported thither even to the Bones of their Dead.

A little below their new Habitation the Coast is much higher than any where hereabout, and it appears to me that they should have placed the City there. It would be but twenty Leagues from the Sea, and with a South Wind, or a moderate South East, a Ship would get up in fifteen Hours. The Night of the 23d we quitted the Boat which had brought us hither, and embarked in a Brigantine, in which we fell down with the Stream

Stream all Night. The next Morning by Day-Break we had paſſed a new Circuit, which the River makes, and which they call the *Reach of the Piakimines.*

We found ourſelves ſoon after in the midſt of the Paſſes of the *Miſſiſſippi*, where it requires the greateſt Attention to work the Ship, that it may not be drawn into ſome one of them, from whence it would be impoſſible to recover it. The greateſt Part are only little Rivulets, and ſome are even only ſeparated by Sand-Banks, which are almoſt level with the Water. It is the Bar of the *Miſſiſſippi* which has ſo greatly multiplied theſe Paſſes; for it is eaſy to conceive by the Manner in which I have ſaid there are formed every Day new Lands, how the River, endeavouring to eſcape by where it finds the leaſt Reſiſtance, makes itſelf a Paſſage, ſometimes one Way and ſometimes another; from whence it might happen, if Care was not taken, that none of theſe Paſſages would be practicable for Veſſels. The Night of the 24th we anchored beyond the Bar, over-againſt *la Baliſe.*

Of the Paſſes of the Miſſiſſippi.

The contrary Wind keeping us ſtill here, we were willing to make ſome Advantage of this Delay. Yeſterday, the 25th, being *Sunday*, I began by ſinging a great Maſs in the Iſland, which they call *la Baliſe*, on Account of a Sea-Mark which they have ſet up for the Direction of Ships. — I afterwards bleſſed it, we named it *Toulouſe Iſland*, and we ſang the *Te Deum.* This Iſland is ſcarce more than half a League in Compaſs, taking in alſo another Iſland which is ſeparated from it by a Gutter, where there is always Water. On the other Hand it is very low, excepting only one Place, where the Floods never come, and where there is Room enough to build a Fort and ſome Magazines. They might unload Veſſels here, which could not eaſily paſs the Bar with their whole Lading.

Of the Iſland Toulouſe, *or* la Baliſe.

M. *de Pauger* ſounded this Place with the Lead, and found the Bottom pretty hard, and of Clay, tho' there come out of it five or ſix little Springs, but which yield little Water; this Water leaves on the Sand a very fine Salt. When the River is loweſt, *that is to ſay*, during the three hotteſt Months of the Year, the Water is ſalt round this Iſland: In the Time of the Floods, it is quite freſh, and the River preſerves its Freſhneſs a good League in the Sea. At all other Times it is a little ſaltiſh beyond the Bar. Therefore it is entirely a Fable, which has been reported, that for twenty Leagues the *Miſſiſſippi* does not mix its Waters with thoſe of the Sea.

Salt Springs.

M. *Pau-*

M. *Pauger* and I passed the rest of the Day with the Pilot *Kerlasio*, who commanded the Brigantine, in sounding and discovering the only Mouth of the River which is navigable; and these are exactly our Observations on the State in which we found it, for I do not answer for the Changes which may happen in it. It runs North West and South East the Space of three hundred Fathom, in going up from the open Sea quite to the Island of *Toulouse*, over-against which there are three little Islands, which have yet nothing growing on them, though they are pretty high. In all this Interval, its Breadth is two hundred and fifty Fathom, its Depth is eighteen Feet in the Middle, the Bottom soft Oose: But we must navigate here with the Sounding-Line in Hand, when we are not used to the Channel.

Of the principal Mouth of the Missisippi.

From hence going upwards, we make still the North West for four hundred Fathom, at the End of which there is still fifteen Feet Water, the same Bottom; and it is to be observed that every where the Anchorage is safe, and that we are sheltered from all the Winds but the South and the South East, which may, when they are violent, make the Ships drive with their Anchors, but without Danger, because they would run on the Bar, which is a soft Oose: Then we make the North West by North East for five hundred Fathom. This is properly the Bar, twelve Feet Water, mean Depth; we must also work here with great Attention, for we meet with many Banks: This Bar is two hundred and fifty Fathom wide between low Lands that are covered with Reeds.

In the *Pass* of the *East*, which is immediately above, we make full West for a League: It is two hundred and fifty Fathom wide, and from four to fifteen Feet in Depth. Then all at once we find no Bottom. In taking again the great Pass at coming off the Bar, we make again the North West the Space of three hundred Fathom, and we have always here 45 Feet Water. We leave on the Right the Pass of *Sauvole*, by which Boats may go to *Biloxi*, making the North: This Place took its Name from an Officer, whom M. *d' Iberville* made Commandant in the Colony upon his Return to *France*.

Other Passes.

Then we must return to the West and by North West for fifty Fathom, and in a Kind of Bay, which we leave on the Left; at the End of this Space there are three Passes, one to the South South East, another to the South, and a third to the West South West. This Bay is notwithstanding only ten Fathom deep, and twenty wide; but these Passes have little Water. We continue to follow the same Rhumb of the Wind, and at fifty Fathom farther there is on the same Hand a second Bay, which is twenty Fathom wide, and fifty deep. It contains two little Passes, which

which Canoes of Bark would be troubled to get thro', and therefore they ſeldom reckon them among the Paſſes. From hence we take to the Weſt for the Space of five hundred Fathom, and we come over-againſt the Paſs *a la Loutre (of the Otter)*. It is five hundred Fathom wide, but is paſſable only for Pettiaugres. Then we turn to the South Weſt for twenty Fathom; we return to the Weſt for three hundred, then to the Weſt by North, the Space of one hundred; to the Weſt North Weſt as many, to the North Weſt eight hundred; then we find on the Left the Paſs of the South, which is two hundred and fifty Fathom wide, nine Fathom Water at its Entrance on the Side towards the River, and two Feet only where it goes out to the Sea. Two hundred and fifty Fathom farther is the Paſs of the South Weſt, nearly the ſame Breadth; never leſs than ſeven or eight Feet Water.—— Hereabout the Country begins to be not ſo marſhy, but it is overflowed during four Months of the Year. It is bounded on the Left by a Succeſſion of little Lakes, which are at the End of that of the *Chetimachas*; and on the Right by the Iſlands *de la Chandeleur (Candlemas)*: It is thought that between theſe Iſlands there is a Paſſage for the largeſt Veſſels, and that it would be eaſy to make a good Port here. Great Barks may go up from the Sea to the Lake of the *Chetimachas*, and nothing hinders from going thither to cut down the fineſt Oaks in the World, with which all this Coaſt is covered.

Means of opening the principal Paſs.

I think it would be beſt to ſtop all the Paſſes but the principal one, and nothing would be eaſier; to effect this we need only guide the floating Trees into them, with which the River is almoſt always covered. From hence it would follow in the firſt Place, that nothing would enter the River, not even Barks and Canoes, but by one Paſſage, which would defend the Colony from Surpriſes; in the ſecond Place, that all the Force of the Current of the River being united, its ſole Mouth would deepen itſelf as well as the Bar. I found this Conjecture on what happened at the two Points cut off, which I mentioned before. Then there would be nothing more to do than to preſerve the Channel, and to hinder the floating Trees from cauſing any Obſtruction in it, which does not appear to me be very difficult.

Breadth of the River between the Paſſes.

As to what concerns the Breadth of the River between the Paſſes, *that is to ſay*, for the four Leagues from the Iſland *Toulouſe* to the Paſs of the South Weſt, it is never more than fifty Fathom: But immediately above this Paſs, the *Miſſiſſippi* inſenſibly recovers its uſual Breadth, which is never leſs than a Mile, and ſeldom more than two Miles. Its Depth also encreases from the Bar upwards, which is the Reverse of all other Rivers, which are commonly the deeper the nearer they come to the Sea.

It would be here a proper Place, Madam, to entertain you with the Causes of the Failure of those numerous Grants, which have made so much Noise in *France*, and on which so many Persons had built such mighty Hopes; but I had rather refer this to our first Interview, and confine myself at present to communicate to you my Thoughts of the Method that Persons should pursue in settling in this Country, if the bad Success of so many Efforts, and of such large Sums advanced to no Purpose, does not entirely disgust our Nation.

Where the Habitations ought to be placed.

It appears to me that the Habitations ought not to be placed on the Side of the River; but I would have them removed higher up the Country, at least a Quarter of a League, or even half a League. I am not ignorant that it is possible to be freed from the Inconveniencies of the common Floods, by making good Ditches; but I think it is a great Inconvenience to build upon a Soil, where if you dig ever so little, you immediately find Water; and of Consequence one can have no Cellars. I am also of Opinion, that they would be great by Gainers leaving the Lands all open to the annual Inundation of the River. The Mud that settles on them, when the Waters are gone off, renews and enriches them: One might employ a Part of them in Pasturage, the other might be sown with Rice, Pulse, and in general with every Thing that requires rich and wet Lands. In Time we should see on both Sides the *Mississippi* nothing but Gardens, Orchards and Meadows, which would be sufficient to feed the People, and would supply Matter for an useful Commerce with our Islands, and the other neighbouring Colonies. In short, I think I could answer for it, having landed twice or thrice every Day as I came down the River, that almost every where, at a little Distance from the Sides, we may find high Grounds, where we might build on a solid Foundation, and where Wheat would grow very well, when they have given Air to the Country by thinning the Woods.

Difficulty of navigating the River.

As to what concerns the Navigation of the River, it will always be difficult when we are to go up it, because of the Strength of the Current, which obliges us even in going down to be very cautious, often bears upon Points that run out, and upon Shoals; so that to navigate it safely, we must have Vessels that have both Sails and Oars. Moreover, as we cannot go forward at Night when it is cloudy, these Voyages will be always very tedious and expensive, at least

till

till the Borders of the River have Settlements near each other, on the whole Extent of the Country, that is between the *Illinois* and the Sea.

From whence proceeds the wrong Notion which they have in France *of this Country.*

Such, Madam, is this Country which they have so much talked of in *France* for some Years, and of which few People have a just Idea. We have not been the first *Europeans* to acknowledge the Goodness of it, and to neglect it. *Ferdinand de Soto* run over it for three whole Years, and his Historian *(a)* could not forgive him for not having made a solid Settlement here. " Where could " he go, says he, to do better ?"

Indeed I never heard *Louisiana* lightly spoken of, but by three Sorts of People that have been in the Country, and whose Testimony is certainly to be rejected. The first are the Mariners, who from the Road of *Ship Island*, or *Isle Dauphin*, could see nothing but that Island quite covered with a barren Sand, and the still more sandy Coast of *Biloxi*, and who suffered themselves to be persuaded that the Entrance of the *Missisippi* was impassable for Ships of a certain Bulk, or that it was necessary to go fifty Leagues up this River to find a Place that was habitable. They would have been quite of another Opinion, if they could have mistrusted those who talked to them in this Manner, and have discovered the Motives which induced them so to do.

The 2d Sort are poor Wretches, who being driven out of *France* for their Crimes, or bad Conduct, true or false, or who, whether to shun the Pursuit of their Creditors, have engaged themselves in the Troops and in the Grants. Both these looking upon this Country as a Place of Banishment, are disgusted at every Thing. They do not interest themselves in the Success of a Colony, of which they are Members against their Inclination, and they concern themselves very little about the Advantages which it may procure for the State: The greatest Part of them are not even capable of perceiving these Advantages.

The third Sort are those, who having seen nothing but Poverty in a Country on which excessive Expences have been bestowed, attribute to it without Reflection what we ought entirely to cast on the Incapacity, or on the Negligence, of those who had the Care of settling it. You also know very well the Reasons they had, to publish that *Louisiana* contained great Treasures, and that it brought us near the famous Mines of St. *Barbe*, and other still richer, from which they flattered themselves they should easily drive away the Possessors; and because these idle Stories had gained Credit with some silly People, instead of imputing to

(a) *Garcilasso de la Vega*'s History of the Conquest of *Florida*.

themſelves the Error, in which they were engaged by their fooliſh Credulity, they have diſcharged their Spleen on the Country, where they have found nothing of what had been promiſed them. *I am,* &c.

LETTER XXXII.

Deſcription of the BILOXI: *Of the* CASSINE, *or* APALACHINE: *Of the Myrtle Wax*: *Of* MAUBILE: *Of the Tchactas*: *Of the Bay of* ST. BERNARD. *Voyage from* BILOXI *to* NEW ORLEANS *by the Lake of* PONTCHARTRAIN.

MADAM, *On Board the* ADOUR, *April* 5.

Arrival at Biloxi.

THE 26th, after having cloſed my Letter, I embarked, and we prepared to ſail; but after we had made one Tack to the South, the Wind coming againſt us obliged us to return to our Anchorage, and to remain there the two following Days. The 29th we weighed Anchor early in the Morning, but the Wind was ſo weak, and the Sea ran ſo high, that in twenty-four Hours we made but fourteen Leagues, which was but half the Way we had to go. The 30th we had neither the Wind more favourable, nor the Sea more calm till towards four in the Afternoon, when a Shower of Rain cleared up the Weather, which was very thick, and calmed the Sea: But after an Hour or two the Miſt returned, and became ſo thick, that not being able to ſee how to ſteer our Veſſel, we came to an Anchor. The next Day as the Fog did not diſperſe, M. *de Pauger* and I went into the Boat, to gain the Road of *L'Iſle aux Vaiſſeaux (Ship Iſland)*; we viſited there ſome Ships of *France*, and we got back to *Biloxi* about five in the Afternoon.

Deſcription of the Coaſt and of the Road.

All this Coaſt is extremely flat; Merchant Ships cannot come nearer it than four Leagues, & the ſmalleſt Brigantine than two: And even theſe are obliged to go further off when the Wind is North or North-Weſt, or elſe they find themſelves on Ground; as it happened the Night before I debarked. The Road is the whole Length of *Ship Iſland*, which extends a ſmall League from Eaſt to Weſt, but has very little Breadth. To the Eaſt of this Iſland is *Dauphin Iſland*, formerly called *Maſſacre Iſland*, where there was a tolerable Port, which a Guſt of Wind ſhut up in two Hours, a little more than a Year ago, by filling the Entrance

trance of it with Sand. To the Weſt of *Ship Iſland* lie one behind the other, the Iſland *des Chats* or *de Bienville*, the Iſland a Corne, and the Iſles *de la Chandeleur*.

Deſcription of the Biloxi.

What they call the *Biloxi* is the Coaſt of the Main Land, which is to the North of the Road. This is the Name of a Nation of Savages which were ſettled there formerly, but who are now retired towards the North Weſt, on the Borders of a little River, called the *River of Pearls*, becauſe they have found in it a poor Sort of Pearls. They could not have choſen a worſe Situation for the General Quarters of the Colony; for it can neither receive any Sucours from the Ships, nor give them any for the Reaſons I have mentioned. Beſides this, the Road has two great Faults; the Anchorage is not good, and it is full of Worms, which damage all the Ships: The only Service it is of, is to ſhelter the Ships from a ſudden Guſt of Wind, when they come to diſcover the Mouth of the *Miſſiſſippi*, which having only low Lands, it would be dangerous to approach in bad Weather, without having firſt diſcovered it.

Of the Caſſine.

The *Biloxi* is not more valuable for its Land, than for its Sea. It is nothing but Sand, and there grows there little beſides Pines and Cedars. The *Caſſine*, otherwiſe called *Apalachine*, alſo grows there every where in Plenty. It is a very ſmall Shrub, the Leaves of which, infuſed like thoſe of Tea, paſs for a good Diſſolvent, and an excellent Sudorific; but its principal Quality is diuretic. The *Spaniards* uſe it in all *Florida*; it is even their common Drink. It began to be uſed in *Paris* when I left it; but we were then in a bad Time for new Trials; they dropt as ſuddenly as they were taken up. Nevertheleſs, I know that ſeveral Perſons who have uſed *Apalachine*, praiſe it greatly.

There are two Kinds, which differ only in the Size of the Leaves. Thoſe of the large Sort are above an Inch long, the others are little more than half that Length. In Shape and Subſtance they are much like the Leaves of Box, except that they are rounder at the Ends, and of a brighter Green. The Name of *Apalachine*, which we have given to this Shrub, comes from the *Apalaches*, a People of *Florida*, from whom the *Spaniards* learnt its Uſe, and this is their Manner of preparing it.

They ſet on the Fire in an earthen Pot a certain Quantity of Leaves, and they let them parch in it till their Colour becomes reddiſh, then they pour boiling Water on them gently, till the Pot is full. This Water takes the Colour of the Leaves, and it froths when it is poured out like Beer. They drink it as hot as poſſible, and the Savages would ſooner go without eating, than miſs drinking it Night and Morning; they think they ſhould be ſick

sick if they went without it, and it is said the *Spaniards* have the same Notion.

Half an Hour after they have taken it, it begins to pass off, and this lasts an Hour. It is hard to conceive how a Drink, which passes so soon through the Body, can be so nourishing as they say it is: It is easier to comprehend that it may cleanse away whatever hinders the Passage of the Urine, and causes Diseases of the Reins. When the Savages would purge themselves, they mix Sea Water with it, and this produces great Evacuations; but if the Dose of Sea Water is too strong, it may kill them; and this is not without Example. I have seen it taken in *France* without so much ado in preparing it, and in the Manner one makes Tea, but only doubling the Quantity, and making it boil near half an Quarter of an Hour; and I make no Doubt but that it has then a great Effect.

Of the Myrtle Wax.

They find here also a Kind of Myrtle with large Leaves, which I knew already was very common on the Coast of *Acadia*, and of the *English Colonies* on this Continent. Some give it the Name of *Laurel*, but they are mistaken: Its Leaves have the Smell of Myrtle, and the *English* always call it the *Candle Myrtle*. This Shrub bears a little Grain, which being thrown into boiling Water, swims upon it, and becomes a green Wax, less fat and more brittle than that of Bees, but as good to burn. The only Inconvenience they have found in it is, that it breaks too easily, but they might mix it with another Wax extremely liquid, which they get in the Woods of the Islands of *America*; which however is not necessary, unless they want to make large Tapers. I have seen Candles made of it, which gave as good a Light, and which lasted as long as our's. Our Missionaries of the Neighbourhood of *Acadia* mix Suet with it, which makes them apt to run, because the Suet does not mix well with this Wax.

The Sieur *Alexandre*, who is here in the Service of the Company in the Quality of Surgeon and Botanist, mixes nothing with it, and his Candles have not this Fault; their Light is soft and very clear, and the Smoke they make when they are blown out, has a Smell of Myrtle very agreeable. He is in Hopes of finding a Way to blanch them, and he shewed me a Mass of it, which was above half blanched *(a)*. He says, that if they would allow him five or six of those Slaves, who are least fit for the common Labours, to gather the Grain in the Season; he could make Wax enough to load a Ship every Year.

(a) This has not been followed, as is said, because this Wax is considerably altered in blanching.

At

At thirteen or fourteen Leagues from the *Biloxi*, inclining to the East, we find the River of the *Maubile*, which runs from the North to the South, & the Mouth of which is over-against *Dauphin Island*. It rises in the Country of the *Chicachas*, and its Course is about a hundred and thirty Leagues. Its Bed is very narrow, and it winds much, which does not hinder its being very rapid. But there are scarce any but the little Pettiaugres that can go up it when the Waters are low. We have on this River a Fort, which has been a long Time the principal Post of the Colony; yet the Lands are not good, but its Situation near the *Spaniards* made it convenient for trading with them, and this was all they sought for at that Time.

Of the Maubile.

It is reported, that at some Leagues beyond the Fort, they have discovered a Quarry; if this is true, and the Quarry abounds with Stone, it may prevent the entire Desertion of this Post, which many Inhabitants begin to forsake, being unwilling to cultivate any longer a Soil which does not answer the Pains they take to improve it. Nevertheless, I do not believe that they will easily resolve to evacuate the Fort of *Maubile*, though it should serve only to keep in our Alliance the *Tchactas*, a numerous People, who make us a necessary Barrier against the *Chicachas*, and against the Savages bordering on *Carolina*. *Garcilasso de la Vega*, in his History of *Florida*, speaks of a Village called *Mauvilla*, which no doubt gave its Name to the River, and to the Nation that was settled on its Borders. These *Mauvilians* were then very powerful; at present there are hardly any Traces left of them.

They are at present engaged in seeking to the West of the *Mississippi*, a Place fit to make a Settlement, which may bring us nearer to *Mexico*; and they think they have found it at a hundred Leagues from the Mouth of the River, in a Bay which bears the Name sometimes of *St. Magdalen*, and sometimes of *St. Louis*, but oftener that of *St. Bernard*. It receives many Rivers, some of which are pretty large, and it was there that M. *de la Sale* landed, when he missed the Mouth of the *Mississippi*. A Brigantine has been sent lately thither to reconnoitre it, but they found there some Savages, who appear little disposed to receive us, and whom they did not treat in such a Manner as to gain them to us. I also hear that the *Spaniards* have very lately prevented this Design, by settling there before us.

Of the Bay St. Bernard.

There is in Truth something more pressing, aud better to be done, than this Enterprize. I know that Commerce is the Soul of Colonies, and that they are of no Use to such a Kingdom as our's our's but for this End, and to hinder our Neighbours from growing too powerful; but if they do not begin by cultivating the Lands, Commerce, after having enriched ſome private Perſons, will ſoon drop, and the Colony will not be eſtabliſhed. The Neighbourhood of the *Spaniards* may have its Uſe, but let us leave it to them to approach us as much as they will, we are not in a Condition, and we have no Need, to extend ourſelves farther. They are peaceable enough in this Country, and they will never be ſtrong enough to give us any Uneaſineſs. It is not even their Intereſt to drive us out of this Country; and if they do not comprehend it yet, they will without Doubt ſoon be ſenſible that they cannot have a better Barrier againſt the *Engliſh* than *Louiſiana*.

The Climate of the Biloxi.

The Heat was already very troubleſome at the *Biloxi* in the Middle of *March*, and I judge that when the Sun has once heated the Sand on which we walk here, the Heat muſt be exceſſive. They ſay indeed that without the Breeze, which riſes pretty regularly every Day between nine and ten in the Morning, and continues till Sun-ſet, it would be impoſſible to live here. The Mouth of the *Miſſiſſippi* is in 29° Latitude, and the Coaſt of the *Biloxi* is in thirty. We had here in the Month of *February* ſome cold Weather, when the Wind blew from the North and North Weſt, but it did not laſt long; and it was even followed by great Heats, with Thunder and Lightening, and Storms; ſo that in the Morning we were in Winter, and in the Afternoon in Summer, with ſome ſmall Intervals of Spring and Autumn between both. The Breeze comes generally from the Eaſt: When it comes from the South, it is only a reflected Wind, which is much leſs refreſhing; but it is ſtill a Wind, and when it fails entirely there is no breathing.

Departure from the Biloxi.

The 24th of *March* I departed from the *Biloxi*, where I had been ſtopt by a Jaundice, which held me above a Month, and I returned to *New Orleans*, where I was to embark in a Pink belonging to the Company, named the *Adour*. I made this Voyage in a Pettiaugre, and I never yet made one more diſagreeable. Five Leagues from the *Biloxi*, the Weſt Wind, which in three Hours brought me there, gave Place to a South Wind ſo violent, that I was obliged to ſtop. I had ſcarce Time to ſet up my Tent, before we were overflowed with a Deluge of Rain, accompanied with Thunder.

Two little Veſſels that ſet out with me, were willing to take Advantage of the Wind, which carried them a great Way in a few Hours, and I was very ſorry that I could not do the ſame, but I ſoon heard that their Fate deſerved rather Pity than

Envy: The firſt was in continual Danger of being loſt, and her Paſſengers arrived at *New Orleans* rather dead than alive. The other was run a-ground about half Way, and five Perſons were drowned in a Meadow, of which the Storm had made a Lake. The Wind continued all Night with the ſame Violence, and the Rain did not ceaſe till the next Day at Noon. It began again at Night, and continued till Day, with Thunder.

Obſervation on this Coaſt.

When we ſail in Sight of this Coaſt, it appears very pleaſant, but when we come nearer it is not the ſame Thing. It is all along a Sand, as at the *Biloxi*, and we find on it only poor Woods. I obſerved here a Kind of Sorrel, which has the ſame Taſte as our's, but the Leaves of which are narrower; and which cauſes, as they ſay, the Bloody-Flux. There is alſo in theſe Parts a Kind of Aſh, which they call *Bois d'Amourette (Lovers Wood)*, the Bark of which is full of Prickles, and paſſes for a ſovereign Remedy, and very ſpeedy againſt the Tooth-Ach.

The 26th it rained all the Day, and tho' the Sea was calm, we made little Way. We got a little farther the 27th, but the following Night we went out of our Courſe above the Iſland of *Pearls*. The next Day we went and encamped at the Entrance of Lake *Pontchartrain*, having left a little before on the Right the River of *Pearls*, which has three Mouths. The Separation of theſe three Branches is at four Leagues from the Sea, and the *Biloxies* are a little above it.

Of the Lake of Pontchartrain.

In the Afternoon we croſſed the Lake of *Pontchartrain*: This Traverſe is ſeven or eight Leagues, and at Midnight we entered the *Bayouc* of *St. John*. Thoſe who firſt navigated this Lake, found it, as they ſay, ſo full of Caimans, that they could ſcarce give a Stroke of the Oar without hitting one. They are at preſent very ſcarce in it, and we only ſaw ſome Traces of them at our encamping; for theſe Animals lay their Eggs on the Land.---After I had reſted myſelf a little at coming out of the Lake, I purſued my Way by Land, and I arrived at *New Orleans* before Day.

Difficulty of the Navigation down the River.

The *Adour* was gone from thence, but not far, and I came up with her the next Day, the firſt of *April*. The Inundation was at its Height, and of Conſequence the River much more rapid than I found it two Months before. Moreover, a Ship, eſpecially a Pink, is not ſo eaſily worked as a Sloop; and as our Sailors were not uſed to this Navigation, we had a great deal of Trouble to get out of the River. The Ship, driven ſometimes to one Shore, and ſometimes to the other, often tangled its Yards and Tackling in the Trees, and they were obliged more than once to cut away ſome of the Tackling, to free us from this Embarraſſment. It was worſe ſtill when we came to the Paſſes, for the Currents always drew us into the neareſt with great Violence. We got even into one of the ſmalleſt, and I could never yet conceive how we could get out again. We came off however with the Loſs of an Anchor, which we left there: We had already loſt one two Days before, ſo that we had only two remaining. Such a bad Beginning, made us a little thoughtful, but the Youth and little Skill of thoſe with whom they had truſted us, gave us ſtill more Uneaſineſs.

The Ship ill commanded.

The *Adour* is a very pretty Veſſel, of three hundred Tons Burthen. It ſailed from *France* with a very good Crew, under the Conduct of a Captain who underſtood his Buſineſs, and a Lieutenant who had a very good Character. The latter was left ſick at *St. Domingo:* The Captain, ſoon after his Arrival at the *Biloxi*, quarrelled with one of the Directors of the Company, who diſplaced him. To ſupply the Places of theſe two Officers, they have choſen a young Man of *St. Malo*, who came three Years ago to *Louiſiana*, in the Station of Pilot's Mate, or Apprentice, and who ſince that Time got the Command of a Sloop in the Road of the *Biloxi*, to go ſometimes to *la Maubile*, and ſometimes to *New Orleans*, with Proviſions. He appears to have every Thing that is requiſite to become a ſkilful Mariner; he loves his Buſineſs, and applies himſelf to it; but we ſhould be very willing to ſee nothing of his little Experience, eſpecially in a Navigation which is attended with great Difficulties.

He has for his ſecond, an Officer who came from *France* in the Quality of Enſign; he alſo is a young Man, very fit to be a Subaltern under Principals of Experience, who would leave nothing to him but the Care of executing their Orders. It would be hard to find a Seaman of more Courage in a Storm, which he has been uſed to from his Childhood, in the painful Fiſheries of *Newfoundland*; and two or three Shipwrecks, from which he has happily eſcaped, has given him a Confidence, which I ſhall be much ſurpriſed, if he does not come into a bad Plight by.

Our firſt Pilot appears a little more experienced than theſe two Officers, and they depend much on the Knowledge he has of the Channel of *Bahama*, which he has paſſed once already. But this is but little to be acquainted with this Paſſage the moſt dangerous that there is in the *American* Seas, and where they reckon Shipwrecks by thouſands. Moreover, I am greatly apprehenſive that a certain ſelf-ſufficient Air which I obſerve in him, will produce ſome fatal Effect. He has two Subalterns,

 who

who are very good natured Fellows; we have fifty Sailors of *Bretagne*, a little mutinous, but ſtrong and vigorous; almoſt all have been at the Cod-Fiſhery, and that is a good School. The Seamen appear to be Men of Judgment and Experience.

In Spite of all theſe Hindrances which I have mentioned, we anchored on the Outſide the Bar the 2d at Night; we paſſed it the 3d, and for Want of Wind we could go no farther. Yeſterday we were again ſtopt all the Day, and this Night we have had a Storm from the South, which made us give Thanks to the Lord that we were not at Sea ſo near the Coaſt. I hope, Madam, to write to you in a ſhort Time from *St. Domingo*, whither our Pink is bound to take in a Cargo of Sugar, which lays there ready for us. I take the Advantage of a Sloop which is going up to *New Orleans*, to ſend this Letter to you by a Veſſel that is bound directly for *France*.

I am, &c.

LETTER XXXIII.

Voyage to the Channel of BAHAMA. *Shipwreck of the* ADOUR: *Return to* LOUISIANA *along the Coaſt of* FLORIDA: *Deſcription of that Coaſt.*

MADAM, *At the* BILOXI, *June* 5.

I Promiſed to write to you immediately from *St. Domingo.* But behold after two Months I am here, as far off as I was then: The Recital of the ſad Event that has brought me back to this Colony, and which has but too well juſtified my Apprehenſions, with ſome Obſervations on a Country which I did not expect to ſee, will make the Subject of this Letter. I am not, however, ſo much to be pitied as you may think. I am very well recovered of my Fatigues. I have gone through great Dangers, but have happily eſcaped from them: The Evil that is paſt is but a Dream, and often a pleaſant one.

The Adour *ſets Sail.*

It was but half an Hour at moſt, after I had cloſed my Letter, when the Wind coming to the North Weſt we prepared to ſail. I thought that the Reſpect due to the ſacred Day of *Eaſter* would have engaged the Captain to have waited till the next Day, eſpecially as it was paſt Noon; but he had few Proviſions, and one Day's Delay might have bad Conſequences. Our

 Haſte

Haste was attended with still worse. We soon lost Sight of Land, and at the End of an Hour's Sail, after having had the Pleasure of seeing the Waters of the River and those of the Sea mix together without being blended, we no longer perceived any Difference, finding only Salt Water.

It may be said, perhaps, that we had quitted the right Channel, and I allow that it may be true; but that Struggle which we observed so near the Mouth, does not shew a River victorious, that opens itself a free Passage, and for twenty Leagues gives Laws to the Ocean. Besides, if this Fact was true, at least in the Time of the Inundation, in which Time we were, how came we to have so much Trouble to find the Mouth of the River? The Difference alone of the Colour of the Waters would have discovered it to any the least attentive.

Observation on the Waters of the Mississippi.

In Regard to this Colour, I have said that the *Mississippi*, after its Junction with the *Missouri*, took the Colour of the Waters of that River, which are white: But would you believe it, Madam, that of all the Waters, that we can take for a Ship's Provision, there are none which keep sweet so long as these? Besides this, they are excellent to drink when they have been left to settle in Jars, at the Bottom of which they leave a Kind of white Tartar, which, in all Likelihood, serves equally to give them the Colour they have, to purify them, and to preserve them.

Description of the North Coast of Cuba.

The 12th at Noon, after having suffered excessive Heats for several Days, and more intolerable still in the Night than in the Day, we discovered Cape *Sed*, which is on the North Coast of the Isle of *Cuba*, and very high. At Sun-set we were over-against it, we then steered to the East, and sailed in Sight of the Shore; the next Morning, at Day-break, we were over-against the HAVANNAH: This City is about eighteen Leagues from Cape *Sed*, and about half-way we discover a very high Mountain, the Top of which is a Kind of Platform. They call it the *Table of Marianne*.

Two Leagues beyond the *Havannah*, there is a little Fort on the Coast, which is called *la Hougue*, from whence we begin to discover the *Pain de Matance (the Bread of Matance)*. This is a Mountain, the Top of which resembles an Oven, or if you please, a Loaf. It serves to reconnoitre the Bay of *Matance*, which is fourteen Leagues Distance from the *Havannah*. The Heat continued increasing, and indeed we were on the Confines of the Torrid Zone: And withal, we had scarce any Wind, and got forward only by Favour of the Current, which runs to the East.

The

The 14th, about six in the Evening, we discovered from the Top of the main Mast the Coast of *Florida*. There is no prudent Mariner, who on discovering this Coast, if he has not at least six or seven Hours Day-Light to run, does not tack about and keep off the Land till the next Day, there being no Coast in the World where it is of more Importance to see every Thing clearly, because of the Diversity of the Currents, which we must never flatter ourselves that we certainly know. We had an Instance of no long Date in the *Spanish* Galleons, which were lost here some Years ago, for Want of the Precaution which I have just mentioned. The Chevalier *d' Here*, Captain of a Ship, who accompanied them, did all in his Power to engage the General of the Flota to wait till Day-Light to enter into the Channel, but he could not succeed with him, and he did not think proper to throw himself away along with him. Our Captain, who had received good Instructions on this Head, had resolved to make Use of them; but too great Readiness to hearken to others had the same Effect with Regard to him, as Presumption had on the *Spanish* General. His first Pilot, who thought himself the most skilful Man in the World, and his Lieutenant, who knew not how to doubt of any Thing, were of Opinion to continue the Route, and he had not the Resolution to oppose them. He proposed at least to make the North East, and the Consequences proved, that if his Opinion had prevailed, we had escaped Shipwreck. But he could prevail only for making the North North East, the Pilot positively affirming that the Currents bore violently to the East. He said the Truth, but it is only when we are near the Land on that Side, as they bear to the West on the other Side, on which we then were.

Shipwreck of the Adour.

At seven o'Clock the Land appeared still at a considerable Distance, and they could not see it but from the Round-Top; but half an Hour after, the Weather growing cloudy, a Sailor observed by the Help of some Flashes of Lightening, that the Water had changed Colour. He gave Notice of it, but his Information was received with Laughter, they told him it was the Lightening that had made the Water appear white. He still maintained his Opinion, many of his Companions were soon brought to agree with him: The Officers would have made a Jest of it still, but they cried so loud, and were so many in the same Opinion, that the Captain ordered the Lead to be thrown out. They found but six Fathom Water; the only sure Step they could have taken was to cast Anchor that Moment, but there was no Anchor ready. They thought to tack about, and perhaps it had been Time enough, if they had used Dispatch; but they

amused

amused themselves with sounding again, and they found only five Fathom Water. Presently after they sounded again and found only three. Represent to yourself, Madam, a Parcel of Children, who seeing themselves drawn towards the Brink of a Precipice, are only attentive to know the Depth of it, without taking any Measures to avoid it.

Now there arose a confused Noise, every Man cried out as loud as he could bawl, the Officers could not make themselves heard, and two or three Minutes after the Ship ran aground: There rose at this Instant a Kind of Storm, and the Rain which followed soon after made the Wind fall; but it soon rose again, settled in the South, and grew stronger than before. The Ship began immediately to lay hard upon her Helm, and they were afraid that the Main-Mast, which at every Shock rose pretty high, would jump out of its Step and split the Ship's Bottom. It was tried in the usual Way, condemned, and cut down immediately, after the Captain had given it the first Stroke with a Hatchet, according to Custom.

Then the Lieutenant went into the Boat, to try to discover in what Place we were, and in what Condition the Ship was. He observed that in the fore Part we had but four Feet Water, that the Bank on which we were wrecked was so small, that it was but just large enough to receive the Ship, and that all round it she would have floated. But if we had escaped this Bank, we could not have shunned another, for we were surrounded with them, and it is certain we should not have met with one so commodious.

The Wind continued to blow violently; our Ship continued to bear hard upon her Helm, and at every Shock we expected it to split. All the Effects of Fear were painted on our Faces, and after the first Tumult formed by the Cries of the Sailors who worked the Ship, and by the Groans of the Passengers, who expected Death every Moment, a deep and mournful Silence prevailed through all the Company. We heard afterwards that some Persons took their Measures secretly not to be nonplushed, in Case the Vessel should go to Pieces: Not only the Boat, but the Canoe also were in the Water, with every Thing in Readiness, and some trusty Sailors were ordered privately to be ready at the first Signal. They assured me afterwards, that they had agreed not to leave me in the Danger.

This is certain, that I passed the Night without closing my Eyes, and in the Situation of a Man who does not expect to see the Day again. It appeared however, and discovered to us the Land at more than two Leagues from us. It was not that, which we discovered at first, and which we saw still at a great Distance, but a low Land, and which appeared to us very unfit

to

to be inhabited. Neverthelefs, this Sight was a Pleafure to us, and gave us a little Courage.

Meafures which they take to fave themfelves.

Then they confidered if there was no Likelihood of getting the *Adcur* afloat again, and becaufe it was good to have feveral Strings to our Bow, they thought at the fame Time of the Means of getting out of fuch a bad Situation, fuppofing it impoffible to recover the Ship. Then they recollected that they fhipped a flat-bottom'd Boat, with Defign to ufe it at *St. Domingo,* to load the Sugars they were to take in there. This was a very prudent Precaution of the Captain, who had been told that in that Country the Loading often detains Ships in the Road much longer than is convenient for the Intereft of the Owners, and the Health of the Ship's Company: But Providence had another View without Doubt in infpiring him with this Thought. This Boat faved us.

I do not well know what paffed the fame Day between the Officers and the Pilot, but there was no more Talk of recovering the Veffel. Many have faid, that all their Efforts for this Purpofe would have been ufelefs; but the Captain complained to me more than once, that they would not fuffer him to make this Attempt in the Way he chofe. They refolved therefore the fame Day to carry all the People to Land, and they laboured all the Morning to make a Raft, that they might not be obliged to make feveral Trips.

However, they did not think proper yet to forfake the Ship, and there were none but the Paffengers that were embarked in the Long-Boat, and on the Raft. At a Gun-Shot from the Ship we found the Sea very high, and the Bifket which we were carrying to Land was wetted: A little Pettiaugre that followed the Boat could with Difficulty keep above Water, and the Raft, which carried twenty-two Men, was carried fo far by the Current, that we thought it loft.

Savages of the Iflands of the Martyrs.

The Boat, in which I was, made Hafte to Land, that it might go to affift the others; but as we were ready to go afhore, we perceived a pretty large Company of Savages armed with Bows and Arrows, which approached us. This Sight made us reflect, that we were without Arms, and we ftopt fome Time without daring to advance. We even thought, all Things well confidered, that it would be imprudent to go any farther. The Savages perceived our Diftrefs, and eafily conceived the Caufe of it. They came near us, and cried out to us in *Spanifh,* that they were Friends. When they faw this did not encourage us, they quitted their Arms, and came to us, being up to the Waift in Water.

We

We were ſoon ſurrounded by them, and it is certain, that embarraſſed as we were with Things in a Boat, where we could not ſtir, it was very eaſy for them to deſtroy us. They aſked us at firſt if we were *Engliſh*; we anſwered them, we were not, but Allies and good Friends of the *Spaniards:* They ſeemed much rejoiced at this, inviting us to land on their Iſland, and aſſuring us we ſhould be as ſafe there as in our Ship. Miſtruſt on ſome Occaſions only ſerves to diſcover Weakneſs, and gives Riſe to dangerous Surmiſes. Therefore, we thought it beſt to accept the Invitation of theſe Barbarians, and followed them to their Iſland, which we found to be one of the Iſlands called *the Martyrs*.

What paſſed between them and us.

But what ſeems moſt remarkable is, that we determined to take this Step upon the coming up of the Pettiaugre, in which there were but five or ſix Men, whilſt we were talking with the Savages; we certainly ran a great Riſque in truſting ourſelves without Arms into the Hands of theſe *Floridians*, and we were well convinced of it in the Sequel: Four or five Men more were not capable of making them change their Deſign, ſuppoſing theſe Barbarians had any ill Intentions againſt us; and I never think of the Boldneſs which this light Reinforcement inſpired us with, but I repreſent to myſelf thoſe Perſons, who cannot go alone in the dark, and whom the Preſence of a Child immediately emboldens, by employing their Imagination, which alone cauſes all their Fear.

However, we were no ſooner landed on the Iſland, than we began to diſtruſt the Officers, having likewiſe but little Ground to depend on the Savages. The Captain of the *Adour* had brought us hither; but as ſoon as he had put us on Shore, he took Leave of us, ſaying, he was obliged to return on Board, where he had many Things to do, and he would ſend us directly whatever we wanted, eſpecially Arms. There was nothing in this but what was reaſonable, and we eaſily conceived that his Preſence was neceſſary in his Ship: But we reflected that he had brought away only the Paſſengers, and that all the Ship's Company would be compleat, upon the Return of the Captain.

The Paſſengers begin to diſtruſt the Ship's Company.

This made us ſuſpect that the Boat, which they ſpoke of to us, was only a Lure to amuſe us, and they had only landed us as People that were a Burthen to them, that they might take Advantage of the Boat and the Canoe, to go to the *Havannah*, or to *St. Auguſtin* in *Florida*. We were all more confirmed in theſe Suſpicions, when we found that we all had the ſame Thought; this

his Agreement made us judge that it was not without Foundation:. Upon which it was resolved among us, that I should return with the Captain to the Ship, in order to prevent unjust Resolutions, if they were tempted to take any.

I therefore declared to the Captain, that since his Chaplain resolved to stay in the Island, it was not proper that I should remain there also; that it was better to separate us, and that I was resolved not to lay from on board the Ship, whilst any Person remained on board. He seemed a little surprised at my Discourse, but he made no Objection, and we set off. I found on my Arrival at the Ship, that they had spread the Sails, to see, as they said, if it was possible to disengage it. But there were many other Manœuvres to make for this End, and they did not think fit to try them.

Several Passengers saved by a good Providence.

In half an Hour the Wind turned to the East, and grew very strong, which obliged us to furl the Sails: But this Storm proved the Means of saving those who were upon the Float, and who had been carried a great Way out to Sea: The Billows drove them back again towards us, and as soon as we perceived them, the Captain sent them his Long-Boat, which took them in Tow, and brought them again to the Ship. These unfortunate People, who were for the most Part poor Passengers, expected nothing but Death, and on our Side, we began to despair of saving them, when Providence raised this little Storm to save them from perishing at Sea.

My Presence was more necessary in the Ship than I had imagined. The Sailors, during the Captain's Absence, were resolved to drown in Wine their Sorrow and Cares. In Spite of the Lieutenant, whom they did not much respect, and whom many did not love, they had broke open the Locker that secured the Stores, and we found them almost all dead drunk. And I saw some Symptoms amongst them of Mutiny and Desertion, from which I judged there was every Thing to fear, if it was not remedied betimes; and the more, as the Captain, tho' liked well enough by the Sailors, knew not how to make himself obeyed by the inferior Officers, the greatest Part of whom were much inclined to mutiny, and who could not bear his Lieutenant.

Trouble from the Savages.

To encrease our Uneasiness, a Company of Savages followed us close, and we conceived, that if we had no Violence to fear from them, it would not be easy to shun their Importunities, and particularly, that we ought to guard well what we were not willing to lose. The most distinguished called himself Don *Antonio*, and spoke *Spanish* pretty well. He had learnt still better the *Spanish* Gravity and Manners. If he saw any one well dressed,

 he

he asked him if he was a *Cavallero*, and he had begun with telling us that he was one, and the most distinguished of his Nation. However, he had not very noble Inclinations; he longed for every Thing he saw, and if they had not been denied, he and his Company had left us nothing but what they could not carry away. He asked me for my Girdle; I told him I could not spare it; he conceived that it was only necessary for my Cassock, and asked it of me with great Importunities.

Who these Savages were.

We learnt of him that almost all the Savages of his Village had been baptized at the *Havannah*, whither they made a Voyage once a Year. They are forty-five Leagues distant from it, and they make this Passage in little Pettiaugres very flat, in which People would not venture to cross the *Seine* at *Paris*. Don *Antonio* farther informed us that he had a King, who was called Don *Diego*, and that we should see him next Day. He then asked us what Resolution we intended to take, and offered to conduct us to *St. Augustin*. We let him know that we took his Offer in good Part, we treated him and all his Company well, and they returned well satisfied to all Appearance.

The Bodies of these Savages are redder than any I have yet seen: We could never learn the Name of their Nation: But although they did not appear to have the best Disposition, they did not seem to us so mischievous, as to be of those *Calos* or *Carlos*, so much decried for their Cruelties, and whose Country is not far from the *Martyrs*. I do not believe that these are Men-Eaters; but perhaps they behaved so well to us only because we were the strongest. I know not what Quarrel they have had with the *English*, but we had great Reason to believe that they did not love them. The Visit of Don *Antonio* might very well proceed from no other Motive than to enquire if we were not of that Nation, or if it would not be too great a Risque for them to attack us.

Disturbance in the Ship.

The 16th I thought myself obliged to go to encourage those who remained in the Island, and to whom the Savages kept the Promise they had made them the Evening before. I passed almost the whole Day with them; and in the Evening, at my Return, I found all the Ship in an Uproar. The Authors of the Disturbance were inferior Officers, and all the best Sailors were of their Side. They wanted to be revenged of the Lieutenant; who till then, as they said, had treated them with great Haughtiness and Severity. The Wine, which they had at Discretion, heated their Heads more and more, and it was scarce any longer possible to make them hear Reason.

The Captain ſhewed on this Occaſion a Prudence, a Steadineſs, and a Moderation, which one would not have expected from his Age, his Want of Experience, and his paſt Conduct: He knew how to make himſelf beloved and feared by People, who ſcarce any longer hearkened to any Thing but their Fury and Caprice. The Lieutenant, on his Part, confounded the moſt mutinous by his Intrepidity; and having found Means to ſeparate and employ them, he carried his Point, and reduced them to Obedience. They had at laſt got from the Bottom of the Hold, the Boat ſo much promiſed, and they had carried it to the Iſland. It was neceſſary to fit it up, and to lodge themſelves till it was ready, and to get out of the Ship Proviſions and Ammunition, to fortify themſelves againſt any Surprize of the Savages. The Captain employed in theſe Works all thoſe whom he moſt diſtruſted; and entreated of me to ſtay on board, to aſſiſt the Lieutenant in keeping the reſt to their Duty.

The Steadineſs of the Officers.

The 17th, at Day-break, there appeared a Sail two Leagues from us. We made Signals of Diſtreſs with our Flag *(a)*, and ſome Time after we obſerved that he lay by to wait for us. Immediately the Lieutenant took the Canoe, and went aboard to aſk the Captain if he would take us all in. But it was only a Brigantine of one hundred Tons, which had been plundered by Pirates, and which for three Days had made many Efforts to get out of this Bay; where the Currents, the Captain ſaid, being ſtronger this Year than had ever been known, had drawn his Brigantine againſt all his Endeavours to the contrary, though he made the Eaſt-North-Eaſt. It is true, that we had this only from our Lieutenant, whom ſome ſuſpected of inventing this Story, that he might attribute to the Strength and Irregularity of the Currents, the Misfortune in which his Obſtinacy had engaged us.

An English *Ship endeavours in vain to relieve them.*

However that might be, the *Engliſh* Captain conſented to take in twenty Perſons, if we would ſupply him with Proviſions and Water, of which they were in great Want. The Condition was accepted, and the Captain approached us in Fact, with Intention to drop an Anchor as near us as poſſible; but a ſtrong Wind from the South riſing on a ſudden, he was obliged to purſue his Route, that he might not expoſe himſelf to the Danger of being loſt, in endeavouring to ſuccour us. The 19th we again ſaw three Ships under Sail. They went to make them the ſame Propoſals as to the firſt, but they could not perſuade them to

(a) This is done by hoiſting the Flag to the Top of the Staff, and twiſting it about it ſo that it can't fly abroad.

accept them. They were also *English*, who complained of being plundered by Pirates.

The same Day, as there was nothing left in the *Adour* that we could carry away, we took our last Leave of her, with so much the more Regret, as that for the four Days which she had been a-ground, she had not taken a Drop of Water; and we went all to Land after Sun-set. We found here some Tents, which they had set up with the Sails of the Ship; a Guard-House, where Day and Night they kept a strict Watch; and some Provisions, well secured in a Warehouse, where they also kept a Guard.

Description of the Martyr *Islands.*

The Island in which we were, might be about four Leagues in Compass. There were some to the Right and Left of different Extents; and that where the Savages had their Cabins, was the least of all, and the nearest our's. They lived there entirely by fishing; and all this Coast abounds with Fish, in Proportion as the Earth is incapable of supplying any Necessaries for Life. As to their Dress, some Leaves of Trees, or a Piece of Bark, suffices them; they have nothing covered but what Decency teaches all Men to hide.

The Soil of these Islands is a very fine Sand, or rather a Kind of Lime calcin'd, every where intermixed with a white Coral, which is easily reduced to Powder. There are also only Bushes and Shrubs here, without a single Tree. The Shores of the Sea are covered with tolerably fine Shells; and they find here some Sponges, which seem to be thrown up by the Waves of the Sea in stormy Weather. They say, that what keeps the Savages here, are the Shipwrecks, which are common enough in the Channel of *Bahama*, and of which they always make their Advantage. We do not see even a single Beast in all these Islands; which seem to be accursed by GOD and Man, and where there would be no Inhabitants, if there were not found some Men solely attentive to take Advantage of other's Misfortunes, and often to put the finishing Stroke to them.

Visit from the Cacique of the Savages.

The 20th Don *Diego* paid us a Visit. He is a young Man, of a Stature under the middle Size, and of an Appearance bad enough. He was almost as naked as his Subjects, and the few Clothes he had on were not worth picking off a Dunghill. He had about his Head a Kind of Fillet, of I know not what Stuff, and which some Travellers would certainly have called a *Diadem*. He had no Attendants, no Mark of Dignity; nothing, in a Word, to shew who he was. A young Woman pretty well shaped, and decently dressed as a Savage, accompanied him, and they told us it was the Queen his Spouse.

We received their *Floridian* Majesties with some Stateliness; however, we showed them some Marks of Friendship, and they seemed very well satisfied with us. But we could discover nothing in these or those Caciques, whose Power and Riches are so highly extolled by the Historian of *Florida*. We said a few Words to Don *Diego*, of the Offer that Don *Antonio* had made to us, to carry us to *St. Augustine*, and he gave us Room to hope, that he would do us all the Services that lay in his Power. To engage him the more in our Interest, I made him a Present of one of my Shirts, and he received it with a great deal of Thankfulness.

Authority of this Cacique.

He came again the next Day, wearing my Shirt over his Rags, which hung down to his Heels; and he let us know that he was not properly the Sovereign of his Nation, but that he held his Dignity under another Cacique, farther off. However, he is absolute in his own Village, and had just then given a very good Proof of it. Don *Antonio*, who appeared to be twice his Age, and who could easily have beaten two such, came to see us soon after, and told us that Don *Diego* had thrashed him soundly, because he had got drunk in the *River*, where, in all Likelihood, they had forgotten some Remains of Brandy. — The most considerable Difference that appears between the Savages of *Canada* and those of *Florida*, is the Dependence which the latter have on their Chiefs, and the Respect they shew them. Also we see not in them, as in the Savages of *Canada*, those elevated Sentiments, and that Nobleness which Independence produces, and which is supplied in civilized States by the Principles of Religion and Honour, which proceed from Education.

Don Diego *excuses himself for not giving us Guides to* St. Augustin.

The 22d, Don *Diego* came to dine with us without Ceremony, dressed as the Day before. He seemed to be much pleased with this Dress, which gave him nevertheless a very ridiculous Air; which, added to his ill Look, made him exactly resemble a Man who goes to make the *Amende honorable* (a). Either from Religion or Antipathy, we could never engage him to eat any Meat: We had still the Remains of a Fish, which he had sent us the Day before, he eat some of this, and drank Water.

After Dinner, we were willing to talk of Business; but he told us directly, that after having well considered of our Proposal, he could neither give us Don *Antonio*, nor any of his People, to

(a) *Tenue*, to do Penance in a white Sheet, with a Torch in his Hand.

conduct

conduct us to *St. Augustin*, because on the Route which we were obliged to take there were some numerous Nations, with whom he was at War. I know not whether they did not then repent of having so inconsiderately forsaken the *Adour*, for after Don *Diego* left us, they sent the Canoe to her; but those who went in it to her, told us at their Return, that the Savages had broke her to Pieces, and that she was filling with Water.

They deliberate on the Course they are to take.

The 23d, the Boat was finished, and they thought in earnest to resolve what Course to take. They had the Choice of two, and they were divided: Some were for hazarding the Passage to the *Havannah*, the others were for following the Coast to *St. Augustin*. The latter Course seemed the safest, the former was the shortest. But if this was a prudent Course, we ought to have done it the Day after the Shipwreck, or rather have sent the Long-Boat to the *Havannah*, to have informed the Governor of our Situation, and to have asked him to send us a Brigantine. The Rigging alone of the *Adour*, would have been more than sufficient to have repaid the Expences he might have been at.

They are divided.

However that might be, the greatest Part of the Ship's Company were of the last Opinion; it was impossible to bring them to any other. They were forty; and they demanded the Boat and the Canoe, and we were obliged to yield to their Request. The Chaplain of the *Adour* was of this Number: If it had not been so, I should have thought myself obliged to accompany them; but it was necessary to divide the spiritual Aids, as we did the Provisions. The next Morning, after Mass, the Chaplain, who was a *Dominican* Father, desired that I would bless the three Vehicles: I obeyed, and I baptized the Boat, and called it the *St. Saviour*. In the Evening after Prayers, I made a last Effort to bring all our People to be of one Opinion: I easily obtained, that the Day following they should depart together, that they should go to encamp in the Island that was farthest from the Land, and that they should determine there according to the Wind.

We departed in Fact the 25th about Noon, and we sailed together for several Leagues; but towards Sun-set, we saw the Boat take the Channel, that they must cross to go to the *Havannah*, without concerning themselves about the Canoe, whose Provisions they carried; and which not being able to follow them, was obliged to join us. We received them kindly, tho' amongst those who were in it, there were some whom we had Reason not to be pleased with. We landed in the Island, where we had agreed all to unite, and where a Company of Savages were come already, I know not with what Design. We were upon our

Guard

Guard all Night, and we departed very early in the Morning.

The Weather was charming, and the Sea fine, and our Company began to envy those that were in the Boat, as having taken the better Course. Some began to murmur at it, & our Chiefs thought it best to seem willing to satisfy them: So they took the Route of the Channel. After two Hours, the Wind grew stronger, and they fancied they saw the Appearances of a Storm; then they all agreed that it was Rashness to engage ourselves in such a long Traverse, in such Boats as our's; for nothing could be weaker than our Boats, which took Water every where: But as to go to *St. Augustin*, we must have gone all the Way back which we had made hitherto, we unanimously agreed to go towards the *Biloxi*.

The Boat takes the Route of the Biloxi.

So we made the West, but we did not advance much that Day, and we were obliged to pass the Night in the Boat, which was far from having Room enough for us all to lay down. The 27th, we encamped in an Island, where we found some Cabins forsaken, some Paths a great deal trodden, and the Footsteps of *Spanish* Shoes. This is the first of the *Turtle Islands*. The Soil is the same as at the *Martyrs*. I can't conceive what Men can do in such a bad Country, and so distant from any human Habitation. We still steered West, and we sailed with such a Rapidity, that could only proceed from the Currents.

Great Currents between the Martyrs *and the* Turtle Islands.

We went a great Way again the 25th, till Noon. Though we had little Wind, the Islands seemed to run Post-haste by the Side of us. At Noon we took the Elevation, which we found twenty-four Degrees fifteen Minutes. If our Sea Charts were exact, we were at the West End of the *Turtle Islands*. It was hazardous to engage ourselves in the open Sea, and if I could have governed, we should have left all these Islands on the Left Hand; but our Officers were afraid they should not find a Passage between them and the Continent. They had great Reason to repent it, for we were afterwards two Days without seeing Land, tho' we steered continually North and North East.

Then our Sailors began to despair, and in Reality there needed only a Gust of Wind, several of which we had often met with, to drown us. Even the calm Weather had its Inconveniencies; they were obliged to row all Day, and the Heat was excessive. The Sailors had Reason enough to be dissatisfied: The Obstinacy of two or three People had exposed us to the Danger in which we found

The Sailors despair.

found ourselves; but the Mischief was done, and required another Remedy, than Murmuring. Since our Departure from *Louisiana.* I could not prevail with the greatest Part to come to the Sacraments, very few had even performed the Duties of *Easter.* I took Advantage of this Occasion to engage every Body to promise to confess themselves, and to communicate as soon as we should come again to Land: The Promise was scarcely made, when the Land appeared.

We steered directly for it, and we arrived there before Noon.

The Inconveniencies of this Coast.

The 4th at Noon we were in 26 Degrees 56 Minutes Latitude. We had always the main Land in Sight, without being able to approach it, because it was bordered with Islands and Peninsula's, the greatest Part of which are low and barren, and between which there is scarce a Passage for a Canoe of Bark. What we suffered the most from was, that we found no Water in them. The next Day we were often stopt by contrary Winds, but we found Shelter every where, and we got a small Matter by shooting and fishing. We wanted nothing but Water: I took the Advantage of this Delay to make every Body keep the Promise they had made of coming to the Sacrament.

It appears that there are few Savages in all this Country.

Our Provisions fail.

We saw only four one Day, who came towards us in a Pettiaugre; We waited for them; but when they had reconnoitred us, they did not dare to approach, and made all the Haste they could back to Shore. The 10th, we were obliged to retrench the Allowance of Brandy, which we had hitherto distributed every Day to each Man, as there was but little left, which we judged necessary to preserve for more pressing Occasions. We began also to be sparing of our Provisions, especially the Bisket, Part of which had been spoiled: So that we were reduced to great Extremities, having often at a Meal only a Handful of Rice, which we were obliged to boil in brackish Water.

But this Coast is the Kingdom of Oysters, as the great Bank of *Newfoundland*, and the Gulf and the River *St. Laurence* are that of the Cod-Fish. All these low Lands, which we coasted as near as possible, are bordered with Trees, to which there are fastened a prodigious Quantity of little Oysters, of an exquisite Taste: Others, much larger and less dainty, are found in the Sea in such Numbers, that they form Banks in it, which we take at first for Rocks on a Level with the Surface of the Water. As we did not dare to leave the Shore, we often entered into pretty deep Bays, which we were obliged to go round,

round, which greatly lengthened our Way; but as ſoon as the main Land diſappeared, our Men thought themſelves loſt.

We meet with ſome Spaniards, *who had been wrecked.*

The 15th, in the Morning, we met a *Spaniſh* Long-Boat, in which were about fifteen Perſons: They were Part of the Crew of a Ship which had been wrecked about the River *St. Martin*. It was twenty-five Days ſince this Misfortune had happened, and for forty-two Perſons they had only a little Boat, which they made Uſe of by Turns, and which obliged them to make very ſhort Journies. This Meeting was a good Providence in our Favour, for without the Inſtruction which the *Spaniſh* Captain gave us, we could never have found the Route which we were to keep; and the Uncertainty of what might become of us, might have inclined our Mutineers to ſome Violence, or to ſome deſperate Reſolution.

Danger of being deſtroyed.

The next Night we were in very great Danger. We all lay in a little Iſland, except three or four Men, who guarded the Boat. One of them, after having lighted his Pipe, imprudently ſet his Match on the Side of the Boat, exactly in the Place where the Arms, the Powder, and the Proviſions were kept in a Cheſt covered with a Tarpaulin: He fell aſleep after this, and while he ſlept, the Tarpaulin took Fire. The Flame waked him as well as his Companions, but in one Minute more the Boat had been blown up or ſunk; and I leave you to judge what would have become of us, having only a Canoe, which could hold but the ſixth Part of our Company, without Proviſions, Ammunition, or Arms, and on an Iſland of Sand, in which there grew only ſome wild Herbs.

The next Day, the 16th, the Canoe left us to go to join the *Spaniards*. We had the Wind againſt us, and we were obliged to go with the Sounding-Line in Hand, becauſe the Coaſt was ſo flat, and ſo paved with ſharp Flints, that at ſix Leagues from the Shore our Boat, which drew but two Feet Water, was every Moment in Danger of ſtriking and bulging. We were in the ſame Diſtreſs the two following Days, and the 20th we encamped in an Iſland which makes the Eaſt Point of the Bay of the *Apalaches*. All Night we ſaw Fires on the main Land, which we were near, and we had obſerved the ſame for ſome Days.

Arrival at St. Mark d'Apalache.

The 21ſt we ſet off with a very thick Fog, which being ſoon diſperſed, we ſaw ſome Buoys, which the *Spaniards* had told us to follow. We followed them making the North, and we found that without this Help it was impoſſible to ſhun the Sand-

Banks, of which this Coast is full, and which for the most Part are covered with Oysters. About ten o'Clock we perceived a square Fort of Stone, with pretty regular Bastions; we immediately hoisted the white Flag, and a Moment after they called out to us in *French* not to come any nearer.

We stopt, and in a Moment we saw a Pettiaugre coming towards us, with three Men in it. One of the three was a *Biscayneer:* He had been a Gunner in *Louisiana*, and he was in the same Employment at *St. Mark*. After the common Questions, the *Biscayneer* was of Opinion, that only the Captain of the *Adour* and I should go to speak with the Commandant, which we accordingly did. This Commandant was only a Deputy, and a Man of Sense: He made no Difficulty to let our Boat come up to the Fort, and he invited our Officers and the principal Passengers to Dinner; but it was after our Boat had been visited, and all the Arms and Ammunition taken out, and carried to his own Magazine, with a Promise to restore them when we should depart.

Description of the Country.

This Post, which M. *Delille* has set down in his Chart under the Name of *St. Marie d'Apalache*, was always called *St. Mark*. The *Spaniards* had formerly a considerable Settlement here, but which was reduced to be of little Consequence, when in 1704 it was entirely destroyed by the *English* of *Carolina*, accompanied by a great Number of the Savages called *Alibamons*. The *Spanish* Garrison, which consisted of thirty-two Men, was made Prisoners of War; but the Savages burnt 17 of them, among whom were three *Franciscan* Friars; and of seven Thousand *Apalaches*, who were in this Canton, and who had almost all embraced *Christianity*, there remained at *St. Mark* but four hundred, who withdrew towards the *Maubile*, where the greatest Part of them are at present.

The Forests and Meadows near the Fort are full of wild Cattle and Horses, which the *Spaniards* let run here, and as they want them, they send some Savages, who take them with Snares. These Savages are also *Apalaches*, who probably went away when the *English* took this Place, and who returned after they were retired. For the rest, this Bay is exactly what *Garcilasso de la Vega*, in his History of *Florida*, calls the Port of *Auté*. The Fort is built on a little Eminence, surrounded by Marshes, and a little below the Confluence of two Rivers, one of which comes from the North East, and the other from the North West. They are but small, and full of Caimans, and notwithstanding pretty well stored with Fish.

Two

Two Leagues higher, on the River of the North West, there is a Village of *Apalaches*; and in the Lands to the West, at a League and half from the Fort, there is a second. This Nation formerly very numerous, and which, divided into several Cantons, possessed a very large Country, is at present reduced to be very inconsiderable. It embraced *Christianity* long ago, yet the *Spaniards* do not trust them, and they do right: For besides that these *Christians*, being destitute of all spiritual Aids for a great Number of Years, are no longer such but in Name, their Conquerors treated them at first with so much Severity, that they ought always to look upon them as Enemies not well reconciled. It is difficult to make good *Christians* of People, to whom their first Treatment rendered *Christianity* odious.

Of the Apalaches.

They told us at *St. Mark*, that a Resolution was taken to re-establish this Post in its first State, and that they expected here five thousand Families: This is much more than the *Spaniards* of *Florida* can raise.-----The Country is fine, well wooded, well watered, and they say that the farther you advance into the Country, the more fruitful it grows. They confirmed to us at this Fort, what the *Spaniards* whom we met had told us already, that the Savages of the *Martyrs*, and their King Don *Diego*, were a bad Sort of People, and that if we had not kept a good Guard, they would have done us some Injury. They told us farther, that a *Spanish* Brigantine being lately wrecked near the Place were we met four Savages in a Pettiaugre, all the Crew had been empaled, and eaten by these Barbarians.

St. Mark is dependent on *St Augustin* for Military and Civil Affairs, and on the *Havannah* in Spirituals. Notwithstanding, it is the Convent of the *Cordeliers* of *St. Augustin* that sends a Chaplain hither: I found one here, who was a very amiable Person, and who did us a very great Service. He informed us, that the Commandant of *St. Mark* wanted to detain us till he had given Advice of our Arrival to the Governor of *St. Augustin*, and had received his Orders. I desired him to ask this Officer if he was in a Condition to support us all the Time that we should be here, since what Provisions we had left, were scarce sufficient to carry us to *Louisiana*.

He acquitted himself very well of his Commission, and his Discourse, accompanied with some Presents, which he hinted to us that we ought to make the Governor, had all the Effect which we expected from it. This Officer granted us, with a very good Grace, some Guides, which we desired of him for *St. Joseph*, which is thirty Leagues from *St.*

Mark; and the Way, as we had been informed, not easy to find.

This obliged us to stay the next Day, and I was not sorry for it, for besides being pretty well lodged in the Fort with the *Cordelier* (a Distinction that was paid to me, and which I owed to my Habit) I was glad to take a short Survey of the Environs of the Fort. They go by Land from *St. Mark* to *St. Augustin*; the Journey is eighty Leagues, and the Way very bad.

Departure from St. Mark.

We departed the 22d in the Morning, and the 25th, about ten o'Clock, our Guides made us undertake a Traverse of three Leagues, to enter into a Kind of Channel, formed on one Side by the Continent, and on the other by a String of Islands, of various Extents. Without our Guides, we should never have dared to engage ourselves among them, and we should have missed the Bay of *St. Joseph*. We were now almost destitute of Provisions, and the Difficulty of finding Water encreased every Day. One Evening that we had dug at ten Paces from the Sea, on a pretty high Ground, and got none but brackish Water, which was impossible to drink, I thought of making a shallow Hole close to the Sea Side, and in the Sand: It immediately filled with Water that was tolerably fresh, and as clear as if it had been taken from the finest Spring; but after I had filled a Vessel, it flowed no more, which made me judge that is was Rain Water, gathered in this Place, meeting with a hard Bottom, and I judge that this may often happen.

Tides at Pensacole.

As soon as we had got a-head of the Islands, we sailed till ten o'Clock at Night. Then the Wind fell, but the Tide, which began to ebb, supplied the Want of it, and we went forward all Night. This is the first Time that I observed any regular Tides in the Gulf of *Mexico*, and the two *Spaniards* told us, that from this Place to *Pensacole* the Flux is twelve Hours, and the Reflux as much. Next Day, the 26th, a contrary Wind kept us till Night, in an Island pretty well wooded, which is ten or twelve Leagues long, and where we killed as many Larks and Woodcocks as we pleased. We saw also here a great Number of Rattle-Snakes. Our Guides called it the *Isle des Chiens (of Dogs)*, and from the Beginning of it, they reckoned ten Leagues to *St. Mark*, and fifteen to *St. Joseph*; but they were certainly mistaken in the last Article, for it is at least twenty Leagues, and very long ones.

The 27th, at eleven o'Clock at Night, we ran upon a Bank of Oysters as large as the Crown of my Hat, and we were above an Hour in getting off again. We went from thence to pass the Night in a Country House, belonging to a Captain of the

the Garriſon of *St. Joſeph*, named *Dioniz*, and at our Arrival they told us very ſtrange News.

Falſe Alarm.

They aſſured us that all *Louiſiana* was evacuated by the *French*; that a large *French* Ship came to *Ship Iſland*, and had embarked there the Commandant, the Director, and all the Officers; that after their Departure, the Savages had killed all the Inhabitants and Soldiers that were left, except a ſmall Number who had ſaved themſelves in two Sloops; that being in Want of Proviſions, they were gone to the Bay of *St. Joſeph*; that thoſe who arrived firſt were well received, but that they would not permit the others to land, for Fear leſt ſo many *French* being together, they ſhould be tempted to make themſelves Maſters of this Poſt, which we formerly poſſeſſed.

All this Story had ſo little Probability, that I could not poſſibly believe it; but it was told with ſo many Circumſtances, and coming from People who had ſo little Intereſt to impoſe upon us, and who being but at ſeven Leagues from *St. Joſeph*, might have News from thence every Day, that it ſeemed hard to think it ſhould be without any Foundation. The greateſt Part of our People were ſtruck with it; and I found in myſelf that theſe general Conſternations are communicated to the Heart, in Spite of our Underſtanding, and that it is as impoſſible not to feel ſome Fear in the midſt of People who are ſeized with it, as not to be afflicted with thoſe that weep. I did not in the leaſt believe what they had juſt told us, and yet I could not be eaſy.

In the mean Time our Company, in Spite of their Deſpair, finding Plenty of Proviſions, and the Servants of the Sieur *Dioniz* very obliging, feaſted all the reſt of the Night. In the Morning our Guides took Leave of us, according to their Orders. We had no further Need of them; for beſides that we could not miſs our Way to *St. Joſeph*, we met with at the Houſe of M. *Dioniz* a *Frenchman*, a Soldier in his Company, and an old Deſerter from *Maubile*, who was heartily tired of the *Spaniſh* Service, among whom he was often almoſt ſtarved, as he ſaid, though they paid him well: So we eaſily engaged him to go with us to *St. Joſeph*, and from thence to *Louiſiana*, ſuppoſing he could get his Diſcharge.

Arrival at St. Joſeph.

We arrived about Five in the Afternoon at *St. Joſeph*, where we were perfectly well received by the Governor. We found there two great Boats of the *Biloxi*, with four *French* Officers, who were come to reclaim ſome Deſerters, but they did not find them here. We had ſeen them the 24th, being *Whit-Sunday*, in a Bark that was under Sail, and which paſſed pretty near us. It is very probable that they had touched at *St. Joſeph*; and to give

give a Colour to their Desertion, they had given out what the Night before had so greatly alarmed us. Two *Cordeliers*, who served the Chapel of the Fort, having heard of my Arrival, came to offer me a Bed in their House, which I accepted very thankfully.

Description of St. Joseph.

For the rest, I do not think there is a Place in the World where one might less expect to meet with Men, and especially *Europeans*, than at *St. Joseph*. By the Situation of this Bay, its Shores, its Soil, and all that Environs it, nothing can make one conceive the Reasons of such a Choice. A flat Coast, open to the Wind, a barren Sand, a poor Country; and which can have no Manner of Commerce, nor even serve for Magazines: To such a Pitch have the *Spaniards* carried their Jealousy of our Settlements in *Louisiana*. We had been guilty of the Folly before them, but it was only for a short Time. There is Reason to think that they also will correct it soon; and that when we have restored *Pensacole* to them, they will transport thither every Thing they have at *St. Joseph*.

The Fort is not situated in the Bay, but on the Turn of a bending Point, and which encloses an Island. This Fort is only built of Earth, but well enclosed with Palisadoes, and well defended by Guns. It has a pretty numerous Garrison, an Etat Major compleat, and almost all the Officers have their Families with them. Their Houses are neat and convenient, and tolerably furnished, but every where in the Streets we sink up to the Ancles in Sand. The Ladies never go out but to Church, and always with a Pomp and Gravity, which is to be seen no where but among the *Spaniards*.

The Day after our Arrival, which was the 29th, there was a great Dinner at the Serjeant Major's. This Officer had been in *Louisiana*, and been highly treated there. He was overjoyed to find this Occasion to make us a Return. He had especially made a particular Friendship in his Journey to *Louisiana* with M. *Hubert*, who was then the principal Commissary there, and who was amongst us. He heard that a Daughter of his Friend, three Years old, who was going to *France* with her Father, had only been sprinkled: He desired they would complete the Ceremonies of her Baptism at *St. Joseph*, and he would be her Godfather. This was performed with great Pomp, and firing of the Guns. The Godmother was a Niece of the Governor's, who at Night gave a magnificent Supper; and by an Excess of Politeness, seldom found among the *Spaniards*, he would have the Company of the Ladies. He compleated all these Civilities, by furnishing us with Plenty of Provisions to continue our Route, though he had not yet received the Convoy that was to bring him Provisions

from

from the *Havannah*, and for this Reason he had refused some to the Officers of *Biloxi*; but our Necessity had touched him extremely.

Departure from St. Joseph.

We departed the 30th with the two Boats, and the Fort saluted us with five Guns. We made seven Leagues that Day, and we anchored at the Entrance of a River, which comes out of a Bay open to the South East. At Eleven at Night, the Wind coming fair, we took Advantage of it, and we steered West North West. All the Coast was upon the same Point of the Compass for twenty Leagues, quite to the Island of *St. Rose*; and we do not find a single Place to get Shelter from a Gust of Wind that should come from the open Sea.

The 31st, at Four in the Afternoon, we had made twenty Leagues, and we anchored behind an Island which shuts up the great Bay of *St. Rose*, the Entrance of which is dangerous when the Sea runs high. Had we been a Moment later, we should have been greatly embarrassed, for the Wind turned all at once from the North East to the South West; and the Waves ran so high the same Instant, that it would have been impossible for us to have passed.

Channel and Island of St. Rose.

The 1st of *June*, about Two or Three in the Morning, the Tide beginning to flow, we re-embarked; and having gone a small League, we entered into the Channel of *St. Rose*, which is fourteen Leagues long. It is formed by the Island of *St. Rose*, which has this Length, but is very narrow; which appears all covered with Sand, and which nevertheless is not ill wooded. The Continent is very high, and bears Trees of all Kinds. The Soil is almost as sandy as at *St. Mark*; but if they dig ever so little, they find Water.————The Wood here is very hard, but subject to rot soon. All this Coast swarms with wild Fowl, and the Sea with Fish. This Channel is narrow at its Entrance; afterwards it widens, and continues the Breadth of half a League to the Bay of *Pensacole*. The Current is strong here, and was in our Favour.

About Eleven o'Clock we doubled the Point *aux Chevreuils*, *(of Roe-Bucks)*; at the Turn of which the Bay begins. We turn to the North, then to the North East. The Fort is a small League farther, and we discover it from the Point *aux Chevreuils*. We arrived there at Noon, and were suprised to see it in such a bad State. It appears plain that they do not expect to continue in it. The Sieur *Carpeau de Montigni*, who commands here, was gone to *Biloxi*, and we found here only some Soldiers. The *Spanish* Fort, which was taken two Years ago by the Count *de Champmelin*, was behind, and there remains nothing in it but a very fine Cistern; the building of which cost, as they say, fourteen thouſand Pieces of Eight. They have been both built in an Iſland which joins almoſt to the main Land, which is not thirty Yards long, and the Soil of which does not appear to be extraordinary.

Deſcription of the Bay.

The Bay of *Penſacole* would be a pretty good Port, if the Worms did not deſtroy the Ships, and if its Entrance had a little more Water; but the *Hercules*, which carried M. *Champmelin*, ran a-ground here. This Entrance is directly between the Weſt End of the Iſland *St. Roſe*, where the *Spaniards* had alſo built a little Fort, and a Bank of Sand. It is ſo narrow, that only one Ship can paſs at a Time: Its Opening is North and South. On the other Side of the Sand Bank there is another Paſs, where there is Water only for Barks, and which is open to the South Weſt. It is alſo very narrow. The Moorings for Ships, in the Bay of *Penſacole*, is along the Iſland *St. Roſe*, where the Anchorage is ſafe.

Arrival at Biloxi.

We departed from *Penſacole* at Midnight, and about Four in the Morning we left *Rio de los Perdidos* on the Right. This River was ſo called, becauſe a *Spaniſh* Ship was wrecked here, and all the Crew loſt.——*Dauphin Iſland* is five Leagues farther on the Left, and is five Leagues long, but very narrow. There is at leaſt one half of this Iſland without a Tree upon it, and the reſt is not much better. The Fort, and the only Habitation that remains here, are in the Weſt Part. Between this Iſland and the Iſle *a Corne*, which is a League diſtant, there is little Water. At the End of this, there is another very ſmall Iſland, which they call the *Round Iſland*, on Account of its Shape. We paſſed the Night here.

Over-againſt the Bay of the *Paſcagoulas*, where Madam *de Chaumont* has a Grant, which is not likely to pay her Expences ſoon, a River of the ſame Name, and which comes from the North, runs into this Bay. The next Day, about Ten o'Clock, one of our Seamen died of a Quinſey. This is the only Man we loſt in our painful and dangerous Expedition. An Hour after, we anchored at *Biloxi*, where they were ſtrangely ſurpriſed to ſee us. I went immediately to ſay Maſs, to return Thanks to God for having ſupported us in the midſt of ſo many Fatigues, and for delivering us from ſo many Dangers.

I am, &c.

LETTER

LETTER XXXIV.

Voyage from the BILOXI *to Cape* FRANÇOIS *in* ST. DOMINGO.

MADAM, *Cape* FRANÇOIS, *September* 6. 1722

I Durst not venture to tell you in my last, as I had done in the preceding Letter, that I should not write any more to you but from Cape *François*, for Fear I should be obliged to contradict myself again, and the Event was very near justifying my Apprehensions. I am here at last, in this long wished for Port, after a Voyage of sixty-four Days, and we entered it at the Time when we had almost lost all Hopes of attaining it. But before I shall enter upon the Recital of the Adventures of this Voyage, I must proceed with my Journal.

Pensacole *restored to the* Spaniards.

The first News we heard on our Arrival at the *Biloxi*, was that of the Peace concluded with *Spain*, and the double Alliance between these two Crowns. One of the Articles of Peace was the Restoration of *Pensacole*, and this Article was carried to *Louisiana* by Don *Alexander Walcop*, an *Irishman*, and Captain of a Ship in *New Spain*. He embarked at *Vera Cruz*, in a Brigantine of forty Guns and one hundred and fifty Men, and commanded by Don *Augustin Spinola*. They say that the Design of the *Spaniards* is to make a great Settlement at *Pensacole*, and to transport thither the Garrison of *St. Joseph*, and all the Inhabitants. They add, that Don *Alexander Walcop* is intended for the Governor: He is a Man of a very good Presence, very sober, and religious.

An English *Interloper at the* Biloxi.

Don *Augustin Spinola* is a young Man, full of Fire, and of a very amiable Character; whose Sentiments declare his high Birth, and are worthy of the Name he bears: He is Lieutenant of a Man of War, and has engaged to serve three Years in *Mexico*, after which he reckons to return to *Spain*, and to make his Fortune there. He was greatly mortified to hear that an *English* Interloper, named *Marshal*, did not quit the Road of the *Biloxi*, where he had traded considerably with the *French*, till he entered it himself. This armed Ship did not even care to sail away, saying, he did not fear the *Spaniards*; but M. *de Bienville* obliged him to it, being unwilling to be a Spectator of a Combat, the Success of which our Officers pretended would not have been favourable

 to

to the Aggressors, though superior in Force. We shall soon see they were mistaken in the high Opinion they entertained of *Marshal.*

Frequent Desertions in Louisiana.

Notwithstanding, that since the Departure of the *Adour*, some of the Company's Ships had brought some Provisions to *Louisiana*, they were still in great Necessity, and Discontent encreased every Day. In Spite of the Care which M. *de Bienville* took to comfort the Inhabitants, we heard Talk of nothing but Schemes for deserting. Besides the Boat which we met on the Route from *St. Mark* to *St. Joseph*, all the *Swiss* that were at the *Biloxi*, with the Captain and the Officers at their Head, having received Orders to go to *New Orleans* in a Sloop, armed on Purpose for them, and which had been well provided with Provisions, instead of taking the Route of the *Mississippi*, had turned, with Colours flying, to the East, and 'twas not doubted but they had taken the Route to *Carolina*; because, being *Protestants*, there was no Likelihood they should go to the *Spaniards (a)*.

A Plot discovered.

The 8th of *June* I discovered a Conspiracy formed to carry off the *Spanish* Brigantine. It was Seven o'Clock at Night when I was privately informed of it, and I was assured that before Nine the Scheme would be put in Execution, the Commandant of the Brigantine not being used to come on board till that Hour. The Conspirators were one hundred and fifty in Number; and their Intention was, if their Enterprize succeeded, to turn Pirates. I sent immediately to inform M. *de Bienville*, who was at Table with Don *Augustin Spinola*, who rose immediately and went on board, and the Major of the *Biloxi* had Orders to begin his Round directly.

These Motions made the Conspirators apprehend that their Design was discovered; and the Major saw only four or five Men met together, who disappeared as soon as they saw him, and he could not take any of them, so that they thought I had given a false Alarm. But besides that, for several Days following, we heard of nothing but of Soldiers and Inhabitants who had disappeared: Some of these Deserters being retaken, confessed the Plot, of which I had given Information.

The English *endeavour to bring over our Allies to their Party.*

The 12th, a Chief of the *Tchactas* came to tell M. *de Bienville* that the *English* made them great Promises, to bring them over to their Interest, and to engage them to have no more Commerce with the *French*. The Commandant, on this Occasion, gave a great Proof of the Talent he

(a) We have since heard that they went to *Carolina*.

has of governing at his Pleasure the Minds of the Savages. He knew so well how to flatter this Chief, that with some Presents of little Consequence, he sent him away very well disposed to continue firm in our Alliance. This Nation would give us a great deal of Trouble if they should declare against us; the *Chicachas*, the *Natchez*, and the *Yasous*, would soon join with them, and there would be no longer any Safety in navigating the *Mississippi*; even if these four Nations should not draw in all the rest, which very probably would be the Case.

About the End of the Month, an Inhabitant of the *Illinois*, who had been to trade on the *Missouri*, arrived at the *Biloxi*, and reported that he, and one or two more *French*, having travelled as far as the *Octotatas*, who in 1719 defeated the *Spaniards*, I mentioned before, they were well received by them, and that for the Goods they carried them, they have received seven or eight hundred Livres in Silver, partly in Coin and partly in Bars; that some of these Savages had accompanied them to the *Illinois*, and assured M. *de Boisbriant* that the *Spaniards*, from whom they took this Silver, got it from a Mine a little Distance from the Place where they met them, and that they have offered to carry the *French* thither, which Offer this Commandant had accepted. Time will shew if these Savages have spoken with more Sincerity than so many others, who for a long Time have sought to draw the *French* to them by the Allurement of Mines, none of which have been yet found real *(a)*.

The 22d I embarked in the *Bellona*, which sailed the 30th.

Departure from the Biloxi.

The 2d of *July* we reckoned that we bore North and South of *Pensacole*, from whence we chose to take our Longitude, because that of the Mouth of the *Mississippi* is not yet ascertained. From that Time to the 20th nothing remarkable happened. We had then the Sun exactly over our Heads, and in our Voyage from the *Martyrs* to the *Biloxi*, we had borne the greatest Heats of the Solstice, without being able to defend ourselves from them in any Manner, no more than from the Dews, which fell plentifully every Night. Yet, would your believe it, Madam, we suffered less from the Heat at that Season, than in the Month of *April* before our Shipwreck?

Observations on the Heat.

Yet nothing is more certain, and I remembered then that I had been several Times much surprised to see People, who were born under the torrid Zone, complain of the great Heats of *France*. We were in the same Case in the Month of *April*, we had the

(a) We have heard no more of this Mine since that Time.

ſame Heats that we feel in *France*, and even in *Italy* in the Month of *July*. In the Month of *July*, during the Dog Days, we were under the Zone, and the Heat was much greater, but it was more ſupportable. This Difference did not proceed from the Winds; we had the ſame, and we had always ſome in both Seaſons. Neither was it only from our being more uſed to them, for we were not ſubject to thoſe continual Sweats, which had ſo much troubled us in the Month of *April*.

We muſt therefore ſeek for another Reaſon, and this is what occurs to my Mind. In the Spring, the Air is ſtill full of Vapours, which the Winter raiſes. Theſe Vapours, when the Sun approaches them, are directly inflamed, and this is what cauſed thoſe heavy Heats, and thoſe plentiful Sweats, which overpowered us in the Month of *April*: We were almoſt always in *Balneo Mariæ*. In the Month of *July*, theſe Vapours were diſperſed, and tho' the Sun was much nearer us, the leaſt Wind ſufficed to refreſh us, by blunting the Power of its Rays almoſt perpendicular over our Heads. Now in *France* the Sun never thoroughly diſperſes the Vapours, as it does between the Tropics; at leaſt they are here much leſs groſs; and this is what produces, not the Difference of the Heat, but the different Senſation of the Heat.

We diſcover the Land of Cuba.

The 20th, we diſcovered the Land of *Cuba*, which three Months before we had made in ſeven Days. Two Things occaſioned this Delay. The firſt is, that we cannot depend on our Obſervations when the Sun is ſo near, becauſe its Rays form no ſenſible Angle *(a)*. For this Cauſe, when we have the leaſt Suſpicion of the Land's being near, we dare make no Sail in the Night. The ſecond is, that the Captain of the *Bellona* wanted to go to the *Havannah*, and as he judged that the Currents bore to the Eaſt, he made the Weſt as much as he thought neceſſary, not to miſs his Mark.

However, he was very nigh paſſing before the *Havannah* without knowing it. They came and told me very early in the Morning that they ſaw Land; I aſked how it appeared, and on the Anſwer they made, I aſſured them it was *Cape Sed*. They laughed at me, and the two Officers of the *Adour*, who were with us, were the firſt to maintain that I was miſtaken. I went upon Deck, and perſiſted in my Opinion, contrary to that of the whole Ship: Our Pilots affirming that we were ſixty Leagues more to the Weſt. At Sun-ſet I diſcovered the Table of *Marianne*, but I was ſtill alone in my Opinion: However, we had the Wind

(a) This Defect of *Davis*'s Quadrant is remedied by *Hadley*'s.

against us, and all Night we only made Tacks to and from the Land.

The next Day at Noon we were ſtill in Sight of the two Lands, which were the Subject of our Diſpute, when upon coming nearer the Shore, we perceived the *Havannah* before us, which greatly pleaſed the Captain, who had a large Parcel of Goods that he expected to diſpoſe of to the *Spaniards* for a great Profit. I was little concerned for his Intereſt; but if we had been further out at Sea, and the Wind had not been againſt us all Night, the Error and Obſtinacy of our Pilots and our Officers would have coſt us dear. The Wind was fair to enter the *Havannah*, and at five in the Afternoon we were but a League off; then we fired two Guns, one to ſhew our Flag, the other, after we had twiſted the Flag round the Staff, as a Signal of Diſtreſs, to require a Pilot from the Port.

Nothing appeared, and it was reſolved to ſend the Canoe to aſk Leave to come in; but as it was already late, it was put off till next Day, and all the Night we paſſed in making Tacks. The 23d an Officer of the *Bellona* embarked to go to aſk the Governor's Conſent for us to water in his Port, and to buy Proviſions, becauſe they could not give us a ſufficient Supply at the *Biloxi*. This was but a Pretence, but I did not know it, and the Captain having deſired me to accompany his Officer, I thought it not proper to refuſe him.

Deſcription of the Port of the Havannah.

The Entrance of the Port of the *Havannah* looks towards the North Weſt and by Weſt: On the Left, at the Entrance, we ſee a Fort built upon a Rock, at the Foot of which we muſt paſs: They call it the *Moro Fort*. It is ſolidly built, and has three good Batteries of Braſs Cannon, one above the other. On the Right there is a Range of Baſtions, which appeared to be newly finiſhed, or lately repaired. The Entrance in this Place is but five or ſix hundred Paces wide, and they ſhut it up by an Iron Chain, which may ſtop a Ship long enough to be beat to Pieces by the Guns, before it can break the Chain.

The Paſſage widens a little afterwards up to the Town, *that is to ſay*, for three or four hundred Paces. The Channel turns from thence to the Left a good Way beyond the City, which is on the Right. ——— This is all I can ſay of it, having never been any farther. I only know that the City occupies the Head of a Peninſula, and that the Side of the Land, which is its whole Length, is encloſed by a good Wall, with Baſtions. It's Aſpect is very agreeable and open, as ſoon as we have paſſed the *Moro Caſtle*. The Streets are well laid out, the Quay large and well kept, the Houſes well built for the

moſt

most Part: There are a good Number of Churches, and which appear tolerably fine; but I never went into any of them: In a Word, a City which contains twenty thousand Souls does not make a greater Appearance; but the *Havannah*, as I have been told, has not near so many.

The Fate of the Interloper Marshal.

Upon my landing I met several of the Sailors of the *Adour*, as well of the Long-Boat as of the Canoe. The first told me, that from the Place where we were wrecked, they were five Days getting to this Port, and almost always in the greatest Danger of being lost. I had no Time to enquire by what Means the second came here. But the Serjeant, who entered our Canoe at the Foot of the *Moro*, to conduct us, took Care to shew us the Brigantine of the Interloper *Marshal*, whom I mentioned at the Beginning of my Letter. It was moored near a Boat so small, that it could with Difficulty carry fifteen or twenty Men, which notwithstanding had taken this Brigantine by boarding her. We must allow that the Privateers of *Cuba* and the neighbouring Islands are brave: Our *Flibustiers* *(a)* have learnt them to fight; but considering the Disproportion of the Force, and the Valour and the Guns of the *English*, they must have been taken by Surprise.

The Governor of the Havannah *refuses Leave to enter his Port.*

The Governor of the *Havannah* received us coldly, and after having heard us, he told us he should have been very glad if he could have granted our Request; but the King his Master had tied up his Hands on this Article, and that he was above all expresly forbid to receive any Vessel coming from *Louisiana*. He added that there were several Places on the same Coast where we might stop without any Danger, and where they would supply us with all the Refreshments we wanted. We were forced to be contented with this Answer, and after having paid my Compliments to the Rector of the College which we have in this City, I re-embarked.

The next Day, the twenty-fourth, at six in the Morning, we were North and South of the Loaf of *Matanza*, and at half an Hour after eleven off *Rio de Ciroca*, where there is a *Spanish* Habitation. But as the Captain was resolved to try if he could not succeed better at *Matanza* than he had at the *Havannah*, and that he had still seven Leagues thither, he took the Resolution to ply off and on all Night; and the 25th at Day-break we found ourselves at the Entrance of the Bay, which is two Leagues wide.

(a) Free *Negroes* and *Mulattoes* of the *French* Islands.

To

To enter it we must at first double a Point, which does not advance far into the Sea, then make the West for a League; then we discover on the Right Hand another Point, behind which is the Fort, and a large Quarter of a League farther the Town of *Matanza*, between two Rivers, which wash its Walls on both Sides. About ten in the Morning, they sent a Canoe thither with an Officer, who did not find the Commandant of the Fort there. He declared our pretended Necessity to the Deputy, but this Officer told him he could not take upon himself to grant the Permission we required; that all he could do for our Service was to send a Courier to the *Havannah*, to know the Intentions of the Governor of that City, who was his General; that if this would content us, we might in the mean Time anchor on the other Side of the Point, where we should be safer.

Description of the Bay of Matauza.

This Answer, and the Declaration, which our Pilots then thought fit to make, that they would not answer for bringing the Ship into the Bay of *Matanza*, because they were not sufficiently acquainted with it, determined the Captain at last to continue his Route with his whole Packet of Merchandize, for the Sake of which he had made us lose at least fifteen Days of precious Time. The next Day, at six in the Morning, we had still behind us in Sight the Loaf of *Matanza*, from which we reckoned ourselves distant between twelve and fifteen Leagues; and the 27th at five in the Morning we discovered from the Mast-Head the Land of *Florida*.

At this Sight we steered North North East; two Hours after we changed our Course, to take a little more to the East; at nine we got again into the Route, and we found ourselves in the true Current, which goes to the Channel of *Bahama*, for we went as swift as an Arrow. We saw at this Instant the *Adour*, which shewed still an End of a Mast out of Water, but the Hulk was almost covered, and we found that she was far from being wrecked over-against the most northern of the *Martyr* Islands, as some Persons believed; for she was over-against us at half past ten, and at half an Hour past one the last of these Islands was still to the North.

Passage through the Channel of Bahama.

About three o'Clock we discovered a Breaker from the Round-Top, close by which we were going to pass, and farther on a Shoal, which ran out a great Way. This Shoal was probably the End of the *Martyrs*, and to shun it, we steered all the rest of the Day towards the South and the East, the Current carrying us always to the North, and towards Night we made the

North

North East. The 28th at Noon, the Pilot judged that we were at the Entrance of the Channel, in twenty-five Degrees thirty Minutes, at half past seven o'Clock at Night he was afraid of being too near the Land, and steered South South East till Midnight with a good Wind. At Midnight he took again his Route, and the 29th we saw no more Land. At Evening we thought ourselves out of the Channel, but for greater Security we continued to make the North North East till ten o'clock.

The Route we must take to go from the Channel of Bahama *to* St. Domingo.

In all the rest of our Voyage to Cape *St. François*, we had almost always little Wind, and sometimes Calms. From Time to Time there arose Storms: The Sky and the Sea were all on Fire; and the Ship leaning to one Side, went like the Wind: But this never lasted long, and a Quarter of an Hour's Rain cleared the Sky, and smoothed the Waves of the Sea, which resembled those Persons of a gentle and calm Disposition, who have sometimes pretty warm Fits of Passion, but who are soon pacified. I believe that what contributes to calm the Sea so soon, after these violent Agitations, are the Currents. They are in Reality very perceiveable in these Parts: On the other Hand, they vary continually, which disconcerts all the Skill of the Pilots.

When we are out of the Channel of *Bahama*, the direct Route to go to *St. Domingo* would be the South East. But the Winds which blow almost always from the Eastward do not permit us to take it, and we must go by a Parabolic Line to the Height of *Bermudas*, which it would be proper to discover if possible; to be assured of the Longitude. For Want of this Knowledge, we are sometimes obliged to go to the Great Bank of *Newfoundland*, before we can be sure of being enough to the East of all those Shoals, which lie to the North and to the East of *St. Domingo*.

Old Channel of Bahama.

Yet they have not always gone so far about to go from the Gulf of *Mexico* to this Island. In the first Times of the Discovery of the new World, after having followed the North Coast of *Cuba*, up to the Point of *Ithaca*, which is the East End of it, fourteen Leagues from *Matanza*, they turned to the Right, and leaving on the Left all the *Lucaye* Islands, amongst which is *Bahama*. This is what they call the Old Channel of *Bahama*. It has Water enough for the largest Ships, but there are so many Sands in it, that at present none but small Vessels dare venture into it.

After

After we were come to the Height of thirty Degrees, thirty-one Minutes, our Pilots judged themſelves enough to the Eaſt, to be in no Danger on making the South, of running on any of the Shoals I mentioned. So they confidently run Southward, and in a few Days we made a great deal of Way, ſailing on a Sea always fine, and carried by the Trade Winds. The 27th of Auguſt, at eight in the Morning, the Sailor, who was upon the Watch on the Round-Top, cried out Land, which cauſed a great deal of Joy, but it was of ſhort Continuance; for the Sailor coming down, they aſked him if the Land was high, and he replied that it was very low, ſo of Conſequence it could only be one of the *Caiquis*, or the *Turk Iſlands*.

Miſtake of the Pilots in their Reckoning.

We were alſo very fortunate in having diſcovered them by Day, for we had infallibly been wrecked if we had come upon them in the Night, and no Perſon had eſcaped, becauſe theſe Iſlands have no Strands, and the greateſt Part of them are bordered with Shoals, which advance far into the Sea, and which are divided by little Channels; where there is not Water enough for Boats. On the other Hand they are very low, and we cannot perceive them at Night, till we are upon them.

But we were not ſafe becauſe we had diſcovered the Danger: The Land before us appeared to be a pretty large Iſland, and pretty well wooded in ſome Places; this made us judge, that it was the grand *Caique*, of Conſequence, that we were forty or fifty Leagues too much to the Weſt. To gain our proper Longitude, we muſt have gone up again to the North above two or three hundred Leagues, which would certainly have taken up five or ſix Weeks Navigation, and we had ſcarce Water and Proviſions enough to ſerve us for fifteen Days, with great Oeconomy. The Captain was greatly embarraſſed; he ſaw the Faults of his Pilots, and might blame himſelf for having depended too much upon them, for not having taken Obſervations himſelf above two or three Times, and for having always preferred the Reckoning of the ſecond Pilot, a very preſumptuous and blundering young Fellow, to that of the firſt, who was more experienced and ſkilful, and who had never approved their Manœuvre.

Difficulties we were under on diſcovering Land.

Neverthelcſs they were obliged to take ſome Reſolution immediately: A Guſt of Wind from the North, that ſhould have ſurprized us, and thrown us on theſe low Coaſts, would infallibly have deſtroyed us. But as they could take no Reſolution which had not its Inconveniency, the Captain would have the Advice of every Body. Some were for making the beſt Way to *Carolina*, where we might arrive in ten or twelve Days, and buy Proviſions.

The Reſolution they take.

sions. This Advice was rejected, and they followed another, which was extremely hazardous, and which appeared to me to proceed only from Despair, this was to coast the grand *Caique* as near as we could till we came to the Opening; *that is to say*, to the Separation of all these Shoals from the *Lucaye Islands*.

All the Vessels pass this Way, which come from *St. Domingo*, to return to *France*, and then there is nothing to fear, because they can take their Time to get out, and this Passage being open to the North West, we are almost sure of having favourable Weather to come out. But to enter it on the Side where we were, we must depend on the North East, and 'tis a great Hazard to find this Wind the Moment it is wanted. Therefore no Body that we know, has ever yet attempted this Passage. In short they resolved to run all Hazards, and they approached the Grand *Caique*.

Description of the grand Caique.

At two in the Afternoon we were but a good Cannon-Shot from it, and we are perhaps the first, who without an indispensable Necessity, ventured to visit it so near in a Ship. The Coast of it is nevertheless very safe, elevated, as it appeared to me, about seven or eight Feet, sometimes a little more, but it is perpendicular, and without any Strand. Its Soil has not at all the Appearance of being barren. Geographers place it directly under the Tropic, which we could not verify, because the Weather was cloudy; but I think it a little more to the South, for there is not certainly three Degrees Difference between this Island and *Cape François*.

Unexpected Success of our Attempt.

We coasted the grand *Caique* till four in the Afternoon, having the Wind and the Currents for us. Then they made a Sailor go to the Mast Head, to observe what we had before us, and he soon came down and told us that he had seen the End of the Island; but that beyond it he saw still low Lands, divided by Channels in which the Waters appeared all white. Upon this Information, we judged proper to change our Course, and we steered North North East. At Midnight we made the South South East, and it looked as if the Wind turned as we would have it; but it was very weak, and the Currents carried us with so much Violence to the West, that at Day-break the low Lands and the Sands, which the Evening before were so far a Head of us, were almost as much behind; and the Passage which we sought began to open itself.

This was the decisive Moment of our Fate, and what gave us good Hopes, was that the Wind inclined by Degrees to the North-East. At eleven o'Clock we made the South East and by South, soon after the South East: But the Currents carried us so much out

out, that our true Course was scarcely South. At Noon we could make no Observation, and the West Point of *Caique* bore North & by North East of us. In short, in an Hour's Time we had cleared the Passage, and I cannot better express to you what appeared on all our Countenances, as we advanced by Degrees into the Opening, than by comparing it to what happens to those Animals that have been put in the Receiver of the Air Pump, which appear dead when they have pumped out almost all the Air, and to which they restore Life by little and little, by letting the Air in again slowly.

We did not dare yet to flatter ourselves that we should be able to gain *Cape François*, which was to Windward of us, but we had *Port de Paix*, or at least *Leogane*, which we could not miss; and after the extreme Danger we had lately passed, any was good, so we could find a Port. At Midnight we had a violent Gust of Wind, but of little Duration, and the next Day, at nine in the Morning, we discovered the Land of *St. Domingo*, but without distinguishing what Part all the Day, because it was foggy. A Ship, which by its Way of working we judged to be a Pirate, employed us a good Part of the Afternoon: We prepared in Earnest to engage her, or rather to defend ourselves, if they should attack us, for we would not have changed a Sail to follow her.

Arrival at Cape François.

At last we discovered that it was only a small Vessel of one hundred and fifty Tons at most, and which probably had been more frighted than we. We judged by her Manœuvre that she came out of *Cape François*, and she appeared deep loaded. All Night we made Tacks to the North East, varying a little, which brought us higher up in our Latitude; and when it was Day, we discovered with a great deal of Joy that we were to Windward of *Cape François*. We saw it plain, were almost at it, but had so little Wind, that we could not enter it till the first of *September*, at four in the Afternoon. Since that Time I have not had a Moment to myself to entertain you about this Country, and my Letter is called for to carry it to a Ship which is ready to sail for *Nantz*. I propose to depart myself in fifteen Days for *Havre de Grace*, from whence I shall have the Honour to write to you once again.

I am, &c.

LETTER

LETTER XXXV.

Description of CAPE FRANÇOIS *in* ST. DOMINGO. *Return to* FRANCE, *landing in* ENGLAND.

MADAM, ROUEN, *January* 5. 1723

I Was but one Day at *Havre*, because I would not miss the Coach for *Rouen*, and I came here to rest myself at my Ease, after the longest and most fatiguing Voyage I ever made. But it is now over, and I am going to take Advantage for the little Leisure I have left, while I wait for the Coach for *Paris*, to finish the Account of my Adventures for these two Years and half that I have been wandering through the World.

Description of Cape François.

Cape François of *St. Domingo*, from whence my last Letter was dated, is one of the Ports of all *America*, where the *French* have the greatest Commerce. It is, properly speaking, but a Bay, which is not quite a League deep, and the Opening of it is very wide: But this Opening is full of Sand Banks, between which we cannot sail with too much Caution. To enter it we must take to the Right along a Point, where there is a Redoubt and some Guns; but it is the Custom before we engage ourselves in these narrow Passes, where two Ships cannot go abreast, to call a Pilot from the Fort; and least the Desire of saving a Pistole, which we must give him, should endanger the Lives of the whole Ship's Company, it has been wisely ordered, that, even though we should enter without his Assistance, we should nevertheless pay the Pilot.

The Town is at the Bottom of the Bay on the Right. It is not considerable, because almost all that are not Artizans, Shopkeepers, Soldiers, or Publicans, live in the Plain, as much at least as the Service permits it to the Officers, Execution of Justice to the Magistrates, and the Business of Commerce to those who are concerned in it; *that is to say*, almost all the People of a better Rank who are in this Place: So that to see the *Beau Monde*, we must go into the Country. And indeed nothing is more charming than the Plain and the Vallies which are between the Mountains. The Houses are not stately, but they are neat and convenient. The Highways are laid out by a Line, of a handsome Breadth, bordered with Hedges of Lemon Trees, and sometimes planted with large Trees, and from Space to Space cut by Brooks of clear Water, cool, and very wholesome. All the Habitations appear well cultivated, and they are really very beautiful Country Houses. We see every where an Air of Plenty, which is very pleasing.

Of the Plain of the Cape.

This Plain is at the North West End of the famous *Vega-Real*, which is so much spoken of in the *Spanish* Histories of *St. Domingo*, which they affirm to be 80 Leagues long; and which, as the famous Bishop *de Chiappe, Bartholomew de las Casas*, pretends, is watered by twenty-five thousand Rivers. Great Names cost the *Spaniards* nothing; these pretended Rivers are for the most Part only little Brooks, the Number of which are really incredible, and which would make of this Royal Plain something more charming and more delightful than the Valley of *Tempe*, so boasted of by the *Greeks*, if it was not under the torrid Zone. There are also some Parts of it where the Air is very wholesome, and the Heat supportable: Such is that where the Town of *St. Jago de los Cavalleros* is built; and we may say the same Thing of the Vallies which are between the Mountains, with which the Plain of the *Cape* is bordered on the South. They begin to be peopled, and they will soon be more so than the Plain itself, because they see few People sick here; and those who come hither from other Parts, recover in a short Time of Distempers, when all Manner of Remedies have proved ineffectual.

Observations.

I visited all the Habitations that are nearest the Town, but I had not Leisure to make many Observations. Moreover, during the Day, the Heat was extreme; and in the Evening, as soon as the Sun was set, the Musketoes, and other Flies of that Kind, did not permit me to walk about long. These little Insects particularly attack new Comers, whose Skin is tenderest, and their Blood freshest. They assured me, that in the *Spanish* Part of the Island they are free from this Inconvenience; but to make Amends, we have no venomous Serpents, and they have many. They also observed to me, that excepting Lettice, all Sorts of Garden Herbs and Roots must be renewed every Year in this Island with Seeds from *Europe*.

What I found here most curious, were the Sugar Mills. I shall say nothing of them, because Father *Labat* has described them much better than I can. After Sugar, the greatest Riches of this Colony is Indigo, of which the same Author has also treated very particularly. This Plant has an irreconcileable Enemy, and which is much more detrimental to it than Darnel to our Wheat. This is an Herb which they call *Mal-nommée*; and

and which, as it grows out of the Ground, bears a Seed, which it ſcatters every where. It grows in a Tuft; and by its Bulk, and its prodigious Fruitfulneſs, it ſo choaks the Indigo, that it kills it; ſo that when it has made the leaſt Progreſs in a Field, it is entirely loſt, and they muſt plant another.

Remark on the Doradoes.

The Coaſts of *St. Domingo* have not Plenty of Fiſh; but if they go a little out to Sea, they find all Sorts. We catched, eſpecially coming from *Louiſiana*, many *Doradoes*, on which our Sailors pretend to have made a pretty ſingular Remark, which is, that when they take this Fiſh in the Increaſe of the Moon, the Fleſh of it is firm, and of an exquiſite Taſte; whereas, if they take it in the Decreaſe of the Moon, it is inſipid, its Fleſh has no Conſiſtence, and is like Meat that is boiled to Rags. It is certain, that we experienced both in the different Times beforementioned; but that this happens always, and that the Moon is the Cauſe of it, is what I will by no Means affirm.

Departure from Cape François.

We departed from Cape *François* the 25th of *September* in a Merchant Ship of *Havre*, named *Louis de Bourbon*, commanded by one of the moſt ſkilful Navigators that I have known: But we had ſcarce got to Sea, when we diſcovered two Leaks in her; ſo that during all the Paſſage, which was ninety-two Days, they were obliged to pump Night and Morning; which, added to the Want of Proviſions, though they had taken in Plenty, but which they never huſbanded for the firſt Month, was the Cauſe that our Captain was ſeveral Times on the Point of ſtopping at the *Azores*. We had been ſtill more embarraſſed, if we had gone into the Snare that was laid for us by a Captain of an *Engliſh* Ship, whom we met half Way in our Paſſage.

We meet with an Engliſh *Ship.*

He came out of *Jamaica* with a Fleet, of which he was at firſt, as he ſaid, the beſt Sailor; but as in loading his Ship, he was ſo imprudent as to leave all his Proviſions in one Place, it happened that by Degrees as they were conſumed, the Veſſel loſing its Equilibrium, loſt by little and little the Advantage that it had over the reſt, and at laſt remained a great Way behind the Fleet. We fell in with him in Reality alone, and making ſo little Way, that in Compariſon of him our Ship, which was far from being an extraordinary Sailor, went like a Bird; and he was afraid that his Proviſions would entirely fail before he could arrive in *England*. He told us the Trouble he was in, and to explain it the better to us, he invited himſelf to dine on board us. They replied that he ſhould be welcome, and our Captain ordered ſome of our Sails to be furled to wait for him.

While

While we were at Dinner, he turned the Discourse on our Route, and asked us whereabouts we thought ourselves. The Captain shewed his Account of the Day before, and he appeared surprised at it. He assured us that we were two hundred Leagues forwarder than we reckoned, which he endeavoured to prove by the last Land he had seen. This gave great Pleasure to the greatest Part of our People, who were already very much tired of so long a Voyage, being continually obliged to contend with violent Winds, and a stormy Sea, in a very crazy Ship. But I had some Suspicion that the *English* Captain said he was so far advanced, only that he might engage us to let him have some of our Provisions. Our Captain, to whom I communicated my Suspicion, told me he had the same Thought, and contented himself with well treating his Guest, and eluded his Demand. He continued to sail by his own Reckoning, which he found so exact, that he entered into the Channel the Day, and almost the Hour, that a little before he said he should enter it.

Arrival at Plymouth.

The 2d of *December* we entered the Port of *Plymouth*, without any apparent Necessity; but our Captain without Doubt had some Business here. We found here the King's Frigate, the *Thetis*, which a Storm had driven in here in a shattered Condition, tho' it was the first Time of her coming out of *Havre*, where she was built. She was commanded by the Chevalier *de Fontenay*, whose Orders were to go to the *American* Islands, in Pursuit of the Pirates, who had lately taken several Ships. As soon as he knew I was in the Port, he did me the Honour of a Visit, before I could have the Convenience of going to pay my Respects to him, and he carried me on board his Ship, where I passed all the Time very agreeably that I continued in this Port.

Description of Plymouth.

Plymouth is one of the five great Ports of *England*, and one of the finest in *Europe*. It is double, and before we enter it, we must pass under the Guns of the Citadel. From thence we turn to the Right, to enter into the Port of the Town, which is the smallest, and from whence one must come out of the Channel, and 'twas here the *Thetis* was moored. They turn to the Left to enter into the other Port, where the King of *England*'s Ships are laid up, over-against a magnificent Arsenal. This Port extends a great Way, and we anchored at the Entrance, because the Winds which blow here are good to go farther up the Channel.

The Town of *Plymouth* is not large, but its Environs, where I used to walk often, are very pleasant. I never saw a better Country: The Weather was very mild, and the Fields as green as in the Spring.

On

On the Night of *Christmas-Day*, after I had celebrated the three Masses, we set sail, and all the next Day we had a fair Wind. Two Frigates of fifty Guns had weighed Anchor two Hours before us, and we soon overtook them. This surprised me, because we sailed but poorly ourselves; but what surprised me still more was, that to see these two Ships under Sail, if I had not seen them prepare for sailing, I could never have believed they were the same that appeared so large to me in the Port; on which they told me, that this proceeded from a particular Construction and setting of the Sails, which was done on Purpose to draw Pirates into a Snare, which in the Sea Dialect makes them call these Ships *Lubber Traps*. In Fact, as they say, the Pirates on seeing them, judging of them by their Appearance, take them for Merchant Ships, and pursue them as a certain Prey. But when they are so near as not to be able to escape, they find somebody to talk to, and are caught in the Snare, without being able to make any Resistance: Therefore the *English*, above all Nations, are most feared by Pirates, and are the worst used by them when they fall into their Hands.

The Ingenuity of the English *to catch Pirates.*

The Night following we went through one of the most terrible Storms that had been seen for a long Time in the Channel. The next Day, tho' the Wind was almost quite fallen, the Sea was in an Agitation enough to terrify the boldest; we shipped some Seas which put us in great Danger: One especially overflowed the great Cabin as I was beginning to say Mass, and hindered me from proceeding; so that when we entered *Havre de Grace* about Noon, every Body asked us how we could hold out in a Storm that was felt even in the Port.

Arrival at Havre de Grace.

But they would have been more surprised at our Escape, when two Days after, our Ship being drawn ashore, they might have seen it drop to Pieces with Rottenness. This was the first News that I heard on my Arrival here. Judge, Madam, how greatly our Lives were exposed in such a Ship in a Voyage of eighteen hundred Leagues, and in a Season when the Sea is always in a Fury; and what Thanks we ought to return to GOD, not only for having delivered us from such an imminent Danger, but also for having concealed from us the Knowledge of it, which alone was sufficient to have killed us a thousand Times over with Fear.

I am, &c.

F I N I S.

www.ingramcontent.com/pod-product-compliance
Lightning Source LLC
Chambersburg PA
CBHW030424300426
44112CB00009B/845

* 9 7 8 3 3 3 7 3 4 4 8 9 4 *